Lady From Savannah

THE LIFE OF JULIETTE LOW

By

GLADYS DENNY SHULTZ

and

DAISY GORDON LAWRENCE

Girl Scouts of the U.S.A./420 Fifth Avenue/New York, N.Y. 10018-2798

Girl Scouts.

National President
Connie L. Matsui

National Executive Director
Marsha Johnson Evans

ISBN 0-88441-147-8

CONTENTS

CONTENTS

ILLUSTRATIONS

ABOUT THE AUTHOR

DAISY GORDON LAWRENCE (1901-1982) was named for Juliette Gordon Low, her aunt and godmother, who was known to family and friends as "Daisy." Although she was not present at the famous founding tea party on March 12, 1912, young Daisy became the first registered Girl Scout when her aunt wrote her name at the head of the troop list. She was active in Girl Scouting throughout her life — "because Aunt Daisy in her will wrote: 'and to my family I leave my friends and especially my beloved Girl Scouts.'" Thousands of Girl Scout visitors remember the family stories that Daisy Lawrence told as a guide at the Juliette Low Birthplace, after it was purchased and restored by Girl Scouts of the U.S.A. in the early 1950s. Those ancedotes and many more are shared in *Lady from Savannah*.

GLADYS DENNY SHULTZ, Mrs. Lawrence's collaborator, began her writing career as a reporter for the Des Moines Register. She went on to become a well-known author of articles and fiction, and was particularly successful with several books of advice to young girls.

LADY FROM SAVANNAH

Girl Scouts of the U.S.A. is proud to reissue *Lady from Savannah* in response to widespread demands for a biography of our Founder, Juliette Gordon Low. In truth, however, this is much more than the story of one woman and the organization she started. It is first of all a chronicle of two great American families — the Kinzies who were founders of Chicago and the Gordons whose name is magic to this day in Savannah, Georgia — that in 1860 produced the gallant, willful, exasperating, generous, and wholly lovable Juliette (known as Daisy) Gordon. The narrative of Daisy's marriage to Willy Low also offers an insider's view of Edwardian high society in England.

The Girl Scouts are most particularly proud that this woman from a background of wealth and privilege was able to envision a youth movement "for the girls of all America," which serves a membership of ever-increasing diversity as the diversity of our country grows.

Betty F. Pilsbury

Betty F. Pilsbury
National President

September 1988

FOREWORD

It must be seldom that biographers have as much source material to draw upon as the authors have had in searching out the story of Juliette Gordon Low. Too often, the biographer must call upon hearsay and his own imagination to fill in gaps and explain riddles. In the case of Juliette Low, we are fortunate in having documentary material that goes back almost to the first founding of America. The Wolcotts of New England are entrenched in the history of the United States. Historians in Wisconsin and Illinois have collected every scrap of information obtainable about the Kinzies. In Georgia, the Gordon name is one to conjure with. Gordon personal letters and memoirs of many kinds can be found in Georgia libraries and museums, and have overflowed into neighboring states.

In addition to all this, Juliette Low's grandmother, Juliette Magill Kinzie, published in her book, *Wau-Bun,* the story of the Kinzies as they pursued their adventurous, romantic way, telling us much that they said and thought, revealing unmistakably what manner of people they were.

Nellie Kinzie Gordon, Juliette Low's mother, carried on this tradition by filling in further Kinzie biographical details in an epilogue to the edition of *Wau-Bun* that was brought out in 1901, and by writing in addition a brief biography of her grandfather, John Kinzie. She kept diaries on her many trips to Europe and throughout the Spanish-American War, in the course of which she became a national heroine. In her later years, she wrote her reminiscences of the early Chicago of her childhood, of her romance, marriage and young wifehood, of her experiences during the Civil War, and in Savannah's dreadful yellow fever epidemic of 1876.

Nellie Gordon, moreover, was a prolific letter writer and possessed the great virtue, from the historian's standpoint, of never throwing away any letters she received, as far as one can tell, from the time she first went to Madam Canda's boarding school in 1853, when she was eighteen.

Nellie Kinzie Gordon had six children, five of whom lived through ripe middle age. They, too, were assiduous letter writers and followed their mother's example of keeping the letters they received, and even copies of some letters that they wrote. Since this was a close and united family, they regaled each other with full accounts of what they did, descriptions of what they saw and conversations in which they took part. The bulk of these letters has been saved.

There are some gaps. Juliette Low's sister Mabel mentions that Juliette had made up a bundle of letters with a notation that they should be burned unread after her death, and her brother Arthur, who was the keeper of the family documents, would undoubtedly have carried out her request. It is supposed that this bundle contained her letters to her husband, Willy Low, and his to her. Juliette Low has referred also to a diary or journal she kept, and her brother has quoted from this diary. No trace of it has been found. It is believed in the Gordon family that if she left her diary behind her, her brother Arthur destroyed it also, presumably because of the references it would have contained to her unhappy marriage. It is known that some letters of a very personal nature were removed and possibly destroyed before the Gordon family archives were divided between the Georgia Historical Library at Savannah and the Southern Historical Collection at the University of North Carolina at Chapel Hill. A group of letters Nellie Gordon wrote to her husband at the end of the Civil War has been lost sight of, though it is hoped that they exist somewhere.

After these deletions, there still remains such a wealth of firsthand material that there has been no need for the authors to invent motives or explanations, except in a few instances. The story we give has been developed from letters and other documents and from the memories of family members. Every quotation is from these sources, none is made up. In the areas where we have been forced to fall back on conjecture, we indicate that this has been the case.

Such masses of material exist, in fact, that it has been necessary to exercise considerable selectiveness. We have not set forth every trifling family disagreement any more than we have been able to include the manifold expressions of love and harmony in their entirety. In some instances we have chosen not to pillory by name persons who are now dead and cannot defend themselves. We feel this is the way Juliette Low would have wished it, even though she had suffered grievous injury from some of these persons. But we have striven to present a faithful over-all picture.

We recognize that it would probably have been the wish of Juliette Low to omit all reference to the unhappy turn her marriage took. Her nieces and nephews believe she loved Willy Low to her dying day and would have wished to shield him. But the very silence that has been maintained on this subject heretofore has given rise to the impression that there may have been something shameful or disgraceful about it. Nothing could be farther from the truth as far as Juliette Low herself was concerned. The catastrophic ending of her marriage had a tremendous impact upon her character and subsequent life. A biography of Juliette Low that ignored the unhappy features of her marital experience would be no biography and would be unjust to the subject besides.

We realize also that in this story there may be a tendency on the part of Juliette Low's mother to emerge more clearly than the subject herself. There are several reasons for this. In the first place, Nellie Gordon described, in vivid narrative form, the important passages in her life. This is something Juliette Low never did. Second, we have many letters exchanged between Juliette Low's parents which give us their innermost feelings about their own relationship and their children. The letters between Juliette Low and her husband are lacking.

Finally, and perhaps this is the most important reason of all, while Nellie Gordon lived she always did steal the show, no matter who else might be present. Her children, and Juliette particularly, were happy to have it so, and rejoiced in the attention their mother received. We feel Juliette Low would not mind if the same thing happens now and then in her biography.

We should like here to acknowledge our thanks to Mrs. Lilla M. Hawes, Director of the Georgia Historical Society Museum; to Mr. James M. Patton, Director of the Southern Historical Collection, University of North Carolina, and Dr. Caroline A. Wallace and Miss Anna Brooke Allan, his able assistants; to Miss Margaret Gleason, Reference Librarian of the Wisconsin State Historical Society; Mrs. Marion D. Pratt of the Illinois State Historical Library; to Mrs. John S. Owen of the National Society of Colonial Dames in Wisconsin; to Miss Barbara D. Simison, Assistant Reference Librarian, Yale University Library; to the Girl Scouts of the United States of America for permission to quote from *Juliette Low and the Girl Scouts* and other assistance; and to the many pleasant people who called upon their stores of personal recollections and stories for our benefit.

GLADYS DENNY SHULTZ
DAISY GORDON LAWRENCE

LADY FROM SAVANNAH

The biographers of Juliette Low have been confronted with one idiosyncrasy in her story for which our subject is in no way to blame. She was christened Juliette, and is thus known to fame and in Girl Scout affairs. But her family and friends never called her anything but Daisy, and thus she is referred to invariably in her personal life. It is inescapable, therefore, to speak part of the time of Juliette Low, and part of the time of Daisy Gordon and of Daisy Low, as she became after her marriage to Willy Low. But she is one and the same, and we beg our readers to keep this in mind. The other Daisy in our story who was the first American Girl Scout—christened Margaret Eleanor, called Daisy in honor of her Aunt Daisy and then further designated in the family as Doots —will be referred to either as Doots or Daisy Lawrence, as she became after her marriage to Samuel C. Lawrence.

CHAPTER I

———————— ☆ ————————

ORIGINS OF AN ECCENTRIC

JULIETTE LOW'S SISTER, Mabel Leigh, used to worry lest, as the years went on, the Founder of the Girl Scouts would be built by legend into a plaster saint, the "perfect Girl Scout." Mabel foresaw that one day a full-scale biography of her famous sister would be written. Would not crucifixion await the biographer reckless enough to portray this sparkling, incredible creature as she really was? Because she had founded an organization for young girls, would it not be considered obligatory to represent Juliette Low as an examplar of all the solemn virtues?

In letters to her niece Daisy Lawrence, Mabel many times expressed her apprehensions on this score. "Daisy [the name by which her family and friends called Juliette Low] was far too warm and human and lovable for that. Her life was a series of adventures. And she was one of the most delightful and maddening people that ever lived, as well as being lovable and good. It is wiser that Girl Scouts should learn to admire her for her charm and gaiety and self-sacrifice, than that she should be set upon a pedestal of impossible perfection."

Perhaps it is fortunate then that those nearest and dearest to Juliette Low have already dwelt, in writing about her, on her idiosyncrasies and whimsicalities. Her brother Arthur, who adored her, called her a brilliant eccentric and went on to say, "It is difficult to describe her with any accuracy because she was so many-sided and unexpected and incalculable. There was nothing conventional or tepid or neutral about her. She had an eager desire to realize life to its utmost, and she would try anything, particularly if she had never attempted it before. What she enjoyed, she enjoyed to her very finger tips; and one reason why she was so eagerly sought after lay in the fact that she was not only very entertaining and amusing when she desired to be, but she was frequently killingly funny when she had no intention of being funny at all."

It is one of the dearest traditions of the Girl Scouts that at an early board meeting, Juliette Low stood on her head in order to exhibit the newly designed Girl Scout shoe, which she happened to be wearing.

Her nephew Arthur Gordon, Junior, has described her habit, when staying in hotels, of putting her jewels in the toes of her shoes, then setting the shoes outside the door of her room, as a way of outwitting possible marauders. (However, her niece, Daisy Lawrence, insists that the jewel-stuffed shoes were placed in the room of Juliette's maid, or a traveling companion, instead of in the hall.)

Another nephew, Rowland Leigh, has expatiated on her habit of inviting people to a party, and then of forgetting all about it. And another habit of attending to business matters in bed, filing her bills in four envelopes labeled respectively: "This Year," "Next Year," "Some Time" and "Never."

Rudyard Kipling reported that "there is a brook, with trout, at the foot of our garden so that if you like (and Daisy did) you can go out after dinner in evening dress and try your luck for a fish. Also there is a high black bridge, under which trout lie, facing a banked stone wall some eight feet high. It was here, naturally, that Daisy got a fairly big one, and equally naturally it was I, in dinner costume, who lay on a long handled net taking Daisy's commands while she maneuvered the fish into the net. We got him, between us, but it wasn't *my* fault for I was too weak with laughter to do more than dab and scoop feebly in the directions she pointed out. And she had her own ways of driving her Ford in Scotland that chilled my blood and even impressed our daughter. But her own good angels looked after her even when she was on one wheel over a precipice; and there was nobody like her."

When in England, she used to drive on the right side of the road "because I am an American," and in her native Savannah she drove on the left side of the road "because I am English." Juliette's sardonic little mother used to call these and many similar performances "Daisy's stunts." It was her propensity for such things as going fishing in full evening dress, with a famous author also in full evening dress to do the dirty work, that won Juliette her reputation for oddity—a trait which endeared her to adults who, like Rudyard Kipling, were a touch fey themselves; and made her an endlessly fascinating companion to the young. Indeed, Ogden Nash's sister, Eleanor Arnett Nash, who was Juliette's young companion on several of her always eventful jaunts, has given us one of the nicest descriptions of Juliette Low. "She had a wicked wit, and a charm I am too word-poor to describe. She was quicksilver and pepper—the whole leavened with humanity and laughter. She was the person I most liked to be with."

But there is no denying that her queernesses made her trying to sober, sensible folk. "I was never an admirer of Mrs. Low," testifies a lady who was dragooned by Juliette Low, as was everyone else she knew who could be helpful, into Girl Scout work. "She was far too irresponsible for my taste. Why, one night she asked me to look after her handbag. 'There are forty thousand dollars' worth of securities in it,' she said, and handed it over to me as if it had been a sack of peanuts. And when she brought some Girl Scout honor pins to a meeting, did she have them wrapped in a neat package as anyone else would have done? Not Mrs. Low. She brought them in in *an old tomato can!*"

Perhaps the greatest contradiction of all is that this social butterfly and world traveler, flitting restlessly from country to country and country house to country house, suddenly in middle age threw all her capabilities, driving power and a large part of her financial resources into an effort completely foreign to anything she had ever done before, showing a tenacity of purpose and an organizing and executive genius that those who knew her best had not dreamed she possessed.

Obviously, Juliette Low possessed many qualities besides eccentricity, and it should be said that her associates have also paid tribute to her artistic talent, her generosity and kindness, her all-encompassing sympathy. Rudyard Kipling—he and his wife, Carrie, loved her dearly—felt that sufficient justice had never been done to Juliette's superb courage and selflessness; "a side of her nature which she dismissed as casually as she would a Customs official," as he put it.

The truth is that the character and abilities and potentialities of Juliette Low were as variegated as the America that produced her. Puritan, bluestocking New England, the aristocratic South and the wild, picturesque frontier had all gone into her making. She was born a Gordon of Savannah, Georgia. A true daughter of the Confederacy, she distrusted "Yankees" as long as she lived. But her own mother was a Yankee, her mother's family as devoted to the Northern cause as the Gordons were to the Southern. If Juliette Low was a phenomenon among human beings, as those who knew her considered her to be, she was an American phenomenon of a peculiar and special kind.

In downtown Savannah today, many of the fine old antebellum houses still face the green squares, shaded by lofty live oaks, that were set apart by Oglethorpe when he laid out his town, and that now break up the solid procession of city streets. It is easier in Savannah than in most important Southern centers to send oneself back into this gracious, quiet world as it was a hundred years ago.

In the most important square of all, called variously Courthouse Square and Postoffice Square, though officially it is Wright Square, just off Savannah's main business street, there is a lofty monument to the first William Washington Gordon, who was Juliette Low's grandfather, several times Mayor of Savannah, builder of the Central of Georgia Railroad. Near by, on the corner of Bull and Oglethorpe, two of Savannah's principal streets, is the tall, stately Gordon mansion, built in 1821 to last for all time by Judge James Moore Wayne, who became a Justice of the United States Supreme Court, and was Juliette Low's greatuncle.

At first, Savannah people who remember the Gordons well —and there are many who do—will tell you there never was a Gordon who was inhibited. Then—for memories go far back in Savannah, encompassing generations long dead—they recall that the older Gordons, and the Waynes and Stites with whom they intermarried, were as solid and conventional citizens as one could ask for. They remember then that it was not until William Washington Gordon II brought home as his bride a little bundle of fun and human dynamite from Chicago that the "wild" strain appeared among the sober Gordons. Savannah retains a vivid memory of Nellie Kinzie Gordon. Savannahians will smile—everyone who ever knew Nellie Kinzie Gordon smiles involuntarily when her name is mentioned. They will say, "Yes, I guess it was the introduction of Kinzie blood that started it all. Things never were the same in Savannah after Nellie Kinzie Gordon came. She certainly sent the Gordon line off in a new direction!"

Nellie's husband W. W. Gordon II—Willie to his wife—used to say that the first time he saw his Nellie, she was "standing on her head on the point of a spear, emitting sparks, and with fireworks going off all around her."

He was speaking metaphorically. In actual fact, their romance began when Nellie, at the age of eighteen, slid down the banister of the Yale Library stairs straight into Willie's astonished presence. Family legend has it that she was equally surprised to see the "demure" Yale senior standing at the foot of the stairs, and overshot the newel post, landing in a heap on the floor, having crushed in transit Willie's hat which had been on the newel post. In which case she undoubtedly swore roundly, for such was her custom even when the provocation was much less.

Now in 1853, when this incident occurred, young ladies did not slide down banisters, and properly reared ladies of any age did not swear. Nevertheless Nellie was a lady—nobody ever questioned that. One thing that set Nellie apart from ladies of the eastern seaboard was that she had grown up in what yesterday had been wilderness, and was still in process of becoming a great new section of America, with accent and mores of its own—the Middle West. Another was that her parental background was an unusual mingling of Puritan, bluestocking New England strains with one of the sturdiest, most venturesome stocks of the western frontier. Back of Nellie Kinzie were men who on one ancestral side had tamed the wilderness, defied royal governors, fought the mother country to gain independence; on the other, of men who had courted the wilderness, plunged themselves into it, made themselves a part of it.

But perhaps more significant still is the fact that back of Nellie Kinzie also, in direct line, were three remarkable women—her mother, her grandmother and her great-grandmother. These women differed from each other in their individual characteristics. But they were alike in that each lived in the midst of the most stirring and colorful events of her era. Each stood beside her husband unflinchingly through hardship, dreadful dangers and in some instances indescribable horrors.

Nellie's gently reared mother had slept with two pistols beside her pillow when Black Hawk and his Sauks were on the warpath in Wisconsin, killing and burning; determined that if her home were attacked, she would at least kill two Sauks before she herself was killed.

Nellie's Grandmother Kinzie had sat in a canoe at the point where the Chicago River empties into Lake Michigan, her youngest children huddled around her, watching the Fort Dearborn Massacre up the lake shore, knowing that in that deadly melee were her husband, her daughter and her nine-year-old son.

Nellie's Great-grandmother Lytle, captured, along with her little son and daughter and three-months-old baby, near Fort Pitt by the Indians in Revolutionary times, had kept an impassive face when her baby was taken from her arms and killed, knowing this was the only way she could save her boy and girl from a similar fate.

Nellie's mother and grandmother are counted among Chicago's most prominent and distinguished women of all time. Wax figurines of Mrs. John Kinzie and Mrs. John Harris Kinzie were in the Chicago Historical Society's original collection of the city's notable women. Their figurines may be seen in the Chicago Historical Society today. Later Nellie Kinzie Gordon's figurine was added to the collection. And it now includes one of Juliette Low, whom Chicago proudly claims because of her Kinzie ancestry.

One cannot attempt to understand the complex, contradictory, courageous personality of Juliette Low, without knowing something about her mother, the merry little madcap who slid down the banister of the Yale Library that day in New Haven one hundred years ago, straight into the heart of William Washington Gordon II. And to understand Nellie Kinzie it is necessary to retrace in some degree the story of her adventurous, colorful forebears.

CHAPTER II

SONS OF THE WILDERNESS

WHEN NELLIE'S FATHER, John Harris Kinzie, died in 1865, the Chicago *Tribune*'s tribute to one of the city's most prominent citizens said, among many other things, "To give the full details of such a life as his has been, would be to retrace the development of Chicago." To combine the full details of his life with that of Nellie's grandfather, John Kinzie, would be to retrace the development of Michigan and Wisconsin and Illinois, from trackless Indian country to a land of farms and towns and vigorous young cities. One wonders indeed that John Kinzie, first of his line in America, has never been made the hero of a frontier novel, for his life as it stood was the stuff of which such novels are made.

His mother had come out to Canada from Ireland in 1758 as the wife of Chaplain William Haleyburton of the First Royal American Regiment of Foot, but her husband dying soon after their arrival in Quebec, she married the surgeon of the regiment, John McKenzie. Their son John, Nellie's grandfather, was born in Quebec in 1763. Surgeon McKenzie, too, did not live long, and his widow married a Mr. William Forsyth of New York City. In the old family Bible which records the birth of five sons to Mr. and Mrs. Forsyth, John is included as "John Kinsey," indicating that he was thus called from his early boyhood on. Why or when the spelling was changed to Kinzie is not known.

The Forsyths moved to Williamsburg, Long Island, but the life there was too tame for John. When he was about ten he ran away from home, stowed away on a Hudson River boat and eventually made his way back to his birthplace, Quebec. There he walked the streets until a kindly silversmith took him in as an apprentice. It has been generally believed that both John and his son John Harris Kinzie got their Indian name of Shawnee-awkee, Silver Man, from the fact that they paid out to the Indians in silver dollars the annuities granted them by the United States government. But Nellie Kinzie Gordon says in her biography of the first John Kinzie that he was given the name because he pleased the Indians by making ornaments and "tokens" for them out of their silver dollars. Two examples of John Kinzie's handiwork exist today. One, a silver bracelet, may be seen at the Chicago Historical Society. The other is a silver cup inscribed with the name Hunter, and presumably made by John Kinzie for his daughter Maria Indiana when she married young David Hunter who later became General David Hunter of Civil War fame—or infamy, according to whether one's sympathies were with the North or South. The cup is now the property of Daisy Lawrence's son, Samuel C. Lawrence, Jr.

Young John stayed with the silversmith for three years, until a friend of his parents ran into the boy on the streets of Quebec, recognized him, reported his whereabouts to the family on Long Island, and Mr. Forsyth came and took the boy home. After this, John seems to have been content to return to school until he was eighteen and his family had moved to Detroit. Then he persuaded his stepfather to fit him out as an Indian trader, and from that time on he was one of the conspicuous figures of the huge, amorphous Territory of Michigan.

Early in his career he was taken under the wing of the famous Indian scout and trader, John Harris, who was mentioned by Irving in his life of Washington. John Harris imparted to the young trader his own great store of Indian lore and Harris' prestige among the Indians protected the youth. John Kinzie acquired the Indian languages with ease, and in his travels among the tribes often dressed as an Indian and passed for an Indian. He respected their customs, and they soon found that his word was as good as his bond. As he neither cheated them nor, being a good trader, allowed them to cheat him, he soon won the respect of the tribes with whom he dealt and the firm friendship of their great chiefs. From the start his business flourished. Before he was twenty-one he had established two Ohio trading posts, one at Sandusky and one at Maumee.

The young widow he chose for his wife, Eleanor Lytle McKillip, had an equally colorful background. Her parents, originally from Virginia, were living at the time of the Revolution near Fort Pitt, which was then on the western frontier. Most of the Indian tribes, including the great Iroquois Nation, sided with the British and raided frontier settlements and farms. In 1779, when Eleanor Lytle was nine, she and her younger brother were seized by a marauding band of Senecas, a branch of the Iroquois, from a field where they were playing. Presently other Indians joined the party, bringing with them Mrs. Lytle, with her three-months-old baby.

Early in the march, one of the Indians offered to carry the baby, apparently as a kindly gesture, then dashed out its brains against a tree. Mrs. Lytle knew that this was done to elicit expressions of grief and pain from her, and that if she complied, the savages might kill or torture the little girl and boy in order to prolong their sport. On the other hand, courage and self-command were the qualities most admired by the Indians and they often left unharmed those who exhibited them. Mrs. Lytle uttered no sound and walked on without change of expression, as though nothing had happened.

Not only did the Indians refrain from harming Eleanor and her brother; the chief of the tribe took a great fancy to little Eleanor, and adopted her as his sister. Eleanor always called the chief Big White Man, for this was what the Indians called him, because of his unusual appearance. He was, however, the famous Seneca chief, Cornplanter. His portrait may be seen today at the New-York Historical Society in New York City. Cornplanter readily released Mrs. Lytle and the little boy to Mr. Lytle when he came with a ransom, but refused all pleas to give up little Eleanor. For four years she lived in the Indian village, the beloved charge of Cornplanter and the Old Queen, his mother. She was given the choicest foods, dressed in the finest garments and treated by the tribe as a princess. The name they gave her, Gron-we-na meant Little Ship Under Full Sail, from which it may be deduced that she possessed the drive and high spirits which were to characterize several of her female descendants. Both Nellie Kinzie Gordon and her daughter Juliette Low were also often called, as children, Little Ship Under Full Sail, and were proud of it.

When the Revolution ended, and peace was made, Eleanor's parents moved to Fort Niagara, because the Great Council Fire of the Senecas was held near there on the American side. Colonel Guy Johnson, the British Indian agent, offered to do what he could to get Eleanor back. Going to Cornplanter's village, Colonel Johnson persuaded Cornplanter to bring Eleanor to the next Council Fire, so that her parents might at least see their daughter and have a chance to embrace her.

Eleanor was now thirteen, and her former life seemed no more substantial than a dream. She promised Cornplanter that she would never leave him without his permission. But when they reached Fort Niagara, where the officers and their wives had gathered with the Lytles to await the arrival of the Senecas, and Eleanor saw her mother, she jumped from the canoe, ran and threw herself into her mother's arms. Cornplanter said, "The mother must have her child again. I will go back alone." Of all the experiences of her Kinzie ancestors that Juliette Low used to tell at Girl Scout campfires, this story was the girls' favorite.

The Lytles, however, did not have their daughter very long. Young folk matured early on the frontier, and at fourteen Eleanor Lytle married a British officer, Captain McKillip, and bore him a daughter, Margaret. Margaret has gone down in Illinois history as an eyewitness of the Fort Dearborn Massacre. Captain McKillip was accidentally shot by one of his own sentries and his widow after this lived with her parents, who had meanwhile moved on to Grosse Point, near Detroit. John Kinzie met her through one of his Forsyth half-brothers in Detroit, who had married her sister.

After his marriage John Kinzie plunged still farther into the wilderness. His first son, named John Harris Kinzie for the elder John's benefactor, was carried when only a few weeks old, in an Indian cradle on the back of a French *voyageur,* to a new Kinzie trading post at Parc aux Vaches, now Bertrand,

Michigan, on the St. Joseph River. Here the Kinzies quickly found their way into the affections of Chief To-pee-nee-bee and his tribe.

However, in his travels through the Indian country, John Kinzie had seen possibilities in M. Le Mai's lonely trading post on the "Chicagoux" River, a stone's throw from Lake Michigan, in a section which at that time was part of Indiana. Just seven years before, in 1796, a native of Santo Domingo had been the first man from the outside world to find his way to this remote spot. The Santo Domingan had gone on to Peoria, and M. Le Mai had taken over. By 1803 when John Harris Kinzie was born, M. Le Mai, too, had had enough of the loneliness and gladly sold to John Kinzie. But it was not until the next year, when Fort Dearborn was built, that Kinzie moved his wife and family from Parc aux Vaches.

Fort Dearborn stood on the south bank of the Chicago River. John Kinzie built his house, the first in the city of Chicago, on the north bank of the river facing the fort, near what is now the north end of the Michigan Avenue bridge, not far from the Wrigley Building. The house, facing the river, was a low building with a porch running along the front. A fenced yard lay between the house and the river, and Lombardy poplars were planted here. John Harris Kinzie as a boy planted two cottonwood trees behind the house. These grew to a great height and served as landmarks for many miles. Behind the house were also the auxiliary buildings—dairy, bakehouse, stables and a dormitory for the French *voyageurs*. Lake Michigan was only about thirty rods away (much filling has been done since 1804!), the intervening sand hills being covered with stunted cedars, pines and dwarf willow trees.

For twenty years the Kinzies were the only white inhabitants of Northern Illinois except for the Fort Dearborn personnel. Little Johnny's playmate was George Washington Whistler, the son of the commandant of the fort. In later years, George was to father the famous painter, James McNeil Whistler. By degrees Kinzie established other trading posts, all contributing to the parent one at Chicago. At "Milwaukie" among the Menominees; at Rock River with the Winnebagos and the Potawatomis; on the Illinois River and the Kankakee with the Potawatomis of the prairies; with the Kickapoos on what was called LeLarge, in the district afterwards made into Sangamon County.

The Kinzies' second child, Ellen Marion, was born in 1805, the first white child born in Northern Illinois outside of Fort Dearborn. Next came Maria Indiana, born in 1807, and Robert, the youngest, in 1810.

That John Kinzie must have been a man of unusual character and personality is illustrated by two incidents of the Kinzies' otherwise peaceful life. In 1810, John killed a rival trader, Lalime, who had made a murderous attack on him. The court-martial which sat on the case—there were no other courts of law than the military—held that Kinzie had acted in self-defense and absolved him of blame. Lalime's friends, balked of legal vengeance, buried the trader's body in the Kinzie's front yard, so that every time Kinzie left his house or returned to it he would have to pass by the body of his victim. If they had thought that this would make Kinzie suffer pangs of guilt, they did not know their man. Nellie wrote in her biography of her grandfather that, instead of avoiding the grave, Kinzie planted flowers on it, tended it as carefully as though it had held the body of a loved one, and was often seen to stand meditating over it. It is evident that this side of her grandfather's nature impressed her.

On August 7, 1812, a friendly Potawatomi chief, Winnimeg, arrived at Fort Dearborn with dispatches from General Hull, Commander of the North Western Army of the United States, reporting that war had been declared between the United States and Great Britain. The island of Mackinac had already fallen into the hands of the British, and General Hull with his army had arrived at Detroit. Expecting that the Indian tribes would come into the war on the British side, General Hull did not believe that the little garrison in the heart of the Indian country would be able to hold out. His orders to Captain Heald, then commanding at Fort Dearborn, were to evacuate if practicable.

As soon as Winnimeg had delivered the dispatches, he sought out John Kinzie and urged that it would be a mistake for the garrison to be evacuated, since the fort had ample ammunition and provisions for six months. But if Captain Heald followed General Hull's orders, Winnimeg said the garrison should leave the next morning before the Potawatomi tribes through whom they would have to pass learned that war had broken out.

Captain Heald rejected the advice, deciding to evacuate, but waiting a week before doing so. Within a day or so the Potawatomis had the news. John Kinzie, knowing that this spelled serious trouble, arranged for his wife and children to find refuge at Parc aux Vaches. The morning the garrison set out—the band was playing the Dead March—an urgent message arrived from To-pee-nee-bee, saying that the Potawatomis planned mischief, and begging Kinzie to go to Parc aux Vaches with his family. Kinzie expressed his appreciation, but said he would stay with the garrison, since the greater part of the Indians were warmly attached to him and his presence might be a restraint against violence. Moreover, John Kinzie kept with him nine-year-old Johnny, perhaps to show his trust in the good faith of the Indians. Kinzie's stepdaughter, Margaret, now married to Lieutenant Helm, one of the officers, elected to go with Kinzie.

From then on ensued an amazing series of events, unparalleled in frontier history and beggaring the most fertile imaginings of fiction writers. Kinzie's Indian friends hovered near, for the express purpose of saving Kinzie, and the members of his family. During the massacre itself and the months that followed it, Indians were constantly popping up like guardian angels, just in time to save a Kinzie or someone Kinzie was known to esteem. Chief To-pee-nee-bee seems to have remained in the vicinity, though out of sight. When the canoe bearing Mrs. Kinzie and the younger children reached the mouth of the Chicago River, he sent orders for the canoe to stop there. At no time did the hostiles threaten those in the canoe, though they tomahawked the helpless women and children in the wagons accompanying the garrison. To-pee-nee-bee personally saved one of the sergeants, as well.

Black Partridge, another of Kinzie's staunch friends, disguised himself with paint so that he might mingle with the hostiles. When Margaret Helm was seized by an Indian, Black Partridge pulled her away, dragged her to the lake and pretended to drown her, though being careful to keep her head above water. For many years a statuary group stood at the foot of Eighteenth Street in Chicago where this incident took place, erected by George Pullman to commemorate the massacre. Now in the Chicago Historical Society, the group shows Black Partridge in the act of rescuing Margaret from her attacker. Winnimeg and another Indian later escorted Margaret to the Indians' camp, which lay along what is now State Street, and the squaw of a chief gave her kindly shelter.

It was due to an Indian who had been raised in Kinzie's household that a truce was arranged which saved the remnants of the garrison who survived the initial attack. Intervention by Indians enabled Kinzie to save the life of Captain Heald, while Mrs. Kinzie ransomed Mrs. Heald from a hostile who was about to scalp her.

After the battle, the Kinzies were allowed to return to their home, and Black Partridge and four other Indians maintained a guard over their friends, to protect them from blood-maddened young warriors. When a group of Indians from beyond the Wabash descended upon the Kinzie house with blackened faces, sign of their malign intentions, Billy Caldwell, chief of the Potawatomi Nation, arrived in the nick of time, shamed the hostiles, and sent them harmlessly on their way. And when the Kinzies were delivered, along with other Fort Dearborn prisoners, to Detroit, Indian chiefs twice besieged the British commandant, who had ordered Kinzie's arrest, and obtained their friend's release.

It was 1816 before the Kinzies got back to Chicago. Two years later Johnny, then fifteen, was taken to Mackinac by his father and indentured to John Jacob Astor's American Fur Company. John's day began at five A.M. and ended at suppertime. After five years on the island he was transferred to Prairie du Chien. Here he learned to speak Winnebago, which up to this time no white man had succeeded in doing, and also wrote a grammar of the language.

General Lewis Cass, Governor General of the vast Michigan Territory, asked young John to become his secretary. For a time John was stationed near Sandusky among the Hurons and Wyandots. He learned their language also and compiled a grammar; in time he mastered thirteen Indian dialects. John's researches are said to have been the basis of Governor Cass' writings on Indian language and customs. Like his father before him, young John entered into the Indian life with zest and won the Indians' friendship by his integrity and fairness. In addition, young John could best the Indians at their own sports, which the Indians admired above all else. He excelled at lacrosse, an Indian game, and had beaten the swiftest runners of the Menominees in foot races.

Visitors to Chicago were rare, usually being relatives or friends who came to stay for a considerable time. But there was Fort Dearborn and its personnel just across the river to furnish companionship for the young Kinzies who remained in Chicago. Maria Indiana, the Kinzies' second daughter, married Lieutenant David Hunter of the Fifth Infantry, U.S.A., a West Point graduate of 1822. This union was to have unexpected consequences in the life of their niece, Nellie Kinzie Gordon, as yet unborn. Robert married the youngest daughter of Captain John Whistler, U.S.A., who was a first cousin to James McNeil Whistler. She was remarkably beautiful and Charles Dickens, on his 1842 visit, pronounced her the handsomest woman he had met in America.

In 1820, General Lewis Cass led an expedition which explored the hitherto unknown regions of Lake Superior, and for the first time traced the Mississippi River to its source. In the expedition was Dr. Alexander Wolcott, Jr., a highly educated Bostonian. The party stopped overnight at the Kinzie trading post on the Chicago River and Dr. Wolcott decided he wanted to settle in this wilderness spot. After the work of the expedition was finished, he became government Indian agent at Chicago and in 1823 married the Kinzies' eldest daughter, Ellen Marion, when she returned from her schooling at Mount Holyoke Seminary.

Dr. Wolcott and young John Harris Kinzie became close friends. When Dr. Wolcott went back to Boston in 1827 for a visit with his Eastern relatives, he took his brother-in-law with him. Juliette Magill, Dr. Wolcott's niece, brought up in Connecticut but then living in Fishkill, New York, happened to be in Boston visiting her Wolcott grandparents. The lithe young athlete from the western wilderness and the girl from New England fell in love at first sight and were married on August 9, 1827. It was for Juliette Magill Kinzie that Juliette Low was named. (Since Juliette Kinzie plays an important part in the succeeding narrative, in order to avoid confusion we shall henceforth refer to Juliette Low as Daisy, the name by which she was called on all but official occasions. Unless otherwise indicated, Juliette will refer to Juliette Magill Kinzie, Juliette (Daisy) Low's maternal grandmother.)

To trace the Wolcott line is to recapitulate the history of Connecticut, in the same way that the Kinzies go back to the beginnings of Wisconsin and Illinois. The first Wolcott in this country, Henry, had emigrated from Somerset County in England to Massachusetts in 1628. Settling in New Town, now Cambridge, he was one of the little group who left there in 1635 to found the town of Windsor, in what later became Connecticut. His son Henry was one of the patentees of the new colony under the Charter of 1662, which was hidden in the famous Charter Oak in 1687. Roger Wolcott, son of the second Henry, was Governor of Connecticut from 1751 to 1754. His sons, Erastus and Oliver, were prominent in Connecticut affairs and both took an active and prominent part in the Revolution. Oliver, one of the signers of the Declaration of Independence and head of the Connecticut militia throughout the war, became Governor of Connecticut in 1796. Oliver's son, Oliver, Junior, succeeded Alexander Hamilton as Secretary of the Treasury, then became Governor of Connecticut in 1817. And so the record continues, each generation of Wolcotts furnishing Connecticut with a governor throughout the nineteenth century.

Juliette was born in Middletown, Connecticut, on September 11, 1806, and grew up there, her family moving to Fishkill-on-Hudson when she was in her late teens. Her father, Arthur William Magill, was a prominent banker, her mother was a great-great-granddaughter of Roger Wolcott, the first Wolcott to become Governor of Connecticut.

Juliette's mother, a highly cultivated woman, had looked after the girl's early education and trained her to be one of those New England women who combined learning with all the womanly and housewifely arts. Juliette's reading had been directed by the Yale-trained Dr. Alexander Wolcott, Jr., Juliette's favorite uncle and John Harris Kinzie's brother-in-law. She had been "finished off" in a boarding school in New Haven and at Miss Willard's Seminary at Troy, New York. Juliette was versed in Latin, spoke French fluently and read

Spanish and Italian. In later life, after many Germans began to settle in Chicago, she learned German as well. She played the piano and organ, sketched, painted in water colors; she was an accomplished housekeeper, notable cook, and a deft needle-woman, whose embroideries were exquisite. No skill was lacking which would have enabled Juliette to take her place at the head of a beautifully conducted household on Beacon Hill, perhaps gathering about her a salon of New England intellectuals.

As against this impressive array of learning and accomplishments, John Harris Kinzie had spent not one day in school. There had been no school on the wild frontier where he was brought up. He was taught to read by a Forsyth cousin who was staying with the Kinzies. Later a discharged soldier from Fort Dearborn instructed the Kinzie children along with those of the officers. However, John was by no means an ignoramus. When he went to Mackinac Island at the age of fifteen, he lived with the Robert Stewarts. Mrs. Stewart, like Juliette's mother, was a highly cultivated woman and made it her responsibility to round out John's sketchy education. In the evening, after the boy's long day at the trading post, she had him read aloud to her; then they would talk over what he had read. "Out of the treasures of her well-stored mind, she imparted much knowledge and helped do away with the deficiencies inevitable from his unsettled and eventful life," his daughter Nellie tells us. It is possible that his wife, Juliette, continued his formal education after they were married, though if this was the case she does not mention it. In any event, when John Kinzie's later life took him into high affairs and into contact with many famous Americans and Europeans of his day, he was at no disadvantage in their company.

And if Juliette never had cause to be shamed by her husband's lack of schooling, neither did John have cause to regret that he had not chosen a bride trained in the ways of the wilderness, as his father had done. She quickly accommodated her housekeeping methods to the rude houses and facilities she had to make do with, while her cultivated mind and command of English gave the northwest frontier what it had lacked up to that time—a historian.

But perhaps the finest gift Juliette brought to her husband

was her spirit of high adventure and her eagerness to share every phase of his wilderness kingdom. Her delight was as great as his when, in 1829, John was offered the appointment as government sub-agent for the upper bands of the Winnebago Indians, with his headquarters at Fort Winnebago near what is now Portage, Wisconsin. Juliette would be living in the Indian country, which had captured her imagination from the time her uncle had gone on the Cass expedition, and then had remained as the Indian agent at Chicago.

John Kinzie was twenty-seven, his wife twenty-four, when they set out from Detroit in September, 1830, for the wilderness life that was the heart's desire of both. At Green Bay they left the lake steamer, *Henry Clay,* and embarked on a thirty-foot boat which was to take them up the Fox River to Fort Winnebago, on Lake Oshkosh. Their furniture would follow in other river boats. But as the regular carriers were likely to be banged about or upset in the many rapids of the Fox River, Juliette took with her her most precious possessions. These included her grand piano, which occupied the greater part of the tiny cabin of the boat. With them, too, went the boxes of silver with which John was to pay the annuities due his Indian charges.

Whenever they passed some lovely vista on the shore, Juliette would run for her sketching pad and pencils. The first edition of her first book, *Wau-Bun,* was illustrated by sketches she made during this trip, when there "was no sign of habitation along that vast and wooded shore. The gigantic forest trees and here and there the little glades of prairie opening to the water, showed a landscape that would have gladdened the eye of the agriculturist with its promise of fertility, but it was evidently untrodden by the foot of man."

Juliette was thrilled by every aspect of the journey, from the frequent portages to the picturesque characters they encountered en route. But what she liked best was the camping out at night along the shore.

"After our chilling, tedious day, it was pleasant to gather round the fire, to sit on the end of the blazing logs and watch the Frenchmen preparing our supper—the kettle nestling in a little nook of the glowing logs, the slices of ham browning and crisping on the forked sticks or 'broches' which the *voyageurs* dextrously cut and set around the burning brands, the savory messes of pork and onions hissing in the frying pan for the hungry Frenchmen. Truly it needs a wet, chilly journey, taken nearly fasting, as ours had been, to enable one to enjoy to its full extent that social meal—supper."

In the early morning the *bourgeois* or leader, who was John Harris Kinzie, turned everybody out with a stentorian "How How How!" The fires were quickly replenished, the kettle put on, in an incredibly short time smoking coffee and broiled ham were served, with toast brought a slice at a time hot and fresh from the glowing coals.

"There is after all," Juliette wrote, more than twenty years later, "no breakfast like a breakfast in the woods, with a well-trained Frenchman for master of ceremonies."

This was picnicking in de luxe style. On their later trips on horseback across the prairie, the only cooking equipment the Kinzies carried was a coffee pot and a tea kettle, each rider having an individual hunting knife and tin cup.

"At table the knife is drawn from the scabbard—those who remember to do so vouchsafe it a wipe on the napkin. Its first office is to stir the cup of coffee, next, to divide the piece of ham which is placed on a traveling biscuit, held in the left hand to fulfill the office of a plate. It is an art acquired only by long practice, to cut the meat so skilfully as not at the same time to destroy the dish. A wisp of dry grass is supposed in most cases to render the knife fit to be restored to the scabbard." This from a girl who had never seen a gentleman attired in a colored shirt until she entered the wilderness, "a spotless white collar and bosom being one of those 'notions' that 'Boston' and consequently New England 'folks,' entertained of the becoming in a gentleman's toilette."

When they were met by their Menominee guide, she was astonished to have him address her with a hearty *"Bonjour, bonjour, Maman!"* Not at his use of French, for she already knew it was the universal language of the wilderness, but at being addressed as Mother by an Indian. John Kinzie explained, "You must make up your mind to receive a very numerous and well-grown family, consisting of all the Winnebagos, Potawatomis, Chippewas and Ottawas, together with such Sioux, Sauks and Foxes and Iowas as have any point to gain in applying to me. The Winnebagos always call me Father by virtue of my office, and the others will do it as a matter of courtesy. You, of course, will be their mother." Juliette promised herself to be as good a mother as she could to her suddenly acquired children. It developed that there were around one hundred and fifty thousand of them.

At Fort Winnebago, Mrs. Twiggs, the wife of the commandant, had been the only white woman in the region for many months. She was so starved for feminine company that she insisted the Kinzies stay in the fort, giving them six large rooms, on three different floors, for their apartment.

Juliette says the bedroom contained a bed "of proportions sufficient to have accommodated Og, the King of Basham, with Mrs. Og and their children into the bargain." But an even more remarkable piece of furniture stood in the corner, a structure of grooved and carved timbers, with swelling pillars and doors that "were not only panelled, but radiated in a way to excite the admiration of all unsophisticated eyes." This served as combined wardrobe, dish cupboard and storage closet. The year before, a young West Point lieutenant had been sent to Wisconsin to complete the buildings at Fort Winnebago. West Point cadets of the day were given courses in drawing, probably with some rudiments of architecture in addition. Evidently the lieutenant had incorporated into the furniture for the quarters all the different styles of architecture that had come his way. The Kinzies called this particular piece The Davis in honor of its creator, but were always careful to refer to it respectfully in his presence.

The winter was cold and hard, but March started in genial and warm. Juliette could not be held back from visiting Chicago, of which she had heard so much. They would travel on horseback, and Juliette set forth in a costume that would have been suitable for a canter in Central Park; fashionable riding habit, which she had cajoled the fort tailor into making for her following a pattern of her own contriving, straw bonnet and kid gloves. She spurned her husband's suggestion that she at least provide herself with blanket socks, and a woolen shawl for her head and shoulders. "Though the wind occasionally lifted my headgear with a rude puff, and my hands ere long became stiff and swollen with the cold, I persuaded myself that these were trifling evils, to which I would soon get accustomed. I was too well pleased with the novelty of my outfit, with my hunting knife in a gay scabbard hanging from my neck, and my tin cup at my saddle-bow, to regard minor inconveniences."

The weather soon turned bitter. There were no towns along the way, not even Indian wigwams, only here and there isolated settlers with whom they might spend the night. At Morrison's, Mrs. Morrison told them she had not seen a white woman during the first eighteen months she lived on the prairie. When at last they reached Dixon's (now Dixon, Illinois), it was to learn that the ferry on which they had counted so much had been swept away by the spring floods. They had to make a perilous crossing of the angry river in a small boat, swimming the horses.

The Kinzies' guide, who had professed to know every step of the way from Dixon's to Chicago, led them astray. Their food gave out. The weather first turned very cold, then a hard snow began. Just before a blizzard struck, they stumbled upon an Indian encampment, on the opposite bank of a river. The Indians ferried them across in a small canoe, one at a time, then the blizzard closed in. They could not have survived it if they had still been wandering on the prairie. But since they did survive, all of these hardships and narrow escapes only made a more thrilling adventure for the New England girl.

And on the return trip, when their wagon of supplies was carried downstream by the current and the harness had to be cut to pieces to get the horses out, it was Juliette who saved the day by sewing the harness together again. In her New England girlhood she had been taught shoemaking, she remarked in her cultured Eastern voice, *as an accomplishment!*

On the trip to Chicago, they stayed at the "diggings"—mines, in the literal meaning of this word—of the son of Alexander Hamilton. Hamilton's was a group of log cabins, low, shabby and most unprepossessing in appearance. Juliette, who had known the Hamilton family in the East, was distressed when the twelve or so miners came in for their meal; for they were a rough lot whom Juliette suspected of being deserters from the army, and they treated Hamilton with thinly veiled impudence. Juliette wondered what Alexander Hamilton's emotions would be if he could know of the desolate life his son had elected for himself. Yet it was perhaps stranger that a lady in whose veins ran the blood of Charlemagne, Alfred the Great, William the Conqueror, and a host of lesser French, Norman and Saxon kings, dukes and earls, had chosen this wilderness as her home, too. For through the Drakes, with whom the Wolcotts had intermarried—the American Drakes were descended from a brother of Sir Francis—Juliette Kinzie could boast if she chose of a truly royal heritage. Juliette appears to have chosen not to boast of it, but her royal lineage was later a source of considerable satisfaction to her daughter Nellie in the family-conscious South.

The Chicago of 1831, when Juliette Kinzie first visited it, still contained, aside from the fort personnel, no more families than could be counted on one's fingers. The fort had been rebuilt on a somewhat different plan, with bastions at alternate angles, and was enclosed by a high picket fence. The Kinzie homestead faced the fort on the north bank of the river, as it had stood for twenty-seven years. The two cottonwood trees John had planted behind the house as a boy now were giants, and John pointed them out to Juliette from far away on the prairie. A little farther up the river on the north bank was the Indian agency house, which was called Cobweb Castle because a bachelor had lived in it for some years and apparently had not been a very good housekeeper. It stood at the southwest corner of what was then Wolcott, but is now State Street, and North Water streets, a solid building of huge logs, hewed and squared, its log outbuildings grouped around it. It was a Chicago landmark until shortly before the Civil War.

The first John Kinzie had died of apoplexy in 1828. The elder Mrs. Kinzie lived in Cobweb Castle, with her son Robert, and her daughters; Ellen Marion, widow of Dr. Wolcott, who had died a few months before, and Margaret Helm, who had divorced her husband. Scattered along the north bank of the river there were now a few other houses, but on the south bank there were no buildings between the fort and Wolf Point, as the forks of the Chicago River were then called. To Juliette, these new relatives at once became "our mother," "our brother Robert," "our sisters." And perceiving the drama and historic importance of the experiences the family had been through, Juliette took down from her mother-in-law and sister-in-law

Margaret their first-hand accounts of the Fort Dearborn Massacre and the girlhood adventure of Little Ship Under Full Sail.

The Kinzie family, under the distribution of land, was entitled to a quarter section or one hundred sixty acres, and during Juliette's visit to Chicago, John's brother Robert returned from Palestine, Illinois, where the land office was located, with a certificate of the family title to the portion of Chicago's lake shore later known as Kinzie's Addition. But the certificate covered only one hundred and two acres, because the Chicago River and Lake Michigan cut off fifty-eight acres on the southern and eastern lines of the quarter. They therefore had the privilege of selecting the remaining fifty-eight acres due them out of any as yet unappropriated land that suited them.

"There is that cornfield at Wolf Point," suggested the elder Mrs. Kinzie. "It is fine land, and will always be valuable for cultivation. Besides, as it faces down the main river, the situation will always be a convenient one."

Robert said, "Listen to her! We have just got one hundred two acres, which is more than we will ever want or know what to do with. Why should we get more than we can possibly make use of?"

Mrs. Kinzie urged that some day they would be sorry if they didn't, but Robert felt it would be greedy to take more land than they could till, and the remaining fifty-eight acres was never claimed. The Chicago Merchandise Mart stands now at what was then Wolf Point.

Another incident of Juliette's 1831 visit to Chicago is worth mentioning. Considerable excitement had been caused by the fact that a settler had been selling milk punch, well-laced with brandy, to the soldiers at Fort Dearborn instead of the plain milk he was supposed to sell, and the beverage had proved so popular that regularity and discipline had suffered to a marked extent. Many years later this episode, recorded in *Wau-Bun,* was to furnish Juliette's daughter Nellie and *her* daughter Juliette Low with a "stunt" in which mother and daughter joined, and which proved a lifesaving one for soldiers in the Spanish-American War.

On their return to Fort Potawatomi, John and Juliette found that several married officers were coming out from the East and that their quarters in the fort would be needed. They lived in makeshift houses, with leaky roofs, which Juliette managed nevertheless to make charming, while John put up a new agency house and outbuildings with $1,500 granted him by the government for the purpose.

The summer of 1832, when the new buildings were going. up, was the one of the Black Hawk War. Indian runners kept bringing word that Black Hawk was about to fall on the whites at Portage and the fort. Juliette was pregnant with her first baby, though she does not mention this fact in her account. She practiced marksmanship and slept with her two little pistols beside her pillow. She begged to stay with John when he decided it was advisable to send her to Fort Howard at Green Bay, while remaining at his post himself. She yielded only when he pointed out that by the aid of his friends among the Sauks and Foxes, he could hope to preserve his life if he were alone; but that this might be impossible if she remained, and they would only perish together. So Juliette went off to Fort Howard, but would better have stayed behind. For Portage was never seriously threatened, and she had a difficult, dangerous journey, with many narrow escapes.

John, meanwhile, attended to his house building, and he built so well that the agency house at Portage continued to stand long after all the other buildings at Fort Winnebago, with the single exception of the surgeon's house, had disintegrated. It was restored by the National Association for Colonial Dames in Wisconsin and dedicated in 1932, the one hundredth anniversary of its building. It may be visited today. Sales from Juliette Kinzie's book, *Wau-Bun*, constantly reprinted as the editions are sold out, go to its upkeep. Here may be seen one of the rude wooden boxes, with the name, Kinzie, carved on it, in which it is believed John Harris Kinzie transported his first shipment of government silver to the Winnebagos. The box was a gift to agency house from his great-granddaughter, Daisy Lawrence.

But the Kinzies' first winter in their new house was saddened by the starving of their Winnebago "children," who had been so anxious to prove their loyalty to John and the other whites that they had left their villages to avoid any contact with the Sauks, and hence had failed to plant their crops. The game on which they could otherwise have lived had been driven off by the troops and the Indian war parties scouring the country. The Kinzies and the other settlers gave until all the food they had was gone. The boatloads of corn John Kinzie had ordered in the fall, foreseeing the emergency, were held in the port of departure because of weather conditions. There was no possibility of getting so much as a barrel of flour. The Kinzies' meals were brought to them from the fort, Juliette saving every left-over scrap to give to Indian petitioners.

By this time Juliette's baby boy, Wolcott, had been born, though of her accouchement under those rude and tense conditions she says not a word. What she does say is that every time a door of the agency house was opened, "some wretched mother would rush in, grasp the hand of my infant, and placing that of her famished child within it, tell us, pleadingly, that he was imploring 'his little brother for food.' "

The rejoicing when the corn boats arrived could not wipe out the painful memories of that dreadful winter. Moreover, John and Juliette were finding that they couldn't make ends meet! Governor Porter took up the Kinzies' situation in a letter to Lewis Cass, who had now become Secretary of War in President Jackson's Cabinet. He pointed out that not only must John Kinzie feed his own family, "but also almost every genteel stranger who comes there, as there is no other house where they can stop," which made the cost of living more than Kinzie could sustain. The upshot was that John was made a full Indian agent, and placed in charge of the Indian agency at Chicago.

"The intelligence when communicated to our Winnebago children, brought forth great lamentations and demonstrations of regret," Juliette Kinzie wrote in *Wau-Bun.* "From the surrounding country they came flocking in, to inquire into the truth of the tidings they had heard, and to petition earnestly that we would continue to live and die among them.

"Among them all, no one seemed so overwhelmed with affection as Elizabeth, our poor Cut-Nose. When we first told her of our intention, she sat for hours in the same spot, wiping away the tears that would find their way down her cheeks, with the corner of the chintz shawl she wore pinned across her bosom.

" 'No! Never, never shall I find such friends again!' she would exclaim. 'You will go away, and I shall be left here *all alone!'*

"Wild-Cat, too, the fat, jolly Wild-Cat, gave way to the most audible lamentations.

" 'Oh, my little brother,' he said to the baby on the morning of our departure, when he had insisted on taking him and seating him on his fat, dirty knee, 'you will never come back to see your poor brother again!'

"And, having taken an extra glass on the occasion, he wept like an infant."

It was, in fact, the end of an era in American history, for already the red men, including the friendly Winnebagos, were being pushed inexorably across the Mississippi, white settlers were infiltrating the deep forests and spreading over the fertile prairies of Wisconsin and Illinois. But as long as John Harris Kinzie lived his Winnebago "children" came to him in Chicago when they had a problem, they always stopped by to see him and counsel with him first when they went to Washington to lay their grievances before the Great White Father there. It was not unusual to have twelve or more chiefs camped about the Kinzie house. Nellie remembered these visits well and often spoke of them to her children and grandchildren. One of her chief treasures in her Savannah home was her collection of Indian portraits of which she had several huge albums. The grandchildren remember that she would always let them look at the portraits, which they loved to do, but they understood that if they soiled or tore a picture swift retribution would follow.

CHAPTER III

─────────── ☆ ───────────

THE WILDERNESS VANISHES
A CITY GROWS UP

JULIETTE KINZIE noted in *Wau-Bun* that by 1833, Chicago had become so much of a place that it was necessary for the proprietors of Kinzie's Addition to lay out lots and open streets through their property. By 1834, when Juliette and little Wolcott joined John Harris Kinzie there, it contained more than fifty inhabitants!

The Kinzies moved into Cobweb Castle, the agency house, and immediately gave their attention to building a church. The one deprivation Juliette had felt in her wilderness life was the fact that there wasn't a single church or minister in the whole area, not even a chaplain at Fort Winnebago. Robert Kinzie gave the land, and John Harris Kinzie and a neighbor, George Dole, contributed the money to build St. James' Church and to call a rector from the East. The first roster contained five names—Mr. and Mrs. John Harris Kinzie, Mr. and Mrs. George W. Dole and Mrs. Magill, Juliette Kinzie's mother.

And so it came about, when a daughter was born to the Kinzies in June, 1835, she could later boast that she was the first child baptized in Chicago's first church, and that she antedated the city of Chicago itself. For it was not until after she was born, though in the same year, that the Illinois legislature appointed a board of trustees for the "Village of Chicago," John Harris Kinzie being its first president.

The child was given the name Eleanor Lytle Kinzie, for her grandmother Mrs. John Kinzie, who had been Little Ship Under Full Sail to the Senecas. But she was called Nellie, and thus we shall call her throughout this book, except as she becomes Mama and Granny in the course of the years.

About 1837 John Harris Kinzie completed a new brick house, which must have been very splendid for the Chicago of that day, at the corner of Cass and Michigan streets. His brother Robert built a large wooden house at the other end of the block, on the corner of Michigan and Rush streets, both houses facing south. The space between was gardened, a picket fence which ran north and south separating the two properties. In the brick house were born five more boys to the John Harris Kinzies, in order John, Arthur, Julian (who died at six weeks of membranous croup), Frank and George. In addition, as time went on John and Juliette Kinzie adopted seven nephews, nieces and cousins.

Robert Kinzie and his beautiful wife died not long after building their big wooden house, and Nellie's uncle, David Hunter, and her Aunt Maria Hunter (the daughter of the first John Kinzie) adopted their two little girls. The Robert Kinzie house was then occupied for many years by Judge Butterfield and his family, their daughter Addy being Nellie's great friend and playmate.

The two yards, comprising a whole block between them, made a children's paradise. A large green lawn about forty feet deep ran across the front of the garden, with a circular bed filled with flowers in the center. Ornamental shrubs and trees were scattered about. A wide graveled walk ran from the piazza steps to the picket gate in the dividing fence, and a similar walk ran down the middle of the garden to the back fence on Illinois Street. There were plum trees, pears, apples, peaches, apricots and nectarines, grape trellises and strawberry beds; English gooseberry bushes; red, white and black raspberries. And every path was bordered with red, white and black currants. At the extreme rear of the garden was a big icehouse which was filled each winter out of the Chicago River, then clear and clean, and a smokehouse in which the Kinzies cured their own hams and bacons. Drinking water was hauled from Lake Michigan in great casks.

Nellie remembered no paved streets in her girlhood, with the possible exceptions of Lake and Clark, on the South Side. When the snow melted in the spring the roads were almost impassable and it became a serious problem for the sewing circle ladies who lived on the North Side to get to the Thursday afternoon meetings. Juliette Kinzie solved it by sending the Kinzies' big two-wheeled cart around to collect as many ladies as could be comfortably seated on the floor of the cart, which was spread with wolf skins and buffalo robes. The mud came up nearly to the hubs of the wheels. When Nellie went to Mrs. Elmore's school on South Michigan, the pupils crossed the river at the foot of Rush Street on a flat scow, which was pulled across the river with a hockey stick on a cable.

But Chicago was growing! "One day Mrs. Elmore told us we must stay after school as she had something very interesting to tell us. 'Children, I want you to know that we have had a census taken of our town, and we have *six thousand* inhabitants! I should not be surprised if some of you children live to see the day when we have *ten thousand!*" When Nellie wrote this, in 1914, she noted that Chicago's population at that time was two million.

Apparently there was a plethora of private schools, for Nellie attended a different one nearly every year, besides putting in a year in one of the newly opened public schools—the school she went to being later named the Kinzie School for her father. She changed schools so frequently, in fact, that one might suspect it was by request of the heads, except that she would surely have said so if such had been the case, for she gloated over every misdeed of her childhood. She had the year in public school because the schools being free, it was thought they were for paupers. To correct this impression, the members of the school board—John Harris Kinzie, of course, was one—sent their own children for a time.

The first board sidewalk built on the North Side (of the Chicago River) ran in front of the Kinzie house on Michigan Street and down the side of their garden on Cass to Illinois Street. Nellie's father, accompanied by Neptune, Nellie's Newfoundland dog, had directed the workmen while they were building it. Consequently Neptune deemed it the Kinzies' private property and for weeks would not allow anyone but Kinzies to walk on it. These boardwalks, used universally in Chicago until the late 1850's, according to Nellie were refuges for the rats with which the city was infested. On a muddy day when the boards would sink down into the slush under the feet of passersby, rats as big as kittens would scurry out from the sides and dart among the pedestrians' feet.

Shortly after General Taylor was elected President, Juliette took Nellie to Washington to visit Nellie's Aunt Maria and Uncle David Hunter. Uncle David had been on General Taylor's staff in the Mexican war. Aunt Maria, like a true Kinzie female, had accompanied him throughout the campaign in a specially built carriage. Nellie's most vivid Washington impression was of being taken to a reception at the White House. There she met not only President Taylor and his daughter Betty, but was presented to Dolly Madison. Still the reigning queen of Washington society, Dolly Madison, was seated in state on a small sofa, dressed quaintly in a black brocaded silk, with elbow sleeves and black lace mitts. She had three little sausage-like curls on each side of her face, surmounted by a white turban with a spray of diamonds on one side. She was treated with great deference and seemed to be enjoying herself hugely.

President Taylor was a broad, gray-haired man with shrewd eyes, a genial smile and remarkably short legs. He had a long chat with Nellie and asked her what she had most wanted to see in Washington. "I wanted most to see you," was her reply, which amused the President very much. Nellie capped this by adding that she would like to have a lock of his hair. Next day President Taylor sent her one by messenger. Nellie cherished the lock but it was destroyed in the Chicago fire in 1871.

One of the most treasured recollections Nellie retained of her childhood, however, was the time her father took her with him on a trip to the northern Great Lakes. He had been one of the discoverers of the copper lodes on Lake Superior, having located the famous Ontonagon mine in Michigan, and having helped to locate the copper mines in Minnesota. Nellie had the experience of traveling by Indian canoe, as her forebears had done so often, propelled by a stalwart Indian, and of shooting the rapids, considered a dangerous and daring feat. On the way back they stopped over at Mackinac Island and she visited her father's boyhood stamping ground.

Nellie, in short, grew up in a community which, while raw and new and still allied to the wilderness, was far from lacking amenities and culture. Her mother was a gentlewoman of distinguished lineage and culture, her father a gentleman by nature and by self-education. Nellie's childhood could not have been happier, her parents more loving. How does it happen then, that Nellie was an *enfant terrible* from the beginning of her life to its end?

In her reminiscences of her childhood and young womanhood—her own title for them was "Chestnuts"—she remarks, "I am sure it will delight my children and grandchildren to learn that I was a very naughty child—what my nurse used to term, 'torn down bad.' " She recalled with satisfaction that she was always the ringleader in the many scrapes she got into in childhood, with Addy Butterfield her faithful follower. One day Nellie and Addy dressed in Mrs. Butterfield's clothes, Nellie putting on the lady's best silk dress, on her head the black curled front with which Mrs. Butterfield hid the ravages of time, a lace cap over this, and Mrs. Butterfield's best crepe de Chine shawl around her shoulders. Addy was no less gloriously arrayed. The little girls went to look at themselves in the pier-glass in the drawing room, not aware that there were visitors. Mrs. Butterfield gave a shriek, then the visitors shrieked, and Nellie and Addy dashed out of the house, over the picket fence, across the garden and up on top of the Kinzies' summer house, shedding Mrs. Butterfield's best finery as they went. "Needless to say, I escaped scot-free, though I dare say Addy was not so fortunate."

One of Nellie's dearest chums at the Misses Whiting's school was a girl named Aurelia. Thereafter, the two girls did not see each other again for more than forty years. Then, when Nellie came to the Middle West to be Chicago's honored guest at the Columbian Exposition in 1893, they met at a reunion of their class.

The first thing Aurelia said was: "Nellie, are you as bad as ever?"

"Aurelia," said Nellie, "I am worse than ever."

Said Aurelia, "Then I love you more than ever!" and the two middle-aged ladies flew into each others arms.

Aurelia also related a tale Nellie had not heard before, and which she greatly relished. When Nellie had returned home from Madam Canda's school, back in 1854, one of her group mentioned that he had called on Nellie the evening before.

"Is she any different?" someone asked. "Has she improved any?"

"Oh yes, decidedly," was the reply. "Now she swears in French!"

Nellie says that she was never whipped but once, and that was for telling a lie. When it was discovered that Nellie had told the truth, that someone else had lied, John Harris Kinzie, who had administered the whipping, was so conscience-stricken "that I escaped many richly deserved whippings in the future, in consequence."

But there are other reasons why it would have been hard for the kindly John and Juliette Kinzie, with their abundance of parental love, to discipline their only daughter. Nellie begins her reminiscences with the death of her older brother, Wolcott, when she was three. "I remembered it vividly, it was such an awful tragedy, and prostrated the whole family. My father lived for twenty-seven years after this but never could bear to have Wolcott's name mentioned. Up to the time of his death he would leave the room hastily if Wolcott's name was accidentally spoken."

Nellie and Wolcott, then six years old, had been playing together in the yard when Wolcott ran off with some other boys, making Nellie stay behind inside the picket fence. In an empty house, the little boys found a bottle of corrosive sublimate, and Wolcott took a swallow. Nellie recalls the scene when he dashed into the house where his mother was entertaining guests at tea and ran to Juliette screaming, "I'm burning up, I'm burning up, it's burning the heart out of me!" Juliette applied white of egg and other remedies but Wolcott died after two days of dreadful suffering.

Then little Julian had died in infancy. But one of the worst fates of all befell Frank, with the yellow curls and soft dark eyes, who was born after Julian and was Nellie's favorite among her brothers. When Frank was twenty months old he fell into a tub of boiling water and was frightfully burned. The doctors said he could not live, but Juliette refused to let this son die, and for six months worked with him day and night. The only thing that gave the little boy ease was for her to walk the floor with him and sing to him, and this she did by the hour. When she was so weary she could no longer stand alone, her husband and Anne Meldrim, a cousin who was staying with them, would walk her, supporting her on either side. It was two years before Frank could run and play like other children, and he remained frail. When the cholera epidemic struck Chicago in the summer of 1850, Frank, then aged six, was one of the first to succumb. Taken ill in the evening, he died the next morning.

There was little time for grieving, for Chicago was sorely stricken—three of the Kinzies' servants died after little Frank—and trained nurses did not yet exist. John and Juliette devoted all their time to caring for the sick, unmindful of the danger of infection to themselves, and even Nellie, then only fifteen, was drafted to sit up with little Amelia White, which made her feel very grown-up.

But one can see the toll taken in Juliette by the loss of her sons. Through great good fortune, the family portraits had been removed from the Kinzie house just before the Chicago fire and sent to Nellie in Savannah. The work of some itinerant painter and crude in many respects, the portraits, nevertheless, are reputed to have been fair likenesses. One of Juliette with little Nellie at three, before Wolcott's death, represents Juliette as a full-faced young woman with glowing skin and smiling eyes, reminding one of the healthy matrons the Dutch masters so liked to paint. Another, made after the death of Frank, shows a hollow-cheeked woman with great, tragic eyes. To this sad woman, it must have been immeasurable comfort to have so glowing and vital a creature as Nellie in the house.

Besides, Nellie had a genius for emerging unscathed from her ecapades. At the school kept by Miss Smith and Miss Thatcher, she drew a caricature of Miss Thatcher on the inside panel of the front door of the school. When Nellie came home from Madam Canda's she called at the school and Miss Thatcher showed her the drawing. The hall had been repainted, but Miss Thatcher would not allow her caricature to be obliterated!

At eighteen she was at Madam Canda's school, in New York City, and visited West Point under the chaperonage of her Aunt Maria Hunter (the Superintendent of the Academy at that time was an able Virginian, Captain Robert E. Lee). The night of the big hop Aunt Maria was so engaged in conversation with Mrs. Winfield Scott that Nellie feared they would miss the hop entirely. The Commandant of the Point observed Nellie's uneasiness and offered to take Nellie to the hop himself. Outside the gate, entirely against the strict West Point rules, several cadets were waiting for Nellie and surged forward when they saw her coming, only to halt in guilty embarrassment when they recognized her escort.

The Commandant remarked drily, "I see you are well taken care of, Miss Kinzie, so I will bid you good night."

"Oh, no, Captain Garnett," exclaimed Nellie, "you must come on to the hop with me. I've been counting on having the first dance with you." The flattered Commandant complied, the cadets perforce trailing along into the lighted hall, where their identities would be pitilessly apparent. As soon as Captain Garnett had had his dance and left, the cadets crowded around Nellie, chiding her for having gotten them into a peck of trouble.

"Stupid," replied Nellie, "I got you out of trouble. You won't hear a word now about having been out of bounds!" And they never did.

Nellie's lifelong refusal to honor conventions which she considered stuffy and hypocritical may have been abetted by several little books of poems for children which had been her own property as a child and which she passed on to her granddaughter Daisy Lawrence. Published in the early 1800's, these are literary and psychological curiosities as well as rarities, full of an unconscious sadism which grew out of the idea that children are adults in miniature. It is evident that the poems made a profound impression on Nellie—in reverse!

She had kept, through all those many years, one book *Good Child* and another, *Cowslip, or More Cautionary Stories in Verse* "by the author of that much-admired little work entitled *The Daisy*." *The Daisy* was not preserved for posterity, but Nellie makes reference to it in her many annotations of *Cowslip*, its sequel. After each dreary little homily in *Cowslip*,

Nellie added another poem of her own devising—at least these are in her unmistakable handwriting—which conveys her reaction.

Her addendum to "Going to School" begins:

> I would not be a good child
> And with good children stand,
> For all the gold and silver
> Within this heathen land!
>
> I could not be so virtuous—
> Oh life would be so tame!
> I would not recognize myself,
> I would not know my name.

After one particularly edifying poem Nellie remarks,

> See how well the little Mary
> Sits up straight and studies grammar.
> I confess I'm so contrary
> That I feel like saying "dammer!"

Her answer to "Quarrelsome Children" has a real bite, forerunner of the vitriolic fury with which, in adulthood, Nellie was to assail the kind of wrongdoers she hated most—hypocrites, those who exploited persons less fortunate than themselves, and betrayers of trusts:

> Ah me! it makes me very sad
> To think that children will be bad.
> To quarrel too is very wrong
> Unless you happen to be strong.
> If you are stronger and can fight,
> Then wrong of course is often right
> And you can spill your brother's blood—
> But you must say " 'tis for his good."
> No matter how he does resist
> If on this phrase you do insist
> You then can kill him "for his good"
> And live on hymns for daily food;
> And raise a psalm, with aspect prim,
> While you decide what's good for him.

Besides the internal evidence of their effect that Nellie has incorporated into the little books themselves, in her letters to Addy Butterfield from Madam Canda's school she mentions their treasured memories of *Good Child* and *Daisy* as an insoluble bond between them. One can imagine the little girls poring over these incredible poems, as today's children pore over the *Pooh* books, steeping themselves in the standards set forth so that they might behave in an exactly opposite way! A child as spirited and intelligent as Nellie most certainly was, might feel obligated to use such mild profanities as reached her tender ears because the excessive punishment of "Improper Words" would so offend her strong sense of justice. Her defense in adulthood was that it was not swearing so long as one did not take the name of the Lord in vain. This she never did—unless she got really mad.

Nellie's reminiscences indicate that she was a thorough tomboy, taking part in the games of her brothers, her adopted cousins and her schoolmates. She boasts that she could beat all the boys at marbles and had a wonderful collection of alleys and moss agates. In winter they used to skate, and Nellie had a fine sled. She rode horseback over the prairie that lay about this rapidly growing, but still-rural community.

At the same time she was carefully schooled by her accomplished mother in all the housewifely arts, including shoemaking, which Juliette had once found valuable in her life on the frontier. And the Kinzie children were required to say the church catechism every Sunday afternoon. By the time Nellie was eighteen, and ready to go off to Madam Canda's, she was a pianist of considerable merit and somehow in her variegated schooling had learned to speak French and Italian fluently and read several other foreign languages. Excellent rider, dancer and skater, graceful, pretty and vivacious, she was the lively center of the group who constituted Chicago's younger set in the 1850's.

The portrait of her painted by Healy in about 1855 shows a very comely girl, though not a striking beauty, with a broad forehead, hair parted in the middle and swept back in two great wings—Nellie's hair was always her chief glory—with just a touch of mischief in the eyes and of petulance in the lips. Nellie must have been on her best behavior for Mr. Healy!

Several of Nellie's friends have hinted that the Kinzies sent Nellie to Madam Canda's in the hope of ridding her of some of her hoyden ways, but there is no evidence that this was the case. Nellie's Aunt Ellen Marion had been sent to Mount Holyoke when Chicago was only a fort and trading post in the midst of wilderness. It was natural that Juliette should have wished her daughter to get an Eastern finishing, and Madam Canda was a family friend. And if Nellie's parents did have a secret hope that her behavior might be toned down a bit by this experience, it was not to be realized.

Madam Canda's school catered to daughters of the best families, but its facilities and regimen sound like those of the English workhouses that Charles Dickens described in his novels during this period. Some sixty boarders slept in dormitories, one large and two small ones, with a teacher in each dormitory. The girls washed and dressed in two large rooms, around which ran rows of cupboards where clothes hung that were in daily use. The rest were locked up in cupboards of which Old Darder, the "dragon of a housekeeper," kept the keys, doling out such items as handkerchiefs on specific days of the week.

Madam Canda had a bath attached to her bedroom, but there were none for the pupils and no place where they could have privacy. If the girls wanted to bathe, they retired to the daily clothes cupboard "carrying our washbasin and other paraphernalia, and did the best we could."

At four o'clock in the afternoon the girls were taken out *en masse* to walk, lined up two by two, with a teacher at each end of the line. This arrangement was calculated to discourage flirtations, but Nellie says a girl from New Orleans did manage to slip a note to a young man during the line of march, but was caught and promptly expelled. However, one might visit friends from Saturday to Monday if properly escorted from the school and back again.

Nellie was generally popular at Madam Canda's, but her special chums were Flo and Ellen Sheffield of New Haven—their father founded the Sheffield School of Science at Yale—and Eliza Gordon, a gentle, shy girl from Savannah, Georgia. Eliza's two brothers, George and William Washington Gordon II, were students at Yale. Nellie met the handsome George in the fall of 1853, and several times he escorted Eliza and Nellie to the opera. The Sheffield and Gordon families were great friends, and the Sheffield girls called the younger Gordon boy Brother Willie just as Eliza did.

At Christmastime, Eliza and Nellie were invited to the Sheffield home on Hillhouse Avenue in New Haven for the holidays, "and of course," wrote Nellie in her reminiscences, "the very first evening Willie Gordon called. He was very quiet and demure; wore his hair quite long, student-fashion, and unfortunately at this time he had a boil on the back of his neck so big that he could hardly turn his head."

In a letter to Willie several years later, Nellie reminds him that she peeped through the curtains at him, presumably before coming in to be introduced properly. Willie's own report of their first meeting indicates that she then proceeded to sparkle and dazzle with her wit and her ability as a *raconteuse*, for which she was famous throughout her life, and as Willie never shone particularly on social occasions, or thought he didn't, the effect, combined with his self-consciousness about the boil, would probably have been to make him completely tongue-tied. Nellie says, "When we went up to bed that night, Eliza asked me anxiously what I thought of Brother Willie and I somewhat scandalized her by saying that I thought he looked just like a Methodist parson."

The next morning Willie took Eliza and Nellie to see the Yale Library (now a chapel), located on what is called the Old Campus. The party got separated, Eliza and Nellie finding themselves at the top of the main staircase. The temptation was irresistible. Nellie slid down the banister, meeting at the foot, to her great surprise, Mr. Willie Gordon, who if possible was more surprised than she was.

It was then that Willie, as sober and conservative a young Southern gentleman as ever was, fell in love with the incandescent little tomboy from the Middle West. Nellie herself doesn't go into that in her reminiscences, but Willie's reaction must have altered the opinion she had gained of him the night before, for she took pains to let her progeny know that "my subsequent knowledge of Willie led me to conclude that his resemblance to any kind of parson was, like beauty, only skin deep."

In a letter to Addy Butterfield, dated December 29, 1853, Nellie wrote, "I am at the Sheffields' and oh they do live so

delightfully! In a charming house facing the great 'Green.'
Eliza Gordon is here too, and her handsome brother Willie
Gordon, who is about nineteen and a *senior* in college, is here
nearly all the time. Yesterday he took us sleighriding in a great
cutter, and we were out the whole afternoon. Today we are
going *twice*, once at eleven o'clock and again at two-thirty. At
night we all dance or play cards." Next Willie was taking
Nellie in the cutter alone and once, when she was cold, he gave
her his coat and nearly got pneumonia.

However, Nellie says in her reminiscences that it was not
until after her final visit to New Haven at the time Willie
graduated in 1854, that "I found that I really cared more for
him than for anyone I had ever met. As I had several little
affairs to settle up at home before I could give him a final
answer, we did not become engaged till he came out to Chicago
the following October."

The engagement lasted for over three years. For one thing,
Willie was not yet in a position to support a wife. Also, they
had several things to straighten out between themselves. One
pertained to religion. Nellie was a devoted Episcopalian and
Willie a Presbyterian. There was also the matter of slavery
to which Nellie, as a good Northerner, objected. In one of her
letters to Willie during their engagement she comments on a
Presbyterian wedding he had spoken of in a previous letter:
"I don't like that. Such a wedding would seem little like one.
My idea is that *church* is the place to be married, where one
has been baptized, confirmed and *catechized*. Then, a party, a
dance, all the old friends, a full house and *no tears*. Weddings
without dancing and music are only to be compared to fu-
nerals."

And in a later letter she says, "I don't like your remarks on
puritanism. . . . Our church and our religion do not forbid
innocent enjoyment. . . . Do you think you've caught a Tartar?
I may express myself rather strongly but remember, I feel anything *like* a slur on my church far more than you ever did my
remarks on *slavery*."

Apparently they arrived at a compromise. Willie bowed to
Nellie's Episcopalianism, later on joining Christ Church in
Savannah, and Nellie forebore to criticize slavery.

For the most part, Nellie's letters to Willie during this period are rather surprisingly sweet ones, filled with frank and open, yet maidenly, expressions of her love and her longing to be with him. The young Yale man had captured her heart completely, and wayward as she was in some things, her love for Willie was as deep and tender as that any man ever had from any woman.

This did not keep Nellie from having a good time during her engagement. Chicago was a very gay place with many brilliant entertainments, in those years just before the Civil War, when the population was pushing ninety thousand. Nellie often went to three parties in one evening. Ball dresses were generally made of light diaphanous materials such as tulle, crepe, tarletan, with low necks, sashes and very full skirts. The thin dresses and freezing Chicago winters did not prevent the belles from piling into a sleigh at the drop of a hat, and often a large party would go out to the hotel at Lake View, ending up with a jolly dance. Visiting girls especially had a good time in Chicago in the 1850's, since there were about four men to every girl.

And a very exciting event was taking place in the Kinzie family. Juliette was shaping her wilderness adventures into the book whose title, *Wau-Bun,* meant Dawn, or Early Day. Her account of the Fort Dearborn Massacre, from the notes she made on her first visit to Chicago in 1831, had been published in pamphlet form in 1837, according to the Chicago Historical Society, which may indicate that there had been a reprinting. She included the massacre story in *Wau-Bun* as well as the story of her mother-in-law, Little Ship Under Full Sail, among the Senecas, and added a description of the Wisconsin wilderness and its people, as she had seen them in 1830. In addition to recording the historic events, Juliette had an eye for the human and colorful and amusing, and the little details of daily living which enable moderns to enter into the lives of people of a bygone era. She described Indian games, told Indian legends, gave the words of the songs the *voyageurs* sang. She wrote, moreover, in such an engaging and lively style that, for all its Victorian quaintness of phrasing, *Wau-Bun* may be read today for pleasure, as well as for its valuable source material.

Nellie was a full confidante in her mother's life and writings, and became her literary executor after Juliette's death. She must have read each chapter as her mother finished it. Derby and Jackson of New York brought out the book in 1856, and Juliette sprang into national prominence in consequence. When a new edition of *Wau-Bun* with added notes by Nellie came out in 1901, the Chicago *Tribune* commented that this book had been Chicago's first literary production. It was Chicago's only literary production for many years.

In 1857 Willie was made a partner in the firm of Tison & Gordon and there was no need to delay the marriage any longer. Willie and Nellie were married December 21, 1857, in St. James' Church. The Reverend Dr. Clarkson, afterwards Bishop of Nebraska, officiated.

It was a daytime wedding and very grand, with six groomsmen and six bridesmaids. Nellie gave the latter their dresses and gloves, which her mother said was the practice in the New England of her day. Nellie's dress was of heavy white satin with an embroidered lace overdress, a wreath of wax orange blossoms fastening down her tulle veil. Willie and Nellie left that evening for Niagara Falls—one suspects not so much because this was "the thing to do," but because it was here that Nellie's Grandmother Kinzie, Little Ship Under Full Sail, for whom Nellie had been both named and nicknamed, was restored to her parents by Cornplanter. Nellie prized all these associations with her family's past. Then on to Savannah, where Mrs. Gordon, Senior, gave a large reception on January 7, introducing the new Mrs. William Washington Gordon II, to Savannah society.

────────── ☆ ──────────

SOMETHING NEW IN THE
GORDON LINE!

T HE GORDON FAMILY, of which Nellie was now a member,
did not go back as far in America as Nellie's own New
England ancestry, but its forebears were of much the same
character. The first Gordon ancestor in America was Peter
Gordon, but his descendants have been unable to find the date
of his arrival here, or anything about his origin. His son,
Jonathan, was born in 1718 and Jonathan's son, Ambrose, was
born on the farm in New Jersey where part of the Battle of
Monmouth was fought, but in the Revolutionary War was captain of a Virginia cavalry unit under Lieutenant Colonel
William Washington, a nephew of George Washington. After
the Revolution, Ambrose found his way to Georgia, married
Elizabeth Meade and named his first son William Washington
Gordon for his former commanding officer. Elizabeth, his wife,
is credited with having defied the United States government
in the War of 1812 to get money to feed her babies. When
trade with England was forbidden, she shipped her cotton just
the same, and accompanied it, sitting on top of the bales in a
rocking chair. She knew the soldiers were too chivalrous to fire
on a woman, or even to stop her!

But through Mrs. Gordon, Senior, who was a Stites—her
mother had been a Wayne—Willie's lineage went back to the

Dr. John Stites who had been a surgeon in Colonel John Hampden's regiment in Cromwell's army, and was credited with being one of the physicians who certified the death of Charles I. When Charles II came to the throne and issued his amnesty proclamation, Dr. Stites was one of the regicides who was excepted from it, and had to flee to Holland. He came from there to Plymouth Colony and later settled in Hempstead, Long Island, where he served the colonists as physician and surgeon throughout the rest of his long life; it is reported he died at the age of 122. His descendants moved on to Elizabethtown, New Jersey. Dr. John Stites' great-great-grandson, Captain Richard Stites, was aide-de-camp to General George Washington and died from wounds received at the Battle of Long Island. Richard Montgomery Stites, the son of Captain Stites, settled in Georgia after the Revolution and married Mary Wayne.

Willie's father, William Washington Gordon I, had been the first Georgian to graduate from the United States Military Academy at West Point, emerging with the rank of third lieutenant. He built the Central of Georgia Railroad which extended across the state from east to west, opened up the hinterland and thus was responsible in large part for Savannah's importance as a port and railroad center. Gordon County in Georgia was named for him. When his wife's uncle, Judge Wayne, left Savannah for Washington to become a Justice of the United States Supreme Court, W. W. Gordon I bought his house at the corner of Bull and Oglethorpe, designed by the famous architect William Jay. It was known from that time on as the Gordon house. Here Willie Gordon and Nellie lived until 1870, when they moved to the Cecil house across the street for two years, then to 17 South Broad and then back to the Gordon house, occupied by Gordons from that time on until 1953, when it was bought by the Girl Scouts of America and made a memorial to their founder, Juliette Gordon Low.

Savannah in 1858, when Nellie Kinzie, now Nellie Gordon, came there to live, was a sleepy old town, with streets of sand or cobblestone—the cobblestones, as in so many of the old eastern seaports, having been brought by ships that used them for ballast when their holds were empty. At every block or two were wells, usually surrounded by a group of domestics come ostensibly to draw water for their several houses, but actually to exchange the latest gossip about their "folks" or their own friends.

Most of the business of the town was carried out on The Bay—a misnomer for Bay Street, which, at the top of a high bluff, parallels the river. Warehouses filled with resin, lumber, hay or that most important of all commodities, cotton, fronted on a narrow lane along the riverside, giving easy access to the numerous boats plying up and down the busy harbor. This lane was reached from the bluff above, by means of cobble-stoned ramps set at intervals along The Bay. The upper rooms, above the warehouses, were cotton brokers' offices as well as cotton-sampling rooms. And here the firm of Tison & Gordon had a proud place on Factors' Walk, as it was called.

Factors' Walk is one of Savannah's interesting sights today, and the old stone walls and the cobbled streets that lead down to the lower level are the same as in 1858, though changes have been made in the buildings above the old basement rooms in which the cotton used to be stored. The Cotton Exchange Building—Willie Gordon was one of the founders of the Exchange and its president from 1876 to 1878—is now occupied by the Savannah Chamber of Commerce but it retains all its baroque Victorian splendor.

Nellie was not coming among strangers. Willie's sister Eliza was already a dear friend, and Nellie had become acquainted with his brother George while she was at Madam Canda's. She visited the Gordons during her engagement. And just to marry a Gordon insured acceptance by Savannah society. But Nellie soon won her own place among this horse-loving aristocracy by riding Captain Charles A. Lamar's stallion, Black Cloud—a feat few men were willing to attempt. Juliette Kinzie, in Chicago, heard from Uncle David Hunter in Washington that Justice Wayne had visited the Gordons and had reported to his wife that Mrs. Gordon's house "is quite a different place since little Nellie came into it. She is the light and life of the house."

But there were pinpricks from Nellie's standpoint. As a bachelor, Willie had lived with his mother in the family mansion and had turned over to her half his salary, which at this time was $1,200 a year. Mrs. Gordon, Senior, took it as a matter of course that the young couple would live with her and that

Willie would continue to turn over to her half his earnings. So every month Willie gave his mother fifty dollars, Nellie twenty-five dollars and kept twenty-five dollars for himself. Nellie says in her reminiscences that "we managed to squeeze by on this for a time, but after babies began to arrive we were very thankful for my dear father's generous help."

Furthermore, Nellie was no happier living under her mother-in-law's roof than are most young wives. Mrs. Gordon had always run her household and everyone in it, and saw no reason to change her ways. We may be sure that Nellie for her part saw no reason to change *her* way, which had been always to do as she pleased. In her reminiscences, written fifty-seven years later, Nellie glosses over this painful period, but at the time she complained bitterly in her letters to her mother in Chicago.

By April the weather was already unbearably hot and another element was added which Nellie took as a personal affront—she found that she was pregnant! Nellie's letters about this to Juliette presumably were burned in the Chicago fire, but Juliette's answers make their contents clear, as well as revealing much about Juliette's own character, and the quality of her maternal love.

On April 12, 1858, she wrote to Nellie: "My dearest daughter: It grieves me much to find that you are so unhappy about what was inevitable, about what any woman who marries has a right to expect. You say that you *hate* children. Had such a sentiment found a place in your mother's heart, what, my dear child, would have been your lot in the days of your infancy and childhood? . . .

"Our Heavenly Father knows what is best for us, and He will send it, whether we will or no. He has undoubtedly chosen the very discipline that is necessary for you—but oh! my daughter, how sad it is that a event that usually and naturally brings such joy to a parent's, more especially to a mother's heart, should be regarded by you as cause for complaint and murmuring. Do not, I entreat you, give way to such feelings. They are wrong—every way wrong. Think of your mother, before the birth of her first child—surrounded by a savage enemy—forced to be separated from her husband, fleeing for safety, she hardly knew whither—subjected to storms and shipwreck and hardship of every kind!

"You must not think, my dear child, that because I reprove your unreconciled spirit I am without sympathy for the real difficulties of your situation. I can feel that it is a great trial for you to be deprived so entirely of William's society, to pass so many lonely and gloomy hours—to miss the cheerful intelligent circle to which you have been accustomed, and to feel that there are so few to whom you are of the importance that you have here to a whole community. . . ."

Having delivered her lecture, Juliette apparently never referred again to Nellie's rejection of motherhood. Instead, wise woman that she was, she sent Savannah-ward a constant stream of lovely materials and patterns and attractive ideas for the baby's layette, together with bits of advice as to Nellie's care of her own self. "It will not hurt you to wear a corset provided you do not lace it too tight. In fact it will be a support. I disagree with Willie on this score. I always wore my corset."

On April thirtieth, at the end of a long chatty letter, Juliette wrote: "You will observe my darling child that I say but little about your *peculiar* sources of trouble. They cannot be helped, and as a Christian, I doubt not you will be able to bear them peacefully. If your mother could only have you with her, nobody else would have to be annoyed, or make you feel unhappy. There are certain parts upon which it is your husband's duty to be resolute. He ought to take care that everything should be planned and provided as you think will most conduce to your comfort. He has taken you from a home where you would ever have found your happiness consulted, and his duty is to see you saved from every annoyance and unpleasant anticipation. You must comfort yourself my darling with the thought that your mother will probably be near you, and that although you may never be permitted to have the nurse you preferred, yet your mother's hands will make all right and safe for you. I shall bring my good Delia who is a person of about thirty-five and a most excellent nurse. If she takes as good care of you as she does of me, you will want for nothing. God will take care of you, and make all things for you good—of that you may be sure, my dearest. Your brothers and cousins send much love. God help you and keep you, and God make Willie a good boy. Take the best care of yourself. Your own devoted mother."

Just how unfeeling the elder Mrs. Gordon really was, it is

hard to say. Her letters to Nellie after Juliette Kinzie's tragic, shocking death are filled with tender expressions of love. As soon as Mrs. Gordon learned that Juliette planned to come for Nellie's accouchement in September, she invited Juliette to stay at the Gordon house, but Juliette declined with gracious dignity.

Throughout the intervening months, Juliette sent a flood of cheery letters, designed to keep up her daughter's spirits in the midst of her trials. These letters, without the writer's having intended it, give us a full length portrait of one of America's superlative women. Juliette presided over a large household, and in addition relatives were always coming for visits of indeterminate length. She was working on a novel, following the success of *Wau-Bun,* and engaged in negotiations with publishers. And now every prominent person who came to Chicago asked to meet the author of *Wau-Bun.* She did an enormous amount of charitable work, and every letter describes a visit to cheer a sick friend or to sit with someone bereft, or to pay her compliments to an old acquaintance.

She wrote Nellie that in one day, working from early morning until late at night, she had gotten together a wedding costume for her niece Gwinney, who was being married in St. Louis—wedding dress, a wreath and veil like Nellie's, and gloves with a little ruche at the top. "I could not bear that poor Gwinney should think that her sister and cousin could be married so handsomely and she want what was respectable." Juliette was a famous cook and entertained a great deal. She frequently made little excursions with her husband, and their devotion to each other obviously had not lessened with the years.

John Harris Kinzie left letter writing to his wife, but her letters give us a picture of him as well. The frontiersman remained a leader in the city he had helped to found. He was kind. His wife mentioned that John could have sent to prison a man who defrauded him. "But you know your father would never do that!" she wrote Nellie.

That summer yellow fever appeared in Savannah, and residents who could do so fled the city. Eliza Gordon, who had married Henry Stiles, went to her mother-in-law's home at Etowah Cliffs in northwestern Georgia. Mrs. Gordon had gone to Willie's other sister, Gulie, at Morristown, New Jersey. Willie, being the junior partner, had to stay in Savannah, and Nellie would not leave him, though everyone urged her to go away at least as far as Huntsville. With Nellie thus "deserted" by the Gordon women, Juliette, who, according to Nellie, "had as little fear of epidemics as I have,". came in the midst of the summer heat to be with her daughter.

The baby, a fine, plump, healthy little girl, was born September 27, and was named Eleanor after her mother, but called Blossom by her doting Grandmother Kinzie. In the family Eleanor was called Nellie and Nell, like her mother, but to avoid confusion she will be referred to as Eleanor through this book. It is intriguing to think of the little drama that must have been played out in the Gordon house after Willie's mother returned; the two grandmothers, equally well born and well bred, circling about each other warily, Mrs. Kinzie unfailingly polite, but keeping Mrs. Gordon at a cool distance which that poor lady was probably at a loss to understand. And Nellie, who was responsible for the performance, was probably enjoying it hugely.

In the summer of 1859, Nellie took little Eleanor back to Chicago for a long visit, and the letters Willie wrote to her show that whatever disappointments Nellie might have had in her new home, her relationship with Willie had grown and deepened. Nor was theirs any tepid Victorian marital "arrangement." In one letter, Willie detailed, with loving tenderness and pride, the steps by which Nellie had arrived at an ardor as great as his own. First there had been her virginal timidity on their wedding night, at finding herself for the first time shut within four walls with "that fearsome creature, a *male*." Next had come what Willie had regarded as her callous toleration of marital relations—"though you never refused me." And then, after the birth of little Eleanor had removed all pain for Nellie, she had arrived at a full womanly response which was the secret joy of Willie's life.

Evidently Nellie was trying to sell some of the lake front property she had either inherited from her Kinzie grandparents or been given by her father, in order to help Willie financially, for he advises her that he thinks $2,000 too small a price for her ten-acre plot fronting on Lake Michigan. "There is, however, no prospect of an advance in lands out West just now and I think you had better sell at some figure. The money will aid us more than the land, so I would advise you to sell for $3,800, which will clear us from our trouble. If you can't get that price, sell for what you can."

Perhaps Nellie's parents had been too indulgent, for there is no denying that Nellie was spoiled. When she was in Savannah, she complained to her mother about the lack of consideration she got from her mother-in-law. In Chicago, she wrote equally complaining letters to Willie about the treatment she received there. Her father was worried by business problems, her brother John criticized her, Juliette was ill and Nellie had household responsibilities. When the baby got sick, there was no nurse. The Kinzie house was always staffed with from four to six servants, besides the good Delia, so that Nellie's duties, except toward her baby, would have been supervisory only. Nellie must have found the temptation irresistible to draw sympathy from her mother and husband, who vied with each other in continuing to spoil her. The gentle Juliette had been moved to indignation at Mrs. Gordon, and Willie fumed over the disregard Nellie's own family showed for his darling's comfort and well-being. He was beside himself when he learned that her parents had let her start off for New York without providing an escort beyond Harrisburg, Pennsylvania. Had he dreamed such a thing could happen, he would have gone to Harrisburg himself, or Chicago, for that matter, to look after her. No wonder his little wife had been dragged down by such an ordeal!

Now the truth is that Nellie was about as weak and helpless as a bulldozer, and so demonstrated on many occasions. The little lady who at different times had General Robert E. Lee and General William T. Sherman working to carry out her wishes and who had the Federal government in Washington jumping through hoops at her behest when she came there, a Confederate officer's wife, in early 1865, could have mobilized the train crew and all the passengers to help her care for one small child, and wouldn't have hesitated to do so had there been any need. She loved Willie's sympathy and permitted him to develop hard feelings toward her family to get more of it. Perhaps the naughtiest thing Nellie ever did was to play against each other, for her own unworthy purposes, her parents and her husband. The time would come, and it was not many years away, when she would regret this.

However, aside from this one area of delinquency, Nellie seems to have been a devoted and most companionable daughter. Juliette's letters reveal the greatest congeniality and harmony between mother and daughter, a sharing of all Juliette's many interests. It is interesting that Nellie always wrote her mother a letter of comfort and love on the anniversaries of the deaths of her brothers, just as Nellie's own daughter, Daisy (Juliette) Low, was to do so long as Nellie lived, on each anniversary of the death of Daisy's younger sister, Alice. Different as Nellie was from her mother, she caught from her a greatness of heart and spirit which was to be her saving grace.

Two of the cousins whom her parents had adopted, Henry Wolcott and Mrs. Caroline Balestier—Mrs. Balestier had been a Wolcott—now lived in New York. Nellie stayed with them long enough to build up her shattered strength and then returned to Savannah by boat, "glad to get back," she wrote in later years, unregenerate still, "to a place where I was loved and no unkind words were spoken!"

Juliette wrote rather sadly that she feared Nellie had not had a very good time at home, but that if she had found dearer friends in Savannah than in Chicago, perhaps it was for the best. Nevertheless, Juliette wished that Nellie and Blossom were back again—"and Willie too, for I would not want him to think that I am trying to *abolish* him, or deprive him of his *white* property."

This was clearly meant as a pleasantry. There is no indication that the Kinzies ever felt aggrieved because Nellie's new family loyalties had placed her on the opposite side of the political fence, though they themselves had joined the recently born Republican Party and, as prominent Chicagoans, were in the thick of the great events then shaping up in Illinois. The kindly Kinzies evidently did not know of the antagonism their Nellie had engendered toward them in Willie and had no idea that Willie might resent their innocent little jokes about the South.

And now Nellie was at it again. The discovery that she was to have another baby the following October caused her once more to fill the air with lamentations and expletives, and in a tantrum she picked up and flounced off to Waynesboro, so mad she didn't write to Willie at all for a while.

Juliette Kinzie and Willie Gordon were alike in a number of ways. Both were mature individuals of the highest integrity and responsibility, both would have sacrificed life itself for the engaging child-woman they doted on. But there was this difference between Nellie's mother and her husband. It was Juliette's way, when someone she loved was at fault, to speak out uncompromisingly but if anything to redouble her expressions of love. She must have sighed when she learned that for the second time, Nellie was rebelling against the motherhood which to Juliette was life's greatest boon. Juliette wrote sorrowfully: "How bitterly should I reproach myself, now that three of my beloved ones are laid away in the tomb, if I had failed to welcome them as they were given me, with all the joy of a mother's heart." But the cup of her kindness to her willful little daughter continued to overflow. In three days' time, she made six nightgowns and six pairs of tucked drawers for Nellie. She was always knitting or sewing something for little Blossom or for the expected baby.

In Willie, however, Nellie had found a man who, while he would not have stopped loving her no matter what she did, definitely withdrew his approval when she acted like a spoiled, unpleasant brat. His letters to her at Waynesboro always contained an expression of his love and his desire to do anything he could for her comfort, but otherwise were curt and cold, in marked contrast to his passionate outpourings when she had been in Chicago. Like Juliette, he could not understand Nellie's rebellion at a natural consequence of a marriage upon which Nellie had entered with loving eagerness, and in one letter he said, "For you I grieve, not only because of your present inconvenience, but because of the repugnance you have always felt lest such a result should be brought about."

As the time for Nellie's accouchement drew near, Juliette expressed the hope that Mrs. George Gordon, who was also expecting a baby imminently, would not name it William Washington if it proved to be a boy. "It means such a confusion and may hereafter occasion the most serious trials to have two of the same name and age. Beg her to wait, and give you the choice of the name."

For Nellie, disappointed the first time in not getting a boy, if she had to have a baby at all, was set on having a boy this time. But the baby, born October 31, 1860, was another girl. They named her Juliette Magill Kinzie for her Grandmother Kinzie, and immediately started calling her Daisy!

The use of a nickname in order to avoid the confusion Grandma Juliette herself mentioned was logical enough, but why Daisy was hit upon is not known. Juliette Kinzie wrote that as soon as Nellie's brother George heard about the new baby he exclaimed, "I bet she's going to be a 'Daisy.' " The capital letter and quotation marks here would seem to have some significance. Had the little book of Nellie's childhood furnished a household word to the Kinzies and did George refer to this?

It would have been characteristic of Nellie to call her child by an uncomplimentary name, just as modern mothers may designate as little monsters the offspring they secretly cherish. When Nellie had gone to Chicago with little Eleanor in 1859, Willie suggested to her gently that while there she refrain from "shockers" such as slighting remarks about himself, her baby, her brother John. It was all very well, he said, thus to exercise her wit in Savannah, where she was known, but among strangers it might not be understood. Willie couldn't get it through his head that in Chicago, Nellie was not among strangers!

Willie himself, as a matter of fact, delivered no glowing account of the new arrival, according to Juliette Kinzie's answering letter to him. "It was with heartfelt joy and Thanksgiving that we received the dispatch announcing our dear child's safety," she wrote, "and last evening your letter containing further particulars of her welfare and of the fat, hearty little stranger, gladdened our spirits and relieved us from nearly all anxiety on their account. I am sorry the new baby is not a beauty. You may remember that the first was not, until a week or more had elapsed. But I am sure that after a very little while she will cease to look like a 'freak' and do credit to the stock from which she is descended."

CHAPTER V

─────────── ☆ ───────────

YANKEE IN THE CONFEDERATE HEARTLAND

NELLIE WROTE many years later that "my little Daisy was a beautiful baby and had a sweet disposition and was very little trouble," from which we may infer that Grandma Kinzie's prediction proved accurate. Nellie continued: "It makes me laugh now when I recall the estimate of her which was so completely reversed when she grew up and turned out to be such a genius. 'Dear little Daisy,' everyone would remark, 'she is so beautiful and good—not clever like little Eleanor, who is as sharp as she can be, but just sweet and lovely, you know.' Daisy loved to be petted and caressed and Eleanor was independence itself, and didn't care what anyone thought or said."

For those who believe that our fate lies not in our stars but in ourselves, and that environment plays a part in shaping character and personality, there is ample explanation for at least some of the changes that were to come about in the baby who to begin with was just sweet and lovely and apparently nothing more. It is already apparent that Daisy's mother was very different from the mother of sentimental songs and Mother's Day greeting cards. Moreover, the Gordon family was soon to be subjected to drastic strains and stresses. The election of "Honest Old Abe" within a week of Daisy's birth was taken by the South, rightly or wrongly, as a sign that compromise would not be possible. South Carolina seceded from the Union on December 20, followed by Mississippi, Florida, Alabama, Georgia and Louisiana on different dates in January, 1861, and by Texas on February 1.

Delegates from these states met in Montgomery, Alabama, in February, to form the Confederate States. They made Jefferson Davis Provisional President. An army and a treasury were set up. On April 12, Fort Sumter was fired on. The United States flag was hauled down on April 14, that of the Confederacy went up. It was war, and a war in which Nellie Gordon's new family and friends and homeland were on the opposite side from her parents and all other blood relatives, and from all the friends of her youth. Her father was appointed paymaster in the Union Army with the rank of major, and with headquarters in Chicago, later being promoted to lieutenant colonel. Her two brothers next to her in age, John and Arthur, volunteered as soon as Lincoln issued his call for troops, John in the Union navy, Arthur in the army. Willie Gordon as promptly offered his services to the Confederacy.

John Harris and Juliette Kinzie begged Nellie to come to Chicago with her children when Willie went to war, but she declined. It has been concluded erroneously for this and other reasons that Nellie was as ardent a Confederate as her husband.

However, Nellie herself says in her Civil War reminiscences, "The only fault I ever found with dear Dr. Axton was a *war sermon* he preached just after the fall of Fort Sumter, which made so strong an impression on my husband that he resolved to 'join the Cavalry.' In other words, to go to the front at once. I was violently opposed to this. Not from any sentiment as to whether the South was right; I didn't give a fig for that. I simply did not want him to run the chance of getting shot. On his part, he didn't care a fig what I wanted. He took the usual 'Gordon' ground of 'duty.' And being backed up by Fred Waring (who had no wife and family to consider) they went to work to equip and carry to Virginia a cavalry company, the Georgia Hussars, to which they had both belonged for years. Willie's grandfather and his father had each been captains of this company, so there was a good deal of sentiment involved.

"There is no use expatiating on the sufferings of those left behind. Fortunately, no one realized what lay in the future,

but thought two or three months of soldiering would be sufficient to settle matters, and that our boys would come marching
home like conquering heroes.

"The Hussars made a fine showing. By way of preliminary
service they were stationed at Skidaway Island, where they had
an opportunity to get some training in the field, were tormented
by red-bugs, devoured by mosquitoes and had to put up with
many distractions and discomforts, all of which they accepted
with delight as their first sacrifice to the 'Glorious Cause.'

"Meantime, Willie now and then got a short leave and came
to town where he held forth on the delights of camp life. I
could not accept his point of view and would

>Strongly blaspheme
>While I rubbed in cold cream."

Obviously Nellie accepted the Civil War with no more enthusiasm than she had accepted the prospect of motherhood.

There had been a decidedly dilettante atmosphere in that
month's training on Skidaway Island, fifteen miles from Savannah. The volunteers were aristocrats, members of the particular militia companies to which their fathers, grandfathers and
great-grandfathers had belonged before them. The Georgia
Hussars was the oldest and hence the most revered, having been
originated by Oglethorpe himself as Mounted Rangers. Next
was the Chatham Artillery, founded in 1777; then in a descend-
ing scale the Guards, who had held their first parade in 1802,
and the Regiment, considered an upstart by the others because
it was not organized until 1808.

The first taste of army life on Skidaway Island was quite an
ordeal for these hitherto sheltered and pampered young men.
Most were used to having body servants, none was used to sleeping in a tent, and the food was a far cry from the plentiful
delicacies they were accustomed to at home. Willie Gordon
had his first experience of sleeping on the ground, and reported
that he was extremely lame and sore next morning. How many
times, in the four years to follow, was Willie to sleep on the
ground in mud or rain or snow or slush, with no covering but
a blanket!

The young men below officer rank, however, valiantly cur-
ried their own horses and did all the cleaning up of the camp.

Besides this there was sabre drill, maneuvering on foot and on horseback, guard mount, sentinel duty and dress parade daily. But they offset the drudgery by having their sailboats brought to the island, and when off duty they would have races or go fishing. The nearest they came to warfare was when a false alarm sent twelve gallant Southerners sailing off to capture thirty Yankee invaders, who perhaps fortunately proved to be nonexistent.

When the month for which they had enlisted was over, the troops returned to Savannah and mustered out. But the war still was not over, somewhat to their surprise, and many of the enlisted men accepted commissions with other Georgia outfits. The rest, the Hussars among them, volunteered to go to Virginia, which was making vigorous preparations to fight. Their services were accepted on condition that the troop itself pay the cost of transporting men and horses. Captain Fred Waring bore the major part of this expense, which amounted to $20,000. In the reorganized group Willie was elected second lieutenant— he had been a lowly corporal on Skidaway—his great friend David Waldhauer becoming first lieutenant. Arrived in Richmond, the Georgia Hussars were mustered into the Confederate service for the duration.

When Willie went off to Richmond, Nellie promptly followed—she remarked that permission to do so was the only consolation she got—taking with her Eleanor, Daisy and a nurse. Nellie had many good friends in Richmond, among the closest being Mr. and Mrs. George Randolph. A brother of Willie's cousin Meta Anderson, Mr. Randolph was Secretary of War for the Confederacy. As Willie was the only married officer in the Hussars, Nellie was able to make herself useful to the Confederacy by keeping the officers' mess of the Hussars supplied with a cook. One William Fisher, whom she dug up, was a particular jewel. He was a splendid forager, able to find chickens, turkeys, eggs and butter if there were any within a radius of ten miles, and a superlative chef. One of his achievements was to serve the officers hot rolls every morning for breakfast. It was not until he had left and his successor said he couldn't give the officers hot rolls in winter because he couldn't get the dough to rise, that it was discovered William Fisher had accomplished this feat by taking the dough to bed with him every night.

All too soon, however, the Hussars were ordered to Centreville, not far from Washington, where the Army of Northern Virginia was in camp, commanded by General Joseph E. Johnston. The Hussars were part of the cavalry brigade under General J. E. B. Stuart.

There were times when Willie, out on patrol, could see buildings in Washington. From Centreville Willie's troop was ordered to Manassas, where the Battle of Bull Run was soon to be fought, and Nellie blithely made plans to meet Willie there. Willie was frantic. He wrote his mother: "It is a wild plan and one I dislike very much. Traveling now with only some chance protector or none at all is neither safe nor respectable for females."

Evidently Willie put his foot down, for Nellie abandoned the plan. Richmond growing constantly more crowded and expensive, she finally returned to Savannah.

And now the Civil War ceased to be a lark, for the women and children in Savannah as well as for the fighting men. Food was hard to get, clothes impossible to buy, and money grew more worthless every day. Had not Grandma Kinzie kept sending boxes of supplies of all sorts from Chicago—which she was able to do because of her husband's position in the Union army and the proven loyalty of the Kinzies to the Federal cause—the suffering of Nellie's children would have been serious. Even so, Eleanor and Daisy grew thin and pale and their baby skins broke out in boils from malnutrition.

The prescribed remedy was a daily dose of sulphur and molasses, to which the little girls looked forward as to a treat. Peanuts, excellent source of nutrition that they are and plentiful in Georgia, were considered unhealthy. Once Eleanor ate one, and then lied about it. "Daisy," Eleanor wrote later, "would have wept over the reproof, but would not have told a lie."

From the beginning of the war, Nellie was an object of suspicion to many Savannah people because of her Northern origin and connections. This suspicion naturally increased when her uncle, General David Hunter, made himself the Northern officer most hated by the South in general, and by Savannah in particular. Uncle David had been stationed at Fort Leaven-worth, Kansas, during the presidential campaign in which Lincoln was elected. Many of the officers were Southern in sympathy and one boasted openly that the South would never permit the inauguration of an "abolition" President. If Lincoln were elected, he said, the Illinoisian would not be allowed to go to Washington. The governors of Maryland and Virginia stood ready to send ten thousand men each to the capital and place Franklin Pierce again in office until they had perfected their arrangements for installing another President. Hunter had considered it his duty to communicate this information to Lincoln.

Lincoln had invited Hunter to accompany him on that historic trip to Washington, and then Hunter had been in charge of a guard of one hundred citizens who had volunteered to protect Lincoln during his early tenure in office. Made a brigadier general after the first Battle of Bull Run, in early 1862 he was given command of the Department of the South comprised of the states of South Carolina, Georgia and Florida. General Hunter's first task in his new command was to reduce Fort Pulaski, which protected Savannah, Georgia's chief seaport and the only seaport left to the Confederacy south of Charleston, South Carolina.

Since the preceding December, Yankee engineers had been placing batteries on Tybee and other islands close to Cockspur, on which Fort Pulaski stood. Early on the morning of April 10, 1862, General Hunter ordered the fort to surrender. The commander refused, and the Federal bombardment began at 8 A.M., continuing without ceasing until the fort surrendered at two the next afternoon. All night long Savannah residents heard the boom of the Union mortars, dropping shells into the fort at five-minute intervals. The Confederates claimed that General Hunter violated the portion of the surrender terms which called for sending the wounded defenders under flag of truce to the Confederate lines, and instead sent the whole garrison to Northern prisons. The *Confederate Military History* says, "This conduct of Hunter accorded with his reputation elsewhere. His brutality was exceeded only by Butler."

Hunter next issued a proclamation freeing the slaves in South

Carolina, Georgia and Florida, and then set up a Negro regiment, recruited from the slaves he had freed! General Phelps, in Louisiana, followed suit. The Confederate War Department at once issued General Order No. 60, decreeing that inasmuch as Hunter and Phelps had "organized and armed Negro slaves for military service against their masters, Major General Hunter and Brigadier General Phelps be no longer held and treated as public enemies of the Confederate States but as outlaws, and in the event of the capture of either of them or that of any other officer employed in drilling, organizing or instructing slaves with a view to their armed service in this war, he shall not be regarded as a prisoner of war, but held in close confinement for execution as a felon, at such time and place as the President [Jefferson Davis] shall designate."

Hunter remained under the ban as long as the war lasted, but he took pains to see that none of his officers in charge of Negro troops should suffer from it. When one was captured and thrown into the common jail in Charleston, Hunter notified the Confederate authorities that unless the man were released from jail immediately and treated as a prisoner of war, he, Hunter, would at once jail all the influential Southerners within his lines and execute three of them for every one of his officers injured. The officer was at once released from jail, but General Hunter's reputation for brutality was not abated.

Hunter's precipitate action in freeing the slaves in his area of command upset Lincoln's plans considerably, for the President had been nursing public opinion along gradually toward this revolutionary step. Lincoln rebuked Hunter publicly. But privately he congratulated Hunter on the performance of his Negro troops, in a letter written a year after the fall of Fort Pulaski.

"MY DEAR SIR:

"I am glad to see accounts of your colored force at Jacksonville, Florida. I see the enemy are driving at them fiercely, as is to be expected. It is important to the enemy that such force shall *not* take shape and grow and thrive in the South; and in precisely the same proportion it is important to us that it *shall*. Hence the utmost caution and vigilance is necessary on our part. The enemy will make extra efforts to destroy them, and we should do the same to preserve and increase them.

> "Yours truly,
> "A. LINCOLN."

Before he received this commendation from Lincoln, Hunter was investigated by Congress for his act, but he stuck stubbornly to his guns. They were fighting this war to free the slaves, weren't they? And besides, recruiting Negro regiments would take the laborers away from the southern fields and force the release of white men from military duty to raise the crops the South had to have. In the end Congress heeded his arguments and called for fifty thousand Negro troops, later making the number larger still. Printable language is inadequate to express the feeling in the South toward General Hunter. He was by far the Northerner most hated in the Confederate States.

History has recorded the trouble General Hunter made for Lincoln by his premature Emancipation Proclamation. He made quite as much trouble for his niece, Nellie Gordon, in Savannah. Not only did a considerable portion of his unpopularity rub off on her, but many claimed that Nellie was a Yankee spy, smuggling out information to her perfidious uncle.

Several of Nellie's Savannah biographers have stated that she met the situation with great dignity and restraint, which doesn't sound quite like Nellie. One biographer puts it a little differently:

"To the honor of her Georgia neighbors, be it said that only one attempted to taunt her about her Northern connections and swift retribution followed. The lady met Mrs. Gordon just at the beginning of the war, and the following conversation took place:

" 'I hear, Mrs. Gordon, that your brother is an officer in the Union Army and all I have to say is that I hope the first shot fired will kill him dead.' To which Mrs. Gordon replied, 'Thank you.'

"A few weeks later this lady's brother, a gallant Confederate officer, had the misfortune to be wounded by a bursting shell, a piece of which struck him in the back. Mrs. Gordon, meeting her at a dinner, where those present had heard the previous conversation, remarked loudly and pleasantly, 'By the way, Mrs.

——, I hear that your brother has been shot in the back. Mine
is very well, thank you!'"

It appears that Nellie simply held her fire for a time when it
would be most effective. That she was well aware of what was
going on, and marked her enemies down for future reference,
is shown by a letter of hers to Willie's particular friend, Lieutenant Waldhauer, in 1865. Nellie wrote from Washington,
where she was busily using her Kinzie connections and her own
potent stock of stratagems and blandishments to get special
favors for her Confederate friends.

"I saw General Rawlins yesterday and got your release from
him—and believe me it gave me great pleasure to do anything
to oblige you. I could have got A—— S——'s at the same time
by saying one word, but in consideration of his father's having
written to Beauregard about me and about my uncle General
Hunter, I concluded not to interest myself in Mr. A—— S——.
I trust his Fort Delaware experiences will do him good and
correct some of his early training!" Fort Delaware was a Union
prison for Confederate captives.

It must have been a strange time for the two tiny Gordon
children. Except for the scarcity of food—and neither was old
enough to remember the days of plenty—they were comfortable
enough in Grandma Gordon's big house, with its enchanting
garden to play in. But their adored papa would appear suddenly after long absence, and after a few days vanish as inex-
plicably as he had come. Eleanor declared she could remember
the day her papa and his brother George went off to war, and
what a sad day it was. It was occasion for joy when Papa or
Uncle George came back to recover from wounds. "Childlike,
we were so happy to have them back, and wounds had so little
meaning for us, that our chief interest promptly became the
dressing of the wounds each day. Daisy and I always begged
to be present when the dressing occurred."

There must have been many days, after word came of a battle,
when Mama and Grandma Gordon went about with strained,
anxious faces, until they heard that the ones they loved were
safe this time, at least. Nellie kept Willie's memory green with
his little girls during his long absences, and she permitted them
to grow into flaming rebels, if not actually encouraging them
to do so. But perhaps their playmates taunted them sometimes

about their great-uncle, perhaps cried out that their mother was a Yankee spy. Considering the nature of children, and the feeling that prevailed in Savannah when Uncle David was riding roughshod over Southern sensibilities, it could hardly have been otherwise.

And as if Nellie didn't have enough to worry about, her quiet Willie found it necessary to fight a duel with a Georgia Hussar! He hastened to be the first to describe and explain the incident to Nellie, knowing well what her reaction would be when she found it out. The orderly sergeant of Willie's company had been wounded in the head and taken prisoner. After he was exchanged and had rejoined the troop, he had exhibited an unaccountable hatred for Willie and had seized every opportunity to insult and injure him. Willie had overlooked it as long as he could, because of the head wound the sergeant had incurred.

"At last, however," Willie wrote his wife, "he had the impudence to hand me a paper which one of the men had written asking me to resign my lieutenancy but giving no reasons for the request. To this paper the writer had affixed the names of a large number of men—some of them absent and at least one of whom afterwards said his name was there without his sanction or authority." Willie had then tried to lay the matter before a court of inquiry, but owing to the almost constant movement of the Hussars, was unable to do so. The sergeant was discharged, and as Willie knew he would go to Savannah and spread rumors attacking Willie's honor, Willie demanded an apology. The apology was refused, in an extremely insulting letter. Willie challenged his enemy—"though I assure you, my dear Nell, that no one is more opposed to the practice and theory of duelling than I am."

Henry Stiles, who had married Willie's sister Eliza, heard about the duel and came to the camp to try and stop it, but it was impossible at this point, as the sergeant was stubbornly determined either to kill Willie, or make him appear to be a "coward and poltroon." Willie's good friend Lieutenant Waldhauer acted as Willie's second, and the duel took place a few miles from camp with double-barreled shotguns at thirty paces, the combatants to wheel and fire at the word.

"God was very good to me," wrote Willie, "and to Him

entirely I ascribe my escape. He [the sergeant] fired first and missed me, while one of my buckshot struck him in the forehead, going through the folds of his hat and glancing over his left eye. When extracted it was perfectly flattened. He was satisfied to make friends after he was shot. I have closed his mouth forever about me and I don't think anyone else in the company will meddle with me."

But Willie's pride of a Georgia gentleman—even Nellie did not realize the diabolical strength of that pride until it was almost too late—suffered some hurt nonetheless. When, in the next election held by the Hussars—the militia companies elected their officers, following the custom begun in Revolutionary times—Willie's re-election as second lieutenant was not completely unanimous, he resigned from the Hussars and joined Mercer's Brigade of Joseph Wheeler's cavalry, fighting with them until General Joseph E. Johnston surrendered on April 26, 1865, seventeen days after Lee's surrender at Appomattox. He became Captain Adjutant of the brigade, was wounded seriously at Lovejoy Station, besides minor wounds on other occasions, and was placed on the Roll of Gallantry for his bravery at Frederick, Maryland, during Lee's Maryland campaign. After the war, however, he rejoined the Georgia Hussars when the Federal government would permit them to meet again, and they consider him their most illustrious member.

But he was still in the Hussars in March of 1862, and since the Hussars had been too busily engaged for Willie to come home on leave, Nellie made a trip up into the Confederate lines in Virginia to see him. The first four pages of Nellie's account of this expedition are missing, but it is plain that she went to Richmond to the home of her friends the Hexalls, and sent a note to General Robert E. Lee at his headquarters, asking the General to tell her where Willie was and to give her his help in getting to him.

"In less than half-an-hour his aide Col. Walter Taylor came to bring a note from General Lee saying that 'the Army had just received orders to fall back, and that the Cavalry was probably in the neighborhood of Madison County' and that 'this was the nearest information he could give me of the *whereabouts of my Willie.*' I kept the precious note for years, and it was at last burned up in the Chicago fire along with a charming one from General William T. Sherman.

"Presently, General Lee himself appeared. He breakfasted with us and gave me many instructions as to my movements and ended by urging upon me the fact that I was *on no account* to go beyond Gordonsville [Virginia]. I promised obedience and told the dear General good-bye. I never saw him again."

The Hussars were in fact at Camp Johnston, near Wolf Town in Madison County, Virginia, but the Confederate lines were in such a state of flux that even General Lee didn't know this. Nellie started off for Gordonsville under the escort of two soldiers, provided by General Lee.

"When the train pulled up in Gordonsville we found the advance body of the Confederate Army had arrived. *Such* a sight! The streets were jammed with soldiers, soldiers everywhere! On the fences, the doorsteps, in the windows. One could hardly make one's way for the crowds of men in gray. My escorts conveyed me to a small hotel with a balcony overlooking the main street. No quarters were to be had, however, so they got me a seat on the balcony and started off on a search for a shelter for me."

In about an hour they returned, reporting that they had found a single room in the house of a shoemaker on the pike, or main road. They appeared doubtful that the lady in whose welfare General Lee himself had taken such an interest would accept such limited accommodations, but Nellie did so thankfully, finding the room clean, though small.

Then it began to rain, and never stopped for three days and three nights. Nellie sat by the one window in her room and watched soldiers, soldiers, soldiers march by.

"Sometimes I would descry a Cavalryman. I would then fly out in the road, halt him and say, 'Can you tell me where the Georgia Hussars are?'

"The answer was always the same, 'Madam, I am sorry to say, I do not know.'

"Twice each day, morning and evening, I posted down to the train in the storm, to see if I could find one of the Company in the newly arrived crowd. I asked every man with a 'G.H.' on his hat, 'Where is your command?' But they had all been on detached duty or sick leave and could tell me no more than that 'the orders to fall back had come after they left, and they were awaiting word of their command themselves.

"The afternoon of the fourth day of the storm I sat at my window looking dolefully out on the pike. The red mud was nearly to the hubs of the wheels. Pedestrians could scarcely pick their way.

"I saw approaching a wretched-looking horse of Gothic architecture, on his back a very dirty, bedraggled soldier, in a soaked and stained overcoat, a grimy slouch hat pulled down over his eyes. I watched the poor wretch without interest. Presently the object pulled up at the gate and as the soldier dismounted I recognized *my lost Willie!* Such a sight as he was!!! He had to peel off his overcoat on the doorstep before he could venture into the house."

Willie was compelled to hurry back to his command early the next morning, but he left Nellie directions for reaching the Garrs' farmhouse, about three miles from the Hussars' encampment. There would be no escort for Nellie this time, and she would have to spend a night along the way, but the shoemaker's sister-in-law volunteered to go with her as far as the halfway house. The two women arrived there at 9 P.M.; it was "dark as Egypt," and the pack of dogs barked at them until the noise brought their master out. Then, says Nellie, "We were welcomed with true Virginia hospitality, all the more cordial when extended to anyone who, like myself, was en route to see a husband who was a soldier at the front."

The Garrs were well-to-do farmers with a comfortable though plain house. Willie got almost unlimited leave, as no fighting was going on at the time, and Captain Fred Waring of the Hussars came over to several meals. "We all enjoyed Mrs. Garrs' liberal table and good cooking, and I began to think, as the Irish preacher said at Killarney, that a great calm had burst upon us!"

The Yankees were drawing near, though, and the little idyll was soon cut short. At 3 A.M. there came a violent knocking at the farmhouse door. It was Willie, with news that the Hussars had received orders at 11 P.M. to break camp. "If I didn't get off by 6 A.M., I should be left in the enemy's lines! I should be captured!" To Nellie, this did not appear at all the terrible fate that it did to her husband. "I thought to myself, 'Why,

all I'd have to do would be to report to the Yankee commanding officer, explain who I was and telegraph to Chicago to my
father. Or still better, request to be sent to my uncle General
David Hunter, who just then was in Washington. Besides, I
had cousins galore within hail on the other side. But I wisely
kept all these ideas to myself and began to pack my belongings."

Now Nellie, coming to the front to see the man she loved,
had wanted to appear well in his eyes and had brought with
her a trunkful of clothes. Mr. Garrs said he could not take the
trunk on the cart in which he had promised to haul Nellie to
Gordonsville. Willie told Mr. Garrs to leave it behind.

Nellie said, "If you leave that trunk, you may leave me! I
don't stir a foot without it. All the clothes I possess are in that
trunk. I have had hard enough work to get them, and as long
as this war lasts I am never going to get any more."

Mr. Garrs, a married man of long standing, could appreciate
this. He said Willie could drive the cart and he would ride
a horse he had hidden away. Nellie relates in her Civil War
reminiscences: "The roads were fearful, red mud and red mud,
the horses plodding along. Willie held the lines carelessly (he
does yet!) and leaned over talking to me eagerly. There was so
much to say, so little time to say it in, and God only knew
when we would meet again, if indeed we ever met at all in
this world."

Suddenly the traces broke. And as fast as Willie and Mr.
Garrs fixed them, they broke again. Still Nellie would not
abandon her trunk. Presently a horse and cart, driven by a
Negro, came down the road. Against the Negro's vociferous
objections, Nellie got in and made him turn around and go
back to his master's house. There she used every wile and trick
at her command to get the owner to lend her Negro, horse and
cart to take her and her trunk to Gordonsville.

She tried pathos first, saying she didn't know what would
become of her if he didn't let her borrow his rig, which would
promptly be returned. The man was courteous, but argued
that if it went off to Gordonsville, he would never see it again,
as the Yankees would grab horse, cart and Negro. Nellie rea-
soned that the Yankees were headed this way, and would seize
the rig anyway if he didn't let her take it. He was unmoved.
Willie, coming up just then, offered the man a twenty-dollar

gold piece for the loan of the rig. The man was momentarily shaken, but still refused.

Finally Nellie said, "If you don't let me take the rig, I shall sit in it right here in front of your house, and sit in it all day and all night and from now on!" That did it. Willie rode off to join his company, and Nellie caught the last train that left Gordonsville for Richmond before the approaching Union army, one of two lady passengers.

The frail little flower who had barely survived the peacetime train trip from Harrisburg to New York just three years before, arrived at the Hexalls' in Richmond that night at nine o'clock, tired and dirty, to find a gay party going on. She sang duets until midnight with the mother of Amelia Rives, the well-known author, and, though entreated to stay on, left the next day for Savannah and her children.

It was in June of this year, 1862, that once more tragedy descended upon John and Juliette Kinzie. Their son John was killed, and shortly after this their remaining sons, Arthur and George, were taken prisoner. Arthur was on General Washburn's staff in Memphis. George, too young for military service, was visiting him there, when General Forrest captured them in a raid, along with most of the officers at the headquarters.

John's death was the harder to bear because it was due to a barbarity that was seldom exhibited in this war between brothers. John and Nellie had had their differences, but one can feel the emotion underlying her terse description of his death in her addendum to *Wau-Bun* written many years later. Her brother was on the gunboat *Mound City* which attacked a Confederate fort on the White River in Arkansas. A hot shot penetrated the *Mound City*'s boiler, blowing up the ship and throwing ninety-seven scalded and dying men into the water. General Frye, the Confederate commander of the fort, ordered his sharpshooters to pick out and shoot the wounded men as they were struggling to get into the hospital boats sent to their rescue. John was shot in the arms and legs as he was being lifted into the boat. "Hearing the victorious shouts of the Union marines, he exclaimed, 'Have we taken the fort? Then I am ready to die now.' The next morning, just as the sun's first rays gilded the horizon, his brave spirit took flight. He was just twenty-three years old, and left a wife barely eighteen.

His little daughter was born three months after his death. From this shock, Colonel and Mrs. Kinzie never recovered."

But the event was happier with Arthur and George, whose imprisonment at Cahaba, Alabama, was destined to be short. As soon as word came of their capture, John Kinzie sent a personal appeal to an old acquaintance. The young West Point lieutenant who had designed The Davis, the remarkable piece of furniture which had graced the Kinzies' quarters in Fort Winnebago, back in 1830, was now the President of the Confederate States. By Jefferson Davis' direct intervention the boys were promptly exchanged. Thus in some measure was wiped out the blot on Southern chivalry made by the commander who had ordered the shooting of wounded men.

Presently, in the midst of all these sorrows and anxieties and difficulties, Nellie found herself once more to be pregnant. Now there was no possibility that her loving mother could come to her aid and support. Willie was too busy battling Union soldiers to dwell very much on her sad plight. He even refused, when he was fighting up in Maryland, to honor her request that he take a little time off and run into Baltimore to buy articles that could not be had in Savannah. "I regret," he wrote with rather excessive politeness, "that I shall be unable to execute your little commissions in Baltimore or any of the towns in Maryland, but really just at this time 'circumstances beyond my control' will render it impossible."

Willie was reported dead. Then Nellie learned that he was alive, but seriously wounded. And it is our guess that bearing a baby under the conditions that obtained in Savannah and in her personal life in 1863, Nellie behaved magnificently. The baby proved to be another girl. They named her Alice, but her older sisters called her Skinny.

The war that was to have been over so quickly dragged on and on. At first the South was winning, and all Savannah rejoiced. But in 1863 came the crushing repulse at Gettysburg. Vicksburg fell. In July, 1864, Willie was taking part in the defense of Atlanta in his own Georgia, against Sherman's army. By September Atlanta had fallen, and Sherman presently started his march to the sea, laying waste Willie's home state as he went.

That summer Willie's sisters, Gulie and Eliza, refugees from

Virginia and north Georgia, had arrived in Savannah with their children to stay with their mother. They filled the house to overflowing, so Nellie took her three little ones and moved to a house at Greenwich, near Thunderbolt, five miles away. It was only a four-room cottage, but it was the first home of her own Nellie had had. As her mother had done before her, Nellie took with her her most prized possessions, the books and pictures she cherished, a piano lent by a friend, and made the cottage charming.

Now Nellie showed the sturdy, Midwestern, pioneering stuff of which she was made. She did countless household chores cheerfully, Eleanor and Daisy working with her, kept chickens, wrote gay letters to Willie about her adventures and the comical sayings of the little girls. The few months at Greenwich were a happy respite. The chickens kept them supplied with eggs, and Nellie beguiled a neighbor into letting her have honey, butter, milk and cream, bartering for them clothes which were more precious than money in the Confederacy. Daisy indicated that she might be clever after all by starting to distinguish the letters of the alphabet. Nellie, delighted, wrote the good news to Willie, who cautioned against pushing Daisy's mental development too fast. "I want no child of mine taught to read at the age of three!"

By late fall, however, Sherman's army was getting uncomfortably close, and it was necessary to go back to the protection of Savannah. Nellie wrote Willie a lively description of their return. The children had been sent ahead in a carriage with their nurse or Mormer, as they called her. Nellie waited for a government wagon promised her for the furniture, but it did not arrive until late afternoon. Then she discovered the piano would not go on it, and scurried around until she found a "wood-wagon." Mattresses were laid in the bed of the wagon, the piano, minus legs and pedals, was placed on them, another mattress was placed on top of the piano and on top of that a clothesbasket filled with books. Last, and on top of all, rode Nellie, steadying the clothesbasket with one hand and holding in the other a plate of butter, her magnificent hair coming down and streaming over everything. The butter, even though some hairs may have had to be extracted from it, was doubly welcome at the Gordon mansion, because it now held many inmates and food was scarcer than ever with Sherman's army cutting its wide swath of desolation across the state, and eating up all the food. After the Federal army was drawn about Savannah on December 10, 1864, and supplies from outside were cut off, there were days when the Gordon women and children knew stark hunger.

Inside the Gordon home there was great activity. The huge mahogany doors, with their handsome embossed brass plates, were painted black. Silver and other valuables were hidden or buried secretly at night. The children reveled in the excitement while at the same time shivering at the thought of the Yankees invading their home.

The boom of the guns grew closer, and finally Savannah was ringed about by Yankees. But Savannah itself was not shelled. The Confederate army in the city escaped over hastily constructed pontoon bridges. Savannah's mayor then met Sherman outside the city and surrendered, no fighting except some skirmishes having taken place during the ten days of the siege.

With daylight of December 21, Nellie's wedding anniversary, Union troops marched into Savannah. And a few days later, who should come calling at the Gordon house but General William Tecumseh Sherman himself, making personal delivery of letters for Nellie, entrusted to him by her family in Chicago!

A number of different versions have appeared of this particular brush of the Gordon family with history. Some persons, accepting the credo that Nellie was a convinced Secessionist, have pictured her as maintaining an aloof and somewhat haughty air in her dealings with the Union general. To clear up the record, we shall reproduce in full Nellie's own account.

"A few days after Sherman's Army marched into Savannah, there was a Grand Army parade through the streets of the city. Everyone's shutters were tightly closed. Eleanor and Daisy, however, stood on chairs looking out of the parlor windows through the blinds and watched the troops marching past.

"Every little while one of them would exclaim, 'Oh, Mama, is that Old Sherman?' and I would answer, 'I'm sure I don't know, I never saw Old Sherman.' After repeated questions, always receiving the same reply, they gave up the attempt to locate him and presently their attention was attracted by the music of the 2nd Wisconsin Band, which passed playing a very familiar air.

" 'Why,' suddenly exclaimed Eleanor in indignant astonishment, 'just listen to that Yankee band playing 'When This Cruel War Is Over.' "

" 'Yes!' echoed Daisy from her chair at the other window, turning around and flinging out both hands in a gesture of intense indignation. 'Just *hear* them playing 'When This Cruel War Is Over.' *And they're adoing it theirselves all the time!'*

"A few evenings afterwards I was seated by the fire, while the two little girls played together. Suddenly the parlor door was flung open and the maid announced, 'General Sherman!'

"To say I was surprised was to put it mildly. I welcomed him and then noticing that the children had retired behind me, I took hold of Eleanor and drew her forward saying, 'General, here is a little girl who was very anxious to see Old Sherman the day of the parade.'

" 'I declare,' exclaimed Eleanor in tremulous tones, 'I never said Old Sherman. It was Daisy.'

" 'Well you said it too, Nell,' retorted Daisy, greatly alarmed. 'You did say *Old Sherman!*'

"The General roared with laughter. 'Why of course you never said Old Sherman,' he said, 'because you and I used to play together when I was a little boy, and now we are going to sit down and talk it all over.'

"With Daisy on his knee, and an arm around Eleanor, he kept them in shouts of laughter till long past their bedtime, and when the nurse came for them I had hard work to make them go.

"As for the General, he fully enjoyed the home fireside and the children, and I was truly glad of the visit and the home letters he had been good enough to bring round to me in person. He told me many amusing anecdotes, and gave me interesting accounts of one or two close calls he had from being captured on his march to Savannah.

"General O. O. Howard's Chief of Staff, General William Strong, was an intimate friend and old playfellow of my brothers John and Arthur. As soon as possible after the occupation of Savannah, he came to see me, anxious to know whether he could be of any service to me or mine. There was nothing in which he could serve me, but I was glad to see him and talk over old times. He one day begged me to let him bring General Howard to call at some time when he could see the children, as the General had four little girls of his own whom he had not seen for many months. I consented, and one late afternoon General Strong called with his chief.

"The children at once made friends, and General Howard took Daisy on his knee. Instantly she noticed he had lost an arm. 'Oh,' she cried. 'You have only got one arm!'

" 'Yes, little girl,' he answered. 'Are you not sorry for me?'

" 'Yes indeed,' said Daisy. 'What happened to your arm?'

" 'It was shot off in battle,' said the General.

" 'Oh, did the Yankees shoot it off?' asked Daisy.

" 'No, my dear,' replied the General. 'The Rebels shot it off.'

" 'Did they!' exclaimed Daisy. 'Well, I shouldn't wonder if my papa did it,' she continued in satisfied tones. 'He has shot lots of Yankees.'

"Tableau!"

The little girls kept the Gordon family provided with excitement, says Nellie. General Howard had Eleanor and Daisy visit him many times at his headquarters and Nellie wrote Lieutenant Waldhauer from Chicago that General Sherman and General Howard had been particularly taken with Daisy. "They came to my house frequently and made a great pet of her, roaring at her comments about Yankees." General Sherman brought candy made with sugar—the first the little girls had ever seen. After it became apparent that the Yankee conquerors were behaving with correctness, Savannah homes were opened to them, and General Carlin of Illinois stayed at the Gordon house. He used to have his band play in front of the house for the entertainment of the little girls.

Probably Nellie herself was no small part of the attraction the Gordon house held for the Union generals. At this time she was a pretty young matron of twenty-nine, as gay and light-hearted company as she had been at eighteen, with the same power to charm anyone she wished to charm. Only extremely insensitive men could have failed to be affected by the sullen hatred all around them, and these were not insensitive men. To have found a friendly fireside in Savannah, and above all a daughter of Chicagoans whom they knew, must have been balm in their disagreeable rôle of conquerors of their own countrymen.

Orders came presently that families of Confederate officers must leave Savannah. General Sherman advised Nellie to go to Chicago, and himself made all the necessary arrangements. He also promised to place a guard over the Gordon house. Nellie, however, declared she would not leave the South until she had seen her Willie. He was now in South Carolina, just across the Savannah River. General Sherman provided a flag of truce to take Nellie to the Confederate lines. Several times Nellie went to the rendezvous and waited for Willie in vain. Still she would not go without seeing him, and again and again went out with a flag of truce until at last she found Willie at the appointed spot and could say her farewells to him. Then and then only would Nellie consent to board a steamer at Hilton Head, South Carolina, bound for New York. General Sherman had asked General Barnard, Grant's chief engineer who had come to Savannah on military business, to look after Nellie and the children as far as Old Point Comfort. There Colonel Lyman of Boston took over. Willie himself could hardly have been more careful of his family's safety and comfort than General Sherman was.

At New York, Nellie was met by her brothers Arthur and George, and the party started for Chicago by the New York Central Railroad, having to sit up all the way in coaches. Between Albany and Buffalo they were snowbound for twenty-four hours, and to while away the hours the passengers began to sing. Someone started "John Brown's Body," followed by "We'll Hang Jeff Davis to a Sour Apple Tree." The little Gordon rebels pricked up their ears and before Nellie realized what they were about were shouting:

> "Jeff Davis rides a milk-white horse
> And Lincoln rides a mule—
> Jeff Davis is a gentleman,
> And Lincoln is a fool!"

Nellie, embarrassed and concerned, tried to silence them, but Arthur and George burst into shouts of laughter in which the passengers good-naturedly joined. After the laughter had subsided, Daisy turned to her mother with tears in her eyes.

"They shouldn't hang Jeff Davis on a *sour* apple tree," she exclaimed, "'cause he's my papa's friend. I wouldn't care if they hung him to a *sweet* apple tree, but they shouldn't hang him on a *sour* one!" This produced more laughter.

It was a tired and bedraggled troop of travelers who descended from the coach at Chicago but the welcome they received was the more enthusiastic for that. The reunion with their daughter was an unbounded joy and comfort to John and Juliette Kinzie, and to them their grandchildren were beautiful in spite of sallow complexions, skinny legs, lusterless hair, and boils.

However, one of Nellie's girlhood friends said excitedly to another, "Have you seen Nellie Kinzie's children? They have tow-colored hair and clay-colored skins, and they look like poor Southern white trash."

The remark was repeated to Nellie, whose comment was: "Well, this is the first time I have ever known So-and-so to speak the truth."

But the exhausting train trip following upon the period of starvation had been too much for a little girl of four. Daisy fell ill with what the doctors called brain fever. For days her life was despaired of. When at last the crisis was safely past and Mama and the grandparents began to breathe freely again, the doctor took Nellie aside and warned her that the danger was not yet over.

"The convalescence will be a long one, and there is always risk of a relapse if she becomes overexcited or emotionally upset. Until she is past the danger point, I must urge you to see that the child is not crossed in any way. Her sisters must be told to give way to her, as well as everyone else." Daisy's strength began to return, but she was cranky and cross and full of whims, in which, by doctor's orders, she was completely indulged. Her family has always believed that it was during this time that the foundations were laid for the stubbornness and refusal to listen to reason which characterized her in adult life.

When Daisy could begin to play again, the little girls had a wonderful time. The Kinzie garden, covering a whole city block, was even more fascinating than Grandma Gordon's. Surely Grandpa Kinzie would have put on his Indian costume and done a war dance for the little granddaughters from Savannah. And they got to see in the flesh the Indians about whom their mama had told them so many stories.

A party of Winnebagos, on their way to Washington, appeared one day in the garden. They were dressed in full regalia, and Eleanor and Daisy were especially intrigued by a squaw who had a papoose and a small boy with her.

In *Juliette Low and the Girl Scouts* Eleanor writes: "Daisy and I were banished from the scene, but we took up our stand behind a trellis thickly covered with honeysuckle. Here we could hear and see everything. Grandfather sat on a soapbox, the Indians, in a circle, on the ground. For a long time after they had taken their places, not a word was spoken. Since ours is a very talkative family, Daisy and I were sure there must be something wrong with Grandfather, although he looked quite well, seated calmly upon his soapbox.

"At last the Chief spoke. He talked at length, stopped, and another long silence ensued. Then a second Indian spoke, followed by silence. And the council continued in just that way until every Indian had spoken and Grandfather had added his opinion at the end." Describing this scene to Girl Scouts in later years, Daisy used to say, "Grandfather had had plenty of time to make up his mind!"

The secesh sentiments expressed freely by the little girls caused laughter here, too, rather than resentment. Even now, Daisy was her papa's girl, and he seems to have been constantly in her mind. Asked what her faith was, Daisy replied stoutly, "My faith is my papa's faith, the Confederate faith!" She explained to a visitor, "I've got a papa down in the Rebel army. I love him *lots!* Sometimes he only has cornbread to eat. Isn't that too bad for such as him?"

Then one day they heard the clanging of cowbells, coming closer as house after house took it up. Grandpa Kinzie burst in, shouting, "The war is over!" Someone began to sing, " 'Mine eyes have seen the glory of the coming of the Lord.' " Daisy and Eleanor jumped up and down, crying, "We've won, we've won!" Grandpa Kinzie put his arms around the little girls and said gently, "No, my dears, you've lost."

Daisy broke away and ran to the gate on Michigan Avenue, where the happy people were now surging past. Perched on the gate, she sang "Dixie" all the way through, at the top of her voice. A kindly neighbor swung Daisy to his shoulder, the Yankee crowd cheered the little Rebel.

But oh, how hard all this must have been for a little girl of four to understand! To have her seriously intended remarks greeted with gales of laughter. To be transported suddenly from a place where the kindest thing ever said of President Lincoln was that he was a fool, to a place where songs were sung about hanging her papa's friend, President Davis, to a sour apple tree. To be told that her brave, wonderful papa's cause had lost, and to see kind, good people shouting joyously because this was so. To be told the Confederacy was gone. Daisy asked, bewildered, "Where did it go?"

She must have turned these matters over, and arrived at extraordinary conclusions. Who knows what defensive mechanisms and subterfuges her child mind resorted to, to keep from being torn apart by emotions and events too violent for a four-year-old to sustain and adult contradictions beyond her power to grasp? By the laws of psychology, we may find at least some explanation here of the unique reasoning methods, so puzzling to her family and friends, for which Daisy was noted in later life.

CHAPTER VI

A MARRIAGE TOTTERS

WILLIE'S GETHSEMANE began with that farewell meeting under the flag of truce, though his first letters to Nellie following it told how wonderful for him the meeting itself had been. One can imagine his emotions when, fighting in the Carolinas, he had received news of the fall to the enemy of his home city, where were gathered all the Gordon women and children. And the ruin wrought in Atlanta, the scorched-earth policy followed by the Union army in its march across the state, compounded his anxieties and his maddening feeling of helplessness.

To be able to hold Nellie in his arms again, to hear from her own lips that none of his loved ones had suffered, seemed a gift of Providence. But no sooner had their goodbyes been said than dark thoughts began to assail him. He had always been a little jealous of Nellie's love for her parents and the close relationship with her mother in particular. Mischievously, Nellie had led him to think that John and Juliette Kinzie did not deserve the love she gave them.

Also, he had never been able to see that in this war, to Nellie there was no enemy. She seems to have kept faithfully her agreement, made before her marriage, to refrain from criticizing Willie's political views in return for his toleration of her religious views. No dyed-in-the-wool Confederate wife could have been more loyal to her husband and his friends than Nellie had been and she had accepted the hardships imposed by her position with gaiety. He seems never to have grasped that so far as she was concerned, the war was a lot of foolishness which had nothing to do with her, except as it affected those she loved.

And so there began to build in Willie's mind an idea that Nellie's departure for Chicago, though he himself had approved it, was a craven desertion to the enemy, from those who truly loved her. "Now you will no longer have to suffer from the unhappiness you have felt for three years because you could not see your mother," was the first indication of the trend his thoughts had taken. On January 14, 1865, he wrote: "The fact of your being in the Federal lines is of course very difficult to bear, but I accept that as the fate of war and will endure it as I would any sacrifice that may be called for. But really what galls me is that you should associate with my enemies upon any other terms than those politeness demands from every lady. . . . Remember you are as much widowed as if death separated us—that you may be made a widow at any moment by the arms of those with whom you are." For Willie would fight on as long as the Confederacy fought, though he must have known by now that the fighting was futile.

From Hillsboro, North Carolina, he wrote tersely on April 29: "This Army has surrendered and the men composing it will be marched to their respective states starting in a few days. I presume we will reach Savannah toward the end of May. My last news of you was your letter of January 30th."

Willie went from Hillsboro to Macon, where his mother had found refuge after she was ordered out of Savannah, stopping in Atlanta on the way to clear his plans with Federal authorities. At first, the bitterness of defeat and the practical problems confronting him took precedence over everything else. "I hope to be allowed to go to Savannah to see Mr. Tison and find out whether it will be possible for me to do anything to make a living there," he wrote Nellie on May 16. "If I should be unable to do the latter I shall, if permitted to, leave the country. . . . You had best stay on in Chicago, till I send for you, for I don't know where to get bread for my mouth and for the present am helpless to fill four or even one more. . . . God bless, comfort and protect you, my beloved. Kiss the chicks and never let them forget that the word 'rebel' means an unfortunate man whom success would have made a hero and a patriot. Again God bless you, darling Nell. Your affectionate husband, W. W. Gordon."

But soon fate itself conspired to direct his understandably bitter feelings toward Nellie herself. Her letters, to which he looked forward so eagerly, did not reach him during this blackest period of all, after the surrender of Johnston's army. Learning that Willie was to go through Atlanta, Mr. Tison had forwarded them to Willie there. Willie, not knowing they were there, had not claimed them. When he got to Macon, he found that his mother had left for another part of Georgia, and so he was denied the comfort of seeing her. Mr. Tison meanwhile had sent Nellie's next group of letters to Macon by messenger. Willie figured out later that he had passed the messenger on the road as he went on to Savannah. When he reached there, toward the end of May, no more letters had come through from Nellie. During those first harrowing weeks, when he was receiving each day fresh evidence of the humiliating hopelessness of his situation and that of his friends and comrades, no letters from her reached him. He could not know that she was trying frantically to get word of his whereabouts, and had a bevy of Union generals tracing him by every avenue they could think of. And by this time, such knowledge would only have added to his resentments. Willie seems to have been in touch with Nellie's movements but perhaps this was through messages she was sending to him constantly by his friends. In his letters to her he made it plain that he was getting none from her at this time, and one can see how this fact fed the feeling that she had deserted him.

Willie found his city bankrupt, business dead, once prosperous firms disrupted. He wrote Nellie that Mr. Tison was going to try to start their firm again. Willie could not be a partner since, as a paroled prisoner, he could not take the oath of allegiance, but he hoped he might be able to work for Mr. Tison, going out into the country and attempting to get from the firm's debtors cotton, foodstuffs or anything else that was salable, and transport it to a market where they might realize something on it.

"If I had a permit to go North, and return when I pleased, I would go instantly to see you and the chicks and return here in a week or two. But I ask no favors and expect none and would be *humiliated beyond endurance* at receiving them through *your* influence and the Federal authorities, military or civil. For God's sake, Nellie, if you love me and respect my feelings, go to your mother and stay *quietly* with her until I can come or send for you."

For as soon as Daisy's condition permitted it, Nellie had gone off to Washington. Some of the thirty-one thousand bales of cotton the Federal army seized in Savannah had belonged to her. Nellie was proceeding on the basis that since she was a Kinzie, she should be indemnified for it. She wanted the money for Willie, and it tickled her sense of humor to play the rôle of a Northerner whose rights had been outraged, in order to get a stake for her Confederate husband.

Nellie's letters to Willie during this period have been lost, though they have been read and their general tenor noted, but a number exist which she wrote to his friend David Waldhauer of the Georgia Hussars, a prisoner at Fort Delaware, having lost an arm in his last battle. Nellie's mind and nature were of a kind to extract the last delicious bit of irony out of the unparalleled situation in which she had found herself during the occupation—the conquerors of Georgia, at the end of their grim, historic march to the sea, petitioning humbly to be allowed to taste her hospitality, the mighty Sherman himself completely subjugated by the small rebel, Daisy. Nellie obviously expected Captain Waldhauer to be as entertained by these events as she was herself. She described gleefully how she held the Federal government in Washington in the palm of her hand, so to speak, and had her family and friends among the Union big brass getting permits, exchanges, or discharges for all the Savannah men who had been captured, with the exception of the luckless A. S. "I can get almost anything I like and Old Abe is *werry* obliging where I am concerned." She asked Captain Waldhauer to pass these details along to Willie. It is plain that her conscience was completely clear, and that she did not dream Willie would take exception to her action.

The Confederacy was now in its last desperate struggles. Nellie wrote Captain Waldhauer: "What do you think about the bill for arming Negroes having passed the Senate at Richmond! After their threatening my brother's life in Savannah because he was reported to have commanded a black regiment, it would be rather rich if my *husband* should chance to be put in command of black troops! Such a life!"

On March twenty-fifth, she informed the Captain that she had "pitched into" Colonel Mulford, Mr. Lincoln, etc., etc., about his exchange, and hoped it would have been effected by the time her letter reached Fort Delaware. "If not, and only on the eve of exchange, I have some messages to send Willie by you. . . . I *must* get to him soon. I don't mean to stay here for all the children have to. Tell him I have written and *written* to him but never heard but twice, both of which letters I wish *had never come and tell him not to write me any more like them!* Such are my orders! . . . If you see Willie, you may kiss him for me as well as yourself."

This wifely scolding of Willie indicates that she did not take too seriously the two letters she mentions, which would have been written soon after the flag of truce meeting, and may have been the ones already quoted.

From Washington, after the war had ended, Nellie expressed to Captain Waldhauer her delight to hear that the Captain had taken the oath of allegiance. "Oh, Captain W., *if* Willie would *only* think as you do! Perhaps he *does* now, and I hope to Heaven he does! I heard from good authority that he wanted to come in and take the oath. I *do* hope so. . . . I am trying to get tidings from Willie. All the officers are so extremely kind to me. General Howard has telegraphed Macon to ask, for me, where Willie is. General Carlin is trying to get a letter and telegram to Bob Anderson at Hillsboro and General Wilcox told me yesterday that if there is anything in the world he could do to assist me in communication with my husband to be sure and call him—he would telegraph, or write or anything. So among us we may soon hear of Willie and his plans."

But fate still decreed that the Gordons should not communicate directly. As Willie failed to get Nellie's letters and Nellie failed to get Willie's, black thoughts took over in Willie's mind. He wrote her that he was willing to take the oath of allegiance but was not permitted to do so. He seemed to take a gloomy satisfaction in recording, in succeeding long letters, further details of the situation he found himself in, along with all the other men who had fought for the Confederacy. He

could not visit debtors of Tison & Gordon on the outlying
farms as he had planned, because to get out of the lines in
Savannah to go in any direction whatsoever required a passport.
No passport was granted anyone who had not taken the oath
of allegiance. And no paroled prisoner was allowed to take
the oath of allegiance. "I am caged here as securely as if my
parole were void." He had scarcely any money, and his friends
were in as bad case as he was. Out of his own little stock, he
had loaned one comrade twenty dollars with which to buy food.
When that was gone, he did not know what his friend would
do.

In a later letter he reported that no one could transact business of any kind without taking the oath, and by the Amnesty
Proclamation of the twenty-fifth of May, although everybody
was pardoned on condition that they took the oath except
certain persons and classes specified, "yet said persons happen
to include every man between sixteen and fifty-five in the Confederacy, (and all over fifty-five with $20,000; all generals; and
governors of states and all civil officers of the Confederate
States) except the Negroes and such renegades as turned Yankee
before the war ended. There are two black regiments and
several white in the city, feeling is not good between them.
Plantation owners are forbidden to visit their plantations. A
Confederate alone or a few together cannot travel in the vicinity
of Savannah without the greatest danger. The poor Negroes
are dying by thousands of smallpox. They are uprooted from
their old life and know no other."

In one letter he said there had been rumors that the Negroes
about Savannah were planning a massacre of their former
masters, who had no weapons with which to defend themselves
and their families. How much truth there was in the rumor
he did not know, but the Union commanding officer had re-
doubled the guard on the city, and at least Savannah had been
spared that horror. Willie foresaw a most difficult period ahead
while the displaced slaves adjusted to their new freedom. In
every letter, Willie would urge against Nellie's return, while
conditions were so unsettled and dangerous.

Unable to get outside of Savannah, and deprived of anything
to do in the city, Willie had plenty of time to brood. He wrote
his mother that he would go to New York "if I am permitted"

—how it must have galled to write that phrase "if I am permitted" in connection with every plan!—in order to try to borrow money to get Tison & Gordon going. When he arrived there, he would have only ten dollars left in his pocket. If he failed to borrow money, he would be stranded. He could not forward any money to his mother because there was no money, nor could there be any until her tenants could start paying their rent again and only God knew when that would be.

Every letter to Nellie grew more desperate in its tone. He was thinking of going to Honduras, as many Confederate soldiers were, or, better yet, to China. He was willing to go anywhere and do any kind of work. But he wanted Nellie to give up trying to get paid for her cotton because it was taking her among *Yankee* officers. He would starve rather than accept any money obtained that way.

And now, his Savannah friends were giving him more things to brood about. Nellie's "great friend Delia" had told him that everyone in Savannah thought Nellie had deserted him. "Your friend Mary Jane regaled me with wonderful accounts of your influence with General Sherman and his confreres. Every one —high and low—says the same thing."

Some of these people were undoubtedly sincere in their praise of the way Nellie had "handled" the Northern generals, and it is doubtless true that all Savannah had benefited from the benevolent mood induced in the conquerors by her hospitable fireside. During this whole time, Willie's sister Eliza was writing most devoted letters to Nellie. But it is also undoubtedly true that many would have viewed Nellie's actions as fraternizing with the enemy, confirming their previous suspicions. Those who had whispered about Nellie during the war would now see a chance to plant poison in the mind of Nellie's husband. Willie, beaten, helpless, frustrated on every side, getting no word from Nellie himself, was in no condition to withstand them.

On June 5 a new and most horrid suspicion seized him. "I see by the newspapers that General Hunter is in Washington. I trust that you have in your recent visit there had respect enough for me and my sentiments towards him to have nothing to do with him. If you have slept under his roof, if you have eaten at his table, if you have availed yourself of his protection or used his name to get pay for your miserable cotton or to procure any other favor from the Yankee Government, I shall never forgive you so help me God!"

Nellie was doing all these things, as a matter of course. Uncle David and Aunt Maria had been second parents to her from her earliest childhood on. Uncle David, moreover, was a direct pipeline to Lincoln while the President lived, and after his assassination, to all the other high government officials. In her personal campaign for her Confederate friends, it would not have occurred to her to bypass so potent a connection.

Yet one can understand Willie's viewpoint too. When Sherman turned toward Atlanta, it had been with the express purpose of destroying or capturing Johnston's army, of which Willie was a member. Willie had been in the engagement at Peach Tree Creek, when the Confederates had "come pouring out of the woods, yelling like demons." But five thousand Confederates had fallen in that battle, as against fifteen hundred Federals, and they had been pushed back into Atlanta itself and then had lost the city. The Union army had had more of everything, excepting only courage.

General Hunter's action in freeing and arming Negroes had not only been a body blow at the Southern economy. It had struck at the hearts of men away fighting, their wives and children surrounded by slaves. To Southern soldiers, it was an incitement to the murder of their helpless families. For Willie, this had become an intensely personal war, as well as one fought for what he considered to be honor and high principle.

Still not hearing from Nellie, Willie stooped to something he could not conceivably have done had he been in his right mind and accustomed character. Nellie had taken with her to Chicago a colored nurse, Ellen, for the children. Ellen had a sister in Savannah named Mary Anne. "Since it seems I am unable to get any word from you as to what you are doing, it occurred to me that I could get news of you by reading your letters to Mr. Tison and Ellen's letters to Mary Anne. I have read them. I find that you went from Chicago to Washington with General Hunter, and I naturally infer stayed with him there. I find that he has been your mainstay and hope in your efforts to get the money for your cotton and that you take as naturally to him as your uncle, as to your father and mother and brothers. Happy woman, to be thus connected with the winning side! . . .

"Perhaps I am presumptuous in addressing the niece of so mighty a one of my masters. Pardon me, I humbly beseech you. I constantly forget that I am subjugated and barely realize that besides country, cause, hope, I seem about to lose (or have already lost) the love, honor and obedience once pledged me. What a pity that one so talented and so highly connected should have thrown herself away on a creature so stupid as to prefer honor and principle to interest and success! What a career might have been open to such a niece if she had only been the wife of a Yankee! . . .

"It is evident from her letters that Ellen is anxious to return to her mother and unwilling to retain the responsibility and care of three children during the indefinite absence of their mother. I think myself a Southern woman would never have left her children thus to a hireling. Poor children! If they are an incubus to you, signify your consent and I will *at once* take measures to place them under the care of *my* mother and will guarantee that though they may not be so well fed or finely clad, they shall at least never want for maternal love."

And all the time Willie was writing these increasingly dreadful and unjust letters to Nellie, each one a whiplash designed to seek out her tenderest spots; all the time he was filling pages with reasons why she should not come back to Savannah now, and making it seem no one wanted her there, he was meeting every steamer that came from the North, in the forlorn hope that Nellie might be on it!

When at last his letters did begin to reach Nellie, they must have fallen on her like bludgeonings. There were so many points the spirited Nellie might have brought up in return— how this war had been none of her making, and how she had endured its privations and anxieties without complaint; how her parents, and she herself, when her brother John had been brutally slaughtered, had not held the barbarous act against Jefferson Davis or General Lee or Willie himself; how lovingly her own mother was caring for her little girls; how serviceable her connections were being to his own friends.

It is the eternal glory of Nellie Kinzie that she saw past the bruising words to the stricken, suffering man who had written them, and recognized their very cruelty and injustice as the measure of his desperation and loneliness. Those who have seen her letters in reply say that they are eloquent documents, reaching heights of nobility. In these letters, Nellie laid aside wit and tricks and stratagems, and held out loving arms to her husband and sweetheart. She pleaded, not her own case, but to be permitted to share with him whatever poverty, hardship, humiliation the future might hold for him. She told him frankly that she thought it would be a mistake for him to leave his country and the city of his birth, where he was so firmly rooted, though if he wished to try his fortune somewhere else in the world, that was for him to decide. But wherever he went, he must take her with him. She wanted no life apart from him.

And so, while Eleanor and Daisy and tiny Alice played happily in the Kinzie garden in Chicago and soaked up Indian lore and grew plump and rosy under Ganny Kinzie's loving spoiling, Nellie in Washington fought with all the power and strength of her woman's heart to save their home and her love.

And Willie's sore, sick heart responded. The moment Nellie's letters began to reach him, he wired her that he would start north the next week. This may have been wishful thinking, for he still could not take the oath of allegiance and could not leave Savannah until he did. Apparently before receiving this telegram, Nellie wired him that her father was ill and she was hurrying back to Chicago. That enabled Willie to give expression to the love and tenderness he had never lost for Nellie, even when writing those searing letters. But he felt self-conscious and awkward in his relationship toward his wife and her people. "I cannot explain to you my sorrow at this new trial for you. . . . I would say how much I sympathize with you and your mother if I thought it would be credited or appreciated."

Nellie's further letters that now began to come in an avalanche must have reassured him about that. And at last the nightmare of immobility in which Confederate sympathizers had been held was beginning to lift a little, with a consequent lift in Willie's spirits. In his next letter Willie called Nellie "my precious one" for the first time since the black mood had descended upon him, and wrote that paroled prisoners under the rank of major were permitted to take the oath, and he had just returned from taking it, "so that obstacle is removed from my going to you." He would leave for Chicago at once.

However, before Willie could start, Nellie wired that the doctors had advised an eastern health resort for her father. He had received a leave of absence and she and her mother and her brother Arthur were accompanying him to New York. They would meet Willie there. But when Willie reached New York, it was to learn that John Kinzie had died en route and the party had returned to Chicago. Nellie wrote, in her addendum to *Wau-Bun,* that as the train approached Pittsburgh, a blind fiddler came through the cars, asking for alms. Her father had reached in his pocket for his purse, but before he could draw it out, his head fell forward, and "he died with a smile on his lips." His death, in the very act of performing a kindness, seemed to Nellie to be the epitome of his whole life.

The Chicago *Tribune's* obituary notice said, "The last of his contemporaries, the death of Major Kinzie turns the final page in the first volume of the annals of this city and surrenders the last survivor of those who looked on prairie and woodland where Chicago now stands. It is rare that the sum of a single human life so honorably enshrines so much that pertains to human progress."

Willie immediately went on to Chicago and the need he found there for his love and sympathy, which he was anxious to give, undoubtedly removed the last bit of strain from his meeting with his wife and her family. No more was ever said about his going to China! The next letters he had occasion to write to Nellie, the following November, were in the old loverlike vein.

The Gordons stayed on until August, no doubt to help settle John Kinzie's affairs and to give Juliette their loving support. It is also believed that Nellie sold some of her lake front property in order to get a stake for Willie. (Her "miserable cotton," and what happened to that project, is never mentioned again!) Whether or not she sold her ten-acre plot at the time of her 1859 visit to Chicago is not known, neither is the outcome of her attempt to sell in 1865. She had Chicago property in later life. Willie had some houses built on it, and Nellie had her own money with which she helped Daisy when Daisy's husband, Willy Low, cut off her funds. But this may have been land which came to Nellie from her parents' estate. Willie was able to feed his family on their return to Savannah, though they had to live most frugally. It seems likely that Nellie's inheritance provided funds for Willie to start in business again.

On August 23, 1865, two hackloads filled with Gordons, nurse and baggage drew up in front of the Gordon mansion in Savannah. The people to whom Mrs. Gordon, Senior, had rented the house when she was forced to leave the city by Federal edict, had fled to Mexico, so it was available for Willie's family. Willie had stayed in the house until he left for the North, but had said nothing about its condition. Nellie, fearing the worst, had refrained from asking questions.

As soon as the hacks stopped, Eleanor and Daisy tumbled out and raced up one side of the portico steps and down the other, wild with joy to be back. Nellie went into the front drawing room, threw up the windows and opened the shutters. The sunlight, illumining the graciously proportioned room, showed that the furniture was all there, though dusty, the glossy African marble of the mantels and hearths was uncracked, and the mahogany doors and their brass fittings were unmarred.

Willie had gone to unlock the back door so the little girls could work off their high spirits in the garden. Joining Nellie, he looked around and said in surprised tones, "It looks all right!" Then he confessed that though he had slept in the house for several weeks, he had been so afraid of what he might see that he went between his bedroom and the front door with his eyes shut! He knew that at Wormsloe, a beautiful estate lying outside the city limits, Yankee hoodlums had deliberately smashed the arms of the caryatids which supported the mantel shelf. At beautiful Wormsloe today one may still see those mutilated caryatids just as the Yankees left them, perpetual reminders of the humiliation and outrage suffered by a proud people nearly one hundred years ago.

But the Gordons had been lucky beyond any imagining. When Willie opened the shutters of the back drawing room, with its fireplace set in the bowed back wall which was a unique feature of the Gordon house, marble, mahogany and furnishings here, too, were unscathed. And so throughout the house. There was dirt aplenty, and evidence of many muddy boots, but there had been no vandalism. Nellie must have sent a silent "thank you" to General Sherman!

The Gordon household utensils had suffered, it was true. On the pantry shelves which the Gordon women had left stocked with set after set of fine china and glassware, nothing remained but two cracked teacups with odd saucers, four old vegetable dishes and two gravy boats. In the kitchen Nellie found only an iron spider and a teakettle. But these were small matters. They could borrow whatever they needed from Cousin Meta Anderson across the street.

Nellie ran over with the precious gift of coffee she had brought the Andersons from Chicago. In the Anderson house, the little Yankee was received with warm, sincere embraces. Not only did Cousin Meta supply the Gordons with dishes and pots and pans, she insisted on sending over wheelbarrows full of kindling and stove wood, to tide them over until Willie could arrange for his own supply.

The W. W. Gordons were home.

CHAPTER VII

————————— ☆ —————————

RECONSTRUCTION

OR A TIME, the Gordons had to live on seven hundred dollars a year. All they needed was still another mouth to feed, as Nellie probably remarked to Willie, for once more she was pregnant. The baby was born the following April, and at last Nellie had her boy, a lively redhead whom they named William Washington for his father and grandfather. In the family he was called variously Willie and Bill. To avoid confusion we shall refer to him as Bill.

His older sisters, Eleanor and Daisy, indoctrinated him early in the Confederate faith. When he was three, Bill disappeared one day. After a frantic search, he and a small companion were found at the Central of Georgia depot, crouched under a seat in a car on a siding. Both little boys were almost extinguished under their fathers' Hussar helmets and had wooden swords buckled around their waists. They were off, they explained, to fight the Yankees up in Virginia! When, as a teen-ager, Bill went to St. Paul's and was surrounded by Yankees, he counted that day lost when he did not have at least two fights before breakfast.

Gradually, the Gordons' economic and household situation improved. Nellie found a German girl who was hired for ten dollars a month "to do everything I tell her!" And one day a colored woman named Liza Hendry came to the door looking for work. Nellie liked her face and engaged her on the spot.

Liza didn't know how to cook, but Nellie took her in hand and eventually the Gordon table became as famous as Juliette Kinzie's was in Chicago. From time to time attempts were made to entice Liza away from the Gordons, but she promised she would never leave them provided Miss Nellie would make her a muslin delaine shroud and Marse Willie would bury her in a "betallic" coffin when she died. Eventually Willie furnished the metal coffin, at a cost of five hundred dollars, and Nellie made the shroud, sitting in her tiny slipper rocking chair, tears pouring down her cheeks and damning everybody and everything in sight; but Liza had been with the Gordons for twenty-nine years before that day arrived. The Gordons loved her not only for her loyalty and good cooking, but because of her quaint sayings. She called turkeys "goblets," granulated sugar was "terrified sugar" and she used to tell the Gordons' friends that "Miss Nellie, she bein' a mother to me!"

One day Nellie found Liza hanging over the back gate, her face sprinkled with flour.

"Eliza Hendry, what on earth are you doing?"

"Why, Miss Nellie, I'se a croquettin'!"

Liza's expressions were adopted by the Gordons, and Daisy frequently used them in her family letters. Liza, for her part, found the Gordons as funny as they found her, and no one could "take off" Miss Nellie in one of her tantrums the way Liza could.

"Miss Nellie, she smell a dead rat in de walls. Well, she sniff and she sniff her way right up to de attic and she say, 'Dat damn rat he under dem floh boahds. What foh he crawl under dem boahds when he come to die? Whyn't he crawl outside?'

"Den de men dey got to drop what dey doin' and come and take up de floh boahds. All de time Miss Nellie sit in a old rockin' chair right spang in de middle of de floh, a cussin' and a damnin' and a rockin' hahdeh and hahdeh. Case de men, dey keep takin' up floh boahds and takin' 'em up and dey don't find no rat. Finally dey got all de boahds up ceptin' right around where Miss Nellie's sittin' and rockin' and still dey ain't no rat.

"Miss Nellie so mad she jump up, she say, 'Damn 'at rat to hell!' she kick ober dat rockin' chair. Cushion fall out, out fall de rat. He ben right dere in de springs, all de time Miss Nellie bein arockin'!"

After a few years the Gordons were living comfortably, if not luxuriously. A small house became available just a few doors from the Gordon mansion and they took it. But Grandmother Gordon's garden was still the play headquarters for all the neighborhood children. It was an enchanting garden. The geometrically shaped, tile-edged flower beds were bordered with violets. Rose bushes, which seemed to bloom perpetually, grew next to the house itself and along the low-roofed carriage house at the back of the garden. High up to the rooftops climbed the sweet banksia rose, spilling its beauty in bursts of sunshiny brilliance and fragrance. Camellia trees, which Willie's father had planted, now were taller than the children and seemed to vie with each other as to which could produce the most blossoms—some pale pink, some pure white and many of the gaudy Doncklaeri, red and white. Right in the middle of the garden stood a pittosporum tree, called "spittosporum" by the children. Its rhododendron-like leaves were glossy the year round, and in early spring its small white blossoms were deliciously fragrant. It was so big that each youngster could have a branch for his very own "house."

Now the Andersons were next door and Meta Junior, Randolph and Elise were handy playmates. A "telephone" was rigged up between the two houses. A small wheel was attached to a window of the Gordon house and another to a window of the Anderson house. A string ran between, over which a basket containing messages could be hauled from one house to the other. The usual message read,

> This very day at a quarter past three
> We all will meet at the Spittosporum tree.

Every afternoon, the elder Mrs. Gordon invited her grandchildren for tea, which was served in the highest style by her colored butler. This was an occasion for genteel conversation and for learning manners.

Winter evenings the Anderson and Gordon children would gather in the Gordon kitchen for a taffy pull. Daisy at this time had long hair like her mother's, which she wore in a thick braid down her back. One night Cousin Randolph Anderson

noticed that the taffy was the same color as her hair and proposed braiding some into it. Daisy, always ready to try anything, consented; the candy hardened. Unfortunately, Nellie's
comments as she had to hack off her daughter's lovely hair have
not been preserved.

Summers they spent on the Isle of Hope, only seven miles
away from Savannah, where Daisy learned to be an excellent
swimmer, and there was boating, fishing and crabbing. At the
age of eight, Daisy distinguished herself by rescuing a three-
year-old who had fallen into the water. She said nothing about
it, and the deed was only discovered when Daisy had to account
to Nellie for the fact that her clothes were sopping wet.

By the summer of 1870, Willie was doing so well that they
could afford a vacation at Amagansett, Long Island. Ganny
Kinzie came east to be with them. Juliette had, of course, kept
in closest touch and it is probable that Nellie and the children
had visited her in the interval. There are many warm, loving
letters in the Gordon file from Juliette to her little namesake.
These are addressed to "Miss Juliette Magill Kinzie Gordon,"
but always begin, "My dear little Daisy."

The death of her husband and dear companion of so many
years had been a hard blow to Juliette, but she had kept up
her usual activities with quiet courage. In 1869 J. B. Lippincott
Company had published her novel, *Walter Ogleby,* laid in the
Hudson River country where she had lived for a time as a
young woman.

The summer began as the most perfect one the Gordons had
ever had. The sandy beach and the surf-bathing never lost their
charm for the youngsters, the cool breezes gave everyone a feeling of well-being. Nellie was expecting another baby in
October. She had been such a valiant little soldier since Daisy's
birth that she well deserved the spoiling her mother and husband together accorded her. Juliette in her turn treasured
every minute with her daughter and grandchildren. At
Amagansett she was correcting the proofs of her new novel,
Mark Logan, and constantly receiving people who came to pay
homage. But there was always time to tell fascinating stories,
to bandage minor wounds and soothe hurts of any kind.

One afternoon in early September, Juliette and Nellie were
sitting on the lawn. Juliette felt she was catching cold, and

sent to the doctor for some two-grain quinine pills to break it up. The pills arrived in an unmarked box, and Juliette hesitated about taking them.

"Nonsense," said Nellie. "They must be quinine since that was what you asked for." To reassure her mother, Nellie popped a pill into her own mouth. Juliette then took two. Presently Juliette complained of strange sensations, but Nellie thought she must be imagining them. When Willie joined them not long after this, Juliette said in a faint voice, "William, please take me into the house. I am really ill."

Another doctor was summoned hastily. Then it was found that the pills had contained morphine instead of quinine. Juliette's case was hopeless. She was dead within four hours. During the rest of that night, the doctor and Willie battled desperately to save Nellie's life.

Eleanor and Daisy, now twelve and ten years old, never forgot that dreadful night. Gentle, loving Ganny Kinzie lying dead. Papa walking Mama up and down, up and down, Mama begging them to let her die, Papa forcing her to keep walking, forcing black coffee down her throat over her protests. It was not until dawn that the doctor at last said Mama was out of danger, and the girls crept shivering into their beds.

It must have been Willie who took Juliette's body back to Chicago for burial—Nellie, eight months pregnant and shaky after her own close touch with death, would not have been able to. Juliette was laid beside her husband in Graceland Cemetery, and the papers were full of enconiums for this lady of whom Chicago was so justly proud. "No woman in the Northwest was more widely known." A great crowd of Chicago's poor, whom Juliette had helped, followed their benefactress to her grave.

The next year the Chicago fire wiped out the Kinzie house and all its contents, but the Chicago Historical Society treasures a few mementos of John Harris and Juliette Kinzie. There may be seen a wallet and cane of John's, and a red silk embroidered shawl that Juliette had worn.

Apparently Nellie never set down on paper her feelings about her mother's death. But when she was a very old lady, she would note in letters to her children: "On this day my dear mother died." Shock at the needlessness of the death as well as grief is expressed in the many letters of condolence Nellie received from all over the world.

Among these are a number from Nellie's mother-in-law, and they are so similar to Juliette's own that they give one an eerie feeling. Both wrote in the same spidery, ladylike hand, using the old-fashioned "f" for double "s"; both ended their letters by writing lengthways across the horizontal lines of the first page; both used the same manifold expressions of affection. Even the ink on both groups of letters has faded to the same coppery shade. It is as though Nellie, in losing one mother, had gained another of identical kind. And this was what the elder Mrs. Gordon intended. Over and over she said, "I have long thought of you almost as my own flesh and blood. Now you will in truth be my very own daughter. I want to be to you everything that your Mother was." Nellie says in her reminiscences that Mrs. Gordon was to her, in fact, as an own mother. If there had ever been any serious friction between the two the circumstances of Juliette's death abolished it.

They had reason to worry a great deal about Nellie that fall. But Nellie came of a stock whose women bore their babies triumphantly through any form of disaster. She seems to have carried her baby to full term, in spite of the morphine poisoning and the severe emotional trauma that attended her mother's death. When Eleanor and Daisy came home from school one afternoon in late October and found the doctor's buggy in front of the house, they were afraid to go into the house at first, for the events of the preceding month hung over the family like a pall. But they found their mother resting easily, having delivered a plump, healthy baby girl. This child was named Mabel, for General Joseph E. Johnston's wife, and amazing to relate she was nearly always called Mabel, though sometimes her name was shortened to Mab. Mabel had the happiest and most equable disposition of any of the Gordon children except the boy who was born in August, 1872, and closed the list. Named George Arthur for his father's brother George and his mother's brother Arthur, he was called Arthur.

Mabel used to refer to herself and Arthur as "after thoughts," and insisted that her sisters Eleanor, Daisy and Alice seemed to her like grownups in her childhood because of the age gap between them. In time, however, this youngest sister and brother were to become the closest to Daisy of her siblings, though she loved them all.

And now that the Gordon family is complete, the relationship between father and mother cemented solidly for all time, mother-in-law and daughter-in-law in loving, close accord, it is time to pause and see what manner of family this was. Nellie, the hoyden carefree girl, had become the mother of six and had weathered the great crisis of her generation. Her character was settled in the mold it was to have until the end of her life.

There were intimations in *Wau-Bun* that Juliette Kinzie, too, had liked her own way as a young wife, and that a spirit of mischief occasionally erupted through her New England dignity. But if she had had wayward tendencies as a young woman, she had learned to subdue them. Her portrait in later life, after all her harrowing experiences, shows a face of utter benignity and serenity, a prototype of the older woman whose soul has found peace through loving-kindnesses. Nellie's portrait, at a comparable age, is of a perky, spunky little person, the eyes alive with gleeful mischief. Things were to happen to Nellie in the intervening years and she was to make things happen but she herself would remain essentially unaltered. Magnificent as she was in many ways, within her family she would be a naughty, captivating madcap to her dying day.

Nellie gave her own great devotion to her husband, and never made any bones about being wife first, and mother second. She herself wrote down, in her reminiscenses of Savannah's yellow fever epidemic of 1876, that when Willie urged her to take the children to safety, leaving him behind to help fight the epidemic, she said, "If you won't go, they can stay here and get yellow fever! What do I care for them in comparison with you, Willie Gordon?"

Yet she was by no means an unnatural mother. When she did lose a child, her grief was excessive. She toiled and sacrificed for her brood. She was more assiduous than most mothers are in recording her children's amusing sayings. And since many of those she recorded are not really very amusing, we conclude that Nellie had a normal maternal pride in her offspring, which affected her usually keen critical judgment. Speech was free in the Gordon household and "cheek" was encouraged, even at the expense of Papa or Mama. Nellie enjoyed a verbal skirmish with her offspring, and being confident of her ability to come out on top, never imposed any handicaps on them.

But they did not all possess her intuitive gift for diplomacy. You may be told in Savannah that the younger Gordons were arrogant. Even the sweet-natured Arthur found himself highly unpopular when he went to St. Paul's in his turn. Part of it was because his mother had outfitted him with a most unsuitable wardrobe, including a coonskin cap which, being many years ahead of its time, provoked derisive remarks. But Arthur also saw that his manner was not endearing to the outside world. He decided he needed to change his personality drastically, and did so in preparation for a much happier stay at Yale.

However, when she felt the children had done something wrong, Nellie's punishments were stern. Redheaded, impetuous, pugnacious Bill was always getting into trouble and being sent to bed for the whole day—his fifth birthday party was canceled because he slopped water on his new trousers. When Bill wrote down stories of his boyhood for his daughter Daisy Lawrence, his wife made him leave out the punishments and represent his mother as gentle and understanding. She feared the truth would too greatly harrow the feelings of his little daughter.

Nellie was superb in emergency or real illness, and warmly comforting in the kinds of suffering she could understand, but she had no sympathy with minor pains or aches. If a youngster complained that he had such a cold he couldn't breathe, she was likely to snap, "Well then, don't breathe!"

This attitude perhaps developed a certain stoicism in her offspring. During the Gordons' stay in Chicago in 1865, they had taken the children to Racine to see a dentist. In the hotel, a heavy window crashed down on Daisy's hand—she was then only four. Nellie says it took Willie and herself at least a minute to get the window up, and Daisy's hand was a bloody pulp. Nellie applied arnica and hot water until the doctor came and the swelling had subsided considerably. The doctor reported that two fingers were broken—Nellie had feared part of the hand would have to be amputated—set them and bound up the hand.

Nellie commented that Daisy behaved magnificently throughout this whole ordeal. When the doctor had finished, she said in a grown-up little voice, "Well I *do* hope we are not going to have any more performances like this one!" One can hear her mother speaking.

It is worth noting that Daisy accepted the many knocks fate gave her later on in the same stoical spirit. No one ever heard her whimper or complain, and no one ever saw her when she was not gay and sparkling. If she was ill or depressed, she kept to herself.

Nellie also recorded that one day Mrs. B. F. Cumming stopped Daisy on the street, kissed her and said, "Daisy, you *are* a pretty little girl!"

"No I'm not," protested Daisy. "My Mama says I am *as ugly as ten bears!*"

Nellie taught her children their catechism of a Sunday afternoon, as she had been taught in her childhood, but her God was the Old Testament one of an eye for an eye, a tooth for a tooth. The iron and great vigor which had characterized the first Kinzie seemed to have skipped a generation, and to exist alongside the culture of Nellie's New England inheritance and childhood home, neither affecting the other. Yet Nellie was a perfectly organized human being, with the ability to marshal all her capacities instantly and direct them unerringly.

And though well aware that they ranked lower than their father in Nellie's esteem, her children didn't seem to suffer from this. As they grew to maturity they became conscious, with a kind of awe, that they were privileged spectators of a rare and wonderful thing—a completeness of love and understanding between their father and mother such as few men and women ever know. They realized that if their mother appeared to love them less than most mothers love their children, it was only because she loved their father more than most wives love their husbands. They worshiped their father, and were content to play, in their mother's affections, second fiddle to "such as him."

William Washington Gordon II was the rock on which this family was built. Arthur wrote of his father: "The watchwords of his life were Duty, Courage, Loyalty. His was the hand of steel within the velvet glove. A dominating yet charming personality, he was easily a leader in every undertaking and in times of storm and stress he was steadfast, immovable, a very tower of strength. He was positive in his likes and dislikes. He neither shirked nor trimmed, and no one could ever doubt exactly how he felt on every subject and about every person."

But though Willie's word was law when he spoke it as law, he was no overbearing father, and he was no more exempt than the children were from Nellie's quick tongue, much as she loved and respected him. One of the stories the grandchildren delight in is an exchange between the two when they were visiting Eleanor at a northern resort. Willie was going to have to return to Savannah before Nellie did.

"Oh, Willie, I hate so to see you go!" Nellie exclaimed. "I think I'll go back with you."

"Now Nellie, you know you are having a wonderful time here. Wild horses couldn't drag you away."

"Maybe wild horses couldn't but one little tame jackass could!"

Willie had an excellent sense of humor and a nice wit, of a dry, quiet kind. But he doted on Nellie and everything she did, he found her endlessly entertaining. He preferred to sit on the sidelines, enjoying the performances she and the children put on between them. And so the Gordon children grew up in a household where there was much fun and laughter, free of the inhibitions typical of most households in that period. They loved their parents dearly, instead of standing in awe of them. They were steeped in the traditions both of the wilderness and of the most dramatic episode in America's history. They quarreled among themselves in childhood, as any group of lively, healthy youngsters will do. But when they were grown, they were the greatest of friends. Through all the separations and the different courses their individual lives assumed, the Gordons remained as closely knit as it is possible for a family to be.

Daisy was much like her mother in appearance and personality. As she grew older, the resemblance was increasingly striking, so that at first glance one may get the impression that she was simply another Nellie Kinzie, operating on an international scale. One is inclined to overlook the fact that she derived from the Gordons as well; and also from the gentle, maternal side of Juliette Kinzie that apparently passed Nellie by.

Daisy as a woman had the brilliance and sparkle and artistic talent that characterized her little mother. Everyone mentions her wit and charm, and manifold examples of her essays into different forms of art indicate that she might have attained fame as an artist if she had applied herself seriously. Like her mother she was an excellent horsewoman, a fine swimmer and good tennis player. But one soon learns that her differences from her mother were as striking as her mother's differences from Juliette Kinzie.

Daisy was as disorganized in her inner being as her mother was organized. Her mind simply did not work like that of the average person. "Given a certain set of circumstances, people will usually act in a certain way," Arthur wrote. "Daisy's response was often that of a weird dream. Two and two by no means made four to her. They made anything she chose to imagine they made, and once she had an idea in her head facts could not change it. The idea remained as *she* visualized it, in defiance of all argument and demonstration to the contrary."

Nellie was a complete realist, Daisy a thoroughgoing romanticist, and she carried her romanticism to fantastic lengths. Nellie had a rapierlike wit, and knew exactly what she was doing and saying every minute. Daisy was often funniest when she didn't intend to be funny, because of a naïveté she retained to the day she died. Nellie would go to any lengths for members of her family, or for those she considered worthy, as is shown in her letters to Captain Waldhauer, but she was not one to distribute largesse indiscriminately. Daisy could not keep money in her hands, because of her generous heart.

Daisy shared Nellie's righteous indignation at wrongs and injustices, and they frequently joined forces in fighting someone else's battles. But Nellie's attitude was more detached—it was the principle of justice she espoused. Daisy was extraordinary in the extent to which she did everything from her heart. Any person or animal in distress evoked a flood of sympathy, and she rushed in to do something, regardless of the circumstances of the fault. The trouble of every living thing she came in contact with was her trouble too, and she felt a personal responsibility for alleviating it. In her we see the great loving kindness which characterized Juliette Kinzie, but without the control of Juliette Kinzie's wisdom.

But the great difference between this fascinating pair was that Nellie was a supremely happy woman, Daisy an intensely unhappy one. Of the five Gordon children who lived to maturity, Daisy was the one who became world famous—and the one who felt that her personal life was a tragic failure. She had an unusual capacity for love, and she was greatly loved. But she was never to know the absolute love of the man she loved, she was to go through life with a hungry heart.

Was it because, in her, the coming together of opposite strains brought confusion and turmoil? Was it because of Nellie's unorthodox nature and manner of handling her children? Daisy's earliest years were marked by tensions and upheavals in which she must many times have longed for a kind of reassurance that Nellie would not have considered it necessary to give, and may not have been equipped to give, being herself so eminently self-sufficient. Or was it that Daisy was fated from the first to have an unusual life, through the play of events upon an unusual nature, compound of New England, midwestern wilderness, and South as she was?

Such questions as these can never be answered to anyone's complete satisfaction. Probably Daisy herself was the last to understand what her motivating forces were. However, the fact that Daisy was away from home so much during her years of growing up and kept in close touch with her family by multitudinous letters, provides a rare opportunity to trace the development of one of the intriguing personalities of our time, from sweet, loving, biddable child to the still sweet and loving, but brilliantly erratic, stubborn-willed woman known to the world as Juliette Gordon Low. We shall trace this development, and interpret as best we can, while realizing that some areas must remain in the mystery land that lies now between inheritance and environment, and perhaps will always do so.

CHAPTER VIII

———————— ☆ ————————

GIRLHOOD

Aᴼᵀᴱᴿ "this cruel war" was at last over, and dear Papa was reunited with his family, it would be hard to find any major unhappinesses in Daisy's childhood, aside from that dire September of 1870. The Gordons' poverty in the years just after the war did not bother the children, for they had everything they needed and everyone in Savannah was poor then. To have been rich would have been the disgrace.

Eleanor and Daisy were close companions, being only two years apart in age. Eleanor continued to be the quick one and was the leader, by her common sense and judgment acting as a balance wheel to Daisy's more fanciful nature. They felt both protective and superior to Alice, who was next in line and three years younger than Daisy. Bill, three years younger than Alice, to the three girls was the "brat" and nuisance most brothers are to sisters a few years older. By the time Mabel and Arthur came along, Eleanor and Daisy were big enough to take a responsible part in their care, and were little mothers to these two babies of the family.

Daisy seems always to have been considered "queer" and Eleanor addresses her sister by a special pet name, Crazy, in the first letters from Eleanor to Daisy that we have. Daisy accepted the nickname with equanimity, though all her life through she could not understand why her reasoning methods and actions were considered strange.

The first school Eleanor and Daisy went to was that of Miss Lucille Blois, who held classes in her home on Hull Street, just down Bull Street from the Gordon house and around the corner. Winter and summer Miss Lucille wore a plum-colored silk, fastened at the throat with an enormous gold brooch. Her spectacles gave her a severe look, but behind the spectacles were the mildest and gentlest of blue eyes. She made learning a pleasure and Daisy was an apt pupil—except when it came to arithmetic and spelling. Daisy's accounts were always kept by a method understandable by no one but herself, while her spelling also remained fantastic and was allied with a propensity for using, in speaking, some word other than the one she meant, so that her conversation was strewn with malapropisms. Her family attributed this particular oddity to the fact that Daisy did not consider spelling important, and it is true that at school she found drawing much more to her liking than word drill. But to have been satisfied all her life to be guilty of outrageous errors in speech and spelling does not accord with Daisy's character, if these were the result of carelessness only. She worked diligently at a whole host of accomplishments, and took pains to master techniques. When she became interested in palm reading, she studied under the great Cheiro himself, and this was typical of her. Moreover, she had a distinct flair for literature. Her letters in adulthood are delightful, though they lack the vigorous punch of Nellie's—as whose letters do not! But she wrote with the same fluid ease her mother exhibited, and her writings, both prose and poetry, have a grace her mother's lack. In addition, her letters show an educated and cultivated mind and are replete with references to books. Hers was a mind to which proper shapes and meanings of words should have come as effortlessly as breathing.

In the light of today's knowledge of learning processes, it is logical to conclude that Daisy's weird spelling stemmed from the same emotional complex as her equally weird reasoning methods. And there may be significance in the fact, overlooked by the family, that Willie Gordon couldn't spell either, in spite of his diploma from Yale. Nellie's spelling and choice of words, on the other hand, are all but impeccable, as is her grammar, while Willie errs occasionally in this last field, too.

Moreover, Daisy did not enjoy the ridicule she constantly

incurred because of her mistakes. One day she burst out, "Well, it isn't my fault, it's because other people drag in such fancy words. I hate people who use big words! They never hope, they anticipate. They don't expect, they expectorate!"

Whereupon Nellie broke in drily, "And I suppose they never swear, they cuspidor!"

The first clear picture we are given of Daisy, after the events attending the ending of the Civil War, is when she was around nine. She was short for her age and thin. Her light brown hair, cut short as a result of Cousin Randolph Anderson's experiment with the taffy, framed a pointed face, whose sharp little nose was sprinkled with freckles. Her enormous brown eyes looked with love upon the whole world, and especially on the world of animals. Daisy was addicted to pets, as her father was, and collected stray kittens and puppies wherever she went. Nellie, who abominated all animals but horses, suffered the pets because her husband and daughter loved them so.

One could fill a book with stories of Daisy's remarkable tenderness for animals. When she was fifteen, a calf had died and the mother cow had gone berserk. She would let no one go near the calf, and was charging wildly about the courtyard, attacking the men servants who were trying to get control of the situation. Daisy heard the commotion, and went to see what it was. The men frantically waved her back, but Daisy paid no attention. As soon as she saw the dead calf, she understood. She walked up to the cow, put her arms around the distracted mother's neck and wept with the cow!

After the disastrous experience at Amagansett, Nellie refused for a time to leave Savannah and Willie in the summer, regardless of heat, yellow fever and malaria, and the children were sent to their Aunt Eliza Stiles' at Etowah Cliffs in north Georgia. They would get on the sleeping car at night, arrive in Atlanta the next morning, change cars for Cartersville and from there were driven seven miles to the big rambling old Stiles house, its double porches overhanging the sheer gray cliffs of the Etowah River. Right after the war, Henry Stiles and his brother Robert had taken the house jointly, and in the summer added to their own broods not only as many of the young Savannah Gordons as were old enough to leave home but the sons of Willie's brother George as well, Percy, Beirne, Cuyler and George, Jr.

What may have been one of Daisy's earliest letters, written to her father from Etowah, records that "Alice has a sweet little peigion, but ugly," and that the Gordon boys from Huntsville had arrived. Percy Gordon and Johnny Stiles had taken the goat wagon, filled it with clover and with Daisy on top of it had driven it to the barn lot.

Sometimes there were as many as twenty children gathered under this hospitable roof, and large as the house was, the beds were all full and the boys slept on mattresses on the floor. These summers at Etowah provided riches of exploring and adventure and imaginative play that are the crown of childhood for those lucky enough to experience them. Etowah was a children's kingdom. Caroline Stiles, Robert's daughter, described it: "The viewpoint of the adults is not known. They did not come into our world. We spent our lives out-of-doors, in the grove and in the park and on the cliffs. Back of the house were the rose gardens and the fruit orchard. And then came our woods, miles of tall pines stretching off as far as you could see across the Georgia countryside, with its soft sands and the redness of the soil everywhere. There the ground was bright with wild flowers of every kind, blue Quaker ladies and Johnny-jump-ups in their season, and many others. Often we would throw ourselves down on the bed of pine needles, listening to the shush of the wind through the branches above us, smelling the tangy fragrance of the pines and looking off toward the distant mountains."

There was much to accentuate Daisy's romantic tendencies. The boys played Indians in the pine woods, hunting with tin-tipped arrows, or refought the Civil War, slashing to pieces the bushes which served for Yankees. Once the girls tried to break in on this fascinating play and the boys got even by assigning Caroline the rôle of the despised Sherman, and Daisy that of a Yankee spy.

But as they grew older, they turned more to theatricals and here Daisy assumed leadership because of her talent for mimicry and acting. Before long, she was writing the plays and directing them as well as taking for herself at least one leading rôle. Frequent benefits were given for the Indians. In the smash hit of the season, which cleared sixty-five cents for the Indian beneficiaries, Daisy took the parts of the Spirit of the Rainbow, Ragged Jim and little Harry in addition to writing and staging the opus.

The cliffs over which the house was built had the strongest appeal for the children in their teen years. Termination Rock was the highest, but the one just below the house was the favorite play place, for it had ledges at various heights for rooms, natural stairways and a beautiful little tower overlooking the water. They dubbed it The Castle of Redclyffe, after a current novel. And whenever they got warm from the play in pine grove or orchard or on the cliffs, they could dash down to the river for a glorious swim.

Daisy wrote some poetry, in addition to her dramatic labors, and did a great deal of drawing. She and Caroline made many paper dolls, and there exist today some beautifully executed representations of the *Eight Cousins,* which Caroline drew and Daisy painted. The two girls also collaborated in writing and illustrating a poem, "The Months," which they submitted hopefully to *St. Nicholas.* It came back, but with a kind letter from the editor, Mary Mapes Dodge.

Daisy's generosity and special thoughtfulness for people as well as for animals were already evident. At twelve, she was writing Papa from Etowah to ask him if he wouldn't ask Mama "if I can't give my doll that Mrs. Austin gave to me to Mary, for I never play with it and Mary has none to play with while Alice plays with her doll." In the same year, Nellie wrote to Daisy, "I don't think you ought to spend *all* your $5 on others— you ought to get one nice present for yourself from Granny, or she won't like it, I am afraid."

When each of the girls in her turn had learned all that Miss Lucille could teach, she was sent to boarding school, the first one being Stuart Hall in Virginia, to which Daisy went off the fall she became thirteen. Nellie continued to exercise vigorous direction over her daughters' activities and to supply them with Savannah news enlivened by Nellie's personal analysis of it.

There are very few of Nellie's letters to Daisy in the files. Possibly Daisy did not keep them. More probably, she kept them all very carefully, then left them in some train or hack, for that is the kind of thing she was always doing. But these few give a good idea of Nellie's attitudes and her conception of her maternal responsibilities: "Mr. L—— committed suicide this morning by blowing his brains out. When a man has not got enough respect for his brains to keep them in his head I don't think his death will be much loss to anybody. . . .

"I especially dislike Mrs. P—— W and I do not visit her and I do not want you to go to her house or visit her under any circumstances. . . ."

"How *came* you ever to *begin* such a book as Hester Morley's *Promise! No!* You *cannot* finish it and I am very vexed that you ever got hold of it. You may read *Lorna Doone* if you like, but I don't think you will enjoy it. *Kate Coventry* and *Jessie Trim* I know nothing about and you can't read them until I do. . . ."

"Your letter with one from Alice enclosed arrived yesterday. Your delay in sending me the length of your skirt, caused me an immense amount of trouble. I was thankful, however, to get it at last. I thought I got your waterproof to put on to run back and forth to the schoolroom? I don't see what you want with shawls besides. I have no old ones, and cannot afford to buy new ones. And as it is only because you think it too troublesome to put the waterproofs on, I think you will have to exert yourselves to do so, for I really have no money to waste. I will have the aprons made. Four apiece. One more scolding before I finish up. I send a list of your words spelt wrong and the right way to spell them. Please study them hard, as you frequently, in fact always, spell them wrongly.

Daisy's Spelling	Right way
SLE*A*VE	SL*EE*VE
IDEA*R*	IDEA
DISGRASE	DISGRA*C*E
SUSPEN*C*E	SUSPEN*S*E

"Please remember that a person's *bust* means *both their bosoms* and according to your description of Alice's 'busts' the unfortunate child has four—two in front I suppose and two behind I conclude, which is certainly more than her share and I don't wonder her dress had to be let out. P.S. If Miss Sarah tells you the price of the ticket to Washington to tell me and you forget it, you won't go because I can't send the money till I know it."

But Nellie also begs "her dear Daisy" not to study too hard and signs herself, "Your loving Mother."

Fortunately, considering what Daisy's future life was to be, Nellie approved of the great English poets and novelists, and Daisy was allowed to browse at will in Shakespeare, Scott, Thackeray and Dickens. She devoured English history as well. Nellie kept Daisy's letters to her, and these give an unusual record of Daisy's teen years, from the inside, so to speak. They are very much like the letters mothers receive from girls away at boarding school today, girl nature seeming to have changed very little. Today's mothers would be principally struck by the fact that Daisy wrote so fully and frankly. She was certainly not afraid of her peppery little mother and confessed all her errors of commission and omission as freely as she set forth her achievements.

One of her early letters from Stuart Hall encompasses both her feeling for animals and her strong dramatic sense.

"We found a little robin frozen to death and we gave it a burial next day at recess. I got a little brown pasteboard box, just the shape of a coffin, and put pins in the edge of the lid, and they looked like silver-headed nails; and I made him a little shroud and a little cap, and laid him out on my doll's bed; and we had six pallbearers and I was parson and we had the services in the schoolroom and they were the Death of Cock Robin.

" 'Who killed Cock Robin?'

" 'I' said the sparrow

" 'With my bow and arrow' and so on. And we sang 'The North Wind doth blow and we shall have snow,' and so on and the girls all stood in two lines, teachers included. And then we all went, two by two to the grave. But I must not forget to say that Miss Kate said we could have English Services in honor of his burial, and we had a real marble stone and on it was written,

> Here lies Cock Robin,
> Snug as a Bug in a Rug.

"Sally L was the chief mourner and she wept and tore her hair and acted just like a chief mourner."

The girls from Georgia enjoyed the cold weather, for then they could ice skate; and they luxuriated in the snow, which was a new experience to them. Aside from these activities, the only exercise was to take walks, the girls marching sedately two by two.

Daisy proved to be very good in languages, though drawing was her favorite subject. "If I get a low mark in French this month don't be surprised because twice Miss B has taken off my marks for drawing in class and it is hard work to pay attention in her stupid old class, but I will try."

Spelling continued to be a stumbling block. She seems to have tried earnestly to better her performance, but to no effect. "A dictionary is no use—half the time I don't even know how the word starts!" Many of her letters contain apologies for spelling, and she was hopeless in music, too, in which her mother excelled. Daisy always enjoyed listening to good music, but seemed to be tone deaf. Aside from "Dixie," which she learned very early, she claimed she never mastered any song but "Susie, Oh My Darlin'," which she used to inflict occasionally on her friends in what she described as a "baritone croak."

Her other affliction was that, being the smallest girl in school, she could not conceal her identity when the "swarrays," which formed the social side of school life, took the form of masquerades. She gave the matter serious thought, and wrote: "At the next masquerade I went as an old man so that no one could tell me. I was stuffed with pillows and had a round piece of pasteboard like a muff box with an awful face painted on it and I put this over my head with a hat on top and you have no idear how tall I looked!"

The big boarding school events, then as now, were the boxes from home, and Daisy was profuse in her appreciation. "Oh Mama, we got the box of candy and my dress and Eleanor's waist, and the idear of you saying you thought I would be reconciled. I think it's perfectly lovely, it could not be prettier. I got my Bible the other day and it is the nicest birthday present you could give me. I will keep it always." This she did, and read it always. Her letters in adulthood are as studded with biblical references as with literary ones, and she had chapter and verse at her finger tips.

At fourteen she was viewing with disgust the crushes of her older sister, Eleanor, not having arrived at that stage as yet herself. "Eleanor and Ida are so devoted, it seems to me they do nothing but kiss, would you ever think Eleanor would slobber with anyone." But she was fond of Eleanor just the same. "She's so sweet, so much kinder and nicer than she used to be."

Her admiring love for her mother is very evident. "Mama, if I am ever half so smart as you or greater, I may 'thank my stars,' so don't be alarmed on that score. And Mama, the principal reason I answered your letter right off was because you called your dear young self, old. *Please* don't again. I got a letter from you on my birthday, it was such a funny little letter, about your loving me. I love you too, my own Mama, more than I can tell."

And a year or two later: "Granny wrote us you are sick, and oh I am so sorry. I hope you are well now. How I wish I could be with you to do something for you." Though she also advises Nellie that "I think Arthur is very smart, but I would teach him something better than 'Yankee Doodle'!"

By 1873, the Gordons' economic situation had improved so substantially that in addition to supporting two daughters in boarding school, they could afford a trip to Europe. Nellie's diary for this expedition is not dated, but presumably it was during the summer while the four older children—Eleanor, Daisy, Alice and Bill—were at Etowah Cliffs. The Gordons took with them Mabel and Arthur and a nurse.

With their entourage, the Gordons made a regular Cook's tour of Europe, and Nellie noted down her impressions of the beautiful and historic things they saw. In London, they were taken to the Tower, the Crystal Palace, Westminster and other points of interest by "the Dickens" who seem to have been Charles Dickens' family. Nellie wished Daisy might have been with them at Westminster to "take off the guide, a most remarkable creature."

They received a pressing invitation from Andrew Low to visit him at his home at Leamington, but declined it because they thought the two small children and nurse—Arthur then was just a year old—would be too much of a burden, and they did not feel they should leave the children behind in a London hotel.

Andrew Low was a Scotchman who had made a fortune in Savannah in the cotton business. He had married a Savannah lady, a Miss Hunter, and had two daughters by her; Amy, who married Sir Henry Grenfell, and Hattie, who, at the time of the Gordon visit, was about to marry Major George Robertson of Widmerpool Hall. Nellie noted in her diary that the Major had an income of ten thousand pounds a year.

In 1849, Mr. Low had built a stately home on Lafayette Square in Savannah. His first wife having died, in 1854 he married Mary Couper Stiles, also of Savannah and a famous belle. Her father, builder of the Stiles house at Etowah Cliffs, had been United States Ambassador to Austria in the 1850's. By Mary Couper Stiles, Andrew Low had four more children —Katy, who never married; Mary, who married Charles Guthrie of East Haddon Hall; Jessie, who married Hugh Graham; and a single son and heir, William Mackay Low, who owed his middle name to the fact that his maternal grandmother had been a Savannah Mackay. Since the second Mrs. Low was a sister of the Henry Stiles who married Eliza Gordon, the Gordon children's Uncle Henry and Aunt Eliza Stiles were also Uncle Henry and Aunt Eliza to the four children of Andrew Low's second wife.

Andrew Low's sympathies were with the South. Returning from England during the Civil War with his wife and Charles Green, a cotton merchant, he brought important papers to the Confederate government. Low was arrested by Union orders and confined for a time at Fort Warren, but his wife smuggled the papers through by twisting around them the fashionable long ringlets which hung at either side of her face. Toward the end of the war, Mrs. Low died in childbirth, the baby dying too, as a result of the privations Savannah residents suffered. Thereafter the Lows had divided their time between England and Savannah. Jessie Low was about Daisy's age, but whether or not the Low children and the Gordon children ever played together in Savannah is not known.

However, the exchanges of civility during the Gordons' London visit indicate a most cordial relationship between the parents. Willie and Nellie called on Katy, the eldest of Mary

Couper Stiles' children, who was very glad to see them. Nellie noted in her diary that Katy was quite pretty "though not as handsome as her dear mother."

Willie paid one hundred guineas for a gold watch at Dent's. And he and Nellie walked and rode about London a great deal, gazing on the exteriors of the houses of British peers of whom their daughter Daisy was later to be an intimate friend.

The next year, 1874, was marked for Daisy by the fact that she received her first attention from boys. It started when she traveled south with two young West Point cadets, "who represented themselves as being Yankees and bitter enemies of Rebels!" She had evidently parried their thrusts with spirit, which aroused their admiration. One of the boys told her she had "liquid brown eyes," and the other declared that a scar which disfigured her brow was really a "great beauty spot."

Daisy was at Etowah, sitting on the topmost branch of one of the high trees and reading a book, when she saw a buggy drive beneath her. She thought it was someone calling on her aunt. Presently one of the maids came running out to the tree and motioned Daisy to come down. She was rushed into the house, hustled into a clean white piqué dress "finished on the edge of the basque with Tom Thumb fringe. My hair, which was bobbed, was slicked down and I was ushered into the drawing room."

Her callers were the young men of the train, and all their talk about being Yankees had been to get a rise out of Daisy. They were as much Rebels as she was, and lived on a plantation about ten miles from Etowah.

"It swept over me that my would-be admirers were two very untruthful, dangerous men and I must have sadly disappointed them if they expected the same lively sallies and caustic repartee with which I had entertained them on the voyage South! For I was tongue-tied, and thus the first glimpse of grown-up life was for me a dismal failure.

"After the cadets had departed my brother tried to reassure me when I asked him if I looked very ugly. 'Sister, you looked so nice none of us recognized you!'" That brother, unquestionably, was Bill!

It was probably at about this same time that Daisy formed her first organization. It was composed of younger girls, and was called The Helpful Hands. Daisy's idea was that she would teach the girls to sew, and they would make many useful articles for the poor. The main trouble with the plan was that Daisy herself knew nothing about sewing, and after she tried to teach the girls to thread a needle with their left hands, the club was given the name Helpless Hands by her brothers and sisters.

Daisy's determination, or bullheadedness as one prefers, would not let her relinquish the effort, and the club made some clothes for the ragged children of an Italian family who had a fruit stall. Daisy admitted their work was not a complete success, "because the Italians were of very warlike tempers, and in one battle which took place in our lane the sleeves of the watermelon-pink garment came completely out, and the boy discarded the garment altogether, racing home sans culottes, pursued by a policeman."

Nevertheless she always insisted that the girls had great fun in their club, and it was not broken up until the great Savannah yellow fever epidemic of 1876 disrupted all Savannah.

The Gordon children all loved their home, and Daisy in particular had been writing very forlorn letters in the spring of 1876. "Oh Mama, you don't know how homesick I am tonight, sometimes I rearly wish I could die, it seems such a long time since I have seen you all and I can't be good in this old school. When I say my prayers at night I'm so tired and slepy that I can't pray for all I want and in the morning I don't have time, and I fly in passions and do bad things all the time, can't you tell me some remedy?"

Between boarding school in winter and Etowah in summer, Eleanor and Daisy had been home very little for the past few years. The remedy they themselves suggested was that this summer they be allowed to stay in Savannah.

Willie and Nellie hesitated, much as they liked the thought of having their daughters with them. The oppressive heat was not the only thing which impelled nearly everyone who could to get out of Savannah in the summer. For some reason then unknown, that was the time when yellow fever and malaria struck. In Savannah, long observation had taught the residents several things: that epidemics occurred with warm weather and were usually ended by a hard frost; that to stay out after dark was to invite infection; that the menace came from the marshes flanking Savannah, being connected it was believed with the noxious emanations of the marshes in hot weather. Some people even built their houses with no windows at all on the east or north, from which directions the miasmas came.

These precautions actually did guard against yellow fever to the extent that they protected the residents from the disease-bearing mosquitoes which bred in the marshes. But ignorant as yet of the true source of yellow fever, Savannahians considered that the disease itself was highly contagious as well as revolting, with the unnatural color it gave its victims, its horrid odor and deadly black vomit. Any person who would nurse the sick, or even venture into a sickroom, was counted heroic.

And so it required considerable argument and coaxing for the girls to get their parents' consent to stay at home in the face of these dangers. It was given on condition that certain rules be observed strictly. They must never go out in the heat of the day, nor go in the sun without a hat. After dark they must stay in the house. Above all, they must never open a window after sundown. Savannah believed firmly that night air was bad: "It gives yellow fever."

The girls were delighted to renew old friendships. Just as before, the crowd would gather in the Gordon home or at the Andersons' next door. The happy summer rushed by, and August was almost over. One Wednesday evening Willie and Nellie strolled over to join the elder Andersons on their piazza. Uncle Ned Anderson, Mayor of Savannah, was there too. It had been rumored that there were some cases of yellow fever in the city.

Cousin Meta Anderson said promptly, to her husband, "Ed, if there is any danger of yellow fever, I hope we can all go away."

Uncle Ned pooh-poohed the idea that there was any danger. "There are always a few sporadic cases, here and in Charleston. There is no more yellow fever here than there is every summer. It's absurd folly to run away from just a scare!"

Friday morning, Alice went over to play with Elise Anderson and her sister, named Meta for her mother. In a short time Alice came back saying that Elise was quite sick and as Cousin Meta did not know what might be the matter, she had sent

Alice home. It was very hot and sultry. The brassy sun beat down. Even the children, playing indoors, were listless and seemed subdued.

Soon after midnight, the Gordons were roused by a violent knocking at the front door. "It's I, Johnny Lewis, Captain," called a voice when Willie stuck his head out of the window. "Sister Belle has just died of yellow fever and Mother wants Miss Nellie to come." Already Nellie was out of bed, getting into her clothes. "You can't go," Willie told her, "it's too dangerous. It would be different if you could do any good. But Belle is dead. I'll go instead and say I wouldn't let you come."

Tears were running down Nellie's cheeks. "She was one of my dearest friends. They wouldn't let me see her alive, no one shall keep me from her when she is dead. Give me a quinine pill and a drink of whiskey if you think they will help any, but go I must." Willie went with her, and both did what they could to comfort Belle's family.

On the way home, Willie told Nellie she must take the children and stay at Etowah Cliffs until there had been a frost.

"Will you come too?"

"I belong to the Benevolent Association. If this proves to be an epidemic, it is the very sort of thing the Benevolent Association was set up to meet. My place is right here."

"Then my place is right here with you," declared Nellie.

"We must consider the children—"

Nellie broke in with her famous and seemingly callous statement, "Not at all. They can stay here and get the yellow fever. What do I care for them in comparison with you, Willie Gordon? You must be crazy!" The argument was renewed the next morning at breakfast with the children present.

And now we are treated to an extraordinary spectacle. For it appears that Nellie went round the table, asking the children in turn if they wouldn't like to stay in Savannah and face the yellow fever peril with Papa. She must have made it sound alluring, for the children were enchanted at the prospect. All, that is, but Daisy! Realistic for once in her life, she was for leaving Savannah immediately.

Nellie reproached her. "Why, Daisy, do you mean to say that you don't want to stay here and die with your family?"

"I'd like to *live* with my family anywhere," Daisy replied, "but I don't want to die here or anywhere else!"

Surely Nellie must have been up to her tricks. Once more Willie was proposing to endanger the life that was so precious to her. She knew he could not be swayed from a path of duty and honor by considerations of self, but if she could set up a situation whereby he would be endangering his children's lives in staying. . . . All this would have gone through Nellie's quick mind in a flash, and is the only possible explanation for her tactics. Probably Willie detected her strategy, for his letters to Daisy in later life indicate that he knew his Nellie through and through. Perhaps he smiled to himself at the way Daisy innocently sabotaged Nellie's little scheme.

Nellie then fell back on a firm refusal to leave Savannah herself unless Willie came too. At last he thought of a solution. "You take the children to Eliza's at Etowah Cliffs and leave them there. I will get board for you at Colonel Davant's at Guyton and I can come up there every night and be in town every day." Guyton was only twenty miles from Savannah on the Central of Georgia Railroad. When Nellie found that was the best she could do, she consented. At least, this plan would get Willie out of Savannah during the perilous nights.

Nellie went over to the Anderson house and offered to take their children with her to Etowah. She found another sad household. Elise's illness had been pronounced yellow fever. The doctor advised against sending the other children to Etowah, as they had been exposed already, and the disease might develop at the plantation, far from physicians able to treat it. Two days later, in fact, Meta, Junior, came down with yellow fever.

It was decided to send Bill, who had not been well, to a cousin in Brooklyn, New York, and he was got off on a steamer sailing that afternoon. He was told he might take two treasures with him in addition to clothing. Like the pioneers of old, he chose his Bible and his shotgun. That night Nellie and the other children left for Etowah Cliffs, Nellie returning to Guyton as soon as she had deposited her offspring with Aunt Eliza. Evidently the older Mrs. Gordon was at Etowah too.

Willie, however, turned out to be a "perfect fraud" so far as his promise to come up to Guyton every night was concerned. "I did not see him except two or three times when he ran up for a couple of hours in the afternoon," wrote Nellie in her story of the yellow fever summer. "But I forgave him, since he was so busy nursing the sick in Savannah."

For fighting the yellow fever, Savannah was divided into districts, and members of the Benevolent Association or other volunteers assumed responsibility for them. Willie's "beat" was one of the largest and he had, besides, many personal friends to look after. His business office was on The Bay, where the atmosphere was considered so deadly that not even a policeman was stationed there. Twelve of Willie's clerks went down, one after the other, with yellow fever.

As soon as Willie had breakfasted, he would take a quinine pill and a drink of whiskey, considered a preventive measure, and then make the rounds of his beat, seeking out the fever cases, administering mustard-plasters, hot baths, medicines, summoning a doctor and arranging for suitable food. In the afternoon he made a second tour of duty, attending to office affairs in between insofar as he could. By night time, he was too weary to get on the train for Guyton.

When Willie died, Savannah's Negro newspaper said that he also visited the Negro hospitals every day to make sure the patients were not being neglected. From 1876 to 1912, the colored residents had remembered his thoughtfulness for members of their race throughout the epidemic.

Every day, heartbreaking sights met his eyes. One morning he went into a house and found the mother dead on one bed, the father dead on another and several little children sprawled on the floor, crying with hunger. In spite of all the volunteers could do, whole families would be swept away. It did not occur to Willie that he would not be struck down in similar fashion. He made his will, and told Nellie he had done so. He also wrote a letter to her, directing her in the minutest detail as to how she should handle the stocks and bonds and real estate that would be left to her. This letter must have been filed with his will and marked to be opened only in case of his death.

If Nellie had seen it during the epidemic, neither wild horses nor tame little jackasses could have kept her from coming to Willie's side, for it is written in the calm acceptance of the fact that Willie was condemned to die, as surely as though he were sitting in the death house of a prison. To his own fate he gives no thought at all. He is concerned only for the welfare of the wife and children he thinks of as already widowed and fatherless, and he looks into the future as far as he can see to give Nellie the benefit of his business acumen.

He mentions that his mother's real estate is valued at about $100,000 for tax purposes. "Should prosperity ever come again to Savannah and thereby the burden of taxes be less onerous, real estate would increase in value and such as is favorably situated would be worth at least fifty per cent more than the present tax value. When said estate is divided at Mother's death, if either the house corner of Bull and South Broad or the house on South Broad, or Carson's stable house on Broughton and Abercrombie, or Clay's house on Abercrombie and Congress comes to the share of you and the children, I advise you to keep them because they are excellent locations and likely to enhance in value." These did indeed prove to be excellent locations—Willie's knowledge of Savannah values was superior to his assessment of Chicago's future in 1859. The letter continued: "This is especially true of the house and garden corner on Bull and South Broad [the present Gordon house]. The house is well constructed, will last with few repairs, and will always be easily rented if you don't want to or can't afford to live in it and will always be salable if necessity compels a sale. Besides pecuniary considerations, my own feelings prompt the wish for it to remain the property of the Gordon name so long as this can be done without the sacrifice of more important considerations.

"My gold watch, chain and seal which I inherited from my father must all go to Willy [Bill]. Let him remember that his name has been respected for two generations and he must keep it unstained. Give my silver watch and crystal seal, my plain gold studs and sleeve buttons to George Arthur. May he be as brilliant in intellect, as good and as much beloved as his Uncle George Gordon was.

"Give my ring to Nelly [Eleanor]. Its intrinsic value is not great, but it came to me from one who loved me very much and I have worn it twenty-two years. Give Daisy my sardonyx studs and Alice my pearl and jet studs. Give Mabel my sardonyx sleeve buttons.

"My dear, dear Mother, and you, my darling wife, will need no mementos of me. I trust your hearts.

"Educate our children as well as your means will allow. *Teach them never to go in debt and that labor is honorable.* Impress upon the girls that an honest man who has learned to work and support himself is preferable to a man born rich—and that a wife to be a helpmate must conform to the means of her husband.

"God bless you, Sweet Heart, and guard and guide and protect you. You have been a loving and devoted wife. No one could have made me happier than you have done. I pray God that we may meet in Heaven to be parted never more; for Christ's sake, Amen."

Later, Willie attributed his escape from the disease to the fact that in 1854 he had a serious attack of dengue fever, which bears certain similarities to yellow fever, and thought this might have made him immune to its so-called "cousin."

However, while the epidemic raged, Willie did not realize he was immune. If he had known that he would die next day as a result, he would have made his appointed rounds just the same. And what a deep contempt those who stayed and helped felt for those who ran away! One of Willie's letters to Nellie states: "Antonine and her husband ran away. Today her body returned in a box. No doctor." There is a penciled reminder on a scrap of paper: "Write Mr.—— in New York and suggest to him that now is the time for him to show his liberality by telegraphing the Benevolent Association at least $1,000. It is what all those who are absent and rich owe to those who remain and take care of the poor and sick."

Nellie also escaped miraculously—she once remarked to Mabel that insects never bit her, and that may have been why. But in 1876, no one knew that mosquitoes carried the disease, and Nellie showed heroism as great as Willie's. For Guyton proved by no means the safe refuge they had thought it would be. Very soon the horror appeared there, and Nellie was in the midst of it.

Elise Anderson died, Meta, Junior, was very ill but survived. When she began to recover, Eddy Anderson, the father, wrote Nellie to find them a furnished house at Guyton. The Andersons had been in Guyton only a few days when Eddy Anderson came down with yellow fever. Nellie spent every day there, helping to care for him.

Meanwhile Captain Fred Waring, who had acquired a wife since he had led the Georgia Hussars off to war, asked Mrs. Davant to take in his wife and himself too. Nellie gave up her room to them. One morning Fred Waring stopped her as she was setting out for the Andersons'. "I'm going to tell Willy Gordon," he said, "that you won't last much longer if you don't stop this nursing."

"Add my epitaph," quipped Nellie. "Killed by the accidental discharge of her duty!" She admitted that the remark was not original, but made Fred Waring laugh, and "to laugh was a good thing in those days. I always was glad when I could get off a joke."

But this was only the beginning. Soon Cousin Meta, too, came down with yellow fever and Nellie nursed husband and wife, with the help of the colored coachman. When the doctor said Eddy Anderson was dying, Nellie insisted that Cousin Meta be brought into his room. The doctor objected that to move her would be as much as her life was worth. Nellie, thinking how she would have felt if Willie were dying, insisted that Meta's life wouldn't be worth anything to her anyway if he died, and on Nellie's insistence, the sick wife was carried in, wrapped in a blanket, and placed in the bed beside her husband. Nellie stood by Eddy at the other side of the bed. "I am sure he knew we were there, though he was too far gone to make any sign. He just passed peacefully away." And when Eddy's body was removed Nellie lay down where he had lain, holding Cousin Meta's hand and comforting her throughout the night. Next morning Nellie had to tell Meta, Junior, that her father had died. "The poor child was dreadfully broken up."

A day or two later Fred Waring came down with the yellow fever, and soon died, Nellie comforting poor Lou Waring as she had comforted Cousin Meta. A doctor who had been coming to Guyton to treat the sick there was suddenly stricken and died. Nellie met his unsuspecting wife at the station and broke the news to her. Then she gave the grief-stricken woman the couch she had been sleeping on herself since relinquishing her room to the Fred Warings.

And still other members of the Davant household were

stricken, Nellie nursing most of them. She was sent for, as well, whenever a patient would not take his medicine. By coaxing, cajoling or outright bullying, Nellie would always manage to get it down. Nellie fought yellow fever as selflessly as her parents had fought cholera in Chicago, but with the special style she gave to everything she did. If any prejudice against the "little Yankee" had lingered on in Savannah after the war, Nellie's courage and devotion to Savannahians in the yellow fever epidemic must have wiped the slate clean.

Daisy unconsciously furnished a bit of comic relief for her part, while all this was going on. The yellow fever did not appear at Etowah, perhaps because of the fidelity with which the Gordon children had obeyed the rules laid down by their parents at the beginning of the summer, perhaps because of the promptness with which they were removed from the city. Amazingly Daisy, with her propensity for entering into the sufferings of others, apparently was giving no thought at all to the yellow fever and to her parents in the danger zone. She was worrying greatly about one of those careless acts which called down Mama's displeasure upon her. Perhaps she had thought all would be well, with Mama safe at Guyton and Papa pledged to spend every night there. Or perhaps Mama's displeasure was more awful to Daisy than yellow fever was! Her other preoccupation was with Alice, now thirteen. The spelling and punctuation, as with all of Daisy's writing reproduced in this book, are taken faithfully from the original: "Oh Mama! I feel perfectly miserable because you're going to give me an awful scolding and I know I deserve it. I've lost my beautiful little ring with the blue forgetmenots on it that Uncle Julian sent from Europe to me!!! This is the way I lost it. Percy Gordon lent me his gold pencil to wear around my neck on a ribbon and I lent him my ring (I know you will say 'the little fool,' but Mama I expect you lent your rings to boys when you were a girl) and of course I didn't know he would lose it but he did and he felt awfully about it and wanted me to take his pencil and he begges me to take it now only of course I tell him I know you wouldn't let me. He lost the ring by the stable gate and I've made Cinanthy look for it and I've offered any of the little cracker girls 50 cts if they find it (which is an immense sum to them) Percy and I have both searched for it.

"And Mama no one here knows its lost except the cracker children and Percy and I and if I had lost it I wouldn't mind who knew it but I don't want a soul to know it now, so please don't mention it in any of your letters to anyone here except me, and when you write to scold me about it please do put 'Strictly Private' on the outside so everybody can't read the letter. Mama perhaps you will be so mad that you won't write to me at all please do my own darling I'd rather have you scold me to death than not to take any notice of me. Oh Mama I feal as if I should die if I don't get home soon. I declare Alice is just unmanageable every time I tell her to do a thing she tells me to 'shut up my mouth' or 'mind my own business' that I 'shan't ordor over her.' I'm sure I don't want to manage her at all, but when she hangs over the most dangerous part of Termination Rock, what am I to do? I don't like to scare Grannie and so I tell Aunt Eliza. She scolds Alice and forbids her to go to the rocks. Alice is always as good as pie before Aunt E. and Grannie, but as soon as Aunt E. turns her back Alice says 'Shut up your mouth' or 'mind your business.' Of course it don't hurt Aunt E. but it sounds so horrid after all she had done for us. Nobody knows that I've written this so please write Alice a private letter and scold her well because I can't stand her much longer. I told her I wished Eleanor would make her behave. She answered, 'Eleanor can't manage me' and when I said, 'Yes she can' Alice replied, 'Well, she'll have a mighty hard job to do it' and I think so myself, and darling please do all I ask.

"Excusez moi s'il vous plait. Your prodigal daughter, Daisy."

All her life long, Daisy's path was to be strewn with lost objects, about which she would feel excessive guilt. And the pattern of the foregoing incident is typical. She would always persuade herself that some other person had done the actual losing—when she left, in a hansom cab in London, General Sir Archibald Hunter's letters describing his Sudan campaign in Egypt, she blamed it on a footman! Also, as long as she lived, Daisy included Percy Gordon, for whom she seems to have had an early infatuation, among those she loved most dearly, though it was a cousinly, rather than a romantic love. And much later, after Percy had become assistant rector of St. Batholomew's in New York, we find him on one of the earliest Girl Scout boards.

Nellie must have breathed a sigh of relief that nothing worse was happening at Etowah, and probably laughed heartily over Daisy's request to keep the anticipated scolding private. She may even have refrained from scolding Daisy about the ring— we do not have her answer. But in the midst of nursing the sick and dying, laying out the dead and comforting the bereft, Nellie found time to write one of her strong admonishing letters to Alice, with an aside for her other warring daughter: "Dear Alice: I wish you would try to obey your Aunt Eliza and keep away from Termination Rock! When you are trying to be good, as I think you are, remember the Bible verse: 'To *obey* is better than sacrifice and to hearken than the blood of rams.'

"There is one more text you better learn by heart: 'A *soft answer* turneth away wrath but grievous words stir up anger.'

"I think this last text would be very useful to Daisy also, and she had better learn it too."

CHAPTER IX

———————— ☆ ————————

GROWING UP

THE FROST came late that year. It was not until the middle of November that new yellow fever cases ceased to appear, and the refugees at Guyton and elsewhere dared to return to their saddened city. By this time the three older Gordon girls were well into their studies at their various schools. Alice had joined Daisy at Stuart Hall, while Eleanor moved on to Edge Hill, also in Virginia, run by the Misses Sarah and Carrie Randolph. In a year or so, Eleanor was sent to the Mesdemoiselles Charbonnier's school in New York City, with first Daisy and then Alice following in her footsteps at Edge Hill.

Daisy's letters from Etowah, written during her fifteenth summer, were still those of a little girl. Those of the next five years give a step-by-step picture of her development from girlhood to maturity, Daisy going through all the phases that any bright, carefully brought up girl goes through, and in much the same way.

Clothes bulked very large in her life, and there are countless discussions of a "blue bunting," which had to be made just so if Daisy were not to fall victim to complete despair, and of a "sheepard's plaid." Daisy would send Nellie well-executed sketches of the designs she had in mind and full details about braid, buttons and other trimmings. With regard to the shepherd's plaid: "The only rub is, where shall the underskirt come from? Where is the black silk skirt Eleanor had? I tremble at my own audacity, *nevertheless I say it out and I'll say it baldly,* have you not got any trimmings I could put on a skirt? . . . I'll bet you'll say, 'Those old black silks have gone to the dogs long ago, and she shan't have such a school dress, rediculous! She has gotten very swollen ideas!' But if you only knew how stylish the sheephard's plaids are and how warm and cheap—only 12½ cents a yard—and how well they wear, you would reconsider the matter my darling."

The second main topic of the letters was finances, complicated to Daisy's way of thinking by the intransigence of Alice, who was a thorn in her older sister's flesh for a year or two: "Dear little Mama: Your last letter was jolly in some respects, but I was very much surprised and disgusted at the scolding in the first part. I have not done a *single thing.* When that $5 came, Alice quietly and composedly took half and though I at first begged her and afterwards insisted that she should divide it as Papa told us, she would not do so until after a big fuss. You may think I am getting to be a perfect miser, but I am *trying* to *save* my money for my Theta Tau badge and I cannot for the life of me! It just runs through my fingers. Besides, Alice has bought every single thing she wanted, and put in money to get suppers as often as I. Now how do you think she did all this when she receives less a month than I? Why, she makes *me* pay for everything we get together! *I* pay for the shoe blacking, pins, for the mending of our clothes, soap, etc. . . . Don't say anything more about money matters in your letters to us, as Alice has paid all her debts to me that she contracted lately, and I don't want to get in a fuss with her, she is so disagreeable, let me keep peace while I can. I *only pity her roommate next year!* P.S. My nose is getting 'tremenormous,' much bigger than yours *ever* was! I am so disgusted!"

After many financial vicissitudes, Daisy finally managed to save the money to buy her Theta Tau badge, so necessary to her middle-teen happiness. When her niece, Daisy Lawrence, also joined Theta Tau at St. Timothy's which was an offshoot of Edge Hill, Daisy presented her with her own precious pin.

Nellie's letters, too, are full of money matters. Even though Willie was doing far better than anyone could have imagined would be possible back in 1865, it evidently required great penny-pinching and inventiveness to keep three daughters in boarding school—and there were three other children coming on! Nellie dug out old material and made over garments endlessly in order to supply her girls with the things they needed. The blue bunting, after figuring in Daisy's letters for three years, underwent a metamorphosis and became Alice's. Nellie required strict account of the girls' expenditures and squelched anything she considered extravagant in no uncertain way. She wrote Alice: "I despise your old clubs! They are always causing some expense!" Nellie herself made all manner of sacrifices, but she was determined that Willie should not be burdened unnecessarily.

In Daisy's sixteenth year, we find a decided mellowing in her attitude toward Alice—just as she had detected a similar mellowing in Eleanor's attitude toward her when she was Alice's age. This new tolerant spirit even extended to Bill, her prime antagonist of old. She sends special love to "my Billy Boy," and in a year or so she is writing that she doesn't know what has come over her, but she has actually let Bill take her pet tennis racquet to St. Paul's!

But a tone of a somewhat different kind is coming into her letters to Nellie. She loves her mother just as much as ever, but it is no longer the blind obedient worship of childhood. She looks at Nellie now from a basis approaching equality and reminds Nellie that she herself had been no angel in her schooldays. From Edge Hill she writes: "Mama, I can't keep all the rules, I'm too much like you. Imagine yourself when at school, on being asked to do something against the rules in order to have some fun, clasping your hands across your bosom and saying, 'How wrong!' I'll keep the rule about studying after the light bell rings, about getting up in the morning too soon and I'll keep clear of big scrapes but little ones I can't avoid."

It would be interesting to have Nellie's answer to that one, but inasmuch as consistency was not a virtue Nellie paid any attention to when it applied to herself, it probably presented no difficulties for her.

Daisy spiritedly refuted her mother's charges of extravagance, in a way she would not have done earlier. "Mama, I have been calculating and these new dresses have cost you, not counting the underskirts, $13.50. Now ain't that shocking and fabulous?"

The outstanding event of Daisy's sixteenth year, however, was that she and Alice spent their Christmas holidays with their Great-uncle David Hunter, in Washington. We are given no hint as to the way this miracle was brought about. A great revolution in Willie's attitude is indicated, for the Gordon girls would never have been permitted to accept an invitation to the Hunter home without their father's express approval. Nellie ruled her own departments of the family with a high hand, but scrupulously enforced Willie's wishes in matters important to him.

Daisy's letters betray nothing but excited anticipation at meeting these relatives whom she had never seen. It appears that Aunt Maria had died, but one of Nellie's cousins—it may be remembered that the Hunters had adopted the orphaned daughters of Robert Kinzie—was married to General Steuart and had two daughters, Minnie and Daisy, about the ages of Daisy and Alice Gordon. The Steuarts were living at Uncle David's home. Daisy Gordon was making Christmas presents for all of them, a large crayon drawing of a dog after Sir Edwin Landseer for Uncle David, and a "lovely fascinater, the lightest blue, in a new-fashioned stich" for her second cousin, Minnie Steuart.

The idea of attending grown-up parties for the first time filled her with both delight and apprehension. In a letter home, she described her fears that she would be considered very unattractive, and would be found wanting in social graces.

This led to one of those rash acts of Daisy's which so aggravated Nellie and reminds one of the taffy experiment that at eight had cost Daisy her long thick braid. There were no beauty parlors to rectify a girl's natural shortcomings, but there was a publication, *The Ugly Girl Papers*. Daisy pored over this, and found that no girl could hope to succeed in polite society if she had white flecks on her fingernails. Daisy had white flecks on her fingernails! *The Ugly Girl Papers* gave a recipe for banishing the dooming blemishes. Without consulting anyone, Daisy bought the ingredients, locked herself in her room, mixed them in her soapdish according to the directions and immersed her finger tips in the concoction. When the prescribed length of time had elapsed, she found that her hands were cemented firmly into the soapdish, and she had to be rescued ignominiously by the teachers. Though her hands were freed after long soaking in hot water, there appeared to be more flecks on her fingernails than ever.

Many girls have done similar things. What distinguished Daisy was that nothing ever killed her faith in the printed word, no matter where she found it. A similar rash experiment nine years later, when she was old enough to know better, was to have drastic consequences.

This time there were none. After the very first party she wrote home that "I had a *glorious* time and lots of attention which I did not expect after my low spirits about parties." There were six "little cadets" from West Point who seemed to her such perfect gentlemen that she was sad when she learned they were going on to Philadelphia next day. At the party Minnie Steuart gave, there were "lots of Princeton students," while at the Ingersolls' lunch she met "lots of Harvard students," among them the son of Senator Blaine "who Uncle thinks a great deal of. He was very attentive to me, but I just thought to myself *what would my father say* if he saw me talking to this *Red Republican!*"

The nicest time of all was New Year's Day, when General Hunter kept open house and one hundred and seventy-five people called. "I wore my white French muslin overskirt and waist over a black velvit skirt, pink ribbins and my pink roman sash. We had everything good to eat and I ate all day. Among the callers was Mr. Grant's son, who looked like a little puppy and who carried on quite a conversation with Alice for which that young lady was quite indignant!" But characteristically, Daisy did not include her Great-uncle David among these despised Yankees and "Red Republicans." She thought him "lovely," and wrote home that he was always giving her hints about easier ways in drawing, which he called "Yankee inventions," and which she accepted gratefully nevertheless.

Daisy formed a fast friendship with the Steuart girls. In later years Minnie, become Minnie Davis, was Daisy's constant companion for a time in France and England after both were widowed. Minnie Davis was a participant in the exciting expeditions and entertainments which marked Daisy's early acquaintance with Lord Robert Baden-Powell. One of the delightful parties was given by Genie Massey, a schoolmate at Edge Hill. This, too, was a lifelong friendship. Genie married Oscar Underwood, and as the wife of the powerful Senator from Alabama, was one of Daisy's most effective helpers in establishing the Girl Scouts on a national basis.

Daisy's graduation from Edge Hill the following spring finds her at the delicate dividing point between girlhood and young womanhood. She yearned for Papa's approval, as much as ever, and she was always to do so. When she was a middle-aged woman, a mild rebuke from Papa could tear her to pieces. And so, the silver medal that she got for drawing, instead of the scholastic medal she had expected, was a crushing disappointment. "It is against the principals of this school to give two medals to one girl (an unheard of thing) so as the drawing medal was a higher honor I suppose Miss Sarah thought I would rather have it. But I would *not*. For Papa told me in his first letter to work hard on everything but drawing and now he won't think I did!"

The attentions she received from the young men who had been invited to the last german of the school year pleased and flattered her—so long as they were in the mass!—but she was not ready yet to be singled out by one young man. "I am very glad I am going to the Rawley Springs with Miss Carrie Randolph, because the Mr. Cockeral I wrote you about danced the german with me, and then the old loon went around telling all the other girls I was the most beautiful creature he had ever seen, that one glance of my eye was more piercing than a thousand words, that I was the light of the room, etc. Now you and Eleanor may laugh at my conciet in repeating these things, but I am real scared, he is not a boy but a man and he has never fallen in love with anyone yet. And he got Miss Sarah's permission to come down here to see me and I know Papa would not like it (because Mr. C. might say things to me if he came) but as Miss Sarah has controll of me she does as she thinks right. So I am glad I will go to the Rawley and get away from it all!"

If anything, Daisy lingered in this "between" state longer than most girls. At the Mesdemoiselles Charbonnier's, in New York City, where she went the next year, she still clung tightly to her home. "You don't know how I love you, my dear little Mother! Neither did I, until you left me." On her eighteenth birthday she wrote Papa: "Can you realize that just eighteen years ago I was a little red-faced baby? But perhaps your memory, which has on several occasions proved very wonderful, can easily recall that night long ago when the nurse placed me in your arms with the remark, 'Just precisely like her Ma!'" When Bill arrived in New York City in January, on his way back to St. Paul's after the holidays, she wrote Willie that "I nearly ate him up, I was so glad to see him! How I wish you had been with him, darling Papa! All I can think of is that *you* will be here in April."

All of a sudden, we find Daisy becoming very sedate. The Mesdemoiselles Charbonnier's school, at least as strict as Edge Hill, was run by two Frenchwomen on the same pattern as one they had formerly conducted at Neuilly, France, for the sheltered daughters of aristocratic French families. The girls had to wear black aprons like French girls, speak nothing but French and the chaperonage, too, was French. The girls could write letters home only on certain days, they had a full escort of teachers to and from the dancing class at Dodsworth's Dancing School and on other forays into the outside world. And when it was observed that the demure troop of schoolgirls drew masculine glances on Fifth Avenue, thereafter they had to go to and fro on Madison Avenue.

The dancing class involved much more than merely learning to dance. The girls were taught how to enter a ballroom, how to curtsy, and most important of all, how to sit. Legs must never be crossed, feet had to rest in a graceful position on the floor, and the skirt had to be arranged in classical folds. The boys learned to be poised under all circumstances, and to acquire an easy grace of manner when making a formal bow or offering an arm to a partner.

Daisy poked fun at the excessive formality of the school and the dancing class, but did not get into even little scrapes. She behaved with such decorum, in fact, that eventually she was privileged—the only girl in the school so honored—to go back and forth alone to her special classes, and even to use Fifth Avenue. She felt her responsibility so keenly that when, one day, she came face to face on the avenue with a young man from Savannah whom she had known all her life, she would not let him walk down the street with her!

Drawing and painting continued to be Daisy's great delight, and now she added painting in oils to her artistic skills. But she no longer neglected French for art. "Snub me no more, my precious mother," she wrote Nellie exultantly, "for I have been studying night and day and in my French Dictée I came out *first*. This explains it all—my faculty of spelling being singularly small, has been absorbed in French Dictées!"

The unkindest cut of all must have been when Arthur, then seven, advised Daisy not to use French in her letters home—Arthur and Mabel had a French governess and learned that language along with English—"because you can't spell in French either!"

Daisy was privileged to go away weekends as her mother had been at Madam Canda's. There were Parker cousins to visit in New Jersey, Churchill cousins at Ossining, still called by the Indian name, Sing Sing, and Wolcott cousins in New York City. Cousin Corty Parker took her to a little party, which she enjoyed immensely. "Oh, if I only have as charming a time next winter among grown people as I had with just girls and boys, I won't dread coming out nearly so much!"

There were evenings at the theater and the opera with Gordon cousins from Alabama, Beirne and George, with whom she had played at Etowah, but no mention is made of any male outside the circle of cousins.

At this stage in Daisy's life, there appears little resemblance to her mother at a comparable age. When she was eighteen, Nellie was cutting a swathe through the young men of West Point, Princeton and Yale, not to mention the havoc she had wrought previously in Chicago. She was handling her elders with the aplomb of a veteran, sliding down banisters, and picking out her life mate from a field of contenders. Daisy seems to have erected squeamish barriers, because she felt inadequate to the requirements of adult society. Was it because she had been assured so positively, when she was little, that she was ugly? Had the years in boarding school, with their few and overwhelmingly supervised social contacts with the opposite sex, led her to fear competition with girls who had attained ease in social situations?

According to her photograph of this period, Daisy did go through a stage of being rather plain. Her hair is pulled back tightly and unbecomingly from a thin, solemn face. It is a thoughtful, almost brooding face, but it would not win beauty contests. And one would not have picked Daisy, at this time, as the Savannah girl most likely to make a brilliant international marriage and scintillate in the highest British and European social circles.

In the summer of 1878 she was thinking of romance, but afraid as yet to embark upon it, and so she scorned the available candidates as she had scorned poor Mr. Cockeral. (Daisy's spelling—what the name really was is anybody's guess.) The Gordons were to gather at Old Sweet Springs, West Virginia, and Daisy and Mabel, chaperoned by Mama's maid, Adele, arrived there first. Daisy expressed amazement when "old Mr. T." turned up, accompanied by his nephew, who was about Bill's age. "I wish they had struck an average and some man more of my age had appeared, for I have practiced Juliet on our balcony and am training Adele to the rôle of nurse. All I need is a Romeo to make a perfect Balcony Scene. The nephew looks as if not loathe to begin a flirtation, but I have said to myself, 'If such things are done in the green tree, what will be done in the dry,' and for fear old T. will follow suit, I avoid flirtations."

After Papa returned to Savannah, leaving the family at Old Sweet, Daisy began her practice of regaling him, when she was with Mama and he was not, with reports of Mama's noteworthy doings. For as Daisy was increasingly impelled to independence of Mama's domination, she also became increasingly appreciative of Nellie's unique qualities, and was happy to be an onlooker while Mama performed, just as Willie was. As the years go on, the comments about Nellie in their letters to each other sound like those of two doting parents, keeping each other posted on the doings of a very dear, precocious and occasionally outrageous child. Daisy also began her practice of decorating her letters with charming sketches.

She told Willie that a blacksnake had invaded the room she and Mama shared. When discovered, it tried to get out through the door, but Mama would not permit this. "She picked him up by the tail, hauled him into the room and stabbed him with her penknife! She stamped on him first, but he got round her leg so she had to use the penknife."

The years since the yellow fever epidemic had been good ones for Willie and Nellie. The death in 1877 of Mr. Tison, the senior partner in Willie's cotton brokerage business, had been deeply regretted by the Gordons, but the firm was now "W. W. Gordon & Company." Nellie proudly sent copies of Willie's new circulars to the girls, so they could show them to the Misses Randolph and others. Willie had estimated Mr. Tison's estate at $300,000. This went to Mr. Tison's heirs, but is evidence of the prosperity of the firm. In 1880, Nellie wrote Eleanor that Willie had $500,000 worth of cotton in his warehouse, much of it already sold.

They had come through the hardships and horrors of the Civil War and its even more soul-trying aftermath. They had fought yellow fever with an identical immolation of self. Their six children were bright and healthy and happy, and, despite the occasional spats common to every large family, they were exceptionally devoted to each other and to their parents. Nellie, slight as ever, seemed to have a boundless supply of energy, and with her flashing wit and fund of stories, was much in demand socially. Willie's main interest, aside from his business, was keeping in touch with his friends of the Confederacy. He rejoined the Hussars after the government allowed them to meet again, and took part in the weekly drills, the occasional "tilts"—where the Hussars performed such expert feats of horsemanship as slicing a lemon in two or spearing rings while riding at a full gallop—and the parades held on Lee's birthday and Southern Memorial Day, which is observed on April 26. It was Willie's great pleasure to bring the Hussars home for some refreshment after one of these affairs. Many a battle was refought around the Gordon dinner table, with Nellie an enthusiastic participant. She went to such lengths, in fact, to make these gatherings successful and enjoyable, that her children gave her the affectionate nickname of The Little Veteran. Thus Daisy often addresses her in letters, beginning with this period and throughout Nellie's life.

The children would not have known that there was a special reason for Nellie to throw so much heart and effort into making these gatherings of Willie's comrades memorable. But Willie understood, and directed loving, appreciative glances at the tiny sparkling lady as she egged on the men who had worn the gray to further stories of Confederate prowess, or made them roar with laughter at her comments.

And what a table the Gordons' was! Nellie wrote down one of her dinner menus in a letter to Alice at the Mesdemoiselles Charbonnier's school in the fall of 1880. Nellie thought herself it was "quite a swell dinner." The courses run as follows: One, oysters on the half shell. Two, strained tomato soup. Three, boiled shad and potato balls. Four, white fricassee of chicken with asparagus. Five, tenderloin of beef cooked with mushrooms, rice, new potatoes with parsley sauce and spinach. Six, stewed shrimp. Seven, venison and green peas. Eight, dressed lettuce and dressed tomatoes. Nine, orange sherbet, strawberries and cream, nuts, candied ginger and prunes, cake.

"We finished off with cheese and crackers, and then black coffee. For wines we had champagne, hock, Château Lafitte of 1864, Yquem, pale sherry and old madeira and burgundy. The orange sherbet was something new. We had a dozen fine oranges with a little round piece cut out of the top, like a cover, and a little bow of blue ribbon in the middle of each cover. Then all the insides of the oranges were scooped out, leaving nothing but the skins and then they were filled up with the frozen sherbet and put into the freezer and frozen *solid*. Then they came on the table in a glass dish and each one was helped to an orange. I got the receipt for angel's food and we made some quite successfully."

It was about this time that Willie built on the Gordon farm, which then lay well outside the city limits of Savannah, a replica of the Kinzie homestead, Chicago's first house, erected by the first John Kinzie. This was purely a love offering to his Nellie, and symbolized Willie's full acceptance of and respect for Nellie's justifiable pride in her family.

Willie and Nellie moved back into the Gordon mansion about 1880, at the elder Mrs. Gordon's request. The house was admirably suited to gracious entertaining. The two drawing rooms were made into a perfect place for dancing, by opening wide the folding doors and pushing the furniture against the walls. Sometimes Nellie played for the dancing, but for a ball a professional pianist and violinist would be engaged. Sometimes there were amateur theatricals, the back drawing room serving as stage, the audience sitting in the front drawing room and hall.

Daisy had had many misgivings about her introduction into adult society, and was astonished, after her debut, to find herself rated one of the prettiest girls in Savannah. Her attractiveness, added to the fact that she was witty and charming and full of fun, quickly made her a belle. Perhaps it is as simple as that Daisy's time had come to blossom, and she blossomed. From her debut on, parties were her great delight.

But Daisy kept her schoolgirl naïveté, and two anecdotes from this period help explain the legendary character she assumed in Savannah, though Eleanor, who had come out two years before, did her best to guide her beloved Crazy through the intricacies of Daisy's new social life. Savannah's most important parties were those given by the German Club, an organization of men which included all the city's socially accepted bachelors. These entertainments were the last word in elegance, and included at least one german, featured by intricate figures and favors which the girls counted and compared afterwards much as Indian braves counted scalps after a battle. The last german of the season was always a moonlight affair held on an island, where a pavilion had been built out over the water. Beaux had been known to entice girls away from the chaperones for a stroll on these occasions. Eleanor, aware of her sister's innocence, warned Daisy, "Be very careful, don't let any man take a liberty with you." Not realizing how unbelievably innocent Daisy was, Eleanor had let it go at that.

On the boat going over to the island, Eleanor was handed a note from Daisy which read: "Come to me at once and bring my shawl with you. Henry has taken a liberty!"

Eleanor, deeming from the note that part of her young sister's clothing had been torn off her, grabbed a shawl from a girl near by and rushed to the scene, followed by her escort and several others who had heard Eleanor's exclamations of horror and indignation. Daisy's costume, however, was in perfect order, and she showed no signs of having been mauled about.

"What did you want the shawl for?" Eleanor asked.

"I'm cold."

"What did Henry do to you?"

"He took a liberty!"

"What did he *do?*"

"I said I was chilly, and Henry—*Henry started to take off his coat!*" It took Daisy a long time to live that one down.

But her reaction to her first proposal was her masterpiece. Eleanor had forgotten to tell her, and Daisy herself did not know because she had been away from Savannah so much, that if a beau asked a young lady to walk to Laurel Grove Cemetery of a Sunday afternoon, it meant that he intended to propose marriage. Just why this particular spot was chosen for these tender declarations is a mystery, but. it was well understood that if the young lady accepted the invitation for the walk, she would accept the proposal as well.

When, therefore, an admirer invited Daisy to go on this Sunday stroll and she said she would like to, he was transported with joy, believing that they were the same as engaged. Arrived at the cemetery, and seated beneath a magnolia tree, the suitor gave expression to his love.

Daisy sprang to her feet, eyes flashing. *"How* can you so desecrate the dead!"

CHAPTER X

———————— ☆ ————————

THE WANDERINGS BEGIN

I T WAS DECIDED in the autumn of 1880 that Alice would go
to the Mesdemoiselles Charbonnier's. She had begged to
be allowed to stay on at Edge Hill, but Nellie was firm.

"Edge Hill doesn't have the advantages you'll get at the
Charbs. You'll like it when you get there. Eleanor and Daisy
both loved it. Remember, you didn't want to go to Edge Hill
from Stuart Hall."

Daisy wished some more painting lessons, so she returned to
the Charbs with Alice. By this time the second and third
Gordon sisters were the best of friends and inseparable companions. Alice had put her naughty early-teen ways behind her
and had developed into a quiet, studious girl. People were
saying that she would be the family beauty.

Nellie was proud that still another lovely flower was unfold-
ing among her daughters, but wouldn't have admitted it to
Alice for the world. She continued to keep a firm hand on the
activities and expenditures of her daughters in New York City,
writing to Alice in the fall of 1880: "I am very much vexed
that you should have caused me to spend $10.50 on the two hats
in order that you might have things *becoming* and to *match!*
I am not able to pay for the privilege and you won't get one
cent's worth of clothes from me till April no matter *what* you
need, so don't expect it!

"Tell Daisy she is welcome to stay on until Tuesday at Cousin

Joe Churchill's, but her Father says an escort *part* of the way *won't* do! She must be under someone's care all the way to New York and get them to drop her at Mdlle. C's, which fortunately is on the route from the 42nd Street depot. I guess Uncle will know someone going as far as New York. It was Mr. Beverly Tucker, Uncle's cousin, who saw Daisy to the cars in New York. It was a very risky chance to take and I didn't dare tell her Papa, he would have been *so mad*. She had better not take such a chance again."

What the risky chance was that Daisy took we do not know, but it was an unbreakable rule of Papa's that a Gordon girl could not travel on any form of public transportation unless escorted. Daisy may recklessly have ridden on the train alone from New York City to Ossining.

In early December, Alice came down with scarlet fever. At first her illness did not seem alarming, but Daisy felt her responsibility as the only family member on the spot, and rose to it with clear thinking and poise. Eleanor seems to have been away from home, Mabel and Arthur were then only ten and eight. Daisy proposed that, if Nellie decided to come to New York, she herself should go home to look after the children. Daisy was of no use at the school, since she was not permitted to see Alice. She had not been exposed to the disease, so she would be no menace to the little ones at home. But Daisy begged to be allowed to stay on at the Charbonniers' if her mother didn't come, "for if Alice should be seriously ill, none of her family will be with her, and it takes almost three days, you know, to reach here from Savannah."

It was decided that Nellie would come, but Daisy stayed until she arrived. On December 10, Daisy wrote Willie that Alice was getting along famously. The rash had left her face, she was "righter" than she had been at any time. But one of the complications set in which made scarlet fever a dreaded disease until the days of modern drugs, and Alice died December thirtieth.

There was no more laughter in the Gordon house. And once more, in a time of family cataclysm, the two older daughters were left to cling to each other and comfort each other as best they could. Nellie surrendered to grief completely. She, who had always despised gloom and the trappings of gloom, swathed herself in black crepe; she mourned ceaselessly and would not be comforted. In addition to her pain at the loss of a child, she blamed herself bitterly for having caused Alice's death, by forcing the girl to go to New York against her wishes. Over and over she would wail that if only she had let Alice stay at Edge Hill, where she had been so happy, Alice would have escaped the scarlet fever. Willie, grieving for his lovely child, was wrenched and preoccupied by Nellie's suffering as well. Eleanor and Daisy had loved their Skinny, too, and though they were now young women, the catastrophic events of their childhood were revived, and intensified the shock of the first break in their immediate family circle.

It was profoundly disturbing to the girls to see their mother's iron strength and courage shattered. There had been security for them in her self-assurance and in the guiding reins she held so tightly, because they knew that their welfare was her first consideration. Now such governance as Nellie exerted was to hold them fast in the backwater of perpetual lamentation in which she had immersed herself. She resented it when her daughters wished to engage in the limited social life the strict mourning etiquette of the day permitted—formal affairs, of any kind, of course were barred. How callous they must be, Nellie cried, to forget their sister so soon, if they wished to have callers or attend an informal gathering of young people.

It was the calm, sensible Eleanor who broke under the strain, giving way to fits of hysterical weeping. For Daisy, there must have been another period of confusion and wonderings and reassessment of her elders during the months that she and Eleanor, clothed in black, slipped quietly about the house and talked in hushed voices. Daisy had just tasted the delights of moving easily and happily in the social life about which she had felt such apprehensions. She was beginning to know her power to attract and charm and divert. Now she was required to sacrifice her youth and her new-found propensity for gaiety in a perpetual mourning which, her healthy instincts told her, in no way benefitted her dead sister.

When her letters begin again after Alice's death, Daisy's attitude toward her mother has undergone still another change. While it appears that in this calamity Nellie's religion did not help her, Daisy's religious sense seems to have deepened as she struggled to find the answer to the "Why?" that youth must ask when a promising young life is cut short. From some inner source the erratic Crazy found a strength to endure and to adjust to what must be. Often from now on, in her letters to her mother she sounds as though she were the wise, mature person of the two. She also, consciously or subconsciously, came to feel that her mother's domination must be resisted. Daisy would have to battle to preserve her individuality, her sparkle and love of life, as her mother never had to do. And with her tendency to extremes, Daisy would battle on occasions when it would have been better if she had not. In the years between Alice's death and Daisy's marriage, we see emerge an unconquerable will in matters Daisy considered vital, before which her parents, strong personalities though they both were, felt compelled to bow.

This new attitude, however, carried with it no diminution of love for her little mother, or failure to respect the grief and the anniversaries to which Nellie clung. On December 3, almost a year after Alice's death, she sent Nellie a letter of utmost tenderness. "How I wish I could speak this to you, my dear little mother, instead of writing it. Tomorrow is Communion Sunday and just a year ago, as you say, Skinny went with me to church. Contrast her lot now to what it was a year ago. Oh my darling, when I think of all she has and when I know her mind is filled with God and Heavenly things, I wonder if she thinks of just one year ago when we took Communion in that dreary church in New York? I could not go to it by myself, so I came here to this little country church, and I will think of you at Communion and she will think of you too."

This letter was written from the North. For after winter and spring and summer had gone by with no improvement in Nellie's state of mind, Willie had realized that it was unfair and damaging to keep Eleanor and Daisy cooped up longer in the house of grief. In September they started off for a round of visits, Eleanor going first to the Parker cousins in New Jersey, Daisy to the Churchill cousins in Ossining. They were permitted to discard their mourning crepe, though continuing to dress in black. From Ossining Daisy went to the home of friends from the Charbs, Grace and Mary Gale Carter, in Cooperstown, New York. The Carter girls and Daisy ran down to

New York for a reunion with alumnae of the Charbs at the Fifth Avenue Hotel where the mother of Abby Lippitt, another of Daisy's chums, chaperoned them. Daisy wrote gaily to Grandma Gordon that the girls slept five in a bed and chattered the whole night through. Then back to Cooperstown to the handsome Carter home, with Lake Oswego, so often referred to by James Fenimore Cooper in his novels, lying at the foot of the lawn. In October, Daisy was in Newburgh, visiting Gordon cousins who had somehow wandered north. She steeped herself in gaiety, and defended herself to Nellie in a letter that was firm, though gentle. "You probably have not thought my grief profound because I throw it off. There is no need to analyze what I feel and it is when I am by myself that I feel it most. . . . There is more than one kind of sorrow and that borne in silence is not less genuine because it is not always seen."

The following summer, that of 1882, Willie gave Daisy her first trip to Europe. Daisy's letters home, as she flew about New York collecting the things she would need for the trip, are full of appreciation and gratitude for her parents' generosity. When a telegram brought the news that Grandma Gordon had died, Daisy's thoughts were with each of her family in turn. "I hope Granny did not mind dying at the last. . . . Kiss dear Papa for me when he comes, Mama, and try to get some rest, dear little Mama, now that the strain of nursing is over. You should just let the house go and patch up your own health a bit. As for Eleanor, ship her off to Baltimore as soon as you can. You know how injurious grief is to her. . . . I went to see Bill—I craved a sight of my own family. . . . I think Aunt Eliza the most unselfish woman on earth. Eleanor wrote me that she told Granny several nights ago when they all thought her dying, that 'She would see Alice.' Dear Aunt Eliza, to think of *our* loss at her mother's death bed, when she has so many dear ones she must have longed to send messages to."

Yet this quality of identifying herself with the pain of others, which was to be Daisy's outstanding trait, did not keep her from writing Nellie, a day or so later, a letter so sharp one might have thought Nellie herself had written it. "You will find when Bill arrives that I have taken *none* of your fine lace, only the pieces from the sleeves which you said I might take. However, I send those too by mail. I've ripped them off the dress. . . . Of course, it is very fine for you to have a memory which retains only the things which suit your convenience. . . . I am not in the habit of perloining other people's property without their consent, nor am I a clept-imaniac. . . . Hereafter what you say had better be taken down in hard type so you cannot forget it. Unwillingly, your Suspected Thief." A postscript said: "Darling Mama, second thoughts are always best and I add a line to say that whatever sounds nasty in the first note, I take it back though I have not time to write it over explaining about the lace."

From now on, we are to find that when Nellie bullied, Daisy snapped back at her in an excellent imitation of Nellie's own vigorous style. This led to a Savannah legend that mother and daughter were constantly at sword's points. As is usual when a strong-minded parent has an equally strong-minded child, here was a point where their likeness to each other, rather than their differences, brought them into conflict. What outsiders could not know was that there was no animus in their frequent arguments, and that they were having a wonderful time. These were sparring matches between two friendly opponents, so equally matched that both could let fly their best blows without fear of doing any hurt.

It is true that Nellie and Daisy tended to respond negatively to any suggestion from the other. When something important was at stake, Nellie or Daisy, as the case might be, would ask another member of the family to present the idea, from whom it would be accepted gracefully. When this technique was employed, it was always in matters which one considered important to the welfare of the other, or others. It is also true that at times, Daisy and her mother were "at odds," as Daisy called it. Daisy might stop writing to Nellie for a while. Nellie called this "Daisy's sulks," and was not troubled by them in the least. Daisy's sulks never lasted very long.

Thus Daisy and her mother got along together as well as two dominating, willful women possibly could. And beneath the surface typhoons ran a strong, never-interrupted current of mutual love. Daisy often displayed a protective attitude toward her little mother, who was so markedly capable of looking after herself. Nellie had a similar protective attitude toward Daisy, in spite of her irate comments. And it is interesting that while

Nellie would always win an argument, she frequently wound up by ceding Daisy the point at issue. Many and many a time Nellie agreed to some madly preposterous project, knowing how foolish it was and not hesitating to say so, but unable to deny Daisy anything on which she had set her impulsive heart. As when Daisy, out riding with Nellie one day in her victoria, saw a dead dog by the roadside, insisted on taking it home and, laying it on her bed, applied Nellie's electric vibrator to it. The dog was not dead, Daisy maintained, only suffering from suspended animation! Nellie grumbled, "If we pass a dead mule, am I supposed to take that in my victoria too?" But she let Daisy put the dead dog in her victoria and probably would have accepted a dead mule if that had been essential to Daisy's peace of mind.

Nellie seems to have realized that Daisy was driven by fever-ish compulsions and could not help herself. Nellie made acid remarks, but always did what she could for this daughter, so fortunate in many ways, so ill-starred in others. Daisy was at her mother's disposal, too, for any venture of hers and ready with her enthusiastic, if not always well-considered support, in every family enterprise.

For all the sharp letters to her mother just before she sailed, Daisy in fact made her first visit to Europe a family enterprise, planning her trip so as to retrace her parents' sightseeing tour in 1873, and to see all the famous paintings, cathedrals and other points of interest which Willie and Nellie had most enjoyed. Then she wrote at length of her own impressions, so that they might be full sharers of her pleasure in whatever had pleased them.

Daisy also visited the Lows at Beauchamp Hall to pay her respects to the man who was her parents' good friend, and her Aunt Eliza's brother-in-law. The Low girls were extremely hospitable, wanting to show Daisy all the sights of London. But of old Andrew she carried away a poor impression. "You don't know *how* I long to see you at times," she wrote Nellie. "I am glad you and Papa are not like other parents I could mention, 'Andrew' among them." Her letters do not mention the son, Willy Low. But the next fall, after she had returned home, Daisy wrote Nellie: "Willy Low has arrived from England. He brings good accounts of his sisters, and also he brought me a little fox terrier which Jessie and Mary sent me out as a present, wasn't that nice of them? He is a dear little dog and I hope you will let me keep him. Willy called the other night and dined here and says he came over this winter in his father's place, as old Low is too ill (or too cranky?) to come himself."

On her return to this country, Daisy had joined her mother at Saratoga Springs. Nellie was still in mourning—Daisy's letters from Saratoga Springs are written on paper bordered deeply with black. But Daisy was rejoiced to see that Mama was improving. She wrote Papa that, while she herself had gained ten pounds in ten days, now weighing 119½ pounds, "what pleases me most is that Mama is so cheery and bright. The waters do her good, she has a splendid appetite, and being with the Walworths, she will discuss the happy past and reminisse of her former frolics, and trots out the ghosts of her old jokes, until you could not tell her from the entertaining little woman she used to be. Don't congratulate her on her improvement, else she will draw into her shell again."

A few days later, Daisy has gone to Cooperstown to see Grace and Mary Gale Carter, the beginning of another extended round of visits. And this was to be Daisy's life pattern from now on. We shall make no effort to trace her wanderings, for our story would become a mere tabulation of departures and arrivals. Until she married and settled—as far as Daisy ever settled—in England, she was shuttling back and forth between friends and relatives in the North and friends and relatives in the South, alighting in Savannah at intervals, to entertain her Northern friends in her turn with a round of parties. Soon, though, she would be off again on her endless quest for gaiety and pleasure. Between 1882 and 1886, Daisy appears to have spent almost as much time with the Carters at Cooperstown, and with Abby Lippitt, her closest chums at the Charbs, as in her own home, with frequent visits besides to other friends and to relatives. This led to many complications inasmuch as Willie and Nellie did a good deal of traveling too, and she would have to get Willie's approval both for her own plans and for the escort without whom she was not allowed to stir a step. On one occasion, Cousin Beirne Gordon had to go from New York City to Newark, New Jersey, in order to escort Daisy back to New York. Willie always paid any expense incurred by an escort.

But keeping all these matters straight required an unceasing flow of letters and frantic telegrams.

Willie and Nellie also kept a firm check on Daisy's associations with young men, though Daisy was now advancing toward the middle twenties. Willie would instruct her to see no more of certain ones, Nellie told her on no account to give her photograph to a man, or to accept a man's photograph. Daisy accepted Willie's orders in good spirit, but begged her mother, "Please, don't try to manage *everything* within ten thousand miles of you!"

Eleanor had lamented to Daisy, in 1882, that she was about to enter upon "old maidenhood," having reached the ripe age of twenty-four without capturing a husband. But Eleanor's visits to the New Jersey cousins had aroused a more than cousinly interest in Wayne Parker, a distant relative, and they were married in January, 1884. Liza Hendry went around muttering to herself because Miss Nell was marrying a Yankee. But when she met Wayne, she too succumbed to his good looks, erect, tall figure and piercing eye, and observed contentedly that "he jest de one tu manage Miss Nell."

The Gordon house, which had grown shabby during Nellie's years of mourning, was refurbished for the wedding reception —the wedding itself was at Christ Church. Matching rugs, woven to order, were ordered from Turkey for the two parlors. Old gold Chinese brocaded silk draperies were hung at the front drawing room windows, over heavy lace inner curtains, while between the two front windows a tremendous gilt mirror was installed, reaching from floor to ceiling.

In May, 1884, Daisy went to Europe a second time, promising Papa in advance that she would not make herself conspicuous, and writing him reassuringly from shipboard that she had been taken up by Mrs. French, whom she greatly admired, and whose approval was a guarantee that Daisy was conducting herself in every way like a lady. In England she joined the two Carter girls and their mother. Colonel Molyneux, a friend of Willie's, saw to it that the American girls had a good time and did all the important and amusing things. He took them to exclusive Hurlingham, owned by the Prince of Wales, to watch cricket and lacrosse; to Lord's cricketing grounds to see the match between the Australians and the "gentlemen" of England; to the opera; to see the Derby. Daisy and the Carters took Colonel Molyneux to Windsor, chartering a coach and four for the journey from London.

On Nellie's birthday, June 18, Daisy wrote her a loving letter from the Lows' at Beauchamp Hall, Leamington, with an intimation that Nellie did not relish demonstrations of affection. "I wish I could give you as many hugs and kisses as you deserve, but probably you feel 'more honored in the breach than the observance'! Do not be angry, but I have never realized properly how dear and necessary you are to me until I am far away from you.

"Mr. Low seems feeble, he wept when he saw me because he took me for you. He considers himself a dying man, although the doctors say he may and probably will live twenty years. He is a great care to the girls and I am very sorry for them, though they are comfortable and happy in this lovely house."

The Lows had begged Daisy to spend the rest of the summer with them. "I don't feel in the least afraid of wearing out my welcome because they have made me so much at home that I am like one of themselves and I know they won't put themselves out to entertain me. As they are tied at home like prisoners by old Andrew's illness, the only way they can have any change is by asking their friends to see them."

Daisy's romantic soul thrilled to the excitement of beholding the places she had read about in fiction and in English history. She had peopled Strawberry Hill in her imagination with the wits of the preceding century. At Hampton Court, she had visioned Anne Boleyn in her happy days when she had had the love of Bluff King Hal. At Loch Lomond and lovely Loch Katrine, she and Grace Carter re-read *The Lady of the Lake* and hunted up every spot alluded to in the poem. "The Mountain pass of Trossachs is enough to make one thank God for being alive and that there are such beautiful things on earth. Strange to say, I had a patriotic feeling as if I was a Scot myself in some distant way, and I don't care if Papa does chaff and say we were probably servants and yeomen of the Gordon clan when our ancestors were in Scotland."

After touring Scotland, Daisy returned to the Lows' for another week before sailing for home. Daisy reported that as soon as she had left the Lows on her first visit, she missed them. "I saw more of Jessie than the others as we are nearer of an age, but they really were too good to me, all of them."

Again, not a word about Willy Low. The only young man she mentioned was Grenfell Kingsley, Charles Kingsley's son, with whom she played tennis at Beauchamp Hall and whom she considered a "very nice fellow." Daisy, who had always been so frank and open with her parents, had suddenly become secretive.

She congratulated Papa on his election to the Georgia Assembly, in which he was to serve three terms, and, with the vagueness characteristic of her about such matters as the workings of government, wanted to know what he would be called now, and hoped that his election wouldn't mean the family would be moving to Washington!

"Thank you again, dearest Papa, for last summer in Europe, the happiest I have ever spent. And now you will probably keep me in this country for the rest of my life and I shall be quite satisfied."

Daisy had never been consciously untruthful. Yet even as she wrote that last sentence, she must have been hoping and dreaming and maybe believing in her heart as well, that "keeping her in this country" or anywhere else would not be Papa's prerogative very much longer.

CHAPTER XI

---- ☆ ----

COURTSHIP AND MARRIAGE

B UT WILLY Low had been discussed in the Gordon family, for Daisy had assured her father, before embarking on the *Servia* for her second trip to Europe, that he need not worry that she would lose her head over the young man. "He does not know that I am coming to Europe, for I have not written to inform him, so there is little likelihood of my seeing him, even if I visit his sisters, for he is never at home. There will be no such friendship between us as you mention between us if we do meet. His education and disposition both make him seem younger than I am, and I have been thrown so much with older men that he is a perfect boy in comparison. His future wife is still in the nursery and my future husband will be blessed with more years of discretion. So be easy, I shall return just as heart whole as I left you."

This is a very interesting statement, and it would appear that in making it, Daisy was being disingenuous, to say the least. Two years later, in April, 1886, Daisy wrote her brother Bill that she was going to marry Willy Low, and told him that they had been in love for four years and "as good as engaged" for nearly two. This indicates that the romance started with Daisy's first visit to the Lows in the summer of 1882, and that an understanding was arrived at during her visit of 1884, from which Daisy had assured her father she would return as heart whole as she had been before.

Never in her life had Daisy been guilty of lies or evasion. She had always confessed her errors frankly and taken her punishment. And it is possible that her peculiar reasoning processes could have convinced her that she was not telling Papa any untruths. Perhaps she had not written Willy Low that she was going to Leamington—but she had written his sisters and they would have told him. If she and Willy were in love, she could have rejected Papa's word "friendship." And if she had already lost her heart to Willy Low, she could promise with truth that her affections would be in the same state on her return to America as when she left.

Willie and Nellie, together, had carried out to the best of their ability the wishes Willie had expressed for his children's future in the moving letter he had filed with his will during the yellow fever epidemic in 1876. They had given and were giving their children as good educations as the era provided— for the boys, St. Paul's and Yale; for the girls, good boarding schools, followed by a select finishing school, which would equip them with all the accomplishments a girl of the nineteenth century was considered to need.

We cannot doubt that Willie had tried earnestly to inculcate in his daughters his other injunction—that "an honest man who has learned to work and support himself is preferable to man born rich." No man could have been more careful of his womenfolk, more thoughtful for their welfare, than Willie Gordon. His strict policing of Daisy's behavior toward young men had been dictated solely by the desire to protect her from gossip—the merest breath of scandal could ruin an unmarried female's reputation in the 1800's—and from young men with whom he thought her happiness would not be safe.

When Daisy's errant heart settled upon Willy Low, she must have known very well that Papa would not approve. He would have ordered her not to write to Willy, not to see him, as Papa had done in the case of other suitors. Daisy could not bear to disobey her father. The obedience she had rendered to him, and still rendered, was based not upon respect for his parental authority, but on her respect and love for Willie Gordon, the man. On the other hand, she could not bear the thought of giving up Willy Low. Once more Daisy was confronted with a contradictory situation, and she solved it by keeping her parents in the dark. And so Daisy, who had been so carefully guided and shielded at every step, deprived herself of her parents' wisdom and guidance in the most momentous decision of her life.

Willy Low must have made an immediate appeal to Daisy's romantic, intense nature. Never in her life was she to see a man she considered more beautiful—her own word. Willy Low's wedding photographs show a tall, slender young man with thick, curly blond hair, and heavy, arched eyebrows, a long, slender, high bred face and finely sculptured features. His deep-set eyes were blue. His mustache perhaps lowers the impact of his good looks for a modern observer, but no doubt enhanced it for ladies accustomed to hair on men's faces. Two women now living who knew Willy Low describe him. One says, "He was as handsome as a Greek god, and the most charming person I have ever met." And the other, "He looked like a Greek god, and was the most despicable personality I have ever encountered."

In later photographs made in Warwickshire, his face had filled out becomingly, and was almost dazzling in the purity of its lines. His tall figure was erect of carriage and graceful. It is not inconceivable that one of the great old Greeks might have chosen Willy Low to personify divine, immortal youth.

To the naïve little girl from Georgia, not yet twenty-two when she paid her first visit to the Lows, this glorious youth must have seemed a prince out of a fairy tale. And to most parents, he would have appeared a match beyond compare. In dollars, Andrew Low was a multi-millionaire—there were not many multi-millionaires in those days even in America—and Willy was his heir. Willy moved in the highest British society, being one of the intimate circle of the Prince of Wales, who was later to become Edward VII. He was extremely attractive to women and his manners could not have been more charming. It was perhaps Daisy's very naïveté, her innocence and freshness, that attracted Willy Low. He had been in and out of amorous entanglements, adored by women, angled for assiduously by matchmaking mamas. Daisy's artlessness and sincerity presumably appealed to him more than her wit and charm, for he set no great value on wit and moved in circles where the women were adept at making themselves pleasant.

But Daisy, naïve as she was, knew that Papa would investigate any young man in whom she showed an interest, and that Willy Low was about as far as a man could be from the responsible, capable young fellows whom Willie Gordon envisioned as the husbands of his daughters. Left motherless at an early age, Willy Low had been reared, and badly spoiled, by his older sisters. Since he would come into wealth that was impressive by the standards of his day, there had been no reason why he should learn any profession or trade. At Winchester and Oxford, he had naturally joined the gilded youth who had no interests beyond sports and society. His friendship with the Prince of Wales would have been no recommendation to Papa, for it was common knowledge that Edward was one of the more convivial princes in England's history.

To Daisy, however, whatever Willy Low was or was not made no difference, after she had been captivated by his beauty and charm. Her love, once given, was irrevocable.

The absence of Daisy's diary and of all letters between herself and Willy Low, together with the absence of his name in Daisy's letters to her family, make it impossible to say how the affair did develop. Mabel thought they became engaged when Willy Low came to America in the fall following Daisy's 1884 visit to his home, though this was conjecture on her part. Except for the two mentions already noted, by the time his name appears in the documents he is Daisy's accepted suitor and Papa, while apprehensive that this love may prove tragic for Daisy, is powerless to influence Daisy, though he tries.

Willie Gordon was placed in an embarrassing and difficult position. He and Andrew Low were good friends, connections by marriage though not related, fellow members of the board of directors of the Central of Georgia Railroad and also involved together in several other business enterprises. He could hardly bar from his home and his daughter's society his own sister's nephew and the son of a good friend and close business associate. And while he could still command Daisy, and she would still obey, it was plain that efforts to discourage her interest in Willy Low only made her cling to him more stubbornly.

What Papa feared for Daisy was not so much that she would make an ill-advised marriage as that she was headed for heartbreak. Willy Low was entirely dependent upon his father and Daisy had formed a very bad impression of the old gentleman. She was so afraid Andrew would forbid the match if he heard about it that she would not let her fiancé tell his father about their engagement. If they were to wait for old Andrew to die, it might be years before they could marry. Papa did not believe that Willy Low was the type of man to stay true indefinitely under such conditions, whereas Daisy had made it plain that, after she met Willy Low, no other young man could touch her heart. Enough of them had tried, without any success.

This was the state of affairs in January, 1885, when Nellie went to New Jersey to be with Eleanor during the birth of her first baby. Bill, Mabel and Arthur were away at school, and Daisy was to run the household and look after Papa. Nellie had had considerable misgivings about leaving Papa to Daisy's scatter-brained mercies but she comforted herself with the thought that the one thing Daisy shone at was entertaining, so Nellie could be sure that at least Willie's desires in this respect would be well taken care of.

To Daisy, life had never appeared fairer. Willy Low was coming, and she was to have the leading part in the Garrick Club play that would be given while he was there. She knew she would have a triumph, for she was an excellent actress and she had given much thought and attention to her costume. Like any girl in love, the supreme happiness would be to have her lover witness her success.

In her photographs of this period, Daisy shows a striking resemblance to the portrait Healy made of Nellie when she was twenty. Soft curls escape from Daisy's coiffure, her face is animated, one feels that she glowed with vitality, she has an aura of happiness. It must have been a radiant young woman who stopped by Dr. H——'s office the afternoon of January 18, 1885, and requested him brightly to administer some nitrate of silver for an earache.

So many versions have been given of this incident that we shall use here the pertinent parts of letters exchanged between Willie and Nellie Gordon on the subject. Daisy lived the greater part of her life in nearly total deafness as a result of this particular escapade. The doctor who permitted Daisy to coax him into giving her the treatment committed suicide a year or two later. There has been a tendency to connect the two events. It is worth noting, therefore, that Willie Gordon, at least, largely absolved the doctor of blame, for whatever comfort this may be to the descendants of the unfortunate man at so late a date.

Willie's first letter reads: "My darling Wife: Today is Lee's birthday, and the military turn out at 2:30. I wanted to give the Hussars a glass of wine after the Parade this afternoon, but as Daisy is in bed I have managed to arrange to give it to them at the Hall.

"Daisy distinguished herself yesterday. She sent me after church to invite Eglinger to dinner and then picked up Robby Mercer in the street and brought him home to dinner, and after all couldn't be at the table herself. She went just before dinner to Dr. H—— and insisted upon his injecting nitrate of silver for her ear, as I understand it through the nose, being the same treatment as that of some New York doctor which she had read about in the papers.

"H—— protested ignorance but yielded to Daisy's importunings and as soon as he had injected the stuff it was evident that something was wrong from the intense pain she suffered. She got home, but after Georgia Chisholm had tried for an hour to relieve her by hot cloths and cotton, etc., we had to send for Dr. H—— and I sent word for him to bring Dr. Read with him. When they came they injected morphine hypodermically and gave her dovers powder internally and made her lie down with her ear on a hot hop pillow. She is out of pain today and I think will do well if she is prudent." Willie had issued orders that Daisy could not take part in the play. When Willy Low called, Papa would not let him see Daisy.

The next day Willie wrote: "Daisy is comfortable this morning and is sitting up in her room painting. Her ear continues to bleed a little, showing that the drum is pierced—either recently or from the reopening of the cicatrix that formed when there was an abscess there six or eight years ago." While the next report was: "Daisy suffered very much yesterday until evening when her ear began to discharge and she became easier and says today that she feels better than for weeks past. I didn't see Dr. Read when he called today and therefore I give you my theory of the case which is that Daisy has had another abscess which has at last broken through the drum as it did before. If my theory is right, Dr. H—— was right when he wanted to lance the bulging eardrum some days ago. That would have relieved her at once and a cut with the lance would, so say Dr. Read and Dr. H——, have healed better than a break by an abscess. If also there was an abscess, then I have blamed Dr. H—— too much for injecting the nitrate of silver, and it only aggravated what already existed.

"Daisy gives an entertainment tonight to five couples, nominally for Miss Genie Massey, who is visiting her, but also because Willy Low is here. Poor child, I am only too glad she can have this scrap of comfort, for I very much doubt his constancy standing the test of years of delay and separation, and by the time Daisy realizes the situation she will be too old to nurse a new flame."

When Willie's letters about Daisy's latest stunt began to reach Nellie, the air around Hutton Park, New Jersey, must have turned a deep purple. She by no means shared Willie's charitable attitude toward Dr. H——. As for what she thought of Daisy—!

"MY DARLING WILL:
"Yours of the 19th just came. I knew Daisy was a pig-headed fool, but I never dreamed she would carry her folly to such extremes! . . . I told Daisy before I left home that if she wanted really *first class* attention for her ear, to wait until we went to Atlanta to see Calhoun, and let him treat her steadily and skillfully until her ear was perfectly well. She sniffed and scorned at the bare idea! . . . What with the doings at home and this tedious *waiting*—they had me come at least two weeks before I needed to—I am so nervous I am almost distracted. Was Daisy out of her mind that she invited Earl E and Robby M of *all men* together? [Apparently admirers of Daisy who did not enjoy each other's company.] Sometimes it does seem as if she were a Boss idiot! I do wish I never had to go away from home. I think of you all the time and how you are bothered and can't have anything the way you want it while I am not there to arrange matters for you."

In answer to Willie's later report she said, "I'm so glad to hear there's no more danger and pain for that poor child to suffer. The next good news will be that you have given that champion idiot Dr. H—— a piece of your mind. I know if you say anything to him he won't forget it in a hurry! I get so furious every time I think of his *daring* to do such a thing under *any* circumstances that if I were in Savannah I should have it out with him myself. I am *sure* you were right in deciding against letting Daisy be in the play. In her letter to me, she didn't seem to mind it very much. She said you said the other day that 'sacrifices would improve her character' and continues, 'Heaven knows there's plenty of room for improvement, and when you return you will perceive, I have no doubt, a shining and brilliant regeneration. That is, if I have any character left. At present it runs the risk of being all chastened and polished away!' Poor little Daisy, I am awfully sorry for her, she is evidently very low in her mind, but her letters are *so* funny they make me laugh."

But Nellie had a more sympathetic attitude toward the love affair than her husband did. "Eleanor says that Willy L. wanted desperately to learn to become a businessman, and went to some friends of his father in London, saying he wanted to come in and learn the business from the ground up. But they said business was fluctuating and it would take him years to learn—in his situation, there was no point in it. They advised him to get his father to buy him a farm. Willy *wanted* to earn his own living. Eleanor says he has been crazy to tell his father about himself and Daisy, to gain his consent, but Daisy won't let him. Eleanor says Daisy is all wrong and urges telling his father. Don't tell Daisy I said this. I am sure Willy Low intends to have it out with his Governor as soon as he gets back.

"My darling, don't be hard on Daisy. Coaxing will do more with her than driving—particularly if she feels you are her friend and if you talk to her in your usual sensible quiet way. She has such confidence in your ability to accomplish anything you attempt, and is so fond of you. She cares much more for you than she does for me, and always believed you sympathize with her more that I do—which is, I think, doing me a little injustice."

A few days later Nellie was writing Willie: "I am so glad you are taking pity on the poor little girl and letting her see something of W. Low. After all, she may never see him again and if she doesn't make herself conspicuous to the Savannah public, what odds does it make whether she sees him now or not? She will not love him any the less if she don't see him, and if he should prove inconstant she will have had this much brightness in her poor little ruined life! I tell you what, I think of her and pity her all the time—and I do hope you'll be as good to her as you can."

After about a week, during which Daisy seemed to be improving steadily, a tremendous swelling developed behind the ear and Dr. H—— urged that Daisy be taken to Dr. Calhoun in Atlanta without delay. Eleanor's baby still refused to make its appearance—the things the frantic Nellie said about her innocent but dilatory grandchild!—and Willie had to drop his business affairs when they were in a critical state so that Daisy would have a proper escort. From Atlanta, Willie congratulated his Nellie upon becoming the grandmother of a twelve-pound girl.

As soon as Nellie could leave Eleanor, she hurried to Daisy, releasing Papa to go back to his business. For a time the specialist feared mastoid trouble, but the swelling subsided, though Daisy's hearing remained impaired, and it took her months to recover her strength.

By May, 1885, however, Daisy was able to start off on her visiting rounds again. Her great chum Abby Lippitt was now married to Duncan Hunter—an Englishman and no relation to Daisy's Hunter kin—and was settled in Providence. Minnie Steuart had become Mrs. Ned Davis. Mary Gale Carter was engaged to marry Hyde Clarke in the fall, and Daisy went to Cooperstown again to be her bridesmaid. There are undertones of wistfulness in Daisy's descriptions of the wedding, the many beautiful jewels Mary Carter had received as presents, the new marital state of her various friends. Willy Low had not proven the inconstant lover Willie and Nellie had thought he would be, but Daisy would still not let him approach his father, and the romance continued in its anomalous state. To see their daughter in a situation of this kind troubled Willie and Nellie, but Daisy remained composed. On Thanksgiving Day of 1885, Daisy chided Nellie about a dream she had had of catastrophe befalling Daisy. "You mustn't dream bad dreams, you dear little Mama, and if you do, pay no attention to them. Waking is bad enough without letting dreams trouble one. And don't worry about me. I am too busy to be either sick or sad."

Willie and Nellie, seeing that they had underestimated Willy Low's devotion to Daisy, appear to have changed their attitude toward the young man. By December, either Daisy felt the time had come to tackle their collective parents on the subject of their marriage, or else Willy Low had the manliness to insist upon doing so. From Savannah, he wrote to his father of his love for Daisy and his wish to marry her. He asked for an income or settlement of some kind that would enable him to support a wife. He also wrote to Willie Gordon: "My dear Capt. Gordon: Ever since I arrived in Savannah I have been trying to get a chance to tell you something and now as I have had no opportunity of seeing you I had better write it. Your daughter Daisy and I love one another dearly, and although at present I cannot see my way to anything definite for the future, I think it is better to tell you everything. I must confess that there is very little to expect from my Father, as he thinks me nothing more than a good-for-nothing boy, and even if we have to wait a long time, we are both willing to do so. I have told you this because I think it is only right and fair that her parents should know it."

There can be no doubt that Willy Low loved Daisy at this time as much as it was in him to love anyone. And it must have been Daisy's self that he loved, for his wealth, social position and personal attractions would have made it possible for him to marry almost any woman he wanted.

These considerations must have weighed with Papa. When Willy Low received no answer from his father, Papa wrote to the old gentleman, mentioning the letter he himself had received from Willy Low with its declaration of the young man's love and his desire to marry Daisy: "I cannot consent to this if you object, but he seems earnest about it and I write to ask your views about it.

"As Willy has no means of his own and no profession from which to derive an income, it will be impossible for him to marry without knowing definitely upon what he can count for support. My own means are not sufficient for me to ensure any amount, worth while considering, to my daughters after marriage. Willy expresses to me a hope that you will agree to his plans, about which I understand he has written you.

"Unless Willy can and will live within such a sum as he will have and unless he is fully determined to live quietly and discreetly, it would be wrong for me to place Daisy's happiness in his keeping. He promises fairly and his amiable disposition and fondness for Daisy should help him."

Old Andrew did not answer this letter, either, but he had his daughter Amy, Lady Grenfell, write to Willy Low, giving his blessing to the union and promising the requested income. It was the April after this that Daisy wrote Bill about her approaching marriage, and Mr. Low's generous settlement.

"The old gentleman behaved very nicely. He said he would give Willy the interest of all his Savannah property as an income during his life time and repair and furnish the Savannah house for us. The income will amount to almost $15,000 a year, or three thousand pounds, which is very handsome of the old man, isn't it?

"When everything was settled this January I determined to tell *no one* except Eleanor. Of course Papa and Mama have known it right along. But now I find that the Lows wish to tell Aunt Eliza and Aunt Maggie; and you, I know, will be more interested in this intelligence than they can be. But do not write or speak of it to one single soul except myself and Papa and Mama and Eleanor. Until I can name a day I do not wish it known.

"I am to live in Savannah, so don't fancy we are to be all our lives separated. In summer Willy may want to see his people but our home will be here and even if we go to England we shall only go on visits. You talked of Willy that day on the stage coach as if you liked him, although you have seen so very little of him. I hope you will know and like him better some day, as I cannot bear to marry anybody whom my family may dislike."

Daisy's happiness was now complete, for once the decision had been made, the family so dear to her accepted wholeheartedly the man without whose love Daisy felt she could not live. It was inevitable that word of so thrilling a match would leak out, and one of the relatives expressed her disapproval of Willy Low's character to Nellie. Nellie lit into Cousin Sally in Willy's defense, over Daisy's protests that silence was the best way to meet such comments. The servants were set to work at giving the old house and the beautiful old furniture, handed down for generations, such a scouring and polishing as they had not had even for Eleanor's wedding. Willie added a third story to the house, and a veranda on the garden side.

In the summer, Andrew Low died. Now it was no longer a question of an allowance, however generous. All of old Andrew's money was Willy's. Daisy feared this would mean they would have to live in England, but they agreed they would spend at least some months in Savannah after their marriage, and of course would come there frequently. Daisy went North, for a final round of visits before taking on the responsibilities of marriage, which, everyone assumed, would "settle her down." At Mary Carter's wedding, Mrs. Carter had implored Daisy and Abby Lippitt Hunter to continue to visit Cooperstown after Mary became the chatelaine of Hyde Hall. Daisy was at the Carter home when Willy Low landed in America, partly on business connected with his father's estate, partly to see Daisy. He lingered for a few days in New York City and managed to get some very unfavorable publicity. It was a stunning blow to Daisy when the New York papers announced that the wealthy young Englishman, William Mackay Low, had gambled fabulously on a polo match. That Willy Low should take to such reckless plunging the moment he got his hands on his father's money gave pause even to Daisy's often foolishly loyal heart. But Willy hurried to her at Cooperstown and explained it to her satisfaction. Daisy then hastened to correct the bad impression she knew the publicity would make on Papa.

"Willy and I are no longer at odds. If you see a lot of rubbish in the papers about his having bet heavily on the polo match, you must not believe it. He said he had laid one big wager for the team, on commission, not for himself. It is untrue that Willy bet $50,000 to $25,000 as the New York *World* said." And Papa, too, accepted the explanation.

However, there were repercussions in Savannah to the betting episode. Willie had wished to take his prospective son-in-law hunting on the splendid game preserve of Mr. Rauers at St. Catherine's Island near Savannah. Mr. Rauers said he could not extend his hospitality to Willy Low. This had been a rebuff unprecedented in Willie Gordon's experience, and had caused quite a flutter. Mrs. Rauers was aghast and persuaded her husband not only to issue an invitation to Willy Low and Willie Gordon to come to St. Catherine's to hunt, but also to invite Willy Low and Daisy to spend their honeymoon at St. Catherine's. Daisy wanted this passionately and she also wanted the insult to her fiancé wiped out. But there was Papa's pride—it was likely that he would never set foot on St. Catherine's again. And if he declined the invitation to hunt, Daisy and Willy Low would be in honor bound to decline the honeymoon invitation too.

This was in October, before the wedding in December. Daisy was in New York with Nellie, buying her trousseau and new fittings for the Low house. She expended much thought on the letter she wrote to Papa, coaxing him, without appearing to do so, to make peace with Mr. Rauers. She spoke of the honeymoon plan as "too charming to come true," since it was what she wanted above everything else. She told Papa how anxious she was that Willy Low should hunt at St. Catherine's, then added, "But I would not want you to accept, dearest Papa, unless it is quite consistent with your dignity. I mean, if you think Mr. Rauers was rude in refusing you at first, why I should of course understand your not accepting now."

Papa must have carried many pictures of Daisy in his mind that October of 1886, the last in which she would be Daisy Gordon. The tiny mite who stood so stoutly for Papa's Confederate faith, who had wept that her dear papa had only cornbread to eat, who had so nearly lost her life because of a war her elders had brought about. The skinny little girl with big brown eyes that filled with adoration whenever she looked at Papa. The boarding school girl, with her amusing, badly spelled letters, the serious eighteen-year-old who on her birthday had thought of Papa and tried to imagine what he felt when she was first placed, newly born, in his arms. He wrote Mr. Rauers, accepting the kind invitation to Mr. Low and himself to hunt at St. Catherine's.

That Daisy was thinking much, and most lovingly, of her parents as she approached her marriage is evident. She chose their wedding day, December 21, for her own. And she carried lilies of the valley for her wedding bouquet, because this had been her dead sister Alice's favorite flower.

December twenty-first was bright and clear, and Daisy, following the tradition of brides, had never looked lovelier than in her wedding finery. The Hughes portrait of her, painted soon afterwards, shows that Daisy had an exquisite figure, slender yet rounded, and with the tiny waist that was a beauty requisite of the period. She carried her head proudly above lovely shoulders and bust, her hair is a soft dark cloud about her broad, high forehead. Her face is oval, her dark eyes seem to hold dreams of happiness. Above them are strong, very slightly bowed eyebrows which give character to her unmarked young features. Her mouth is overly large for classical perfection, but its lines bespeak generosity and gentleness. While Daisy's photographs resemble Nellie when she was young, in this portrait there is nothing of Nellie, but instead a striking likeness to a daguerreotype of Willie, made in 1865 when he was thirty-one. Willie Gordon, soldier, man of action, responsible citizen and family head, astute, hard-working businessman, in the daguerreotype has a dark, poetic, almost feminine beauty. Daisy's portrait shows this same dark, brooding, romantic quality.

Daisy wore the jewels that were her bridegroom's gifts to her, —among many others—the engagement ring that was a half-loop of large, graduated diamonds, a huge diamond crescent and a beautifully designed diamond star. Billow, as they decided to call him to avoid confusing him with Daisy's father and brother, had personally picked out each stone that went into these pieces, and had designed the settings. Before platinum was so much as thought of, Billow always had diamonds set in silver, believing that they showed to better advantage against white metal than against gold.

It was an entirely white wedding. The bridesmaids were: Daisy's sister Mabel (afterwards Mrs. Rowland Leigh); the groom's sister Jessie (afterwards Mrs. Hugh Graham); Mary Couper Stiles (afterwards Mrs. Edward Swan); Gulie Harrison (afterwards Mrs. Randolph Cuyler), and Abby Lippitt Hunter. The bridesmaids' dresses were of white chiffon, embroidered in floss silk, with enormous sashes of white moiré. Their tiny white chiffon bonnets were surmounted with curling ostrich tips and tied on with coquettish bows. Each wore the groom's gift to her, a charming diamond brooch in the shape of a daisy, with the date 1886 along the stem. The ceremony was held in Christ Church. Bishop Beckwith of Georgia and the rector of Christ Church officiated.

After a wonderful wedding breakfast at the old house, Billow and Daisy dashed out of the front door under the traditional shower of rice and left in a carriage for the boat which would take them to St. Catherine's Island, where they were to spend their honeymoon. But the honeymoon was not the idyll they had anticipated. After a day or two Daisy's good ear began to hurt, and soon the pain was excruciating. She was forced to go in to Savannah to a doctor—not Dr. H——. Examination revealed that a grain of the "good luck" rice had lodged in the ear and it was badly inflamed. Therewith went the professional reputation of another Savannah doctor, for it was rumored that in removing the grain of rice, this man injured Daisy's eardrum irrevocably. In any event, Daisy spent much of her honeymoon ill and in pain. And after the infection was healed, she found that she was totally deaf on that side.

CHAPTER XII

DAISY ENTERS HER
FAIRY KINGDOM

IN EVERY OTHER WAY, however, it seemed that Daisy's most fanciful dreams had come true. She had married her fairy tale prince, and now she entered her fairy tale kingdom. First in order after the honeymoon was to have the stately Low mansion on Lafayette Square for her own. The big square building, with its gardens and carriage house, occupied a whole city block. Two lions, at the top of the steps, guarded the entrance, a touch of elegance with a particular appeal for Daisy. When she had her own home in England, she asked Willy for lions for that place too. She would stop and pat their heads whenever she went in or out.

Inside, the large, well-proportioned rooms of the Low house live up to the dignity of the exterior. The downstairs ceilings are the highest in Savannah, though old Savannah houses are noted for their lofty ceilings. A wide hall runs from the front door to the veranda overlooking the enclosed garden at the back. On the left of the entrance is a small room used at that time for smoking—in the Victorian era, no gentleman ever smoked in a lady's presence; on the right, a door leads to the front and back drawing rooms. Opposite the back drawing room is a spacious dining room and just outside its door is the stairway leading to a landing and the bedroom floor above.

Besides the gracious dignity of the house itself, there were associations which made it the more precious to Daisy. Here had once presided Mary Couper Stiles Low, whom Daisy's mother had loved, and whose beauty and grace were still remembered in Savannah. Here Billow had lived as a little boy. One of Daisy's favorite authors, Thackeray, had been a guest here, the first time in 1853, while Andrew Low was still a widower following the death of his first wife. Three years later, when he next came to America, Thackeray again was a guest at the Low house, "now decorated," he wrote, "with a pretty little wife and baby since I was last here." The pretty little wife was Billow's mother. Thackeray lingered with the Lows for a considerable time, and wrote part of *The Virginians* in their home, using the Lows' butler, Tom Milledge, as his model for Gumbo. And General Robert E. Lee, whom Daisy reverenced above all other men except her own father, had stayed under this roof when he visited Savannah after the Civil War.

Daisy had kept much of Andrew Low's furniture—the rosewood Victorian sofa and chairs in the drawing room, the desk Thackeray had used, and other pieces. Her taste was unerring, and when she had finished her redecorating, there was not a more charming house in Savannah.

The months spent in the Low house after her marriage were probably the happiest in Daisy's life, in spite of the fact that her ear still bothered her a good deal, and the doctors insisted that she cut down on her social activities. But Willy Low's business duties were not arduous, and he was as pleased as Daisy to have his own house. When Billow could not be with her, Daisy occupied herself with a labor of love—making a copy, in oils, of the nearly life-size portrait of her mother, done by Healy when Nellie was twenty. It would require an expert to tell wherein Daisy's copy falls short of the original.

As Daisy's strength and health came back, she was able to indulge in the entertaining at which she had always shone. She had a large staff of servants, with Mosianna Milledge, daughter of the Tom Milledge whom Thackeray immortalized, presiding in the kitchen. Mosianna's cooking rivaled Liza Hendry's, to the latter's acute discomfort and jealousy. All the

Low parties were delightful, but their dinner parties soon became famous.

Daisy would have liked to stay in Savannah forever. Her family and home city were all the dearer to her in her happiness. Also, she had the same misgivings about her ability to cope with social life in England that she had had prior to her debut. It was summer before Billow finally could get her off to England. She was somewhat reassured when, on shipboard, she made a conquest of Lady Bovill, an elderly peeress who reminded her a great deal of Granny Gordon. She wrote her family that "Lady Bovill and I had some comfortable talks together. She made me promise to call on her in England, and I will do it. I begin to think that the English are not so formal and hard to know after all. This will be a good friend for me, if I can talk things over with her in the future, as I did on the steamer."

But hardly had Daisy and Billow stepped into their hotel in London when she began to be deluged with attentions from Billow's sisters and his friends. In 1887, the British Empire was at the peak of its power and glory and wealth and pomp. Now Daisy was to be a participant in the tradition-laden ceremonials and festivities, instead of the tourist onlooker she had been during her two previous visits to England. The great naval review, which was the British navy's compliment to Queen Victoria in her Jubilee year, took place the Saturday following their arrival, and the Lows witnessed it from a private yacht along with Billow's sister, Amy Grenfell and her husband, Sir Henry Grenfell. There had never been such a naval review before in England—the harbor was filled with ships and yachts, flag-decked from stem to stern, and the supposedly stolid British shouted with wild enthusiasm when the royal party went past. At night the illuminations and the colored balls of light fired from the sides of the ships made the scene appear like a fairy naval battle.

After this exciting introduction to her new life, Daisy was plunged immediately into fitting out not just one house, but two. The Lows planned to take their time about finding a permanent home. Meanwhile Billow simultaneously rented a house at Leamington, near Beauchamp Hall, his boyhood home, and took a ten-year lease on a grouse moor near Blair

Atholl in Perthshire, Scotland. They at once took possession of the house at Leamington, and Daisy shuttled back and forth to London on shopping tours. Daisy wrote home: "Issacar was an ass, that stooped between two burdens, and I resemble him at present." Billow's sister Hattie and her husband, George Robertson, stayed at the same hotel as the Lows, and his sister Mary accompanied Daisy on her rounds of the shops. Alfred Grenfell, Sir Harry Grenfell's brother, called every day and made himself useful in many ways. Daisy was surrounded and supported by Billow's family, as by her own in Savannah.

Daisy knew it would please Nellie to hear that the brother of the Marquis of Queensbury was at a little party Alfred Grenfell arranged at his house on the Thames. "The brother's name is Lord James Douglas, and he took Angel Maxwell and me in a boat called a punt, and punted us all over the river. I tried to learn to punt, but it was no good. Alfred's house is the quaintest one you ever saw. It is called Bishop's Farm, and was an old church property. I am sure it was built at the time of the Ark. The fireplaces are so large that two people can sit inside the chimney, and the black oak mantle pieces run up to the ceiling. Over each fireplace was a motto, carved in old English, and I have copied two for your benefit. One is

> "Lette noe one carry from this corner hence
> Things uttered here in friendlie confidence.

"The other reads,

> "Life is mostly froth and bubbles,
> Two things stand like stone.
> Kindness in another's troubles,
> Courage in your own."

Lude, their place in Scotland, proved to be as rich in romance and tradition as Alfred Grenfell's house. The Duke of Atholl, their landord, held a meeting of his clan every year at Blair Castle. No gentleman was allowed on the dance floor unless he wore kilts, and the Laird thoughtfully provided kilts for his Sassenach guests. Also, at these clan gatherings six pipers always played throughout the dinner. Daisy had felt a mystic kinship with Scotland and the pull of the Scottish blood that was in her veins, on her first trip there. Lude in a way was a coming home for her.

She seems, in fact, to have slipped into Billow's life in England as easily and successfully as she had slipped into the social life of Savannah. This was the Edwardian social life, established, after he came of age, by the Prince of Wales, later Edward VII, and as different as he could make it from the prunes and prisms behavior imposed on the peerage for so long by his mother, Queen Victoria.

"Froth and bubbles" though the Edwardian life was, it followed a well-defined pattern, built about country estates, the London season, fox hunting, racing and game hunting. In August, September and part of October, "everyone" was in Scotland for the grouse shooting and deer stalking. Winters were spent in house parties at country estates, except for trips to Paris or other parts of the Continent or travel in far lands. The house parties might be gathered for the race meetings, at Goodwood, Ascot, Newmarket, the Derby at Epsom, or the Grand National at Aintree, which "everyone" attended, or local racing events. Aside from the serious business of watching the races and betting on them, the house parties were given over to fun and frolic. Parlor games were the vogue, and the high-spirited might engage in such perilous sports as sliding down banisters, balancing on trays; while a great deal of ingenuity went into playing practical jokes.

There would be occasional elaborate balls to enliven the winter season, and many fancy-dress dinners at the house parties, gotten up on the spur of the moment and with the costumes improvised. These last were favorite entertainments in Scotland too. And there was hunting to hounds, which provided the principal color of country life. The London season, with its formal dinners, balls, luncheons, opera and theater parties, was held in the summer, before the time for moving on to the grouse moors, the deer preserves and trout-filled streams of Scotland.

Since Billow and his friends were of the intimate circle of the Prince of Wales, the Lows followed the pattern faithfully. The Prince was a racing enthusiast, having his own racing stud. Billow, like the other young bloods who could afford to do so, followed suit. The young Lows attended all the racing meets far and near, except that, for some reason, Billow would never allow Daisy to go to the Newmarket races. They were members of house parties at great country estates of England or Scotland when they were not having gay house parties of their own. Billow belonged to the Warwickshire Yeomanry, which gave notable balls. The most stunning photographs of Billow are those in his uniform.

This was not an intellectual life. The Countess of Warwick once wrote that Britain's select social set recognized that books must be written and pictures painted, but considered the persons who performed these services as beneath their personal notice. Their patron, the Prince of Wales, disliked books, adored shooting and racing and the company of pretty ladies, and the noble Britons whom he favored with his friendship were of the same turn of mind.

Daisy was superbly equipped to shine in such a setting. She was not an intellectual, though she did love books and art. Like her mother, she was interested in larger events only when they concerned people she cared about. She had her mother's faculty for witty comments, and for making the most of an anecdote. In fact, if Willie and Nellie had known from the beginning the position Daisy was to occupy, they could not have given her better training for it. She had been well schooled in social graces, beginning with Grandma Gordon's afternoon tea parties up through Dodsworth's Dancing School and the thorough grounding she got in French at the Mesdemoiselles Charbonnier's in New York City. Her parents had given her freedom after her years of formal schooling to move in high social circles in the North as well as in the South, and to accustom herself to different practices and mores. Her outdoor accomplishments, riding, swimming and tennis, were precisely the ones most useful to her in her new life, while her talent for gracious entertaining, shaped in a home and city where hospitality was raised to a fine art, enabled her to take her place at once as a successful hostess.

Her British life, in fact, was very much a continuation of the one she had lived in America, except that her friends and companions now had names famous in English history, and for the most part lived in castles or manor houses or, in some instances, palaces. Her love of gaiety, which had manifested itself so strongly after the bleak period following Alice's death, fitted her temperamentally to find zest in every ball and every dinner. She never did grow weary of such things, to her dying day.

Her main problem was with English servants, whom she found to be a very different breed from the happy-natured Negroes she had been accustomed to all her life. Evidently her English staff had sized up their generous, merry, informal little American mistress as someone they could deal with to suit themselves. During Daisy's first summer at Lude, she and Billow ran over to Edinburgh, and the servants proceeded to hold high jinks. They capped their impudence by giving a ball, inviting the surrounding tenants, gillies and gamekeepers, and serving refreshments out of Daisy's storeroom. Mary Low, who had not yet married Charles Guthrie, was staying in the house and was awakened by sounds of revelry in the night. She told Daisy about it. Daisy, investigating, learned that this was the second ball with which her staff entertained the countryside in her absence. It was Daisy's custom, as the years went on, to give a party each season for the servants, tenants, gillies and gamekeepers. But for the servants to dispense her hospitality without permission was rank impudence, and evidenced contempt for their employer. As Daisy put it in a letter home: "Mrs. Jobbings, the housekeeper, thought she could dispense with my lieve but she recconed without her host. It is not ettiquet for the housekeeper and ladies' maid to dance with under servants or any that wear livery, so their being very few valets, Mrs. Jobbing extended her invitations to the neighbors. Counting my visitors' maids and men, I have eighteen servants in the house and Heaven knows to what extent they added to this number."

Daisy, softhearted as she was for any in her employ who suffered misfortune, was not to be intimidated. Daisy held the housekeeper responsible and dismissed her without ado. "I had an interview with all the others in which I informed them that the housekeeper had furnished the example this time, but the next time such a performance occurred in my house, I would sack everyone concerned in it. It has served as a terrible warning to them." Again, we can hear Nellie's accents!

Daisy continued her kindnesses, nevertheless, to those of her staff whom she considered deserving. A scullery maid whom she had had to dismiss for dereliction of duty came down with heart trouble, and the doctor said it was the result of overwork in her previous post. Daisy promptly sent the girl to a hospital, paying all the bills. It was most disillusioning when Walton, a butler whose expenses she had paid through a siege of inflammation of the lungs, took to drink in her second summer at Lude, when Billow was away, and the insolence of the butler who succeeded him was carried to such lengths that Daisy had to take to her bed for several days to quiet her nerves. In time Daisy mastered the art of inspiring the necessary awe in an English staff, without ceasing to follow her kindly instincts.

At length the Lows found the house they wanted and Billow bought it in 1889. It was Wellesbourne House, in the heart of Warwickshire, and had originally been built by the Granvilles of Wellesbourne Hall for their butler. The Granvilles had sold it and it had been added to by its various owners. Daisy speaks of it as a small house and it was small in comparison with the castles and great manor houses owned by many of Billow's friends, but its photographs make it appear large and imposing by American standards.

It stood almost inside the village of Wellesbourne, a white stucco house covered with ivy and surrounded on front and sides with a velvety lawn, while in back there was a kitchen garden and two greenhouses. The house had a narrow entrance hall, with a good-sized dining room on the left and a billiard room on the right. There were two small, low-ceilinged drawing rooms, their French windows opening on the lawn. At the back was a large square hall, into which the smoking room opened, with a wide staircase ascending to the bedrooms.

On the bedroom floor, there were two large guest rooms over the dining room and billiard room, and two small bedrooms. Daisy's room was over the smoking room, Billow's was next to hers. In addition there was a small room with white furniture which became Mabel's after she began spending much of her time in England. A swing door led from these apartments into the servants' quarters, and to the one bathroom. The Lows and their guests had baths in their bedrooms morning and evening, but the gentlemen loved to splash about in the bathroom tub.

The stables were huge and elegant, but not big and elegant enough to suit Billow, whose racing stud had become his principal interest in life. He also wanted a mechanical organ, the most expensive kind it was possible to buy, in the square hall of the house. While the alterations went forward, the Lows made a trip to Egypt, Daisy's first, but by no means her last.

Sir Francis Grenfell, a cousin of Amy Low's husband, was sirdar, or commander-in-chief of the Anglo-Egyptian forces. The sirdar's nephew, Jack Maxwell, was his aide. The Maxwells were already good friends of Billow and Daisy. The young Lows were shown every courtesy, honor and assistance it was in the power of the sirdar to extend.

Back in England, Daisy learned that she had been invited to appear at Court. Presentation to Queen Victoria was very important for Daisy as the wife of an Englishman in high society, especially since she was American by birth. Her own social position was not assured until she had received this cachet of approval. Accompanied by her maid, Josephine, she dashed over to Paris to procure a gown worthy of the occasion. Daisy paid sixty pounds for her presentation dress, a little more than three hundred dollars then, and apparently a huge amount even for the wealthy Mrs. Low to pay for a gown, for Daisy was most apologetic in confessing her extravagance to the folks at home. It was white satin, with the skirt perfectly plain, but overhung with festoons of ostrich feathers, the whole covered by a film of tulle. Each festoon was decorated with a bunch of plumes, of three feathers each, like the crest of the Prince of Wales. A band of feather trimming crossed the bodice from one shoulder to the waist, and Daisy thought the gown would have rejoiced the heart of an Augusta, Georgia, girl "as Mama says they love ostrich feathers." Daisy wore, besides, three feathers on one shoulder and like every other lady admitted to the Queen's presence, was required to wear a tulle veil with three plumes on her head. The rule of the Court also required a six-yard train. Daisy's was of white silk, lined with pink satin, and brocaded in a feather design.

When she dressed for the presentation, she put on all her diamonds including a flight of diamond swallows—pins in graduated sizes which had been a post-nuptial gift from Billow—on one side of her bodice, and diamond stars along the feather banding on the other side, where they "glittered through the feathers like the Milky Way." She carried a white bouquet.

Daisy's sponsor was the Marchioness of Hertford, whose daughter, Lady Margaret Seymour, had become a great friend of Daisy's and who accompanied her mother and Daisy to the Court. Daisy therefore drove first to the Hertfords' in Eaton Square. She wrote her family in Savannah: "They were waiting for me in their coach, which looked like a hearse or a Noah's ark draped in velvet, and the coachman's and footman's liverys were precisely the same as those worn in the time of Queen Elizabeth. Lots of the old coaches were very extraordinary—some like the pictures of Cinderella's coaches in the fairy tales. And one white livery, turned back with blue velvet, silver and blue cocked hats and blue silk stockings, was most gorgeous.

"I felt just as Thackeray describes Becky Sharp when she went to Court, and although I don't agree with his sarcastic assertion that no woman can be vertuous without going through that august ceremony, and that it set a seal upon her honesty, still I did, like little Becky, 'Look out for number one'; and in the rush and tear through the Palace to get to the throne room I felt more as if I were in Billingsgate than in Buckingham, and I used what few wits I possessed to keep my clothes on my back and myself on my legs. There are such hundreds of people that, if one stops to sit down and rest, one loses ground that is never regained, and although we started out at three o'clock it took us until six to walk through seven rooms. At each door we were stopped by ropes which were held by Gentlemen-at-Arms, who also wore beautiful costumes. One of the gentlemen was old Mr. Phillips, who married a cousin of the Lows. He arranged all the trains and stood just outside the throne room. It gave me confidence to see a familiar face in that crowd. Of course, everyone was very sorry to crowd and push and everyone apologized continually, but my train weighed tons and my bouquet pounds! I disposed of the bouquet by perching it on the bustle of the lady in front of me and, quite unconscious of the service she rendered, she carried it the length of all the rooms! Lady Hertford knew the ways of the Court and saved time by going through the doors unknown to the uninitiated.

"Some of the conversations of those around us were very amusing. One lady said she had once worn pale green gloves to match her gown and the Lord Chamberlain made her take them off as only white are allowed at Court, so although her hands at once became as red as fire, she had to go without gloves."

Daisy had derived wide-eyed enjoyment from her glimpse of royalty and of the medieval panoply with which the British Court and nobility surrounded itself on state occasions. But she never lost the faculty of finding fun in Old World solemnities, as she had found fun in the solemn formalities of the Mesdemoiselles Charbonnier's school. And her British friends did not consider her the less charming because of it.

At last the house and stables at Wellesbourne were ready, and the Lows moved in. For a girl who had steeped herself in English literature and history and romance, there could hardly have been more thrilling surroundings. Near at hand were real castles of the kind into which Daisy, her brothers and sisters and cousins, had transformed the rock below the house at Etowah in their imaginative play. And the real castles surpassed their most extravagant imaginings. The great pile of Warwick Castle rose up from the banks of the Avon River. Not far from it were the ruins of Kenilworth. There were Stoneleigh Abbey, Stratford-on-Avon and Charlcote, where Shakespeare was brought before Sir Thomas Lucy for poaching. And the great families of the neighborhood went as far back in time as their homes. There were still Grevilles at Warwick Castle, Leighs at Stoneleigh, Lucys at Charlcote, and they all became Daisy's intimate friends.

Others of the Lows' close circle, in addition to Lord and Lady Warwick, were the Earl of Warwick's only sister, Eva, and her husband, Frank Dugdale, nicknamed Duggie; the Earl of Aylesford and Baron of Guernsey, Charlie; Sol who was Viscount Dungarvan and Baron Boyle of Youghall until he became the Earl of Cork and Orrery on the death of his father in 1904; Lady Olive Cairns; Lady May Grey Egerton. Lady Grey Egerton appears the prototype of the healthy English beauty, but she had been a Cuyler of Georgia before she married Sir Brian Egerton, twelfth baronet, and was connected with Daisy through both the Gordon and the American Churchill families. When Daisy, too, married an Englishman and settled in England, she and her distant cousin became very special friends. Their lives were to run parallel in other ways than in their marriages to Englishmen.

The foregoing names appear in the Wellesbourne visitors' book on practically every page, the peers, following British custom, signing their last names only. Sometimes the names are written large, sprawled all over the page, sometimes as small as could be managed. Sometimes they are made into designs, or written upside down. And on the occasion of one Yuletide house party, silhouettes of the entire group and of other close friends occupy several pages.

Frequent visitors were Jack, Louise and Angela Maxwell; and Lord Arthur and Lady Ota Wilton, lessees of Houghton, a palatial country seat that had been rebuilt by Robert Walpole, Prime Minister to George II and father of Horace Walpole. Bob and Alix Beech, two other intimates, occupied Meggernie Castle in Scotland, the property of Ian Bullough, Mrs. Beech's son by a previous marriage. Both Houghton and Meggernie became second homes for Daisy, in the same way that the Carter place at Cooperstown, Hyde Hall and her sister Eleanor's home in Hutton Park, New Jersey, were places in America to which she could invite herself whenever she pleased.

In the visitors' book, at one time or another, are the names of most of the elect in the society of their day. Lord Cornwallis West; Alwyne Greville, a brother of the Earl of Warwick, and high in the favor of Edward and Alexandra; Anna Cassel, daughter of Sir Ernest Cassel, the financier who gave Edward good advice about his investments. Anna Cassel married Lord Ashley, and became the mother of the present Lady Mountbatten. We find also Lady Randolph Churchill and the Duke of Marlborough with his duchess, who had been Consuelo Vanderbilt.

A very close bond was maintained with Billow's sisters, all of whom married men of wealth or distinction or both, with the exception of Katy, who did not marry at all. Katy Low, eldest of the children of Mary Couper Stiles Low, had had much of the responsibility for her younger sisters and her brother, Willy, after their mother's death. A woman of force and character, she became a true sister to Daisy. Hattie Low died not long after the marriage of Daisy and Billow, but her widower, George Robertson, remained one of Billow's closest friends.

The Low girls had loved Daisy before Willy Low fell in love with her. And the titled Britishers from whom Daisy's friends were mainly drawn not only took up the little American in a social way. They took her to their hearts as well, as Daisy was to learn when her time of trouble came. They must have enjoyed her ingenuous enchantment at everything she saw, and perhaps Daisy filled their preconceived notions of an American girl, with her complete naturalness, her keen sense of humor, her sparkling wit and charm. For Daisy remained entirely herself, just as Nellie had altered none of her Midwestern ways for New York City or Savannah, and talked to her new friends exactly as she talked to her older ones in America.

Warwickshire was fox hunting country, and her first winter at Wellsbourne Daisy, along with Billow, hunted with the North Warwickshire Hounds. No one had told her, it seems, of the custom of tying a ribbon on the tail of a horse that kicked, so that other riders could stay clear of his heels. Daisy had a spirited mount. When it lashed out furiously at another horse, its rider demanded to know why Daisy hadn't tied a ribbon to her horse's tail.

"Whatever for?" Daisy wanted to know.

"Because he kicks!"

"That is just the reason why I would *not* tie a ribbon to his tail! If you wish to do so you can, but I'm not going to. An ancestor of mine once tried to brush a fly off the hind leg of a mule. He got kicked in the head, and was never the same after that!"

It is a little strange to find in the visitors' book the names of people who figured in the most flamboyant scandals of the Edwardian era. For Daisy, tolerant with every other human weakness, was as strait-laced as Papa could have wished when it came to infractions of the moral laws. Perhaps Daisy's own innocence and naïveté kept her from knowing about the purple passages in the lives of some of her new friends. But there is a hint in a letter she wrote to her father in 1898 that she had

had to make some compromises with her principles for Billow's sake. Willie Gordon had been concerned because Daisy, on one of her many visits to America, had been seeing an American society woman of dubious reputation. Daisy wrote him, "M—— amuses Billow, and he always asks her to dine, and with such gay ladies I always think it wisest to be friends, even if I did not really like old M——, which I do. But in showing her attention with Willy Low, I will not compromise the family, so no harm will be done. If I could choose my friends, it would be different, but it doesn't answer for Willy and me to stand on a different footing with anyone, and his attitude is always friendly. . . . I know you have my best interests at heart, but after all, everyone knows best when their own shoe pinches!"

Daisy loved beautiful things, had always taken a great interest in clothes, and now she could surround herself with beauty. Billow's gifts of jewelry were princely in the early years of their marriage. She could have her ideas about gowns carried out by the leading Paris *couturiers,* and indulge to the full her penchant for trailing negligees of real lace. By the late 1890's, as the influence of the aged, frugal Victoria waned and that of the Prince of Wales ascended, British ladies were paying several hundred pounds for a gown in Paris and thinking nothing of it.

Daisy had the gift of her mother and grandmother for setting a notable table, and took a special pride in offering Georgia delicacies to her guests. Papa sent over peach-fed hams from Belmont, his farm in the country north of Savannah, barrels of sweet potatoes and even green corn. Mama kept Daisy supplied with various kinds of pickles including those made from Ogeechee limes, a curious fruit which grows only along the banks of the Ogeechee River, near Savannah, and pepper vinegar. This last item, very foreign to the bland British cuisine, brought tears to the eyes of Liney, Daisy's stolid Scotch head gardener, when she rashly gave him a taste. Her purpose was to encourage him to induce the somewhat dry pepper plants Mama had sent over to live and flourish in English soil. "There's nothing like this vinegar for giving flavor to soups and sauces," Daisy urged him. "See, isn't it different?"

"It is certainly different, ma'am," Liney acknowledged when he could speak.

One of the contradictions of Daisy's nature was that in spite of her inordinate tenderness for birds and animals, she entered with zest into the various kinds of hunting and shooting that were an essential part of English county life. This may have been another secret sacrifice that Daisy made to Billow's happiness, and another proof of her determination to let no inclinations or prejudices of her own come between them.

Daisy also assumed her community responsibilities as a member of the privileged upper classes, and we find the name of Mrs. William Mackay Low among those of the titled ladies who presided over booths at bazaars which were opened by members of the royal family.

But immersion in pleasures and excitements beyond anything she had ever dreamed of by no means lessened her feeling for her family. At her pressing invitation Bill visited her at Spring Hill, before she settled at Wellesbourne, and so did Eleanor with her two little daughters, Alice and Lalla—Lalla had been named Eleanor, after her mother and grandmother, but was never called that, in accordance with the Gordon tradition about names.

These glimpses of her beloved family, however, were not enough. Daisy's thoughts turned to the youngest brother and sister, for whom she had always had a more maternal than sisterly affection. Arthur was now seventeen, Mabel nineteen. In the spring of 1889, Daisy wrote Nellie: "Now there is one thing I want very much, and that is for you and Papa to let Arthur come over and be my guest for the entire summer. I will pay all his expenses, and as he will not be needed at home, I pray and entreat that he may come. There are many times that I am alone, and if I only had *one* member of my family with me, I could be so happy. . . . In the past, whenever Billow went off to the races, etc., I have picked up my duds and gone to London or some place, but I think that a bad plan. Firstly, my place is at home, and then too knocking about is not good for my health—it only makes me restless. Arthur and I could be great companions and he would be such a comfort. I know it is useless to ask for Mabel, but if you can spare Arthur, do let him come. I shall not say one word

Juliette Magill Kinzie
and her daughter Nellie

Wolcott Kinzie,
Nellie's elder brother

Portrait of Nellie Kinzie two years before her marriage to W. W. Gordon, II. The original was by G. P. A. Healy but this is from the copy painted by Juliette Low.

Captain William Washington Gordon, II, of the Confederate Army

The Gordon children: Mabel, Eleanor, Juliette, Arthur, Alice, Bill. Juliette was then about fifteen years old.

Portrait of Juliette
Gordon Low painted soon
after her marriage

Willy Low *(seated center)*,
wearing the uniform of the
Warwickshire Yeomanry

The parrot Polly Poons was one of Juliette Low's
favorites among her many pets.

Head of Daisy Gordon Lawrence, modeled by Juliette Low, at the time Daisy Lawrence was made the First Registered Girl Scout. The original is in the Juliette Gordon Low Birthplace.

Portrait of the first William Washington Gordon, modeled by Juliette Low

The wrought-iron gates designed and made by Juliette Low.
Now at the entrance of Gordonston Memorial Park, Savannah.

Headquarters of the first American Girl Guides. The building
is at the back of the garden of the Low house in Savannah.

Sir Robert Baden-Powell, Lady Baden-Powell and Juliette Low,
in 1919

Juliette Low working at her desk in the first National Girl
Scout Headquarters in New York City

to him until you decide, and if Papa decides against it, Arthur had better not know I made the proposal."

We suspect that Daisy's plea of loneliness on this occasion was a stratagem for giving Arthur a summer in England. Nellie, tart of tongue though she remained to the end of her days, could never resist a proposition necessary to Daisy's happiness, and Daisy knew it well. Papa was not so easily influenced, but Nellie could usually bring him around, given time. She got his consent for Arthur to go, and this was the beginning of the close bond between Daisy and the baby of the family which was to continue throughout her life.

The next summer, that of 1890, while the Lows were still at Spring Hill, Mabel came for her first extended stay. She was introduced to county society at the Rugby races, where the Lows had a tent of their own and gave lunch to one hundred people. Everybody asked who Mabel was, and she became rather indignant at being described always as "Mrs. Low's little sister."

Soon, however, Mabel made her own place among Daisy's friends. Mabel at twenty was a rarely winsome bit of femininity, closely resembling Daisy with the same slight but beautifully rounded figure, the same natural curls escaping about her lovely, fresh, dimpled face. From 1890 on Mabel spent every summer and several winters with Daisy, until she, too, married an Englishman and had her own home in England.

Daisy had long been begging Papa and Mama to come over. She wrote to Nellie in 1890, "I keep thinking all day and dreaming all night of having you and Papa here. Oh! do try and come. I so long and yearn to see you both. Don't press Papa to make the decision. Even if he says 'no' now, wait, and perhaps he will come when the heat is intense and the work is dull. What a welcome you shall both have!"

In 1891 Nellie and Willie did come over, bringing with them Arthur, Bill and Mabel, who had gone back to Savannah in the meantime. When they reached the Albermarle Hotel in London, they found a Mr. Rowland Leigh waiting for them, "to see Mabel, I presume," Nellie remarks in her diary, and as usual Nellie was right. A younger son of Baron Leigh, Lord Lieutenant of Warwickshire, whose magnificent estate Stoneleigh Abbey was and still is one of the show places of the county, the Honorable Rowland Leigh had fallen in love with Mabel, and was her faithful suitor for seven years before Papa would consent to their marriage in 1898.

From a group photograph made at Wellesbourne in 1891, we can see how tiny Nellie was, with the figure of a girl, dressed in trim, stylish outdoor clothes, looking about half as big as and not a day older than the young English women in the picture, contemporaries of Daisy. If it were not for the "Mama Gordon" Daisy has written over Nellie's head in the Wellesbourne visitors' book, and the fact that Willie is at her shoulder, one could not believe that this slim youthful little person was the mother of five grown children, and a grandmother as well. Willie, also short and slender but wiry, looks more like an older brother to the effulgent Billow, who stands near by, than like his father-in-law.

Very soon after the Wellesbourne visitors' book was started, the names of other American relatives and friends begin to appear in its pages. Daisy's intimates from the Mesdemoiselles Charbonnier's, Grace Carter and Mary Gale Carter, the latter now Mrs. Hyde Clarke, appear there, together with Mary Gale's husband, almost as often as do the close British friends. Abby Lippitt Hunter and her husband, Duncan, were guests in 1894. Not only did Eleanor Parker, and her husband, Wayne, come often, but numerous Parker cousins signed the visitors' book as well. Georgia Chisholm, who applied the hot fomentations when Daisy persuaded Dr. H—— to administer the silver nitrate, was a guest, as was Nina Anderson Pape, of the Anderson cousins in Savannah. There are Stiles galore. Daisy, while acquiring hosts of new friends of various nationalities, seems never to have dropped along the way an old friend or even a remote family connection.

Whenever anyone she knew in America planned a European trip, Daisy would send an urgent invitation to visit her at Wellesbourne or Lude, and would offer to pay the extra traveling expenses that would be involved, in the case of all relatives and of any friends whose travel budgets would be strained by the trip. She would take her American guests to Warwick Castle and Kenilworth, spreading a picnic lunch just outside the ruined tower where Amy Robsart had her room. The party would explore the ruins and the King's plaisance where Lady Amy used to walk. Another favorite picnic spot was a lovely sward on the bank of the Avon. Daisy had mastered punting by this time, and would convey her guests and the baskets of food to the place by boat.

Every winter Daisy visited America, returning with Mabel, and would slip back into her old life there as if she had never left it. There would be the round of visits to her Northern friends, just as before her marriage, and Daisy never came back to this country that she did not run over to Etowah Cliffs to see Aunt Eliza Stiles.

And on each visit to Savannah she managed to add to the legend she had begun in her debutante days. Most accounts of her idiosyncrasies say somewhere, "Everyone in Savannah knew Daisy Low and loved her." Meaning that everyone in Savannah knew that Daisy would behave in completely incalculable ways, but that Savannah loved her anyhow.

Savannah had its own protocol, quite as rigid as that exacted by the otherwise easygoing Prince of Wales. As soon as Daisy and Mabel arrived from England, all Nellie's friends would "leave cards." This was a necessary prelude to seeing the Gordon girls in the flesh or inviting them to any sort of entertainment. Daisy and Mabel, in their turn, must leave their cards within three days.

On one occasion they hired a carriage from the livery stable for this ceremonial return of cards, with Sawed-Off-Johnny as their driver. Daisy found that she had left her card-case on the table in the library and asked Johnny to run in and get it for her. According to custom, the coachman went to the door of each house visited and left the cards, the ladies remaining in the carriage. As the afternoon wore on, Daisy asked Johnny how many of her cards still remained. "All I got now is de ace and de jack o' spades, Miss Daisy," he replied. In behalf of Mrs. William Mackay Low, Johnny had been distributing playing cards at Savannah's most august houses! Although Daisy never assumed any airs, and was careful not to drag titles into her conversation while at home, Savannah was well aware that Daisy Gordon now moved in exalted social circles indeed. There was conferring back and forth among the dowagers about the playing cards. It was well known that the

Prince of Wales was sportively inclined—was it possible that this was another of his innovations? Everyone drew a sigh of relief when it developed that it was only another of the amusing mix-ups in which Daisy was always involving herself.

She enlivened British society, too, in the same way. On one of her visits home Daisy persuaded Mosianna Milledge, who had been her cook during the time she and Willy lived in the Low house after their marriage, to return to England with her. So superbly did Mosianna perform at Wellesbourne that the guests frequently would insist that she be called in after a meal so they could congratulate her. Lord Warwick could never remember Mosianna, so he called her Mozambique; a name Mosianna preferred to her own. His title, the Earl of Warwick, was equally difficult for Mosianna to get in her head. Hearing him addressed by the English servants as "My Lord," she solved her problem by calling him "My Gawd," which delighted the Earl quite as much as his name for her delighted Mosianna.

One summer Daisy went up to Lude earlier than usual, leaving tickets and instructions for Mosianna to follow in a day or two. At a junction point in Scotland, it was necessary to change trains, and Mosianna was ejected onto the station platform. The English pronunciation had been bad enough for Mosianna to get used to, the Scotch was completely beyond her. She could understand nothing the railway guard said to her, and her deep Southern accent was just as incomprehensible to him. Mosianna was on the verge of panic when suddenly she caught sight of a familiar figure in the middle of a crowd of fashionably dressed men and women. Mosianna shouldered her way through the group that surrounded the Earl of Warwick, threw her arms around his neck and sobbed, "My Gawd, I sho is glad to see you!"

"Why, Mombazique, whatever are you doing here?"

"I'se tryin' to git to Miss Daisy, My Gawd, but dey done put we-uns of'n de train an' ah don' know whut ah gwine do. Dat feller," glaring at the railway guard, "he don' even talk English!"

Lord Warwick patted her back comfortingly. "Don't you worry, Mombazique. We're on the way to Miss Daisy's ourselves, and you shall come right along with us." And so Mosianna arrived at Lude under the escort of the Earl of Warwick and friends. Mosianna told Daisy that "My Gawd is jus' lak de white folks back home!"

Mosianna got too homesick for Georgia after a while, and Daisy had to let her return. But the Earl of Warwick always asked after Mombazique when Daisy had been in America, and as long as Mosianna Milledge lived, the colored folk of Savannah were never allowed to forget My Gawd.

CHAPTER XIII

UNDERNEATH THE SHINING SURFACE

I T IS CHARACTERISTIC of Daisy that in her letters home during the early years of her marriage, she never mentioned the handicap imposed on her by her deafness. It must have been a terrible blow, and it must have presented particular difficulties in meeting new people, before whom she was anxious to appear at her best on Billow's account. Hearing in her "good ear" had been destroyed completely by the "good luck" rice. Hearing in the other grew worse. It was embarrassing to have to ask to have remarks repeated, frustrating to be the hostess at a dinner party and see everyone laughing at a joke she had not heard. Nevertheless Daisy never railed at fate, and indulged neither in self-pity nor in self-reproaches for a deed that could not be undone.

Instead, she established in her new circle a reputation as a wit and *raconteuse*, equal to that Nellie held in Savannah. She was the life of every party, and so amusing that everywhere she went, groups gathered about her to hear what she had to say. Daisy Lawrence once asked her aunt how she managed to be the center of things wherever she was. "I got tired of straining to hear conversations that weren't particularly interesting anyway. I decided it was simpler to take things into my own hands!"

People might realize, after a session with Daisy, that she had done all the talking. But at the same time she contrived to make them feel that it was some quality in them that had moved her to pour out a spate of anecdotes and funny personal experiences. Samuel Lawrence, her nephew by marriage, counts her the most fascinating person he has ever known. Eleanor Arnett Nash comments that Daisy had the great gift of making other persons feel that they were fascinating. Her interest in people was genuine, as the record of her whole life attests, so this was not merely a stunt. And when people were in trouble, she always managed to hear their stories.

From this time also dates the gradual growth of Daisy's natural naïveté and impulsiveness into the downright eccentricity for which she became famous. Shut off from much that went on in the outside world, thrust back upon her own resources, more and more she followed her individual course without regard to the opinions, suggestions and sometimes convenience of those about her. She quickly learned to turn her deaf ear to anything she did not wish to hear.

This habit frequently involved her in imbroglios, but these furnished her with further entertaining stories. One she used to tell often was an incident that took place in Scotland. Out walking, Daisy came to a stream where the bridge had been washed away and a log thrown across in its place. A peddler was standing by, leaning on a cane. Daisy asked him civilly to lead her across the log, for her deafness interfered with her sense of balance. He shook his head and started to say something, evidently in dissent. "Come now, it will only take you a minute, I'll tip you well." Daisy seized his elbow and impelled him to the log, paying no attention to his mumblings. "Now you walk across, I'll follow with my hand on your shoulder." It was plain there was no use arguing with the woman. The man got on the log and inched across, tapping the log with his cane as he went. Daisy, her eyes closed tightly, inched along after him. When they were safely on the other side and Daisy opened her eyes, she saw that he was blind!

"Why on earth didn't you tell me!" she exclaimed.

By this time the man was mad enough to yell. "I kept trying to, ma'am, only you wouldn't listen!"

It was a harder blow to Daisy to have her doctor tell her,

after her first hunting season in Warwickshire, that she must not ride to hounds any more. Before she married, she had put her horse at a small jump, the horse had shied and she had strained herself. She had suffered a further strain in hunting and now the principal winter occupation of the county folk was denied her. One of the few indications she ever gave that she had a battle to fight beneath the surface of her seemingly enviable situation was in a letter to Mabel, after Papa, Mama, Bill, Mabel and Arthur had returned to Savannah in 1891. "I can hardly face the loneliness of the coming winter, now that I cannot ride any more." Daisy after all had not lived in Warwickshire very long, and while she had made warm friends, they were in the circle who would be off after the hounds.

Daisy's mother and grandmother had both gone through periods of hardship, danger and difficulty without the help of their husbands. But in their cases the separation had been forced by what the husbands considered to be their duty. No other consideration could have kept either Willie Gordon or John Harris Kinzie from his wife when she needed him. From the time she was a tiny girl, Daisy had beheld Willie's loving solicitude for Nellie whenever she was ill or unhappy. Throughout all the exciting adventures and vicissitudes Juliette Kinzie describes in *Wau-Bun,* there runs a continuing theme. "John, of course, was thinking of my comfort first of all," or "John thought only of my safety."

But Billow was not a Willie Gordon or a John Harris Kinzie. It probably did not enter his head that he should deny himself any of the hunting or other rugged sports he enjoyed, and from which Daisy was now cut off. Billow went his way, spending more and more of his time, as the years went on, in far-flung game-hunting expeditions with his men friends. Once more Daisy, alone and unaided, had to figure out her personal course as best she could.

She turned to her artistic skills, for which she had had little time in the constant press of social engagements. While Billow and her house guests and her Warwickshire friends were away at the hunt, Daisy first of all carved a mantelpiece for the smoking room. Above it she hung Billow's portrait on horseback in his red hunting coat, done by Palmer. Next she made oil paintings of dogs in the Warwickshire pack, to hang about the room. When the hunt came Wellesbourne way, she would give her friends lunch. And she made her hospitality so delightful that they formed a habit of dropping by for tea after the hunt.

Her next venture was to make a pair of iron gates for the entrance of Wellesbourne, and this was an undertaking indeed, for Daisy had never worked with metals. She loved adding new skills to her collection, however, and went about it in the businesslike way that was to characterize her thereafter in any new enthusiasm. She hired a forge and took lessons from a blacksmith who was expert in the refinements of his craft. Under his direction, she made her own tools, then set to work on the gates, decorating them with daisies beaten out of copper. When they were installed at the entrance, Daisy had a right to be proud of her winter's work and her friends were greatly impressed.

There was one drawback, however. Her arms became so muscular as a result of pounding iron that when the London season came round the next summer, she found that she could wear none of her Paris gowns, with their tight leg-o'-mutton sleeves!

Ill health was added to Daisy's handicaps. In January, 1893, she had an illness while she was visiting Eleanor at Hutton Park. Papa had urged her to come to Savannah in order to recuperate fully before hurrying back to England. Daisy had replied that the weather in England would be better for her, and that she had compelling reasons, not stated, for wanting to get back there. Later she wrote that on the ship she had been allowed to use the best cabin on board as a sitting room, so that she need not go up and down stairs, and that the doctor and ships officers were doing all they could to make her comfortable; from which it may be inferred that the trouble whatever it was, had been rather serious. From this time on she had periods of suffering from "internal abscesses" as they are called in the letters. What these were, in modern medical terms, is a mystery. In those days people did not talk about "female" disorders, and no symptoms are given. But Daisy frequently went to the Continent for "cures," and frequently had to miss entertainments because she was not feeling well.

Even this she turned into a kind of advantage. She never

inflicted her personal unhappiness on those about her. When she had received a crushing blow, it was her custom to hide herself away and stay apart until she could return as her usual gay, sparkling self. Probably she often used illness as her excuse for absenting herself, and there is at least one instance where this was certainly the case. In any event, she never let her physical frailty interfere with leading a full and superabundantly active life.

The hardest blow of all was to have the years go by, and the longed-for babies fail to appear. Both the Lows very much wanted children. To Willy, as an Englishman of position and substance, it was vastly important to have an heir to carry on his name and inherit his wealth. Daisy, from early childhood, had exhibited her Grandmother Juliette's capacity for abounding maternal love. Her choice of her parents' wedding day for her own was more than a compliment to them. She had thought of it as presaging the start of a family life as happy as theirs had been. It was Mabel's understanding that Daisy had a miscarriage in the early years of her marriage so that she had reason to hope, especially in view of the notable fecundity of both her family and Willy's. But though the many doctors she consulted in England and on the Continent could find no reason why she could not have children, it is the family's understanding that she never became pregnant again.

Denied the natural outlet for her maternal impulses, Daisy poured out on pets her great tenderness for small, helpless things. She always had a mockingbird from her native Georgia. When one died, her parents would send another. In 1890 she wrote Nellie: "My mockingbird is such a dear, and so cheeky! I let him fly about the drawing room and he jumps on my head and in spite of remonstrances he scolds and bites my hair, and snatches the pen from my fingers when I try to write. Let us hope that he will 'nothing exterminate nor aught set down in malice'!" There was her blue macaw, which she called "my beautiful Blue-bird"; her parrot, Polly Poons. But best of all she loved her dogs, and always had a number of these, usually of the toy variety. They slept on her bed, accompanied her everywhere. The pages of the Wellesbourne visitors' book contain almost as many photographs of little dogs as it does of people.

Daisy by no means confined her maternal, protective impulses to animals. She did not engage in the organized charities that furnish heart's ease for many wealthy women with empty lives. Billow did not wish his wife to be on charity boards, to engage in settlement work or trail her long skirts through slums. Daisy's charities had to be private, and they were another thing she never spoke of. How many unfortunate persons she assisted can never be known, for those that are known were discovered by accident. But she could not pass by a human being in distress any more than she could pass by an animal in distress. Quite frequently those she helped would have chosen other types of aid, for she was as eccentric in her benefactions as she was in other matters. Yet quite as frequently Daisy's odd, unorthodox methods worked out for the best. And her brand of charity was distinguished by the fact that though she gave liberally of money, she gave even more liberally of herself.

A woman in Wellesbourne village developed a disease that was very loathsome in appearance and was thought to be leprosy, so that everyone avoided her. One afternoon a week Daisy would disappear mysteriously, never saying where she had been. Mabel learned from one of the villagers that Daisy spent the afternoon with the unfortunate woman chatting, making the woman feel that she was still part of the human race. Another of her regular ports of call was the workhouse at Stratford-on-Avon, where she would joke and laugh with the destitute old people. Mabel learned of this when at Christmastime Daisy received thirty smudged and thumbmarked Christmas cards from one of the old men there; and when the matron wrote next day asking Daisy if she wouldn't please return the cards, as the old man had stolen them from the other inmates!

No one could ever convince her of the danger of picking up strays and tramps. One Sunday morning, returning from early church service, Daisy found a shivering, starved-looking wanderer just outside the gates of Wellesbourne. She took him with her to the kitchen entrance, but he refused to go in. Daisy flew into the kitchen, seized from the hands of an astonished footman the tray of early morning tea he was taking up to a guest, and ran out doors with it. The tramp reached eagerly for the hot tea, then shrank back saying, "No, it is poisoned!" Daisy realized the man was not mentally normal—all the more reason to get some warm food into the poor creature. She coaxed, "If I drink and eat with you, will you take it?" He said he would. So Daisy got another spoon and between them they spooned up the tea, then shared the bread and butter bite by bite. Daisy took the empty tray into the kitchen. When she came out again, the man had disappeared. The next day the man, an escapee from a mental institution, was found dead of exposure under a hedgerow some miles away. Daisy wept, and thus the incident of the preceding morning came out.

"But the man was insane—he was probably dangerous!" Her friends protested.

"He wasn't dangerous, he was just so terribly frightened. If only I hadn't let him get away!"

Daisy felt the same obligation to help, rather than blame, persons suffering from human frailties, provided they were not in the realm of morals. Another of the early succession of butlers took to drink. Daisy had acquired more confidence with her English servants, and this man had proved faithful and competent aside from the one defect. Instead of firing the butler, Daisy suggested to him that they make a pact. She would refrain from drinking anything but water for six months if he would do the same—not an easy bargain for her, since water was never served at English dinner parties. The man agreed, and they signed a paper to this effect. Both kept the contract, and by the end of the six months the man was cured.

So far as we are aware, the trip to Egypt in the late 1880's was the only extensive one that Daisy ever made with Willy Low. Billow's increasing absorption in sports took him to extremely remote countries, for types of hunting in which the ladies of that era did not take part. It was routine, in the circle Billow belonged to, to run over to Africa to hunt big game; to Albania to track goats in the wild Albanian mountains; to India for pigsticking or elephant shooting. In May of 1893, Nellie, Daisy and Mabel were all at Eleanor's at Hutton Park, with Willy Low expected back from Japan any day. What particular sport it was that called Billow to Japan we are not told, but he would hardly have gone there to study flower arrangements, and Daisy had not been invited to go along.

She must have reconsidered the decision she had expressed to

Nellie in 1889, that her place was at home, even during Billow's absences, and that flitting about only made her restless. Or perhaps this argument, too, was part of what appears to have been her plot to give young Arthur a delightful summer. In any event, in 1891, she went to Egypt under the chaperonage of one of the Mesdemoiselles Charbonnier who had been her preceptresses at school in New York, in a party which included several married couples.

In all these various ways, Daisy met her various problems. But it would appear that her family, too, moved quietly to her support. For understandable reasons, Daisy concealed from her father and mother those difficulties of her situation which struck at her heart. But Nellie would have read between the lines, and it must have been because of Billow's increasing tendency to wander far afield that after 1891, Mabel was allowed to spend the greater part of her time with Daisy, and that Arthur was permitted so many trips to England by his parents.

Daisy's relationship with Eleanor remained as warm and fond as ever, but Eleanor had many duties with her rapidly enlarging family, and in doing all a wife could do to help her husband build his career. She visited Daisy often, but with her children, and could not stay long. Bill, in the early 1890's, married beautiful Ellen Screven—called Ellie in the family—and settled down to practice law. He had a small son, named William Washington for his father, grandfather and great-grandfather, and always called simply B.

But Mabel and Arthur were footloose as yet, and Daisy could count on them always. The two youngest Gordons had come into prosperous and less troubled times than the older ones: they had had advantages denied their elders, though never grudged, for Mabel and Arthur, in spite of having their full quota of Kinzie-Gordon spirit, were notable for their sweet dispositions. Often, when differences arose among the more volatile members of the family, they were called upon to be peacemakers. Even Nellie once wrote in her diary, apropos of nothing in particular: "Dear Arthur! Since the day he was born he had never given me one moment's worry or trouble!" Arthur, who was twenty-one in 1893, soon ceased to be the "baby" brother to Daisy. He became her full confidant, she began turning to him for counsel, and developed for him much the same kind of doting love she gave her father. There can be no doubt that the frequent presence and support of this brother and sister, the admiring, uncritical love they gave her, were a strength to Daisy in sustaining the rôle she had set herself, of being a woman without a care in the world.

Very early in 1895, the new Earl and Countess of Warwick took up residence in the castle, an event of prime importance in Warwickshire, and one that was to introduce a red letter year in Daisy's life. There was a succession of festivities, the grandest being the *bal poudre*, or "fancy dress ball with powder," given by the Warwicks, and one of the notable parties of the time. All the county folk roundabout had house parties, the one at Wellesbourne including among others Sol Dungarvan, of the regular Wellesbourne standbys; Alwyne Greville, brother of the Earl of Warwick, and his wife; and George and Alice Keppel. George Keppel was a younger son of the Earl of Albemarle, but it was his wife, Alice, upon whom the eyes of the world were focused. She had captivated the Prince of Wales as had none of the many other ladies with whom his name was connected, and remained the favorite until his death as King Edward VII.

Since this is the only time the names of the Keppels appear in the Wellesbourne visitors' book, and in the letters available Daisy never mentioned Alice Keppel until King Edward VII died, we assume that it was as a favor to some distinguished individual that the Lows included the Keppels among their guests. There is no indication that they were particular friends of the Lows.

The Earl of Warwick considered that the *bal poudre* was the most brilliant function ever held at the castle within his recollection. Four hundred invitations were issued, and Lady Warwick had selected the reigns of Louis XV and Louis XVI for the masquerade, so that all should wear powder. Besides the elaborate costumes necessitated by this period, the ladies were required to have equally elaborate coiffures. The Earl mentions in his memoirs that every hairdresser in London had been called to build these towering structures for the ladies at the various house parties, as Willy Low learned to his dismay when he tried to get one for the ladies at his house. Billow thereupon brought a French hairdresser over from Paris.

The weather was terrible, with great banks of snow everywhere, and the Frenchman had a stormy passage across the Channel the night before the ball, catching the first train next morning for Warwickshire. "He had tried to conquer the *mal de mer* on shipboard and the cold in the train by a prolonged course of spirits, and he arrived at Wellesbourne totally unfit to undertake any work at all," says the Earl.

The gentlemen of the house party held a council of war, then met the situation by taking the Frenchman outdoors and rolling him in a snowbank until he was sufficiently sober to function. Mabel has added in the margin of Bill's copy of the Earl's memoirs, "I was the first woman to have my hair dressed and Alwyne Greville sat in my room to protect me while the Frenchman, steadying himself with one hand, worked with the other!" But the Earl of Warwick testified that not one head was awry when the Wellesbourne party arrived at the castle. *"Vive ?'Entente!"* he added.

Daisy had a notable personal triumph at the only slightly less brilliant Warwickshire Yeomanry dance. One of Billow's quirks was that he had never presented his wife to the Prince of Wales. Whether this was because he feared the Prince would not approve his choice, or because he feared that the amorously inclined First Gentleman of Europe might approve his choice too warmly, we do not know. Daisy later confessed that often she herself did not know the reasons for Billow's actions.

But on this night, the Prince saw Daisy dancing with Sir Francis Grenfell, and asked to have her presented. Frank Dugdale was the gentleman the Prince had delegated to lead Daisy to his presence. But Lord Warwick, seeing what was going on, came up and asked Daisy to let him present her to the Prince. Daisy had been well schooled before her presentation at Court, but she had no idea what one was supposed to do upon meeting the Prince of Wales in a less formal setting.

She wrote home, describing her big moment: "I felt like the little girl who, when reproved as to her manners, said to her mother, 'Please tell me beforehand, when I go to Heaven am I to shake hands with God or only bow to him?' Personally, I did both, and H. R. H. was very gracious. He said he had known Willy for years and didn't know *I* existed, that it was a great shame to hide me away, and so on. He sent for Willy and said next time he came to Newmarket I was to be taken there also. Then, to everybody's amazement he asked me to dance a valse. It is years since he danced a round dance, and I was the only woman in the room he danced with."

The Prince of Wales did not ask to have ladies presented to him unless they were attractive to look at, animated and diverting, so we may be sure that Daisy possessed these qualities in full measure. What pleased Daisy most about the incident, however, was that "Willy was *very* pleased!"

Billow, however, changed none of his ways. He still would not let Daisy go to Newmarket, he still left her behind when he went adventuring. In the spring he was "off on that blessed yacht," belonging to one of his men friends. Daisy could not even write to him, for he was either at sea or else shooting in Albania where there were no post towns. Daisy now took what was for her a revolutionary step. Though she had always shrunk from new social situations, feeling the need of support, she went to Egypt with only the much younger Mabel as a companion. On this trip, she demonstrated that she could strike out for herself and again had a personal triumph. The two attractive, spirited Gordon ladies made a great hit wherever they went. The British officers whom they met squired them everywhere and dined and feted them.

Among the new friends Daisy acquired were two brothers-in-law of Abby Lippitt Hunter, Daisy's great chum from Mesdemoiselles Charbonnier days, Captain George Hunter and Colonel Archibald Hunter. The latter was the Governor of the Sudan and "a big Mogul around here," responsible for protecting Egypt proper from the dervish fanatics who hovered just beyond its southern border. At Aswan, Daisy and Mabel dined every night with officers and were given a gala party by the officers' mess. The affair almost broke up when, as a special compliment to the guests of honor, the native band began to play "Marching Through Georgia." Daisy and Mabel got up and started to leave the room, chins high, eyes blazing with indignation. They consented to stay only if the band would play "Dixie" by way of reparation. Mabel played the tune on the piano, Daisy whistled it, until the band was able to produce a satisfactory rendition, and the evening ended happily.

Colonel Hunter took the ladies to his headquarters at Wadi

Halfa, where they met more officers. There being no women at this remote, dangerous post, the two were in great demand at the impromptu dance which was promptly put on. A breakfast was arranged for them at Sarras, the farthest outpost of the Anglo-Egyptian army, but they had to return to Wadi Halfa hastily and breakfastless when word came that dervishes were trying to cut the railroad. They had the thrill of going over the First Cataract at Low Nile, in the first boat ever to attempt this feat. Foreseeing war with the dervishes, Colonel Hunter had wished to find out if it could be done, and yielded to the pleas of Daisy and Mabel that they be allowed to go too.

Not only did Daisy prove that she could make her way socially anywhere. The Egyptian trip was the beginning of Daisy's special friendships with high-ranking British military men. Two of the officers she met in Egypt were to become her suitors after she was widowed. She was brought into touch with a side of the English life and character very different from that of Willy's circle; and through these friendships, into intimate touch with English history as it was made.

This was an experience in which her family shared. That summer Colonel Archibald Hunter visited Wellesbourne at the same time as Willie, Nellie and Arthur. Willie and the English soldier took an immediate liking to each other, Colonel Hunter was greatly impressed by Arthur and made him a kind of protégé. Nellie had the sober, responsible Englishman roaring with laughter at her stories and witticisms.

It was during this summer that Nellie came into her own in the English life. On her 1891 visit, she had evidently determined not to be impressed by any aspect of Daisy's exalted position, in spite of the fact that Billow's friends had accepted Willie and Nellie enthusiastically and called them "Puppa" and "Mumma" just as Billow did. Her only comment in her diary about it was that Wellesbourne was "very nice." On her 1893 visit, after a continuous round of luncheons, teas, dinners, tennis parties and cricket matches she had written in her diary "this seems to me a very unsatisfactory mode of life. It is nothing but a rush after amusement and you don't get a great deal of that out of it either."

However, it may well have been her association with Daisy's titled circle that stirred Nellie's interest in her own ancestry.

Nellie had been a complete Gordon since her mother's death, identifying herself wholly with her husband, the family, and Savannah affairs. Perhaps she was reminded now that through her New England mother, she could match pedigrees with practically anyone. In 1893, she started the Georgia chapter of the Society of Colonial Dames of America very soon after the national organization came into being, in sharp contradiction to her hitherto lifelong avoidance of any organization except her church. She instituted the marking of historical spots in Georgia, and was responsible for erecting the statue to James Oglethorpe and the monument to Tomo-Chi-Chi, the Indian chief who had been the great friend of Oglethorpe and the first colonists. Both may be seen in Savannah today.

In 1893, also, Chicago had recalled to her that she had reason to be proud of her Kinzie blood as well as of the Wolcott and Drake. She was invited, as the oldest living Kinzie, to be Chicago's honored guest at the Columbian Exposition. The Columbian bell was rung in her honor, and she was given a dinner by the Chicago Historical Society. From that time on Nellie was a professional Chicagoan, and discovered quickly that her stories about the Kinzies and early Chicago were one of the best conversational gambits she had. Colonel Archibald Hunter entreated Nellie to write down all her stories, experiences and jokes, putting in his order on the spot for a dozen copies as soon as the book came out.

On this visit, Nellie entered into the English social life with a zest equaling Daisy's own and in the course of the years many of Daisy's British friends, friends of Willie and Nellie too, visited the Gordons in Savannah. She also introduced an English friendship that proved a delight to all of them, and particularly to Daisy. The granddaughter of Carrie Balestier, who had been Nellie's favorite among her foster sisters, had married a writer who had attained some fame, and who lived at Rottingham, four miles from Brighton. Nellie wrote to Carrie Kipling and she came to lunch. All the Gordons were charmed with Mrs. Kipling, finding her both handsome and clever. Nellie noted in her diary: "Mr. Kipling came to call on Willie today and made himself most agreeable. I have promised Mr. K. some lily bulbs from my Savannah garden and Carrie some information about her ancestors, especially the Drake line, which she wants on account of her children." The Drake line was the one starred with kings and queens.

The Kiplings soon ranked among Daisy's closest friends. Frequent visits were exchanged between Wellesbourne and Batemans, as the Kipling estate was called. The handsome Carrie was fond of her new-found American kin, and Daisy and Rud, as they came to call him, had a host of things in common. He shared her tenderness for children and animals; and when they were together, their badinage kept the rest of the company convulsed with laughter. Carrie maintained an affectionate correspondence with Nellie, and Kipling used Nellie as a character in several stories.

When the war with the dervishes that Colonel Hunter had foreseen broke out in 1896, the Gordons in Savannah followed its course with as deep interest as anyone in England. Throughout the campaign Archibald Hunter wrote long detailed letters to both Daisy and Arthur, describing the battles and skirmishes. Willy Low, who had been inclined to be jealous of this friendship of Daisy's, opened one of Hunter's letters by mistake and was so intrigued by Hunter's account of the most recent battle that he carried it about with him and read it to his friends.

All the officers Daisy had met in Egypt, as well as Jack Maxwell and Sir Francis Grenfell, were involved in the war and a number won great distinction. Archibald Hunter's aide, Neville Smyth, was awarded the Victoria Cross for saving a group of correspondents from a dervish who had played dead, then had risen suddenly from a heap of the slain and run amok. Hunter himself emerged from the campaign as General Sir Archibald Hunter—Daisy wreathed his initials in laurel in the Wellesbourne visitors' book as her own tribute. "The whole world is at his feet," she wrote to Arthur.

Daisy's already strong bent for hero worship and admiration for things military, inculcated in her in early childhood, was greatly accentuated. Thus when, at the end of the Egyptian war, Daisy's special heroes were made the subject of attack by "a youth named Winston," at a house party at Warwick Castle, the little American flew to their defense and routed the enemy as successfully as the Anglo-Egyptian army under Kitchener had routed the dervishes. Young Winston, she explained in an indignant letter to Papa, was the son of her friend Lady Randolph

Churchill and had covered the war as a correspondent. He had started the Warwick Castle affray by announcing that he had just written a book about the campaign in which he had made the leader of the dervishes the hero, Lord Kitchener the villain. Major Haig, who was also present—he was to become Marshal Haig in World War I—told Daisy that young Churchill had been very disliked in the Sudan, "though his book is clever and he is quite a genius in his line and only twenty-five years old." Daisy took Churchill's remarks jokingly until he disparaged Neville Smyth's feat, claiming it was an absurd farce to award the Victoria Cross for killing only one man. That made Daisy furious and the sparring match became a free fight. Churchill turned his guns next on Jack Maxwell, though Lord Warwick had told him Maxwell was a good friend of Daisy's. Daisy looked the young man up and down with unutterable scorn and said, "I can see that Jack must have snubbed you!" This made young Winston so furious in his turn that he shut up. It is probably one of the few times in Winston Churchill's life that he retired from an argument in disorder. Lord and Lady Warwick enjoyed the encounter thoroughly and had kept egging Daisy on. Afterwards Lady Warwick said to Daisy, "You mustn't mind Winston. You see, he has English cheek and American cheek combined!"

When Billow's lease expired on Lude, the hunting lodge at Blair Atholl, he rented Mealmore in Invernesshire, Scotland. This was very wild, rough country and the hunting was superb. Sir Charles Mordaunt, a frequent Wellesbourne guest, also had a notable shoot at Inverness. Cawdor Castle was not far away, and Moy, the near-by castle of The McIntosh, was another to delight Daisy's romantic heart. In front of Moy's main door stood the anvil, dear to Scotchmen, which had helped save Bonnie Prince Charlie when he took refuge with The McIntosh. Word of his hiding place leaked out and the Earl of Lowther, with a thousand men, marched to attack Moy and capture the Prince. A scullery maid overheard the plan and ran all the way to Moy to give warning. There were only five men at Moy, one of them a smith. But the five deployed themselves in strategic spots, and when the Earl of Lowther's force drew near, shouted the war cries of the various clans while the smith beat frantically on his anvil. Thinking they were surrounded by six or more clans, the Earl of Lowther and his men turned back. This was another story Daisy loved to tell the Girl Scouts, in later years.

The McIntoshes were already good friends—the name of the daughter, Mamie, had appeared in the Wellesbourne visitors' book a number of times—and Daisy became an ardent devotee of Bonnie Prince Charlie. She wrote her family how Mamie McIntosh had recently put the seal on this incident after centuries had elapsed, to the delight of Invernesshire. The Edwardian Earl of Lowther had come to the castle. Inscribing his name in the visitors' book, he remarked that he believed he was the first of his line to be a guest of The McIntosh.

"That is true," said Mamie demurely. "One of your ancestors started for Moy, but he never got here!" Daisy claimed that retort was worthy of Nellie herself.

"Darlings, I can't wait for you to come to Mealmore," she wrote her parents. "You will love every inch of it and of Moy. The McIntosh sends you a special invitation, Papa, even though you are a Gordon!"

Willie and Nellie were to have come the summer of 1898, but they didn't get there. "Circumstances beyond his control" prevented Willie. Though in 1898 Willie Gordon was sixty-four, he was off to the wars again. And this time Nellie went right along with him, and so, eventually, did Bill, Arthur and Daisy!

CHAPTER XIV

———————— ☆ ————————

TO WAR, *EN FAMILLE*

IN THE SPRING of 1898, war clouds arose between the United States and Spain. Daisy was furious when some British officers joked about the conflict that seemed impending. Spain might not present much of a military threat to the United States, but if war came, her father and brothers might be involved. Rowland Leigh, Mabel's fiancé, was the only one in England who understood her anxiety, she wrote. It had been a relief to find, when she visited Savannah, that the men of her family were against going to war with Spain. But by June of that year, she was frantic.

"The whole family seems demented!" she wrote Arthur vehemently. "When I came back to England last time, I left you all with strong principles against a war over Cuba, and now you are *all* bitten with the war craze and *Mabel* actually writes, 'It is all right. Both boys will now go to war, as fresh volunteers are called for.' I can't see why it is all right. I think it is all *wrong*. I am miserable about it! I shall certainly come back to America if you continue to make me anxious. *There* is a threat!"

On March 21, the board of inquiry which had investigated the sinking of the battleship *Maine* in the harbor at Havanna, with the loss of 266 American lives, had made its report: the ship had been blown up by deliberate intent. President McKinley demanded that Spain withdraw its forces from Cuba by noon of April twenty-third. Before this message could be delivered to the Spanish government, the American Ambassador in Madrid was handed his passport. Spain was going to fight. And the moment this fact became apparent, Willie Gordon, along with his former Civil War commander, Joseph Wheeler, offered his services to the Federal government. This simple act was to set in motion a train of unexpected events, political, historical and personal, and in the end was to involve all the Gordon family but Mabel, who had other things on her mind at the moment.

The Savannah papers made special note of the fact that W. W. Gordon and Joseph Wheeler had responded immediately, for their action had more than ordinary significance. The South, though conquered, had never become reconciled. And least reconciled of all were the citizens of Georgia. Too many cellar holes still gaped, too many chimneys stood stark and alone where there had been stately mansions, to let Georgia forget Sherman's march to the sea. Joseph Wheeler and W. W. Gordon were prominent Georgians and highly respected. No one had fought harder for the Southern cause than they had. Where these men led, others would follow.

The Federal government in Washington recognized an opportunity to heal old wounds. President McKinley immediately made Wheeler, who had been a major general in the Confederate Army, a major general of volunteers, along with Fitzhugh Lee. A brigadier generalship was also offered to Georgia. It was generally assumed that this would go to W. W. Gordon, though he had been only a captain in the Civil War.

According to Nellie's Spanish-American War diary, "the politicians at Atlanta" took a hand in the game. The appointment was a political plum, they wanted one of the party faithful to receive it. Willie's Confederate comrades then went to work with might and main to get it for Willie. Wayne Parker pulled all the strings he could as a member of Congress, Eleanor assisting in the ways known to adroit Washington hostesses.

Willie alone did nothing to advance his candidacy. The whole time, Nellie says, he "bucked like a steer" at the very idea that any exertion should be made in his behalf. "Who was *he* to have such an honor, what had *he* ever done, and all such nonsense, was all you could get out of *him!*"

The Georgia delegation in Congress was the focal point, for

the man they recommended would presumably get the appointment. Willie's advocates agreed to a caucus of the Georgia delegation, which proved to be a tactical error, for the man put up
by the "Atlanta politicians" got the nod. It appeared to be
defeat. Eleanor was entertaining at a dinner party when she
received the word. She burst into tears and had to leave the
table. But so many protests came from Georgia that the man
approved by the state delegation was dropped. When the Secretary of War sent to President McKinley the commission for the
brigadier general from Georgia, it carried the name of Governor
Atkinson.

President McKinley, however, had evidently been doing some
investigating. He ran his pen through the name of Governor
Atkinson. He wrote in, instead, the name of W. W. Gordon.

Willie was informed by telegraph on May twenty-seventh that
he was the brigadier general chosen from Georgia. Says Nellie,
"Then came wild whoops and laughter and dancing around
the room till the telegraph messenger thought he had got into
a lunatic asylum." And after this came telegrams and letters of
congratulations by the hundreds. Once again, Daisy was a hold-
out from her family's ardor for self-immolation. She wrote
darkly to Mabel: "Mama has sent me a letter of great happiness
about Papa's being made a general, but if he is given a post of
great danger, she will change her tune!"

Nellie thought Willie looked very handsome in his new blue
uniform. In her diary, he becomes "my General," and even in
letters to the children, she refers to him proudly as "the General." She followed him to Miami, this time with his full approval, when he went there to take over his command, the 2nd
Brigade, 1st Division, 7th Army Corps. Willie had expected
to have Bill and Arthur on his staff, and had taken them with
him to Miami. It was a disappointment to all three when
Willie learned that he would have no voice in choosing his
aides. Moreover, Bill and Arthur would have to get commissions before they could be considered for staff duty. They went
off to Washington to hang about in the anterooms of officials
in the War Department. Nellie put her agile brain to work
to think what she could do.

She had had her lesson, in the Civil War, about using petti-
coat influence openly in her husband's military affairs. The

Gordon men, with their Georgia pride, wanted to earn such honors as came their way. So she resorted to strategy. General Lloyd Wheaton had been captivated by Nellie's conversational pyrotechnics, and had made a practice of seeking her out at dinners and other social affairs. One evening he mentioned that he had been impressed by her son Bill. That gave Nellie her opening. She expatiated upon Bill's virtues, and those of her other son, Arthur. She told the General how anxious they were to serve too, and how pleased Willie would be to have his two sons with him. In no time at all, General Wheaton was directing Nellie in a letter campaign to the War Department on behalf of her sons, telling her whom to write to and just what to say. He probably exerted some personal influence, as well. Soon Bill and Arthur were telegraphing triumphantly that they had their commissions—Bill was made a captain and later a major—and were being assigned to their father's staff. None of the Gordon men ever knew of the part Nellie had played.

And Willie, delighted as he was to have his two sons by his side, was careful to show no favoritism. Bill's wife, Ellie, had come to Miami. Soon after her arrival there Willie rode horseback, in a driving rain, to the house where she was staying; came in, sat down by the fire, and chatted comfortably with Ellie for a while. Presently he remarked, "My aide is sitting out there on his horse in the rain. May he come in for a cup of coffee?" The aide was Bill, and it was when he came in, dripping, that Ellie first learned her husband was on his father's staff.

Nellie had not been in Miami very long before she became exercised about the living conditions of the troops concentrated there. The soil at the camp site was not deep enough to hold the tent pins down. A sample of the water, sent to New Orleans for analysis, revealed that it was full of typhoid germs "and every other horror." Nellie suspected that locating the camp in so unsuitable a spot had been a "job" to benefit Mr. Flagler, the Florida tycoon. Willie had tried to get distilled water for the men of his brigade, but the machinery at the factory was out of order. He had issued orders then that the men should boil their water, but it was hard to make them do so. The men were going down with typhoid in droves. In spite of all Willie could do, deaths were increasing, the men were demoralized and the officers discouraged. In Willie's 2nd Texas alone, there were four hundred sick men.

Nellie visited the army hospital and found it a "positive disgrace. The sick men were housed in tents, which were set up, in spite of warnings from the residents, in a location most unsanitary and apt to be overflowed when a heavy rain set in. They did not have sheets or pillows, in many instances. There were no mosquito nettings. I saw desperately ill and dying men lying with flies crawling into their mouths and mosquitoes buzzing over them! The attendants were inefficient. Men were discharged from the hospital and sent back to their commands before they were able to resume their duties, and they had relapses. Hell fire is too good for the people who have pulled strings to locate an army camp in such a damnable hole for their own profit!" she blazed.

Nellie was thoroughly aroused, and it was as though a new species of hurricane had hit the Florida coast. Various members of the hospital personnel began to wish they had never been born. But Nellie did not stop with this. She decided that what was needed was a convalescent hospital, where the men dismissed from the army hospital, but not yet fit for duty, could recover completely. Nellie took it upon her herself to provide one.

She went to see Mr. Flagler. What she said to him she does not disclose, but she emerged from the interview with the promise of a huge, barnlike building. It had no floor, but Mr. Flagler's manager would see that one was put in. Nellie went down and stood over the workmen, the floor was finished in a day and a half. Willie contributed one hundred cots, Daisy sent mosquito nets and fans. The Georgia Colonial Dames contributed money, with which Nellie bought a big refrigerator and other necessities.

Then Nellie went to the ice plant run by the army, to engage fifty pounds of ice a day. She was told she could not have it, because there was not enough to supply the officers and the hotel. Nellie threw a tantrum. What business, she demanded, had the officers or hotel guests to get any ice at all when it was needed for the sick! She ended her tirade with a dire threat. "I will have the ice, and if you don't send me fifty pounds every day, I will come down here and take it by force!"

The thought of this tiny lady wresting ice from the United States army by force had its humorous side, but it must have been terrifying too. When Nellie Gordon was on the warpath, it would have required more courage to oppose her than to face Spanish bullets. Laughing, the manager gave in. "If you want the ice as badly as all that, I'll send you fifty pounds every day." And the ice was delivered faithfully.

This was Nellie's hospital, the patients in it were "my men." She was amused to receive a visit from "some fool woman" who evidently had taken Nellie to be a kindred soul. "She talked to me about the Red Cross and the W.C.T.U. She was much surprised to learn that I knew nothing about either one."

As soon as she could after she learned of her mother's enterprise, Daisy came over to America to help, but there was a matter she had to attend to first. At about the time the Battle of Santiago was raging, Nellie complacently noted in her diary that her daughter had entertained H.R.H., the Prince of Wales, at Wellesbourne at luncheon. "Lady Randolph Churchill, the young Duchess of Marlborough and Lord and Lady Warwick were of the party. The Prince made himself very agreeable and everything seems to have gone off very well."

Calmly as Nellie took this honor accorded her daughter, for Daisy it had been the supreme test of her art and skill as a hostess. The Prince was a stickler for carrying out every item of royal etiquette. If Daisy fell short in any detail, Billow would be deeply humiliated. A list of the Lows' most select and amusing friends must be made up, submitted to His Royal Highness and approved by him. The menu must be truly fit for a king, the service must be without flaw. Rowland Leigh helped her with the protocol, Daisy thought every conceivable point had been covered. The day of the luncheon, Lady Warwick arrived early, with a roll of carpet under her arm. "Whatever is that for?" asked Daisy.

"I thought you might not know that one must always put down a red carpet for royalty to step down on from the carriage and walk on into the house." This was the one detail that had been overlooked. Thanks to Lady Warwick's thoughtfulness, Daisy was saved, the affair was completely successful. Again, Billow was pleased.

Immediately after this event, Daisy sailed for America and the deep South, in the worst of the summer heat. She arrived just in time to help Nellie with the first consignment of eighty men, the lowest number the hospital ever had. Often it was filled to its capacity of one hundred. The staff was limited to a steward and two orderlies. The "convalescents" had typhoid, dysentery, measles and some were very sick, especially those with typhoid. There were always at least twenty who could take no solid food, and finding proper sustenance for the "liquid" squad was a great problem.

Daisy spent her first days in Florida making beef tea, jellies, oyster broth and heating up canned soups for the liquid squad, on a kerosene stove in the bathroom of Nellie's room at the hotel, there being no kitchen facilities as yet in the convalescent hospital. As she literally stewed over the stove in the hot little room in the Miami midsummer, it must have been hard for her to realize that so short a time before she had been stewing figuratively over such things as protocol and red carpets for the feet of royalty. "Daisy is working like a little brick," Nellie wrote in her diary. "I only hope she doesn't make herself ill."

Nellie herself made quantities of "koomis," which from the recipe she gives appears to have been similar to yoghurt. The two ladies bought up all the arrowroot and tapioca the town had. Then they were at their wit's end. On one of her marketing errands, Daisy's eye fell on a shelf full of Mellin's Food. She bought a big supply, and Nellie instructed the steward just how to prepare it on the new stove that had now been installed in the hospital. Then she went to summon her liquid squad to dinner.

Not one of them could be found! Their mysterious disappearance was soon explained. A Mellin's Food wrapper had been left on a table, the men had seen it. They stated with male dignity that they were neither babies nor nursing mothers and that they would starve rather than eat that kind of food. There flashed into Nellie's mind the incident at Fort Dearborn, so many years back, which Juliette Kinzie had described in *Wau-Bun*—the milk punch a farmer had supplied to the soldiers to their enthusiastic approval. Nellie summoned the steward. In the presence of the insurgents, she asked him, sternly,

"Did you remember to put the brandy into the punch I had

you make for the men?" Naturally he had not, this being the first he had heard about it.

"Bring me the brandy bottle," she ordered. Nellie made a great show of stirring the liquor into the Mellin's Food mixture, "with the result that the scrimshankers came struggling in and took their new food from that time on with great satisfaction." Milk punches à la Fort Dearborn thereafter became the great standby of the Gordon ladies, and they would go down a very sick man when he refused all other sustenance.

Each morning, after the routine duties were completed, Daisy would scour the surrounding countryside for butter, eggs and milk. One day there had been an unusual run on milk punches. When evening came, their milk supply was exhausted. Daisy found to her great distress that there was none to be had in the town and there were several typhoid patients who required milk throughout the night. At 9 P.M., she started out, accompanied by an orderly, to find milk. She remembered that she had seen cows in the yard of a woman up the street, and went there. The woman, however, had sold the last drop of milk to some soldiers.

"What time were the cows milked last?" Daisy asked her.

"At four o'clock."

"Then there should be enough milk now to see our very sick men through the night."

"Maybe," the woman allowed, "but my hired man has gone home—he does the milking."

"I'll milk the cows," Daisy said.

Daisy had done some milking at Etowah Cliffs when she was a girl, but it had been many years since she had had any practice in this rather difficult art. Nevertheless she persevered, while the orderly held the lantern, and carried a full pail of milk back to the hospital.

It is safe to assume that no hospital before or since was ever run quite like this one. One can imagine Nellie darting about, doing the work of at least three; responding with devastating ripostes to the patients' affectionate teasing; coaxing or scolding as each individual case required; Daisy pouring out all the tenderness of her sympathetic heart, smoothing bedclothes, rubbing backs, cheering up the discouraged.

Even Nellie could not control the men who were nearly

well. In spite of her entreaties and chidings, they would slip off and wander about the streets before she thought they should, and she had no real authority over them. At length Nellie took away all their clothes and left them nothing but pajamas. "That will put a stop to their wanderings," she wrote in her diary.

But it didn't, quite. Willie had supplied instruments to the musicians in his brigade, and they gave a concert which all the officers in camp attended. Suddenly there was a commotion. In filed a group of poker-faced men from Nellie's convalescent hospital, garbed in pajamas, with their military leggings strapped on over the pajama legs! Nellie says General Wheaton went into such convulsions of laughter that he nearly fell off his horse.

In August, Willie was ordered to Jacksonville. Nellie then turned over her convalescent ward to Dr. Caleron, who had supplied the medical supervision and in whom she had confidence. He made it a typhoid ward, which Nellie considered a good move. Colonel Maus, head of the medical department, visited Nellie's convalescent hospital when he came on a tour of inspection with General Fitzhugh Lee, and was so impressed that he asked his wife to start a similar one at Jacksonville. Mrs. Maus took a large, empty hotel at Pablo Beach, put in beds and other equipment, and Daisy went to Pablo Beach and ran the hospital for Mrs. Maus until a suitable matron could be found to take charge of it.

Nellie had no part in this enterprise, for Willie had scarcely arrived at Jacksonville before his orders were changed. President McKinley appointed him a member of the three-man commission to arrange the peace terms with Puerto Rico (then spelled Porto Rico), the other members being Admiral Schley and General John R. Brooke. It was a great honor, and Nellie nearly burst with pride. She wrote in her diary, "The papers are full of complimentary notices of my General all over the country. Bless him! At last it has come, the recognition he deserves! And in such complimentary form! We hear he was the President's special selection."

The problem was what this new development would do to Mabel's plans. Papa having at last consented to her marriage to Rowland Leigh, Mabel had been trying frantically to find a wedding date that would permit her warlike family to be present. Now Nellie had to wire her that once more the day must be changed. Nellie wrote in her diary, "Mabel, poor child, is sick and nervous and I am very anxious about her. I shall join her, and if she wants me, I will stay with her instead of going to Porto Rico. . . . I do hope it can be arranged to have her wedding before her father leaves."

And so Nellie started for Savannah, Willie seeing her on to the train at Fernandina. Then occurred the incident which made Nellie Gordon a nationwide heroine.

Willie had only just left her, when a group of desperately sick soldiers was hurried into the sleeping car. Some were assisted in by one or two fellow soldiers, others were carried in, still others were thrust through the windows. They lay gasping and nearly fainting on the seats or on the floor in the aisle where the sickest had been laid.

The two porters began hurriedly to make up the berths. Nellie called for a pillow for one poor chap whom she had had put on the seat with her, and told the porters to give pillows to the other sick men, while she fanned first one, then another and got them ice water. "Just as one of the men had been lifted from the floor onto a berth, three soldiers brought in a boy who I could see at a glance was death struck. His eyes were set and staring, he was delirious, waving his arms wildly, and was in a cold sweat. His brother, quite a young fellow, was with him and evidently was greatly distressed." The brother of the dying boy was the only well man in the group aside from their captain, Elias Salisbury. They were being sent back to their home in Goshen, Indiana. Captain Salisbury was not a doctor, and no doctor had been provided, no nurses, no medicines. And there was no time to get any, for as soon as the last sick man had been incontinently hustled aboard, the train started.

Nellie took command. She turned her attention first to the dying man, Private Charles Perry, sending to the rear car for a doctor she was told was aboard. She had the porters bring brandy and ice water and succeeded in getting Private Perry to swallow some. She and the brother, Corporal Perry, rubbed the dying man's feet with brandy and fanned him. The doctor said at once that Private Perry could only live a short time.

The brother was frantic. "Oh, can't we keep him alive to see Mother?" he begged. "It will kill her if Charlie dies!"

Then he turned to Nellie. "If he must die, won't you pray for him?" And Nellie prayed, then sat beside the dying boy, wiping the sweat from his face and pushing the damp hair back from his forehead, as she knew his mother would have done. The doctor touched her shoulder. "Please don't lean over him so closely," he cautioned. "He has typhoid, and you shouldn't let his breath strike your face."

Nellie snapped, "I have slept in the same bed with yellow fever, I am not afraid of typhoid!" Six hours after they left Fernandina, Private Perry died. As he lay *in extremis,* another man began to hemorrhage, and still another to rave with delirium. As soon as Nellie had gently folded the dead boy's hands on his breast and closed his eyes, she applied herself to those in greatest need of attention. She asked about food, and was horrified to learn that no provision had been made for feeding the invalids on their three-day journey to Goshen.

Nellie called the porter. "Bring me all the milk you have," she ordered.

"I am not allowed to sell more than one glass of milk at a time," he told her.

"I will take six glasses right now and you just go and bring them as fast as you can." The six glasses of milk were promptly forthcoming. Nellie laced the milk liberally with brandy, handed the glasses around, and instructed Captain Salisbury to feed the men on milk punch, milk punch, milk punch until they got home, "And if anybody says you can't have the milk, shoot him!"

The crowning horror was that the authorities who had loaded an obviously dying man aboard the train had given Captain Salisbury no instructions as to what to do with the corpse. They were in the deep South, and it was August!

This was a situation beyond Nellie's choicest expletives, and she reacted to it with the warm thoughtfulness and nobility she could display when the cause was worthy. She sent telegrams to Savannah—to Agnes, her housekeeper, to prepare a bedroom for Corporal Perry; to Mr. Dixon, the undertaker, and to Colonel Maxwell, of the Florida and Peninsula Railroad, to meet the train. Both men were at the station when the train pulled in. Nellie gave Colonel Maxwell a review of conditions in the Pullman car of sick men. He held the train while food was put aboard for the journey on to Goshen, told the train crew to do everything they could to help Captain Salisbury. Mr. Dixon took charge of Private Perry's body, while Nellie got the brother into her carriage, took him to the Gordon house, made him eat supper, take a warm bath and go to bed. While he slept, Mr. Dixon embalmed Private Perry's body and placed it in the handsome coffin it had been Nellie's wish to provide. All next day the body of Private Charles Perry lay in state in the front drawing room of the Gordon house, a laurel wreath on the coffin, his brother keeping watch beside it. Savannah people filed past, honoring the stranger who had volunteered to fight for his country, and had died so needlessly and so far from home. Nellie's minister came and said a prayer. At midnight, Nellie saw the "poor Corporal" off on the train for Goshen with his brother's remains, Colonel Maxwell having made the necessary arrangements.

Next morning, the editor of one of the Savannah papers phoned Nellie. A reporter had happened to be at the station when the train came in. From the train crew and the Goshen men who were able to talk, he had received an account of the deplorable situation, and of the "fiery little angel of mercy," as the men described Nellie, who had come to their assistance. The story had gone out sizzling over the wires, and the editor wanted Nellie to know that it had created immense excitement. The Atlanta paper was out with big headlines, the New York *Sun* had an indignant article, papers as far away as the West Coast had telegraphed the Savannah editors to rush them pictures of Nellie. A very short time before, General Gordon had been in all the papers through his appointment as peace commissioner. What his wife did was news, and her selfless devotion to the sick boys from Goshen got bigger headlines in many places than the Peace Commission had.

The biggest headlines were in Chicago, which was as proud of its Nellie Kinzie Gordon as Nellie was of her general. The papers for August 24 carried long dispatches from Savannah, recounting every detail of the tragic journey, hailing Nellie as "the good angel of the American soldier," in the Kinzie tradition of courage and service, and recalling the exploits of her parents and grandparents.

An enterprising reporter had traced down Nellie's brother Arthur, who was employed in one of the Chicago municipal departments. Arthur Kinzie was pleased, though not surprised, to hear what his sister had done. "I can just see her," he is quoted as saying, "taking command of the railroad car, turning the other passengers out of the berths and putting the sick soldiers in. It is exactly like her."

Nellie, when she had time to set down the incident in her diary, did not tell it quite that way. She remarked that as soon as the other passengers realized the dreadful condition of the sick men, they quietly evaporated. But if they had not, she would certainly have requisitioned their berths.

It was stated that had it not been for Nellie's milk punches and other ministrations, more of the men would have died en route. There was nothing in Goshen, Indiana, that Nellie couldn't have had. Thanks to the newspaper stories, she was receiving grateful telegrams from Goshen before the sick men got home. The minister of the First Goshen Presbyterian Church wrote her: "They are 'our' boys, and inasmuch as you have done it unto them, you have done it unto us. You are praised by all the good people, who will ever hold you in kindest remembrance."

There were beautiful and touching letters from the Perrys, and from the families of the other men, which moved Nellie deeply. "I shall value them and keep them as long as I live," she wrote in her diary.

And oh, the fuss and fanfare when Willie got to Savannah, with his 2nd Louisiana, 2nd Texas and 2nd Alabama regiments! Officers and men marched to the Gordon house with a band, to serenade Nellie. Her former convalescents begged her to let them know if she ever needed an eye or an arm or a leg, or their collective lives for that matter.

When Willie took leave of his brigade, his staff gave him a badge in the form of a jewel-studded United States flag with an accompanying note: "It is your flag, and we hope you will wear this on your loyal breast, over the heart of a true soldier." The entire brigade presented him with a marvelous gold watch, which had four different dials, showed the changes of the moon, struck the quarter hours and, as Willie said, "struck for cocktails every half hour." But Willie felt badly about the watch. When he went off to war, he had left behind the one hundred guinea gold watch he had bought at Dent's in London, taking with him a big, battered silver "turnip." It grieved him that the men had concluded it was the only watch he had, and chipped in from their meager pay to buy him this elegant one.

Mabel decided to be married on October 30, after her father's return from Puerto Rico. That freed Nellie to go to Puerto Rico too, and she set out for Washington ahead of Willie, for she had some business there. When she had returned from putting Corporal Perry and his brother's body aboard the midnight train for Goshen, she had not gone to bed until she had written a blistering letter to Colonel Studebaker, commanding officer of the 15th Regiment, Indiana Volunteers, to which the Goshen boys belonged, describing the episode, expressing her opinion of the surgeon who had permitted men in their condition to leave camp without either a doctor or a nurse, and promising that "I will make it my duty to report the Major in charge of the medical service at your camp to Surgeon General Sternberg at Washington and to give this outrage such publicity as will in some measure punish those responsible for it."

The papers had already attended to the publicity angle. Furthermore, the whole disgraceful disregard of the health and lives of American soldiers in the camps had been brought to public attention through the dramatic incident of the Goshen boys. Reporters continued to harry the War Department and the Surgeon General until the last volunteers had returned home. Perhaps it is owing to Nellie Gordon, in some degree, that in every war since the Spanish-American, our service men have had the best medical attention our government could provide, in this country and abroad.

To Nellie, the Surgeon General offered abject apologies, explanations, and assurances that the bad conditions were being righted. She felt it was a good time to get in a stroke for the convalescents in the hospital Daisy was conducting at Pablo Beach. It would help their morale, she suggested, if they were given a furlough home before having to report for active duty again. The Surgeon General said he had issued such an order some time back.

"A statement did come from you," Nellie told him, "but it was worded so vaguely no one could be sure just what it meant. It hasn't been acted on."

Sweat broke out on the Surgeon General's forehead. "I'll issue another one immediately," he said. Then he struck the desk with his hand. "By George, I'll make it a telegram!"

"That's very good of you, General," murmured Nellie sweetly. "I am sure the men will appreciate it. I'll get off a telegram myself to Pablo Beach to tell them yours is coming!"

There is one episode of the peace negotiations—not recorded by Nellie, but a family legend—that is worth repeating. The grandees who represented Spain were violently opposed to ceding Cuba and Puerto Rico to the United States, as was demanded. They were getting nowhere. Finally the little General from Georgia arose. "Gentlemen," he said to the Spaniards, "I can understand your feeling, and I sympathize. I was on the losing side of the War between the States. I, too, had to give up things most dear to me, because I was part of a beaten army. I, too, have known the shame and heartache of defeat, but defeat is not dishonorable when one has fought bravely. I implore you to accept our terms, and as I had to do, make the best of your situation." When the interpreter repeated Willie's statement, the grandees looked at each other in amazement. They talked excitely in Spanish among themselves. Then they announced that they would accept the terms.

The commission adjourned October 12. Across the street from her hotel, Nellie could hear a Puerto Rican band practicing "The Star-Spangled Banner" and "Yankee Doodle." When the day came for the ceremonial raising of the United States flag, Nellie watched from a balcony of the throne room of the Catalina Palace, Willie stood with the other notables and their staffs at the right of the big entrance. Just at noon a cannon was fired, the first of a salute of twenty-one, and the Stars and Stripes were run up. Every hat came off, the troops saluted, the band played "The Star-Spangled Banner." At the exact moment the American flag was raised above the Catalina Palace, it went up also over Morro Castle and San Cristobal. Spain was uprooted at last from the West Indies.

Willie and Nellie had planned to start for home as soon as the ceremonies were over, and Willie could have returned with

Admiral Schley, but Nellie couldn't, as no women were allowed on army transports. It appeared that Nellie could not sail at all, since no ships but transports were available. Willie would not leave without Nellie. And there was Mabel waiting in Savannah, and the wedding date drawing near! Nellie wrote in her diary that she cried nearly all night for two nights, but mostly she cussed.

Finally an appeal was sent to President McKinley, and he ordered a special dispensation for Nellie. She and Willie and Bill, who had come as his father's aide, embarked on the twenty-second of October on a transport carrying the 6th Massachusetts back to Boston, the three Gordons occupying the captain's cabin. They would have been comfortable, Nellie remarked, but for the croton bugs and roaches that ran over them during the night. She had put such a strain on her vocabulary in dealing with the United States army that she let the navy off lightly.

The honors for Willie went on and on. When they reached Boston, Governor Wolcott of Massachusetts came out to meet the transport.

Nellie found Willie hiding away in the cabin. "Why, Willie, what are you doing here? The Governor has come aboard. You must come and be introduced to him."

Willie wouldn't budge. "Colonel Rice of the 6th Massachusetts deserves the honors. According to military procedure, I would put him in second place if I were present. I don't want to do that."

But Willie's absence was soon discovered, he was dragged out of his hiding place and to the front of the regiment, where he was introduced to Governor Wolcott. Special deference was paid him, despite his efforts to divert attention to Colonel Rice.

Then Nellie feared that everything was going to be ruined. As the notables embarked in launches to go ashore, the 6th Massachusetts band struck up "Marching Through Georgia!" Of all the things they could have played, to choose that! But Nellie was the one who flinched. Willie gave no sign that he heard.

Ashore a telegram awaited them, saying that Mabel had put off her wedding until the thirty-first, so they were able to accept Governor Wolcott's invitation to drive to the State House and watch the review of the 6th Massachusetts from his office windows, and meet prominent Bostonians. Governor Wolcott must have been a relative of Nellie's in some degree, but she does not so much as mention this. It was Willie's day, Nellie wanted all the glory to be his. On to Savannah next, where they arrived in plenty of time for Mabel's wedding. Mabel and Rowland Leigh accompanied Willie back to Washington where he was to report to the War Department, and the Leighs went with him to call on President McKinley. Mabel, very pretty in one of her trousseau costumes, thanked the President charm-ingly for his kindness in arranging to get her father and mother home for her wedding.

The President replied as charmingly, "Why, I looked upon this wedding as a sort of international affair. I felt it was my duty as Chief Executive to do all I could to help it along!"

President McKinley flattered Willie by asking him, as a personal favor, not to apply for mustering out. "I may have need of you again." Willie replied that he would be at the service of the President and the War Department for any task they wished to assign him.

Nellie's Spanish-American War diaries end with the notation that Willie was awaiting orders to go to Macon, to take charge of the 2nd Brigade, 1st Division, 1st Army Corps, which it was rumored would be sent to Trinidado, Cuba. Apparently the orders never came. Perhaps the War Department had realized that where Willie went, his fiery little wife would go too, and felt it needed more time to recover before Nellie was unleashed once more against the United States army.

And perhaps it is as well. So far as it concerned the Gordon family, there couldn't have been a better war than the Spanish-American. The President of the United States himself had recognized the sterling worth of modest, quiet, little Willie. All America had paid tribute to Nellie's great, warm, fighting heart. Bill, Arthur and Daisy had been privileged to serve under the parents they so admired and adored. That their rôles were inconspicuous, all the honors going to Papa and Mama, was exactly as they wished it. The emergency had welded together a country long divided, and Willie had played his part in this. It was a good place to stop.

CHAPTER XV

————— ☆ —————

THE FAIRY KINGDOM FALLS

JUST WHEN the first ominous cracks began to appear in the walls of Daisy's fairy tale kingdom, we do not know. To her family, as to the rest of the world, she maintained her rôle of happy wife. It was Mabel's belief that all went fairly well, in fact, for some years. Billow was selfish to the core, but at the same time generous and kindhearted in his own way. During the years before Mabel's marriage, when she spent so much time with the Lows, Billow was always insisting on paying her travel expenses, and they had amicable fights about it. If Daisy asked him for fifty pounds, he would give her two hundred. He might hurt Daisy and cause her anxiety by going off without telling her where he was going or how long he planned to stay; but when he returned it would be with a gorgeous piece of jewelry for her. He was genuinely fond of "Puppa" and "Mumma," and in 1893 Billow loaned his father-in-law $100,-000, the money arriving in Savannah in American gold eagles, three boxfuls of them. Willie Gordon mortgaged his wharves in Savannah as collateral, engaging himself to pay ten per cent interest and to repay the money by February 1, 1894. The Gordon files contain Billow's receipt in full for the loan, dated January 31, 1894.

Daisy, equally loyal to both her countries, would permit no criticism of any Englishman, much less of Willy Low. Throughout Daisy's life she had had before her the example of her mother's attention to her father's welfare and desires. She had the same capacity for a great and selfless love, she devoted herself to Billow's wishes and happiness as Nellie had devoted herself to Willie Gordon's, giving way to him in everything. The trouble was that even though she may have had tongue in cheek when she wrote her father in 1884 that Billow was far too immature for her, she had spoken truly. Billow remained a gay, irresponsible bachelor, with a schoolboy's sense of humor, popular with men and women alike, but riding heedlessly over Daisy's loving heart.

He would tease Daisy by saying that he was going to ride in the Grand National, throwing her into a fever of anxiety. "It is such a dangerous thing to ride in a steeplechase, and with no chance of winning, it seems as if he were jeopardizing his life for nothing. There have been four dreadful accidents in the hunting field this season, and steeplechasing is more dangerous than hunting." Yet Mabel was sure that though he often entered a horse in the Grand National, Willy never rode it himself, and did not even ride in the local steeplechases. It would amuse him at times to talk in deliberately low tones, to make Daisy more conscious of her deafness. This charming, grown-up child was aware that Daisy's love made her defenseless against him, that he could hurt her at will, and he hurt her often. All this Daisy kept to herself. There is every evidence that Willie and Nellie refrained from any interference in her marriage, though it must have seemed a strange one to them.

Arthur seems to have been the only Gordon who dared probe into Daisy's affairs, so carefully did she guard her husband from her family's disapproval. In August of 1897 she wrote Arthur: "Now let me satisfy your brotherly curiosity by saying that Billow and I are still at odds. He says he is very annoyed at something, he forgets exactly what it is, but he means to give me a real dressing down. So as he puts it off from day to day I may escape altogether. He is a most unusual sort of man and one never knows exactly when he is or isn't chaffing. He was very much amused at your comparing him with Providence, which is similarly unpredictable." A short time later she was commenting that "my old husband went to Doncaster today. Frank Dugdale and I are alone, until Amy comes. First time I have ever been alone with a male guest without Billow. *He* arranged it—he has been so dear and nice. Like Scotch weather, when he is bad he is awful, but when really nice, sweeter than summer!"

It was not until the summer of 1899 that Daisy told Arthur frankly, "I see so little of Billow I feel there is no human affection for me except in the family." She had grown so unhappy that she had thrown herself into organized charity, in spite of Billow's prejudices against it. "I have become a second Mrs. Jellaby! I had thirty parsons to tea yesterday! This would be the irony of fate for Willy, who hates parsons, if he knew he had to pay for their entertainment!" Arthur, however, was pledged not to disclose these things to other members of the family, and evidently did not.

When Willie and Nellie visited England again in 1900, Willie became ill and was ordered to Brighton by the doctor. Billow was as assiduous in his attentions as Daisy, placed his electric coupé at his parents-in-law's disposal and every day sent hothouse fruits and other delicacies from Wellesbourne. Willie and Nellie would never have accepted these attentions from Billow if they had known how unhappy he was making Daisy. Papa would have had matters out with Billow then, as he was to do a few years later.

Of course, they guessed. Beginning with 1900, in her travel diaries and in her letters to Willie Gordon when they were separated, Nellie always speaks of this daughter as "our Daisy," or "our little Daisy." It is as though to her the brilliant, seemingly successful woman of the world were still their little girl, impulsive, heedless, so loving, so tenderhearted, so vulnerable. Papa withheld his consent to Mabel's marriage to Rowland Leigh those many years because Willy Low had given him a poor opinion of Englishmen as husbands. He had to be thoroughly convinced that "little Rowley," as Daisy called him, was very different from Willy Low.

At late as 1901, Daisy was still barring her parents from her confidence, writing Arthur: "Mama has tried not to say much to me, but I know she thinks if she was in my place she could manage Willy and engineer things much better than I do. But every heart knoweth its own bitterness and although I am sure there is much to be desired in my character, still I don't think anyone else can judge quite fairly."

Daisy had taken to heart the motto over Alfred Grenfell's fireplace, which had impressed her so much that she had copied it off for Nellie:

> Life is mostly froth and bubbles,
> Two things stand like stone.
> Kindness in another's troubles,
> Courage in your own.

She had met her own difficulties with courage, those of others with loving-kindness. Once more, out of her lonely ponderings, she had evolved a philosophy. Eleanor had lost one of her little boys, and in January of 1901 wrote Daisy begging her to come. Daisy replied that it did her heart good to have her sister turn to her, to have anyone need her.

"You say your life has been happier than mine. My dear, if I had been struck the blow you have felt I would neither have the sense nor the courage to acknowledge any past happiness. But happiness is not the sum total of life. I am beginning to believe there is almost as much satisfaction in bearing pain bravely, as one grows older. One's own individual life is such a small part of the working of the big world; and if one lives up to the very highest level of one's powers, one can only fulfill a tiny part of God's reasons in putting us here, and one's own affairs dwindle into supreme insignificance as compared with the scheme of existence as a whole—just as nobody counts the myriad little insects that die to make a coral reef and yet they have their uses and have not lived in vain."

In early 1901, old Queen Victoria died, and at long last Willy's friend became king. And in the summer of 1901, Daisy's marriage came to a crashing end.

Her letters to Arthur betray an increasing feeling of desolation. Even to Arthur, however, she did not express the full bitterness her heart was beginning to know. In early August she wrote that once more she would be entertaining in Scotland without Willy Low. The McIntosh was to look after the men who would come to shoot at Mealmore, she would have a woman friend to help entertain them. Billow was at Nauheim taking the cure, and his doctor had persuaded him to stick it out. "He drinks only water and smokes three cigars a day instead of thirty and writes letters all day long."

What she did not say was that Willy Low was not alone at Nauheim, and that his companion on this occasion was not one of his men friends but a woman. The first mention of Mrs. Bateman occurs in a letter from Daisy to Arthur in January, 1901. Her party for one of the balls had consisted of Lord Alletumney (Daisy's spelling), Sol Dungarvan, Lord Warwick, and a Mr. Glyn. "The women are Lady St.Oswald, a very handsome Mrs. Bateman and a beautiful girl, Elspeth Campbell, the Duke of Argyle's niece." Mrs. Bateman's name is not inscribed in the Wellesbourne visitors' book, in fact there are no entries at all between early 1900 and January 1904, when Daisy was no longer mistress of Wellesbourne. Mabel, writing many years afterwards of the breakup of Daisy's marriage, thought it was in 1895 that Willy Low first met Mrs. Bateman, a very beautiful widow, though she said she could not remember the exact year, and the indications are that it was around 1900. But Mabel said she well remembered Willy Low's receiving a letter from Mrs. Bateman thanking him for sending her flowers. He laughed and said he had never sent her flowers. Mabel was told by friends of Billow's that Mrs. Bateman fell desperately in love with him, and that eventually he became infatuated with her.

Soon everyone was talking about the affair. Willy Low and Mrs. Bateman were going about together openly. At Nauheim, the handsome widow and Willy stayed in the same hotel. "Her attitude was that as she and Willy were not being clandestine, there could be nothing wrong." Mabel believed there had been women before in her brother-in-law's life, but the affairs had not been serious and had not lasted long. Daisy had borne them in silence. Daisy kept to herself whatever she thought about the affair with Mrs. Bateman, until it took a turn that could be neither ignored nor endured. A letter to Mabel, August 21, 1901, from Mealmore, speaks mainly of the shooting, which had been exceptionally good. "The first day they got 397 brace with seven guns and almost 500 brace the second day. Willy has come back from Nauheim, looks well, has gained a stone in weight. P.S. There are no women here except Ota [Lady Wilton]. Mrs. Bateman comes Friday."

Mabel was preparing to go to Meggernie Castle, when she received a letter from Daisy begging her to cancel her visit there and come at once to Mealmore. "I need you desperately, darling, or I wouldn't ask it." Mabel hurried to Mealmore, and found an incredible situation. As soon as Lady Ota Wilton had left, Mrs. Bateman had taken over. Mrs. Bateman's room was at the head of the staircase, Willy's at the foot, Daisy had been relegated to another wing. Mrs. Bateman was giving orders to the servants in Daisy's presence. The butler would say to Daisy gravely, ignoring Mrs. Bateman, "What did you wish me to do, Madam?" Willy was poisonously rude to Daisy.

Mabel thought Mrs. Bateman believed she could employ the long-suffering Daisy as a screen. Daisy had too much self-respect and dignity to be used in this blatant fashion, but her actions show the compassion and protectiveness she felt for Willy even now. Stay she could not, but she would not go until Katy Low, whom she had sent for also, could arrive to lend the propriety of her presence to the ménage. In the painful interlude, Daisy needed someone there who cherished her, and so had asked Mabel to come.

Mabel's view of Mrs. Bateman, naturally not a sympathetic one, was that the lady's "beauty was equaled only by her stupidity. She was always talking about how it was her sad fate that the husbands of her friends should fall in love with her. She actually said to me that Willy's family should be grateful to her for taking care of him. Willy was sitting listening and grinned when I answered that he was quite capable of looking after himself, and I did not think he was worth looking after!" Daisy, so full of spunk when it came to standing up for other people, was too crushed to take her own part in the face of Mrs. Bateman's insolence and Willy's rudeness. Mabel had enough spunk for two. She would fly at Willy when he said something nasty to Daisy. He took her thrusts in good part, and remained as nice to her as ever.

As soon as Katy Low arrived, the two sisters left, Daisy going back to Wellesbourne to pack and get off for Savannah as quickly as she could. Rejected, abased, wounded as only the tenderhearted and all-giving can be wounded, she felt that there alone in all the world was love she could count on. From one standpoint, it may have been a fatal step. She was never to set foot in Mealmore again, never again in Wellesbourne, so dear to her, into which she had put so much of herself.

Now her marital difficulties could be concealed from her parents no longer. Willie Gordon had a talk with his son-in-law in Paris. Daisy's heart still clung to Willy, she had urged Papa to deal with him gently. Directly after the nightmare experience at Mealmore, before she left Wellesbourne, Daisy had written Mabel that Willy had sent her one hundred pounds to defray a big doctor bill Mabel had incurred. "I did not tell him I had already helped pay. I mentioned this so you will realize how fond he is of you."

And Willy, in this interview with Papa, declared he did not want a separation or divorce, apologized for his behavior toward Daisy, asked for time in which to break off gracefully with Mrs. Bateman. Papa carried this message to Daisy in Savannah. She waited for Willy's word that the situation had been cleared up, that she might return home.

The following February she was still waiting, and wrote Mabel that witnessing her sister's happiness with "little Rowley" on their recent visit to Savannah, "seeing what happiness life can contain, helped to keep my own heart from withering away from bitterness and callousness." By summer she was growing very concerned, writing Papa from Washington that she felt she should not go to Saratoga with him and Mama. "I ought to get back to England before Ota Wilton, Barbara Brand and other friends go to Scotland, if I am to show myself to the world and prevent gossip." Willy Low, meanwhile, had sent her no money beyond the five hundred pounds he had given her when she left England the previous fall. "I don't like to ask you or Papa to advance me money," she wrote Arthur. "I must not leave myself short in England as I have no bank, now, where I can overdraw, and you will be too far away to come to my aid and my pride revolts at asking any of his sisters to advance me a sum of money."

By June 19, nearly a year after she had fled from Mealmore, the blow had fallen. Willy wrote her that Wellesbourne was shut and he had let Mealmore—Daisy now had no home in England to return to. He would leave it to her, he said, to decide whether or not to come back, but he did not think they would be happy together and asked her consent to live apart. "Please talk this over with your father," he requested. Just why it is hard to say.

Papa wrote Willy a brief letter—it must have been at Daisy's urging again that he restrained the grief and rage he and Nellie felt in equal measure—requesting Willy to make a settlement on Daisy and place a sum of money for her support in the hands of his brothers-in-law, George Robertson and Sir Henry Grenfell, to administer as Daisy's trustees. Daisy wrote briefly to Willy, agreeing to the separation. It was not what she wanted —she consented out of pride and hurt. This was to prove a costly error.

It was now, with her marriage wrecked, her life in ruins, that Daisy displayed the strength, the ability for clear, straight thinking that had lain concealed beneath the gay, frivolous, illogical exterior. She wasted no pity on herself, no emotion of any kind on Mrs. Bateman, until it became apparent that Willy was a very sick man and that his open flaunting of the affair was alienating him from his family and friends. Then she wanted Mrs. Bateman punished; but for what Daisy thought she was doing to Willy, not for what she had done to Daisy.

After Daisy returned to England, she learned that her friend, Lady Ota Wilton, had intruded in Daisy's affairs, telling Willy, after his interview with Papa in Paris, that she had heard from Daisy that Daisy did not mean to return to him. "She made him believe it was absolutely over between him and me. I honestly believe she meant to help me and thought by scaring Willy she could make him behave himself; but she had made real mischief." Daisy was aghast, but the damage had been done. She wrote Nellie about it, to excuse Willy for having broken his word to Papa. Then she put it from her mind.

The courage it required for Daisy to return to England and face Willy's friends and family can be deduced only from her expressions of incredulous relief when she was received with warm love. She had imagined that, as a woman openly separated from her husband, she would be snubbed, since in the early 1900's wives were expected to hold on to their husbands. Most of her circle in England had become her friends through Willy, they were devoted to him, and she supposed would side with him. Willy's sisters adored their only brother. She could not expect them to transfer their loyalty to her. But a settlement must be arranged, and though either Arthur or Papa would gladly have acted for her, she felt she had already brought enough trouble and inconvenience on her family. This must be her responsibility.

As soon as she arrived in London, she had breakfast with Katy Low and Amy, told them of Willy's letter, and that the marriage was at an end. She said to each of them separately, "If it comes to a point where you feel obliged to choose between Willy and me, I will quite understand your choosing Willy and nothing will ever alter my love for you, even if we never meet again."

They replied with expressions of deepest love and sympathy. Amy Grenfell said she would be settled in her new house in September. Daisy must bring her boxes there and stay as long as possible. Katy Low invited Daisy to go on a trip with her. In a letter she said, "How *could* anyone possibly blame *you,* dearest Daisy?" Daisy wrote to Jessie and Mary and received replies in similar vein. As the word spread, Daisy was caught up on a tide of affection and support. "All around there is a unbroken wave of sympathy for you. You have many friends and you must let them help you all they can," wrote one of Willy's closest associates.

Alix Beech asked Daisy to spend the whole three months of the Scottish season at Meggernie, invitations to other great houses flooded in. There is a pitiful letter in the files from old George Granville, of Wellesbourne Hall, who was dying. "You will forgive me, I know, if I write you a line as we have been friends so very long and neighbors, and say how sincerely I sympathize with you in your great sorrow, but I truly hope Willy will do all he can for you, which can never make up for the great wrong he has done you.

"I have been very ill and am still very bad and I know now I can never recover. I am afraid there is no chance of your ever living at Wellesbourne. I wish you were, true friends are scarce and all new people here now."

No, Daisy could never live at Wellesbourne again, and her Warwickshire neighbors were as grieved because of it as Daisy herself. A letter signed "Edelweiss," apparently the Honorable Mrs. Mordaunt, expresses their sorrow, and contains a prophecy as well: "The Wellesbourne lions make me cry and the gates hurt worse still and you are so brave and good. And you will not lose faith but will hold fast to all that is more worth living for and will yet make your life not only a success, but a help to others who under the same circumstances would have gone under and so failed to learn the lessons God is teaching by such adversity as yours."

To Arthur Daisy wrote: "I see how morbidly sensitive I was when I imagined I would be ostracized as a woman separated from her husband."

Daisy had a great need just then of human affection, and the kindness and loyalty of her English friends touched her immeasurably. Yet she did not want to have their support at Willy's expense. One of his very close friends told her of meeting Willy on Bond Street and cutting him dead. "Please please don't cut Willy off," Daisy begged. "He needs his friends now more than ever."

Daisy set herself to adjust to her new situation, with no diminution in her outward gaiety. From Meggernie she wrote Nellie proudly that she had made herself a very pretty dress bodice. "They all say it is very nice. I begin to like sewing and being my own maid. Don't waste your prayers asking for my happiness, just pray that I will have enough money to be comfortable and contented." After her visit, Alix Beech wrote Daisy that "you are absolutely the most delightful creature that has ever been to Meggernie."

But there was a never-ending ache for Wellesbourne, a growing sense of her own inadequacy as a woman and a wife. When Daisy learned of the death of Duncan Hunter, Abby Lippitt's husband, she wrote Nellie: "Poor, poor Abby! Yet it is easier to lose one's husband as she has done, than as I have done. At least she can look back and know she made him happy, but I can only look back on failure."

And Willy refused to consider a settlement unless Daisy would grant him a divorce. According to Mabel, the divorce was Mrs. Bateman's idea. She wanted to marry Willy, in order to mend her damaged reputation. Daisy did not believe in divorce, she had married Willy Low for all time. Probably for years he had been to her a difficult, much-loved child, rather than a husband, and one cannot cast out one's child from one's heart, however outrageously he may behave. Willy was withholding money from Daisy as a means of forcing her to consent to the divorce.

Daisy was out of funds entirely, with the settlement as remote as ever, before she let her parents and Arthur know what Willy Low was up to. Separate drafts came at once from Arthur, Papa and Mama. Papa insisted that Daisy should not be humiliated further by Willy about money. He would support his daughter, and would be happy to do so. Papa, in fact, had sent to Daisy through all the years of her marriage to a rich man, the allowance he had given her before her marriage. He had done the same with Mabel. Nellie continued this loving gesture after Willie's death. Now Papa proposed to increase Daisy's allowance to a sum that would permit her to live comfortably and with dignity, wherever she wished. Mama, again acting separately, offered the same thing.

Daisy expressed her affectionate gratitude for their desire to "act as my banker," but explained why she must get a decent settlement from Willy Low whatever the cost to her feelings. "If I accept less than is due me, it will be thought that I have ceded my rights because I have committed some fault and dare not claim them." As would indeed have been the case. She did accept their temporary support as a loan, to be repaid when Willy had done the right thing; as she believed eventually he would.

It was not until Daisy had been introduced to the hard facts of the English law that she wavered in her determination against divorce. When at last she took her troubles to a lawyer, she learned that her letter to Willy Low, agreeing to the separation, barred her from claiming an immediate settlement on grounds of desertion. Without Willy's co-operation, which he would not give, she would have to wait two years to establish desertion. She had no option for obtaining financial support under the law except to bring divorce proceedings, or else sue her husband for restoration of conjugal rights. "I will not appear before the world as a person who clings to a man who is kicking her aside, and I now know that by English law my only chance of getting support is through the divorce court."

But there were obstacles in the way of a divorce, as well. In England a divorce was granted only for adultery and cruelty, or for adultery and desertion. Willy would concede desertion, to get a divorce. But so far as the adultery requirement was concerned, he insisted that Mrs. Bateman's name be kept out of the case. To use another woman instead would be collusion, which was against the law.

Mabel was present at a meeting between Willy and Daisy in her lawyer's office. Willy turned to Mabel and said, "If Daisy names Mrs. Bateman she will kill herself, and I will do the same and Daisy will be to blame."

Daisy answered quietly, "I am in no way responsible for you or Mrs. Bateman."

Willy said to Mabel, "Mrs. Bateman means it."

Whereupon Mabel retorted, "I know she has just ordered in Paris a most expensive evening coat, so I fear there is no such luck!"

The result was stalemate. Willy refused to consider a settlement unless Daisy would bring suit for divorce without naming Mrs. Bateman; Daisy and her lawyer refused to be parties to collusion.

Unfortunate in so many of her "worldly arrangements," to use Mabel's phrase, Daisy was most fortunate in her lawyer, Sir George Lewis. The situation was one of extreme delicacy, for at that time husbands had much the best of it under English law—wronged wives now are in much better case in England. Both Willy and Mrs. Bateman were without scruples. Willy, always unpredictable and undependable, became more so. Sir George threaded his way through all the complications with consummate skill, knowing when to apply pressure, when to feign indifference so as to force the other side to come to him. He was a good friend besides. Daisy was an equally good client, following his instructions implicitly, never once letting herself be goaded into a rash action. The Gordons, of course, were behind her in a solid phalanx, and sometimes their concern and indignant loyalty became too much of a good thing.

Again and again she had to explain to Papa why it would not do for her to drop the distasteful, endless negotiating with Willy and let Papa support her, reiterating that if she gave up her rights, it would be considered she had done something wrong, which she had not. "Besides, it is utterly unfair to expect you to support me, no matter how willing you are. My position as neither maid, widow or wife will be a difficult one at best but it becomes at once misunderstood if I cease to live in the style befitting Willy's wife. I still think divorce wrong, but it is the lesser of two evils."

Arthur was concerned about Daisy's dubious status as "neither maid, wife nor widow." Though Daisy turned forty-two the fall her troubles became public property, her thirty-year-old brother appointed himself arbiter of her conduct. If she took any trips, she must always have some one of her immediate family along as a chaperon. She must refrain from lunching or dining in public places and in her home must never receive single gentlemen, only women or married couples! Daisy, dismayed, showed this letter to Katy Low who simply laughed. Katy answered it, assuring her "dear boy" that while a woman in America who was separated from her husband might have to enter a nunnery, "the part of society that matters in this country is very just, I think, and you need have no fear that this very deplorable and unfortunate affair will reflect in any way upon Daisy with her true friends, who I know will be as ready to shield her from harm as her own people.

"If she were to do as you say she would probably attract more attention to herself than otherwise," continued this sensible woman. "In fact, if Daisy continues to act as she has always done socially, no one can cavil at her. She has always been particular even when erratic."

For three years after her return to England, Daisy was kept on tenterhooks. Her heart was lacerated over and over, her tenderest feelings trampled upon. She could make no plans, for some new development was always coming up. If she ran over to the Continent or to America, she was likely to be summoned back.

Yet Daisy, who in early wifehood had taken to her bed because of the insolence of a servant, went through the ordeal unflinchingly. In early 1903, she wrote a little poem which was found in her journal after her death:

> Only thyself, thyself can harm,
> Forget it not—and full of peace
> Ignore the noise and world's alarm,
> And wait till storm and tumult cease.

It was her own idea to live as frugally as possible until she knew what her financial situation was to be. She did not mind doing without things for herself, believing this was good for her character, which she was always to feel needed improving. But it cut deep to be unable to offer to pay travel expenses for friends and relatives, to have to keep her purse closed, or try to keep it closed, when she came across need or suffering, now that she was an object of family charity herself. She could continue to give of herself, and this she did. Her heart grieved over the widowed Abby Lippitt Hunter, she could not bear to have her so far away. At length she persuaded Abby to come with her four children to Europe, so that Daisy could minister to her.

Part of the time Daisy had a house, but when her funds ran low, she would leave her boxes at Mrs. Lewis' hotel and go about to her various friends. Mrs. Lewis' name appears in the letters frequently. A notable cook who had once worked for Daisy and then had gone on to cater to royalty, Mrs. Lewis was deeply sympathetic with her former mistress, and through her friendship with Baker, Willy's valet, kept the Low family informed of developments after Willy had estranged himself from his sisters. Daisy also spent a good deal of time with Mabel and Rowland Leigh in the tiny house they then had in London. One day Mabel entered her street to see a crowd collected around her doorstep. When she got up to the house, she found that Daisy and a monkey were the attraction. Daisy had come upon an organ grinder with a monkey; she thought the monkey looked hungry. Not trusting the organ grinder to feed the animal if she gave him money, she had brought both to Mabel's house, and was regaling the monkey with choice hothouse fruit someone had sent Mabel. The monkey would take one bite of each offering, then throw it on the paving.

When a whole year had gone by and the storm and tumult showed no signs of ceasing, she revealed at last the shame and agony in her heart, in answer to a loving letter Nellie had written on Daisy's forty-third birthday. "You say: 'You all love me but that is not the love I want.' Indeed I have learned to realize that's the *only* love that endures, and I crave it. You also say I am a comfort to you all, but I know for the past year I have been a thorn in the flesh and I would give anything if I could spare you all this trouble I am causing you. But the worst part of all will soon be over after the money is settled. Then the shame and loneliness will be softened by degrees and there is so much for you to be proud of in your other children that you will be compensated for the disgrace Willy has brought on me."

Her feeling of self-abasement became complete when she learned that Willy Low was drinking himself to death, that Katy Low thought his brain was affected. She withdrew her objections to a divorce on Willy's terms. "I simply cannot believe that it is more moral to uphold the marriage laws when, in my case, they have become a dead letter, than to let a man chuck away his life because he cannot be quit of me!"

A bitter end to the dreams the painter had caught in Daisy's soft, brown eyes in her early married years.

Daisy had been worried about Willy's health for some time, but had felt a delicacy, as a rejected wife, about inquiring into it. Now she asked Willy to come and see her, in Sir George's presence, writing Mabel afterwards: "I know Papa and Mama will think me very weak to be affected by anything Willy could say, but even that man of experience, Sir George Lewis, was touched. Willy has gone through Jimmie Guthrie's mental breakdown with him, and knows he himself is doomed. His mind has taken the sombre outlook—Jimmie's view was all *coleur de rose*. For days at a time Willy never utters a word. But he broke down with me and wept. He was just as incoherent and agitated when he told me he 'would have to be shut up' as he was that time when he said Mrs. B. was going to take poison. As Sir Lewis said, it would have been positively inhuman to do anything but soothe him and I did reassure and calm him."

Daisy added, "Mrs. Lewis told me Mrs. Bateman was moving heaven and earth to bring on the divorce at once as she meant to marry him the minute she could do so, whether he was all right or not. It will be a fearful retribution if she has him slip through her fingers now and loses all his money and has to face society with her tarnished name which she hoped to whitewash by marrying him and living it down. Eva Dugdale said she and Frank met Mrs. B. in Bolton Street and cut her dead. Mrs. B. can't marry Willy for a *year* after the divorce!"

But in spite of the anger and revulsion Daisy was beginning

to feel toward Mrs. Bateman, Daisy promised Willy that she would do all she could to get the divorce without naming Mrs. Bateman, provided he would stop drinking and would go to a rest home. Willy promised, and did go to a rest home for a time.

But now that Willy had his own way, he created further difficulties by declining to bring in, to establish the adultery charge, any other woman than Mrs. Bateman. That, he said, would look as though he had been unfaithful to Mrs. Bateman! Daisy, with her purity and abhorrence of sordidness, was spared no humiliation that a husband could heap upon a wife.

Summer of 1904 had come before a way had been found around the various obstacles. It was agreed that Daisy's lawyer would prove desertion by pleading that Mrs. Bateman's presence in her house had forced Daisy out of it, that Willy had asked her not to return and that he had deserted her for two years. For the adultery charge, Willy would furnish proof that he had registered at a hotel with a woman as man and wife at a time previous to his affair with Mrs. Bateman. Daisy signed the divorce petition. The case would come to trial in October or November; Sir George thought it would take not more than thirty minutes. Willy had made a settlement of £2,500 a year on Daisy, insured by £10,000 which he had in the Chalmers Guthrie firm, the family business of Mary Low Guthrie's husband, in which Willy Low had invested a large part of his fortune. Nellie whisked Daisy off to Franzensbad for the mud baths there and for the change of scene she badly needed.

But the case did not come to trial in October after all. Willy's mind broke down as he had foreseen would happen; he had to be confined in an asylum for a time. The doctors' diagnosis was a paralytic condition which would be steadily progressive until he died of it; at any time he might have a seizure which would cause general paralysis or death.

Now, looking back, they could trace the steps by which Willy's endless pursuit of pleasure had brought him to this unhappy pass. For many years, Willy had been in the habit of drinking port every evening after dinner for hours. He had never shown signs of drunkenness, but had far exceeded the alcoholic limits even of that day of copious drinking. In recent years his formerly amiable disposition had turned to irritability, he was often morose—Mabel understood that several times he had had fits. After Willy was placed in the asylum, Lord Warwick told Mabel for the first time that Willy had gone berserk when the Earl was tarpon-fishing with him in Florida, and had attacked one of the party with a knife.

Daisy's fury against Mrs. Bateman had been mounting steadily. She had written Mama when the settlement was being negotiated, "Everybody must be patient and not try to help me, as I find even the lawyers can't make Willy do as much as I can and if you saw his poor palsied body and realized the constant torment that woman keeps him in, you would know he too suffers. Baker [Willy's valet] told Mrs. Lewis that Mrs. B. wrote or wired every day to Willy and was killing him."

Daisy had her divorce case put on the reserve list—to go on with the proceedings when Willy was in so pitiable a state was unthinkable. But he made an astonishing recovery, soon being released to the care of his sister Katy who, together with Amy Grenfell, nursed him at Wellesbourne. By November of 1904, Willy was well enough to give a big luncheon at the Warwick races. There was a little house party at Wellesbourne that Christmas—Katy Low, Harry and Amy Grenfell and George Robertson, all family except for Jack, Louise and Angela Maxwell—the first entry in the visitors' book since February of 1900, except for Blanche Brand's name in October, 1901, perhaps Daisy's guest while she made her preparations to flee to Savannah.

But alas, for the loving hearts that had stood by Willy so loyally! Willy asked Amy and Katy to invite Mrs. Bateman to Wellesbourne and act as chaperones. When they refused, he ordered them to leave Wellesbourne that very day and never return. Mr. Gasquet, Willy's business agent, tried to get Daisy to have Willy declared insane. This Daisy refused to do even though it would have given her control of the situation. To force her to comply, Mr. Gasquet cut off her allowance. She went to the heads of Chalmers Guthrie, asking them to see that her allowance was paid out of the £10,000 that were held there as surety. Then it was found, to the consternation of the company heads, that the £10,000 had been withdrawn. Willy might live for years, unable to attend to his affairs, yet meddling with them. "I hope if God thinks it best for Willy to live, that He will in His infinite mercy let me die," Daisy wrote to her parents at Christmastime. "I would not undergo any more of this Hell on earth that I have been suffering."

Nellie began praying fiercely that Willy Low would die. This must have struck Daisy with a special horror. She was deeply religious, and her Lord was the gentle Christ. Daisy could not have prayed for the death of Willy or any other human being, except as a merciful release from suffering. To her, it would have been a mortal sin. It must have seemed to Daisy a compounding of all the ills she had brought on her family, that her cry of despair had moved her little mother to imperil her soul. But to beg Nellie to cease on this account would have been worse than useless. Nellie would have replied that she would gladly burn in hell through all eternity if she could send her daughter's tormentor there a little sooner, and she would have meant it too.

Daisy solved her problem by writing Nellie that she had been quite ill. "You had better be careful, Mama, how you pray for Willy's death. It looks as though God has gotten your orders twisted, and if you keep on, you may end by bringing about mine!"

Now came a letter from Billow reproaching Daisy for dropping the divorce suit. "Daisy: You have broken your word to me. You have put the divorce on the reserve list while I was ill. You promised me on your solemn word of honor to divorce me. I think it is very unkind of you. Please go to Sir George Lewis at once, to continue proceedings."

Daisy replied with dignity that she had put the divorce on the reserve list because of his illness. "If I go into court and tell the world how you have treated me and also say (as I have told you all along that I must say) why I have left you (though I shall not mention a name) then the judgment against you will be severe. I did not want to cast this slur on you, unless you were well enough to derive some satisfaction from my taking such a step. You know me to be honorable. You should not therefore accuse me of being a liar. I have complied with your wishes and today I went to see Sir George Lewis."

Once more the ponderous machinery of the law had to be set into motion. In the files is a copy of the letter Willy wrote Daisy to prove adultery. "It is now two and a half years since we lived together and I believe you feel that I have treated you very badly. Perhaps I have, but anyway I feel you ought to know that you can get rid of me and gain your freedom if you wish to do so. One fact is as good as several. If you choose to go yourself, or send someone to the Arlington Hotel, Eastbourne, you will find that I was there sometimes with a lady, registered in the names of Mr. and Mrs. Low. I feel it is a matter of honour, after two and a half years of desertion I am bound to make this confession."

There are ironic echoes here of the letter Willy Low wrote to Papa in 1885, telling him of his love for Daisy. Did Daisy catch the similarities in phrasing when this strange document was put into her hand?

Again the case was set for trial. Papa was going to come over to be with Daisy. But the Low sisters, too, had been undergoing great strain these two and a half years. Katy had been a tower of strength for all of them, and Amy, Mary and Jessie had continued their devoted friendship with Daisy. But now Jessie, apparently unaware of the intricate maneuvering, wrote an hysterical letter to Daisy, claiming that Daisy knew Willy had gone to a hotel with an innocent woman, and that she was divorcing him because she wanted money. Daisy at once asked Sir George to stop the divorce proceedings. Willy was furious with his sister, ordered her to apologize to Daisy and said he would never speak to Jessie again if she did not apologize and if Daisy did not forgive her. He wrote humbly to Daisy, "You have been honourable to me and tried to keep your word. If you can forgive the past, I hope you will."

Mabel's indignation knew no bounds. She wrote Mama, "I have done with Jessie!" But Daisy wrote Willy Low, "I freely and frankly forgive the past. I only beg of you not to go yachting alone with men. You have been too ill. If Mrs. Bateman does not join you for the yachting trip, ask Katy to go with you. You cannot ask her to go with Mrs. Bateman. I have not asked a favour of you for four years, but I do ask this, dear Willy. Katy has been loyal to you and has harmed no one."

The fat was in the fire, however, so far as the divorce was concerned. Daisy cabled Papa: "Don't come, divorce uncertain, Willy worse." There was a most painful interview in Sir George's office. Willy could not see why Daisy, who had always given him everything, was again interfering with his plan to marry Mrs. Bateman. Why could they not all be good friends, even though he had another wife? Sir George tried to make him understand that since Jessie had charged collusion, no court would grant a divorce unless Daisy named Mrs. Bateman. What Daisy thought and felt, we can only imagine.

There was one last meeting between Daisy and Willy Low. He came to see Daisy at the house she had rented at 40 Grosvenor Street, and Mabel and her husband happened to be there. He was a piteous sight, unshaven, the beautiful facial lines blurred, his clothes spotted and untidy. He had been sent by Mrs. Bateman, to make another plea for a divorce without naming his inamorata, and he repeated dutifully the things she had told him to say. Daisy replied gently that it was impossible for her to do anything, as the King's Proctor would certainly intervene unless the true adultery grounds were given. Mabel reported that "Willy acquiesced quite amiably and then asked to see Rowland and me. He was affectionate in his manner, most anxious to be friendly. He said to me sadly, 'I can't understand why Puppa won't be friends with me.' "

In June, 1905, Willy died suddenly at Ruthven Castle, where he was staying with Mrs. Bateman. He was taken with a fit while going to bed, never regained consciousness and according to the doctors, did not suffer.

In her own indescribable sadness, Katy thought of the shock his death would be to "our dear little Daisy." She sent a hasty note to Mabel, asking her to break the news to Daisy before she heard it from some other source. Daisy was staying with her great friend and distant cousin, Lady May Grey Egerton, because Lady Grey Egerton needed her just then—she, too, had been deserted by her husband, whom she divorced the next year. Mabel went to Lady May's house, and gently and lovingly told Daisy that Willy was dead. Daisy said sadly, "We all adored him and must feel that death was best for him, since his health and his brain were gone."

Mrs. Bateman took charge of the funeral arrangements—before his death Willy had signed a paper ordering this, and also asking that his sealed dispatch box be sent to Mrs. Bateman. Daisy determined to go to the funeral, in spite of the fear of the

Low sisters that if Daisy were there, Mrs. Bateman might create a scene, "either fainting by the grave or throwing herself into my arms as though she and I were the only ones who had cared about Willy!"

Mrs. Bateman had chosen the churchyard near Widmerpool Hall, the home of Willy's brother-in-law Major Robertson, for the interment, which did not please George Robertson as he imagined Mrs. Bateman would be making constant visits to the grave. "Even in death, she will not let him go." He invited Daisy to join the Low family at Widmerpool Hall and go to the funeral with them. Daisy declined, thinking it best to go under the escort of Mr. Gasquet, Willy's business agent. Eleanor Parker was in England and would go with her, Mabel and Rowley would join her at the church. She wrote to Sir George Lewis, "I told the Low girls that so far as I was concerned, Mrs. Bateman does not *exist*, and it takes two to make a scene, and if she chooses to make one and no one interferes, it will soon be over. I know Willy when alive wished for her and would have expected her to be at his funeral. Therefore she is welcome to go to it and personally I don't want to see her thrust aside. I am going myself because by showing this mark of respect, I also show the world that I bear no malice and that I realize Willy was not responsible for his actions."

Daisy knew Mama would not understand a mark of respect for a man Nellie would never forgive as long as she lived, so Daisy wrote her the same reasons, with the added one that "Willy would understand and would not object if I were to go." She went on to say, "I feel that although I am glad he is dead, since his condition was so dreadful and hopeless, yet for the sake of those years long ago when I loved him, that I would like to see his poor suffering body laid to rest, and if I who am so full of human faults can forgive him, does not God also pity and love him?"

The funeral passed without untoward incident, and the Low sisters were glad that Daisy had gone. Katy wrote to Mabel that "dear Daisy has won the admiration of everyone by her quiet dignity." And to another friend, "She was so calm and dignified, and we were all so glad she should take her proper position before the world. It was very hard for her, poor girl, but it ends many complications for her. I trust that after a time she has much happiness to compensate." Many of Willy's former friends wrote to Daisy, expressing their appreciation for her magnanimous spirit, and their admiration for the quiet composure with which she had endured this last painful ordeal.

Everyone thought Willy's death was the end of complications for Daisy. Instead it was the beginning of new ones.

Daisy had planned to walk back to Widmerpool Hall with the Low family after the funeral for the reading of Willy's will, but changed her mind, and was later glad she had not gone to Widmerpool. Mr. Gasquet began to read the will, Willy's sisters became so upset that they begged him to stop, and the will was never read at all. Wellesbourne was to go to Amy Grenfell, and after her death to Katy. One gathers that these sisters also received money. But Mary and Jessie were not mentioned. Aside from several minor bequests, Willy's entire estate, including the Low house in Savannah and all of his American properties, were to go to Mrs. Bateman. But he did not forget Daisy. A codicil revoked the generous bequest he had made to her in a will drawn up in 1898, and requested Mrs. Bateman to pay Daisy her £2,500 a year while Daisy lived. After Daisy's death, this money, too, was to be Mrs. Bateman's.

Mr. Gasquet conveyed the news to Daisy and urged her to fight the will, though begging her not to tell anyone he had so advised her, as he was supposedly representing Willy's interests, and hence those of Mrs. Bateman. She could not upset the whole will, Mr. Gasquet told her, but she could prove by the doctor of the asylum that when Willy made the codicil cutting Daisy out of participation in his estate, he had been mentally ill. Further investigation showed that Mrs. Bateman's own lawyer had drawn up the codicil, just before Billow went into the rest home at Daisy's request, which Sir George Lewis said was utter folly. He thought he could get Mrs. Bateman to "divulge" all—Daisy's word—without going into court.

To learn that while Daisy had been filled with pity and anxiety for him, Willy had planned this ultimate ignominy for her; that he had arranged that two of his sisters should be deprived, for Mrs. Bateman's sake, of any share in the money that had come from their father, took away Daisy's will to fight for herself. Soul-sick and revolted, she said she would use what leverage she had to force Mrs. Bateman to grant Mary and Jessie amounts comparable to those given Amy and Katy under the will. She wanted nothing for herself.

Papa and Wayne Parker agreed that the dignified course was for Daisy to accept her £2,500 a year and not contest the will on her own account. It was Arthur who pointed out that in this case Mrs. Bateman would be paying Daisy's allowance to her and might claim that Daisy was a pensioner on her bounty. She might also say that Daisy had not dared fight the will because her own record was not clear. Arthur was for having George Lewis "scare Mrs. Bateman out of all of it" and immediately took ship for England to help his sister in this new emergency. When Daisy went to Sir George Lewis' office to decide what should be done, she was flanked by three Gordons, Eleanor, Mabel and Arthur. Bill was ready to come at once if he could be of help. Arthur kept in close touch with Papa and Bill by cable.

Having had time to think over Arthur's analysis, Papa, too, was now for fighting the will openly and demanding that it be set aside altogether. Daisy expressed her own decision in a letter to Sir George Lewis written August 4, 1905. "I wish to do nothing that looks like defrauding Willy's sisters. I wish to get only what Willy intended me to get when he was himself. Therefore I hate to insist on *no* compromise, because if I fail to win my suit, I leave the sisters in no position to ever gain anything."

Once again Daisy was plunged into negotiations and maneuvering of the utmost delicacy. Sir George did not want to protest the will on grounds of insanity, for it might then be charged that Willie was insane when he had made the settlement on Daisy, and Daisy might lose her settlement without breaking the will. He also pointed out that (at that time) a man in England could leave his innocent wife and children out of his will, and nothing would break the will except proof of undue influence. Sir George could prove immorality but not undue influence. He therefore did not wish to go into court, but to use the threat of court action as a means of forcing Mrs. Bateman to disgorge. Meanwhile, no mention of Sir George's real intentions could be allowed to leak out.

It settled down into a war of nerves, and again, the erratic

Daisy was not the one who cracked. She had, incidentally, the wholehearted support of the Chalmers Guthrie firm. Willy was by far the largest stockholder. If Mrs. Bateman got his whole estate, she would control the company! But Daisy had many other people to stand out against in following the course she had settled upon. Mr. Gasquet apparently was now doing his best for Mrs. Bateman. Daisy became oppressed at times with the attitude of the Low sisters, with the exception always of Katy. Amy refused to surrender Wellesbourne in return for a money settlement. It seemed to Daisy that Mary and Jessie were interested only in the money they would obtain. Judging from later letters, some friction must have arisen, as nearly always happens where large sums of money are involved.

Daisy had her own indignant impulses to contend with at times. As Mabel remarked, at least now the battle was with "that woman," and Daisy no longer was torn by the loving and pitying impulses which had moved her time and again in dealing with Willy. Once she wrote Arthur with every word underlined: "All I want is as much as I was left by Willy's 1898 will, but the woman is a mixture of cowardice and avarice and I long and hope for her to make such difficulties that Sir George will be obliged to fight—show her up!" But she was careful to do nothing to upset Sir George's delicately poised apple cart— perhaps only lawyers who have had clients in similar cases can appreciate her self-restraint!

We do not have Mrs. Bateman's side of this affair, and all we are told of her background is that she had been married to an older man, and that she inherited a fortune from him when he died. It would be interesting to know what were the motives that had impelled this beautiful, already wealthy woman, apparently with a high social position, to throw discretion so completely to the winds in pursuing her affair with Willy Low, and to give herself the further bad name among decent people of seizing his estate at the expense of his wife and sisters. In that day, however, psychology was an infant science, and we are given only the views of the Gordons and the Low sisters regarding Mrs. Bateman. Daisy showed her magnanimity and fairness in the letter she wrote to Sir George Lewis about Willy's funeral. It was not in her to hold a grudge, even against the woman who had wrought such havoc in her own life and

Willy's, if Mrs. Bateman had shown the least desire to do the right thing. We can only deduce that Willy, bent on self-destruction as the culmination of a lifetime of self-indulgence and irresponsibility, had found a woman also neurotically bent on self-destruction, though she employed different means. One of the hardest crosses for Daisy to bear must have been that the woman for whom she had been put aside proved to be avaricious and greedy.

Money troubles were added to her other difficulties. Either Mrs. Bateman had refused to pay the allowance, or Daisy had rejected it from her hands. Daisy wrote Mama October 28, 1905, thanking her for a birthday check of ten pounds and saying she had told Mabel that "on the first of April I must commit suicide, for my money will only last until then, and if this will isn't settled I must just peg out as I'd rather die than go in debt again, so you see by sending me a present of money you unwittingly prolonged my life! Mabel thinks the 1st of April an appropriate date for me to die!"

George Robertson, who was involved in the dispute—perhaps as executor of Willy Low's will, though his connection is not clear—began urging Daisy to waive her fine points of honor in favor of a quick settlement, in which her £2,500 a year would be guaranteed beyond peradventure. This suggestion was made once more at a meeting between Daisy, George Robertson, Mr. Gasquet and Sir George Lewis. Daisy said, "Which of you three men, if your wives had done wrong with some man, would accept a sum of money from that man?" Dead silence. A number of times, Sir George and Mrs. Bateman's representatives agreed on various settlements for Mary, Jessie and Daisy, only to have them rejected by Mrs. Bateman.

It also burst upon Daisy unpleasantly that having a well-defined status at last as an authentic widow, free to marry if she chose, had its disadvantages. She wailed to Mabel from Hackwood, Basingstoke, that she was finding herself viewed as a designing female! Sol Dungarvan had made his metamorphosis to Sol Cork, having come into his earldom upon his father's death in 1904, and he was in the same house party. The Earl of Cork and Orrery, we assume, was a good catch. Though he was paired off with another lady for the house party, he kept seeking Daisy out and making his jokes at her expense, with

Daisy retorting in kind, just as they had always done. "The whole thing is that Sol *knows* he is safe with me, and has always been terrified of showing attention to eligible girls, but knows *I* don't want to marry him." But Sol's partner and her friends were looking at Daisy askance, as was even Daisy's dear friend, Lady Ota Wilton! This sort of thing bothered Daisy more than the amount she might eventually receive from Willy's estate.

It was not all heartache and problems, though. At Dinard, where Daisy had gone for a while after Willy's death, she wrote Mabel that she was very contented and happy and surrounded by friends. "Louise Maxwell is here, and asks me to lunch and dine. Mrs. Lawrence takes me to drive to all the old châteaux in her beautiful motor car, the Fitzgibbons are very attentive." Abby Lippitt Hunter had a villa just across the road from where Daisy was staying, and Daisy spent the mornings with her. "We sit in the garden and rest and get fat and in the afternoon we are very gay!"

From the time of the separation from Willy Low, until Willy's death, there is little mention of General Sir Archibald Hunter. He had taken part in the Boer War, and then had gone out to India as Commanding General, Western Command of India. Not long after Willy's death, Daisy wrote Mama that Sir Archie was at Simla with "Kitchener of Khartoum" but would be in England before long. The correspondence had been maintained, however, and Sir Archie's faith and support had been a source of strength and comfort to her through the grueling aftermath of the separation. When the crisis about the will arose, Sir Archie had advised Daisy to follow Arthur as a guide, even before Papa and Mama.

In the October following Willy's death in June, Sir Archie wrote Daisy a long letter, telling her that he loved her. He advised her to confide in Arthur and follow his guidance in this matter too. As much as the Gordon men, Sir Archie wished to guard her against gossip, which had not touched Daisy herself to date, and wanted her to have the protection of the men of her family, even though it might militate against his own interests and desires. "It speaks well for your own life, Arthur, that a man like A. H. should look up to you as a standard to guide you and me," Daisy wrote her brother, placing her own affectionate interpretation on Sir Archie's delicacy and punctiliousness where she herself was concerned. "I can't explain now, beyond saying he doesn't think he is worthy of me, and though that is untrue, he is right to say it is impossible. But I am glad to know he cares for me. *That* makes all else insignificant."

What "it" was is obvious enough, but why was it impossible? Sir Archie's letter declaring his love is not among the available documents—it is conceivable that Arthur destroyed it, after her death, with other letters which revealed the more than friendly feeling other men were to have for Daisy; Arthur seems to have looked upon romance as not quite proper for his middle-aged sister. The record is clear, however, that while Willy lived, Sir Archie had concealed the depth of the feeling he must long have had for Daisy, while Daisy's whole capacity for romantic love had been centered upon Willy. They had nothing to reproach themselves with. It seems far-fetched that Sir Archie, at least, would have considered their own friendship before Willy's death as a deterrent to their marriage, after a suitable interval had elapsed.

There may be an explanation in a poem Daisy wrote during this period.

> When we are young, and heart to heart
>   Whispers of things untried, divine,
>   Before the dregs are in the wine
> Or disillusion plays a part—
>   When we are young, is it not true,
>   That love's eternal, when it's new?
>
> When we are old, and time has bred
>   A callous tolerance in love's stead
>   Blessed are the eyes whose clearer view
> Can read the wisdom of the whole,
>   The deeper meaning of the soul,
>   The Love Eternal—old or new!

It was to be many years before Daisy would be able to find the clearer view of her tragedy, to read the wisdom of the whole. She was to torture herself over the debacle of her young love and dreams until, like her Grandmother Juliette, she found the deeper meaning of the soul in the purposeful use of her many abilities. By then the time for romantic love had gone by. Before he wrote his letter, Sir Archie had been in England and had seen Daisy. It may be he recognized that her bruised and battered heart should not be asked to entertain a new love.

Daisy spent the Christmas holidays of 1905 with Lord Arthur and Lady Ota Wilton, lunched the day after New Year's with Lady Olive Cairns, who lived near Southampton, and then went on to France to join Abby Lippitt Hunter, after a tempestuous Channel crossing that lasted eighteen hours. She had barely greeted Abby, when a wire came from Sir George Lewis telling her to return at once.

She wrote jubilantly on the sixth of January, 1906, to "My dearest Father, Mother, Brothers and Sisters and all my dear ones. . . . I took the same cockle shell boat, and we were *twenty* hours making the crossing. It was worth all that journey to hear from Sir George himself that the case was settled and see the sparkle and delight in his brilliant eye. I met him at his own house. After the interview, he said, 'Now come upstairs to see my wife!' Lady Lewis beamed with delight over my enthusiasm, for Sir George has indeed been my earthly Providence. Mrs. Bateman is very ill. She has only asked one thing, and that is that I shall not in future say unkind things of her. She never can sleep, but always thinks she is in a Court of Law."

Mrs. Bateman had agreed finally to grant Mary and Jessie an amount comparable to what Amy and Katy received under the will. Daisy got £40,000 in discharge of her annuity, £10,000 of this to be paid within three months, and 3½ per cent interest to be paid on the balance until it was paid in full; £20,000 besides in six months time, at the same interest; her allowance paid up to date, with £2,500 at once; and £50,000 in shares in the Chalmers Guthrie firm, as soon as the will was proved.

This was in addition to all of Willy's holdings in America, including the Low house in Savannah, which Daisy had been particularly anxious that Mrs. Bateman should not have. The Georgia statutes required three witnesses to a will, whereas Willy Low's had had only two. Through this lucky chance, Willy Low was held under American law to have died intestate, hence all of his property and investments in this country reverted to his widow.

As nearly as can be figured, after the estate was settled Daisy received in all something like $500,000 which in the early 1900's would have bought very much more than a million would to-day. The greater part of her English inheritance, however, was in shares in the Chalmers Guthrie Company. Daisy never felt comfortable about this company, but then she was suspicious of anyone with whom she had business dealings. She and Mrs. Bateman held an equal number of shares in the company. After the estate was settled, the only mentions of Mrs. Bateman are in this connection, which seems to have been less embarrassing than might have been imagined, because Mrs. Bateman tried to keep out of Daisy's way.

The long ordeal was over and Daisy had attained the objective upon which she had focused since 1902—that no one should be able to say she had not dared claim her just rights because of some blot on her own record. There had never been a stain on the Gordon name—what had impelled Daisy most strongly in her long effort was that no stain should accrue to the Gordon name, through weakness or cowardice on her part. Now she stood completely vindicated before the world.

November 26, 1906, Daisy wrote to Papa: "All my money bothers are now at an end, for I met, by appointment, Sir G. Lewis, Mr. Gasquet and George Robertson and they, or rather George handed over 22,000 pounds, which is the whole amount due, and my heart is full of thankfulness. 'Sweet are the uses of adversity,' for I can appreciate the blessings I now enjoy, ten-fold. The Psalms at Church today had two lines that applied to me—'It is good for me, that I have been afflicted; that I might learn thy statutes. The law of thy mouth is better unto me than thousands of gold and silver.' I feel like singing Peans of Praise, first to God, then to you and Mama, for the love and sympathy you have given me, then to Sir G. Lewis, and then to little Mabel and Arthur and all my brothers and sisters and to the host of friends that have held out kind hands during the dark years that I now hope are over forever."

All Daisy had to do now was to find something to live for.

CHAPTER XVI

———————— ☆ ————————

BACK INTO THE SUNLIGHT

A SHADOW was lifted from the entire Gordon family with the lifting of the shadow from Daisy's heart. She went through a period of depression, it is true, following her first joyful reaction to her triumph over Mrs. Bateman. She wrote Nellie: "I am just an idle woman of the world, with no real work or duties. I would like to get away from the world somewhere and work at sculpturing—start to do some work in life."

This feeling seemed to pass, however, and soon she was involved more deeply with "the world" than she had been even during her life with Billow. The Lows had never had a house in London, Billow having shared bachelor quarters with several men friends, while Daisy and Mabel stayed at Claridge's Hotel when they came for special events of the London season. During the years that she struggled with humiliation and abasement, Daisy had not felt like taking part in the London social scene. Now, soon after her financial affairs were settled, she bought the house at 40 Grosvenor Street which she had rented prior to Billow's death, and number 39, next door. She took a box at the opera. From this time on she immersed herself in the London season every summer. Her letters to Nellie are filled with accounts of memorable first nights at the theater, operatic events, balls and receptions at London's great houses. However much Nellie might affect disdain for the follies and fripperies of British high society, she gloried just the same in the evidence that her daughter had a secure place in it, and Daisy was well aware of this.

For the Scottish season, Daisy rented Lochs, a small place near Meggernie. Meggernie, belonging to Ian Bullough, the son of Daisy's great friend Alix Beech, was another enchanting castle, with conical towers, slit windows in its thick stone walls and half a ghost—that of a lady who had been cut in two by her jealous husband. Daisy, visiting Meggernie in winter when the landscape was covered with snow, wrote Eleanor that it looked just like the fairy castles the two of them had conjured out of their imaginations when they were children.

From America, once again, came visitors to Grosvenor Street and Lochs, almost in a steady stream. In addition to Daisy's contemporaries, the guests now included her nephews and nieces, and sons and daughters of her old friends, as each grew old enough for adult entertainments. Parents of girls had no need to worry in entrusting their young daughters to Daisy's care. She was a demon chaperon, guarding her charges' welfare as zealously as her own had been guarded in her girlhood and young womanhood, sometimes more zealously than the charges themselves considered necessary. But they had a marvelous time. Daisy would give lovely parties for them, Sol Cork could be counted on to give a dinner for any young feminine guest of Daisy's. The nephews and nieces would be invited to stay at the Kiplings' on the ground of the very tenuous cousinship, and at the castles and manor houses where Daisy was an intimate.

The sons of Daisy's English friends were growing up, too, and Ian Bullough would have groups of them at Meggernie for the deer stalking. The young men would come to Lochs of an evening to banter with Daisy and often took her with them when they went shooting. She wrote home about the fine buck Hugh Grosvenor had shot when out on the hills with Daisy. Proudly she described the big stag she herself had shot after a seven-hour stalk in the rain. These young chaps, who found Daisy a delightful companion as did the military men of her own age, called her "Daisy." Whereas the letters from her close friends among the high British brass were always addressed sedately to "Mrs. Low."

From 1906 on, Daisy spent her winters in America, partly in Savannah, partly in the accustomed rounds of visits to relatives and old friends. She was gayer, more sparkling than ever, more deeply committed to the social round than ever, apparently more determined in the pursuit of pleasure. The dark years were never referred to. She drove them firmly underground— perhaps too firmly for her ultimate good.

On December 21, 1907, Willie and Nellie would have been married fifty years. Daisy, putting aside the ache this date, her wedding day, too, held for her, threw herself enthusiastically, along with the other children, into making the golden wedding a joyous and memorable celebration.

For days ahead of time, gifts and congratulatory notes poured in from many states, and from many parts of the British Empire. The gifts were magnificent, the one from the children being a gold coffee service, the tray of crystal with gold edge and crest, the coffee pot, cream jug, sugar bowl and sugar tongs of solid gold. But all agreed that the most magnificent of all was the Georgia Hussars' present to Willie—a gold loving cup eighteen inches high, engraved on one side with the picture of a cavalry-man riding a prancing charger, on the other with an inscription wreathed in oak leaves for strength, and in laurel leaves for valor.

The description of the reception took up columns on the society pages of the Savannah papers. Nellie appeared in white brocaded satin, embroidered in gold and finished at the neck and sleeves with beautiful point lace. This had been made for the occasion. But on her head she wore the wreath of wax orange blossoms she had worn in 1857. Daisy had gilded it, and declared it looked like solid gold.

Daisy's gown was of rare old lace embroidered with pale pink coral beads. The coral design was laid on folds of cream satin over the lace bodice, extending in a panel down the front and outlining the graceful skirt. She wore all her diamonds, as she had when presented at Court. Eleanor and Mabel, Bill's wife, Ellie, and Arthur's new wife, Margaret, were also gorgeously arrayed. The little General must have been very proud of the bevy of Gordon ladies.

Daisy's brilliance was particularly commented on, on this occasion. It is significant that as soon as the guests had left and Daisy had gone to her room, she became violently ill. She called the illness "cholera morbus"—one suspects it was an emotional repercussion. But it did not prevent her from getting up the next morning and starting off for India, accompanied by Grace Carter, one of her triumvirate of closest chums from the Mesdemoiselles Charbonnier's school, and her niece Beth Parker. This was another triumphal tour, for a number of the officer friends she had made on her Egyptian trip of 1895 had now moved on to high posts in the subcontinent. In addition to General Sir Archibald Hunter, who was a very big mogul indeed in India, there was Neville Smyth, now a major, whom Daisy had defended so stoutly against young Winston Churchill. There was also Lord Mahon, who, under Sir Archie's command in the Boer War, had relieved famous Mafeking, held for ten long months by an officer little known up to that time, one Colonel Robert Baden-Powell. Hunter provided a servant to look after the American ladies throughout their travels over India and would have provided an aide-de-camp as well, but Daisy declined the aide-de-camp, on the ground that she knew very well the officer delegated would have hated the assignment. However, Lord Mahon and Neville Smyth—Sir Archie was in Burma, inspecting his command there when they arrived—saw that the ladies got comfortably from place to place, and that they were "as gay as butterflies," wherever they went. The party spent a week as the guests of Sir Francis Younghusband, the first Westerner to penetrate to Lhassa, at Jammur, where the Maharajah of Kashmir held his Court in winter. Sir Francis was the English adviser to the Maharajah, and Daisy and her party were entertained with oriental splendor, which Daisy adored. She managed, through the help of Lord Mahon, to get to the Khyber Pass, where troops were massing for an attack on the Afghan tribes, and to other places in India of which her friend Rudyard Kipling had written.

But to Daisy, the most notable part of the whole marvelous experience was the kindness shown by her officer friends when at Agra the three Americans came down with chicken pox, thought at first to be smallpox. Lord Mahon at once telegraphed that he was on his way to look after them, several telegrams a day came from both Neville Smyth and Archibald Hunter. And when the hotel at Agra in which they were quarantined closed and no other place would take them in, Neville Smyth moved out of his charming bungalow at Mhow and installed them in it. Later Daisy learned that Major Smyth had had to hire more servants to take care of his guests and buy a complete kitchen equipment, since he had been eating at the mess. Also, that the bungalow into which Major Smyth had moved had been available because there had been several cases of plague in it and no one would live there! Daisy, greatly affected, wrote home that "my own father and brothers could not have done more, when I was ill, than these officers!"

It was the only kind of attention Daisy wanted, now, from the male sex. She avoided romantic advances, as she had in her schooldays. During her forties and fifties, she held the devoted affection of a number of fine, prominent Englishmen—it might be said that, in an eminently respectable way, she was the darling of the British high command. There can be no doubt that if she had been receptive, more than one of these friendships could have developed easily into love. For some years after Willy Low's death, she used her wit and social skill to keep their friendships.

But it was only in such subtle, scarcely discernible ways that her scars betrayed themselves. Daisy displayed the depth of her nature only when circumstances demanded the courage, resolution and uncommon sense she could summon when things were grim. Throughout her years of crisis, the deeper side had held sway. She had acted with extraordinary poise and dignity, her thinking had gone straight to the heart of her difficulties, there had been only occasional flashes of her "lighter side"—which covered, in addition to her love of fun, weird reasoning processes, actions impossible to understand by any known standards of human behavior. With the crisis behind her, she stepped back into her rôle of charming zany, spreading confusion and happiness impartially as she went her erratic way.

Savannah used to view her annual descent with mingled anticipation and apprehension. It meant lovely parties for the grownups, glorious picnics for the smaller nephews and nieces and their friends.

But at least half the time Daisy would forget all about having asked people to her house. Her nephew, Rowland Leigh, describes one occasion when she had invited a large company to a ball. He got there a little late and found all the guests assembled, but no hostess. Volunteering to investigate the situation,

he went up to Daisy's room and found her comfortably en-
sconced in bed, going over her bills. Her deafness had kept her
from hearing the noise of the arrivals, the hum of conversation
below.

"What are you doing here?" she demanded rather sharply,
when her nephew invaded her room.

"Do you realize you're giving a dance downstairs?"

"Why, so I am! I'll be down in five minutes." And he says
she was.

After a long succession of maids of various nationalities,
Daisy at length acquired a Scot, Bella MacDonald, who stayed
with her to the end and eventually took over the functions of
housekeeper, major-domo and social secretary. Bella became
almost as much of a legend in Savannah as Daisy herself. When
luncheon guests arrived at Daisy's house to find that their
hostess was off attending somebody else's party having forgotten
all about her own, they would say good-naturedly to Bella,
"Mrs. Low has invited us to lunch, and we intend to be fed!"
Bella would see that they were.

Daisy bought her first car in Savannah, and her home city
went with her through her pangs in learning to drive. In those
days drivers' licenses had not been thought of. The adventurous souls who acquired automobiles went out a time or two
with the dealer to find how to start and stop the thing, otherwise they were on their own. In addition to her inexperience,
Daisy ignored alike the rules of the road and the laws of physics,
which intensified the perils.

Her neighbors always dropped whatever they were doing to
watch when Daisy prepared to start off in her "motor," as she
called it. The servants would push the car out of the garage,
and maneuver it around until it faced in the direction in which
Daisy wished to go. Then the cook would take up a stance in
the street in one direction, the butler in the other. Daisy would
start the engine, with much sputtering and backfiring. At her
signal, the cook and butler would stop the traffic coming from
both directions; the car would give a sudden leap, either forward or backward, Daisy never knowing in advance which it
was going to be; and then off she would go down the wrong side
of the street, waving happily to her audience. Even the intrepid

Willie Gordon quailed when Daisy suggested taking him out in her motor.

Savannah citizens quickly learned to get out of the way when they saw her coming in her car. But inanimate objects could not do this. Carrying out the intricate maneuver of turning a corner, Daisy one day ran into a little wooden house at the junction of Gaston and Bull Streets, where Armstrong Junior College now stands. She came to a stop inside the dining room, where the astonished family was eating lunch. She backed out, got to a phone, told her brother Bill what had happened and asked him to handle it for her.

"What did you say to the people when you crashed through the side of their house?" he asked wishing, lawyerlike, to know to what extent she had committed herself.

"Why, I didn't say anything. I didn't think it would be polite to bother them while they were eating!"

When Daisy turned her carriage house over to the Girl Scouts, she precipitated a crisis in the Judge Meldrim family. One morning Ellie, Bill's wife, called Mrs. Meldrim and told her, under pledge of secrecy, that Daisy planned to ask Judge Meldrim if she might keep her car in his carriage house.

"I thought you might want to do something about it," whispered Ellie, in conspiratorial tones.

Mrs. Meldrim tried to phone the Judge at the Court House to warn him, but he was on the bench and could not be reached. "It was a real dilemma," Jane Meldrim Hewitt recalls. "Daisy was so gracious and charming that everyone wanted to please her. There was room for a second car. Father was what you might call gallant, and a great friend of General Gordon's besides. What would he do? We waited breathlessly for Mother to break the news when Father got home that night.

" 'My dear,' she said, handing him his mint julep, 'Daisy Low wants to use our garage, and I'm not sure it is a very good idea. What do you think?'

" 'I think it is too small,' replied Father calmly, taking an approving sip of his julep.

" 'Too small?' we all gasped in unison.

" 'Yes,' said Father. 'I told Mr. Bryson, on my way to the Court House this morning, that I would take an electric coupé for Mrs. Meldrim and the girls. It will fill the garage.' We could hardly believe our ears. To have one car was epoch making in Savannah in those days. Two for one family was unheard of.

" 'Yes,' went on Father, reflectively, 'Mr. Bryson has been trying to sell me an electric for some time. I thought the price was too high. But when Arthur said—'

" 'Oh, you met Arthur Gordon this morning?'

" 'Yes, on my way to the office, and he mentioned something about Miss Daisy's plan. He said the General thought I ought to know. And then I dropped by Bryson's and ordered the electric. So when Miss Daisy asked me—'

" 'You saw Daisy too?'

" 'Yes. She was waiting for me when I got to the office. I certainly hated to have to tell her there wouldn't be room for her car in our carriage house.'

"There was a pause. 'But Peter,' said Mother, 'can we afford the second car? You said the price was too high.'

" 'No price is too high!' said Father."

But it was in financial matters that Daisy's peculiarities shone to fullest advantage. Though she now was a well-to-do-woman, her money troubles were not done with and never were done with. It was not that Daisy didn't try. When her fortune was placed in her hands, she determined with all her might to administer it wisely. She got the best advice—her English consultant foretold, in 1906, the American panic of 1907—and distributed her cash in a variety of industries in a number of different countries, so that economic doldrums in one industry or country would be balanced by prosperity in another. She used both her Grosvenor Street houses and the Low house in Savannah much of the time as income properties, renting them out when she could do so to advantage. She was so bent, in fact, upon proving herself a good business woman that she became a veritable Scrooge.

When George Robertson turned over the £22,000 which had set her to singing "peans" of praise, she at once asked Papa if he wouldn't borrow some or all of it. "It is there in the bank, and they will only pay me four per cent and you will pay me five per cent, won't you? Every day that it remains uninvested means a loss. That is why I suggest lending it to you at five per cent." Daisy would have given Papa every penny she possessed, she would have given him her life. That it was a rather poor return for all his generosity to ask him to pay higher interest than she could get elsewhere, did not occur to her.

She seems to have imposed blatantly upon her family in other ways, going around in Savannah without money in her purse, so that whoever was with her had to pay for things she bought; borrowing sums and then forgetting all about it. Everyone in the family had been delighted to help Daisy when she was in trouble. But now that she was better off financially than any of them, Papa decided the time had come to speak to her about these matters. Daisy was so hurt that when Papa and Mama came to the boat to see her off for England in May, 1907, Daisy begged them to excuse her and did not appear! As was her custom when she had reacted ungraciously, no sooner had the boat sailed than she was overcome with contrition. "I should have seen you, but feared I would be cross and mar our parting. I want to ask pardon for what crossness I have shown. . . . I am really grateful to Papa for telling me my faults. It gave me a shock at the time, for fear my family thought me, a rich woman, sponging on you. . . . I shall try hard to keep some change always about me. Some silver dollars sewed in my belt would be uncomfortable to wear, but easy to get at and use as ready money, and hard to give to beggars—my loose cash always goes to beggars. . . . I love you so much!" A typical Daisy idea —to sew silver dollars in her belt. Whether or not she carried it out is not recorded.

She would quarrel with Savannah workers and tradespeople over their bills and refuse to pay them. Eventually these would be laid on Willie's doorstep. Daisy once tearfully begged Papa and Mama to stop paying her bills, for then she was under obligation to repay Papa or Mama. These tradesfolk were robbers, she insisted; she paid all her honorable bills. Finally Papa thought the time had come to set Daisy straight about this habit too. She had refused to pay a carpenter's bill for fixing boards on the roof, because the man had not also painted the roof.

Papa wrote, dictating the letter to his stenographer: "It is natural for you to want to manage your own affairs and it is your legal right to make a bargain according to your own ideas— if you can get the other party to consent to the bargain you propose. Unfortunately, you are so inexperienced that you don't express in the terms of the bargain all the details which turn out to be desirable. In this case . . . you are not only making an illegal demand for something to which you are not entitled, but you make yourself ridiculous in doing so. I write you frankly, because you need to have the truth laid before you and the unpleasant task devolves upon your father, when there is no one else to do it.

"You are very generous toward those who arouse your sympathies. In business, you are suspicious of being imposed upon and so inexperienced that you frequently fail to get as good results as you would if you had some confidence in the honesty and expert knowledge of the people you employ.

"Your methods of making contracts and paying your bills may be adapted to England, but not to Savannah, and I do hope, for your own sake as well as for the peace of mind of your relatives and business representatives, that you will reform. Your loving Papa."

Daisy was deeply wounded, unable to see how she had been in the wrong, and up in arms because Papa had dictated his little scolding. She wrote him to "pay the carpenter anything you choose, only pay it quickly, because each month since he finished work, his bill has increased." She said she was glad to follow Papa's advice and glad to be corrected by him. "But please hereafter write it yourself. What you say to me whether fair or unfair is meant for me alone and not for the benefit of the office or your clerks. I would be very much obliged if you would neither pay nor try to pay any of my bills, as we are so far apart and life is short and it is not worth while the angry letters sent 3000,000 miles away across the sea. . . . Much love."

In a letter to Arthur she said she felt inclined to insert this notice in the Savannah papers: "To all whom it may concern: General and Mrs. W. W. Gordon refuse to be responsible for Mrs. Low's bills or any accounts of hers. All persons presenting her bills to her parents will be prosecuted with the utmost rigor of the law!"

She hurt Papa's feelings in her turn when she disregarded his advice about a Venezuelan investment he had gone to considerable pains to investigate at her request, because she got a "better tip, from a big Wall Street broker." Daisy mulled this over for a while, then wrote Arthur that she really ought not to bother Papa with her business affairs, he was too old. "Though he seemed to enjoy it—digging up information about investments—when I was in Savannah." Papa may perhaps have considered that he would have been better off if he had supported his daughter, as he had suggested in the beginning, instead of having the thankless task of trying to help her run her affairs.

She once wrote Arthur: "I hope it has not put you in an awkward position for me to have said I would sell the lot for $15,000, and then cable that I refused to sell the lot? When I saw the plans I realized how I hated the idea of a garage there with horns tooting day and night so I cabled and refused."

Daisy's inability to add or subtract correctly also caused complications for Papa and Arthur and W. W. Gordon & Company. One Sunday morning, when Daisy was in Savannah, she phoned Arthur to come to her house at once. He found her surrounded with bankbooks and bills, as usual having gone to bed to do her sums.

"Arthur, I'm ruined!" she cried in tragic tones. "I have overdrawn my bank account and I have no more money!"

Arthur said, "I am on my way to church. I will see you later."

When he stopped in again after the service he found Daisy in the best of spirits, cheerily singing "Susie, Oh My Darlin'!"

"I thought you were ruined," Arthur commented. "What are you so happy about?"

Daisy replied airily, "After you left I took a phenacetin pill and then discovered that I had a large balance in the bank!"

When Daisy got back to England from her trip to India, she wrote Papa as airily that she had returned with just two pounds left to her name. She would appreciate it if Papa and Arthur would send her various sums owed her by members of the family and by W. W. Gordon & Company.

Arthur replied, irately for him, that she must have taken a phenacetin pill before she wrote this letter. "You are about $1,000 wrong in your estimate of what is due. On Nov. 14, 1907, you owed the firm $972.40. You seem to have overlooked this trifle. On Jan. 1, you had overdrawn still further and owed the firm $2,119 (not 200 pounds or $1,000 as you state in your letter)." He concluded sarcastically, "I am sorry you are so hard up. I hope you haven't speculated or loaned too much to friends."

A few weeks later he wrote, without sarcasm this time, "You speak of having the fact brought home to you that you are using capital and not replacing it. I think your principal difficulty comes from *anticipating income.* You are too impatient to wait *until* you get your income before you spend it. If you would deny yourself the pleasures of making your friends happy, sit tight and live inside your income for a few months, you would accumulate a fund *from your income* sufficient to take trips and give people pleasure, and all without the harassing feeling that you are in debt and hard up. Forgive these sage remarks."

Daisy thanked Arthur for his sage remarks, but when Margaret, Arthur's wife, asked Daisy to visit them, she declined. "I must 'sit tight' and set my house in order so that I shall never again 'anticipate income.' "

Oddly, she took admonitions from Nellie about money in good spirit. Not long after she had thrown his own words back at Arthur, she wrote Mabel that "Mama has been writing me the *sweetest* letters all along. She has certainly spoken words of wisdom about my money affairs, and none of her letters have made me cross, as you feared they would do. Though I don't agree with all her advice, it is charmingly put to me and so sweet that I twice woke up in the night and thought how awfully sensible she is and how right to tell us children when we are wrong."

She had some quirk, however, about having her financial and mathematical procedures questioned by any male, even by her adored papa and younger brother, even by General Sir Archibald Hunter. This quirk seems, in fact, to have brought her long and deeply cherished friendship with Sir Archie to an end. From the first, she had been suspicious of the Chalmers Guthrie Company, in which when all was settled she held sixty-eight thousand shares. She began probing into the way the company was being run.

She wrote Arthur: "The chairman is Charles Guthrie, holding sixteen hundred shares, a country squire whose wife by her influence keeps the Low family quiet. Among the directors are Mrs. Bateman's lawyer, Mr. Taylor, who keeps Mrs. Bateman quiet. . . . I don't wonder we can't get dividends if the six directors are paid £2,000 a year each. . . ." Daisy had told Sir Archie, too, about her dissatisfaction with the Chalmers Guthrie firm and she felt he had not shown a proper sympathy. Eventually she wrote Arthur that Sir Archie was in London, but she had not seen him and had no intention of seeing him. "He wrote me a very sarcastic letter when I reported to him the last meeting of the Chalmers Guthrie Company." It appears to have been a permanent break.

So far as we know, Daisy did not suffer any substantial loss through the investment in the Chalmers Guthrie Company. Her income seems to have been constant enough until World War I brought business to a standstill. But Daisy was always having money troubles just the same. She was continually running short, getting overdrawn at the bank and with W. W. Gordon & Company, writing Arthur frantically to speed a payment of $200 or even less, to save her from financial ruin. This was because she was as generous in her private affairs as she was miserly when it came to business arrangements. She would promise Arthur that she would stop lending money to her friends, she would listen gratefully to Mama's suggestions about curbing her generosity, but she could never resist an appeal, or an appearance of need. Her generosity made trouble for her many times. On one occasion she had leased 40 Grosvenor Street to the former Lady Randolph Churchill, who had married Mr. Cornwallis West, but allowed the friend of a friend, who had been unable to find lodgings, to stay there until Mrs. West was ready to move in. The lady, whom Daisy herself had never met, immediately took the ground that Daisy had rented her the house, and refused to vacate. Daisy had a hard time to get rid of her.

"I must be a fool!" Daisy wrote Mabel. "Certainly very odd things happen to me.

"I had a little London house and it was very gay.
I lent it to a lady to occupy one day.
She used my things, abused my things and then refused to go.
I would not lend my house again for all she could bestow!"

Yet the Misses Phillips, Daisy's neighbors on Lafayette Square in Savannah for many years, remember that one day Daisy had just finished telling them she must get a good rental for the Low house, because she needed the money badly, when a young woman dropped in, tired out from house hunting.

"I can't find a thing that Charlie and I can afford."

"What a coincidence!" exclaimed Daisy. "I have been looking for a responsible couple to live in my house and take care of it for me. Of course there would be no rent." When the young woman demurred at occupying the stately house without paying anything, Daisy insisted, "I wouldn't know what to do with any more money. It would just be an embarrassment to me!" Often she took a needy family into one of her houses in Grosvenor Street while she helped the husband find work. If both happened to be rented, she would ask Mabel to take a needy family into her house, an arrangement that did not always work out to the Leighs' satisfaction. Once Daisy managed to get into the bad graces of both Nellie and Eleanor with one of her charitable projects. Daisy found a post with Aunt Eliza in America for Mrs. Cowie, a widowed mother she had taken under her wing—she felt that the best way to help was to enable people to help themselves, which was a sound enough principle. But the Cowie baby got sick and was unable to travel, Daisy sent the mother on to America just the same, renting a cottage in the country and hiring a nurse to care for the children. That it would be simpler to have the woman delay her departure and take care of her children herself was the sort of thing that did not enter Daisy's mind. When Nellie had a fit because Daisy had separated the children from their mother, Daisy couldn't understand it.

Later, Daisy herself, with Bella's help, took the children to America and had a lively set-to with the immigration officials on her arrival in New York Harbor. Bella, being a Scot, and the small Cowie children, being English, were viewed with deep suspicion. Afterwards Daisy used to declaim dramatically, "Ellis Island almost touches the Statue of Liberty, where all the freedom of the United States is concentrated in one stone. In reality we are slaves!"

She became more and more indignant under the cross-examination to which she was subjected about these "dangerous" aliens. When asked to name an American citizen who would if necessary support the Cowie children, Daisy gave the most awe-inspiring name she could think of off hand, that of the Honorable Wayne Parker, member of Congress. It created the "sensation among the fossils" she had hoped it would. Asked more respectfully this time what the nature of Mr. Parker's interest in the children was, Daisy burst out laughing.

"Gentlemen, nobody would be more astonished than Mr. Parker to hear even of the existence of these children!"

Daisy maintained that it appealed to the "macabre Yankie" sense of humor of the Immigration officials to saddle a congressman with the maintenance of two children he had never heard of, and they voted unanimously to admit the Cowies. Daisy thought it all very funny, but Eleanor was not amused. Devoted as she was to her sister Crazy, Eleanor got very upset when Daisy drew Eleanor's politician husband into her unorthodox enterprises. New Jersey voters did not know and love Daisy the way Savannah did, Eleanor was always afraid that some "stunt" of Daisy's would put Wayne out of politics. To smooth her down, Daisy sent affidavits to the Department of Immigration, obligating herself for the support of the Cowie children. "Though how the incident can possibly ruin Wayne's career I cannot see!" she wrote a bit snappishly to Eleanor.

And while Daisy complicated the lives of Papa and Arthur with her business vagaries, and often ran afoul of her mother and sisters through her other peculiarities, her tenderness and consideration for the different members of her family were unremitting. Bill and Ellie lost a baby in 1908. Daisy arranged to spend with Ellie the daytime hours, while Bill had to be at his office, so that her sister-in-law might have company for "her poor lonely heart." Daisy took a special fond interest in Bill's son B., who had been rendered completely deaf by an illness in his babyhood. She was always inventing compelling reasons for B. to visit her in London or at Lochs. B. had become a fine tennis player, so Daisy would make it her business to see that there was a tennis court available for B. and someone about who could give him a good game.

When she heard, in England, that Papa had a cold, she insisted that Papa, Mama, Arthur's wife, Margaret, and his little daughter, Mary Stuart, should come to her at once. Arthur could follow later. As usual she pleaded her own need of them. "I am aching with loneliness, dearest Papa, and I beg

you, darling, to come. . . . You shall carve for the family, you
shan't be asked to go out in any motor. . . . I've got my house
in order and I know I can make you comfortable. I want you,
my honey, I want you!"

Her full heart went out to her friends in the same way. "Daisy
had the sweetest smile of anyone I have ever known," one
Savannah lady remembers. And another, "I think the most
notable thing about her was her sympathy. I have never seen
such agony on a human countenance as when Daisy told me
that Katy Low had cancer."

Savannah, which knew Daisy well, continued to love her
dearly in spite of her oddities. And Arthur and Papa, who
knew her even better, continued patiently to untangle her
financial messes. They must have exchanged wry smiles and
headshakes over many of her letters, but it is remarkable how
seldom they complained. For one thing, it did no good. For
another, perhaps the Gordon men came, like so many of Daisy's
associates, to have a certain pride in Daisy's erratic performances, and would not have changed her if they could.

The years slipped by so agreeably that Daisy appeared to
have forgotten all about her desire to do "some worthwhile
work." It seemed to be enough that she had established a
reputation as a notable London hostess. Her affairs were
usually small but very select, and her food was unequalled. By
this time her former cook, Mrs. Lewis, had three hotels in
London and one in Paris and was "far too big a swell to cook
herself." Nevertheless when Daisy gave a dinner party, Rosa
Lewis would come and do the cooking. Daisy wrote a lyrical
description of a Derby Night dinner. "Those who were there
have told everyone they met that it was the best dinner ever
served. I have become famous through my cook! Such is the
power of good food on London society!"

Mrs. Lewis, on her side, attributed much of her early success
as a cateress to the Southern recipes and characteristic delicacies
she had first encountered when she was with the Lows. In the
book she wrote, *Queen of Cooks and Some Kings*—it created
something of a stir in England when it came out in the early
1920's—she had a good deal to say about Willy Low and Daisy,
and about General and Mrs. Gordon, taking pains to impress

upon her English readers that "they were your real American aristocracy—from Savannah." Willy Low, she said, had brought over the first Virginia hams ever seen in England, and used to give them to her to serve to King Edward and his brother, the Duke of Edinburgh. "It was the greatest thing, in those days, to have a Virginia ham." Mrs. Lewis used sweet potatoes, which Mosianna Milledge had taught her to prepare in a variety of ways, as the *pièce de résistance* at her dinners for royalty; and at charity bazaars made waffles by Nellie's famous recipe, and served them in their long-handled irons. The irons were copied from those Daisy brought with her when she came to England to live. Eventually Jackson's in Picadilly began importing Virginia hams, sweet potatoes, terrapin soup, canvasback ducks and brandied peaches, which Daisy's English friends had enjoyed either at her table or when they visited the Gordons in Savannah. These were in great demand. According to Mrs. Lewis, the growing of sweet corn was started in England as a result of the corn Willie Gordon had sent to Daisy at Wellesbourne.

In the summer of 1909, Willie asked Daisy to lend her skill as a hostess to himself and Nellie, for a very special occasion. An unaccustomed pride shows through the formality with which Willie invited Daisy to come to Savannah earlier than was her habit to help them get the house ready to receive the President of the United States, William Howard Taft, and to stay and help them entertain him.

Willie had been on cordial terms with the White House beginning with President McKinley's incumbency, numbering Theodore Roosevelt, too, among his admirers. With President Taft there was the bond that both were Yale alumni. Willie had helped organize the Yale Alumni Association in Savannah, and had served as its first president. He had urged the erection of a memorial at Yale to the students from North and South who had lost their lives in the War between the States. In the spring of 1909, he attended a meeting of alumni at Yale, over which Taft presided. A committee was appointed to plan the memorial, and Taft made Willie Gordon its chairman. The two struck up a warm friendship.

Daisy was only too happy to put at her parents' disposal her own experience in entertaining the man who now was King of England. They must find out all about presidential protocol, she wrote. Perhaps Wayne Parker could help with that, through his connections with the State Department. There must be no slip-ups, such as the one Daisy was spared, when she entertained the Prince of Wales, only through Lady Warwick's thoughtfulness in bringing the red carpet. Daisy felt the house should be redecorated from top to bottom and sent her mother such a long list of things to be done, that Nellie replied:

"Please send me five hundred pounds *at once* to buy all the expensive articles you describe! I shall get the new lace for the door curtains. I *may* indulge in four pairs of new curtains for the library. I don't understand about the red, white and blue bunting for decorations, as I heard your Papa say we should only hang out our big U. S. flag over the front porch, which will be quite *enough*. . . . I may buy some new tamboured muslin curtains for your room—but *don't touch my drawing-room curtains! Those are sacred!* I think *one* coat of fresh paint on the woodwork of the halls would be an advantage, but why we should paint all the walls from attic down I cannot see." Nellie then relented enough to say that Daisy needn't send the five hundred pounds after all, that was only a joke. But as for protocol, Nellie felt that when one Yale man was visiting another, both would know how to conduct themselves without any help from outsiders.

When Daisy arrived in Savannah she was amused, but not surprised, to find her mother in the midst of such a renovation of the Gordon house as it had not had in its entire history. All the second floor bedrooms, which were to house the presidential party, were being repainted, and redecorated to have every item in each room match the new color scheme. The day of the President's arrival, no one was allowed to write a letter, for the seven desks in the house had been made ready for the President and his entourage. Daisy arranged flowers of appropriate colors in every room, the Gordon ladies put on their finest dresses to receive him. Nellie boasted in a letter to Mabel the next day that there wasn't a speck of dust from the garret down.

It is unlikely that President Taft would have noticed it if there had been. There could not have been a more delightful guest, or one easier to entertain. When the party arrived at eight in the evening, Nellie asked the President if he would like a little light refreshment. He said he certainly would, gave his arm to Nellie and they led the procession to the dining room. Seeing that Bill's nine-year-old daughter (now Daisy Lawrence) was among the company, the President insisted that the little girl sit next to him, and soon had her chattering to him as happily as if she had known him always. The President admired the huge yellow chrysanthemums that Daisy had chosen as a centerpiece. The child selected the biggest of all and placed it in the President's lapel.

Nellie's "light refreshments" consisted of hot turkey bouillon, boned turkey, Virginia ham, salad and hot rolls. The President ate two helpings of everything and drank four bottles of ginger ale, then went off to the official banquet at the De Soto Hotel! He still wore the yellow chrysanthemum in his buttonhole. Whenever anyone commented on his outsize boutonniere—it could scarcely be ignored—he would say, "It was given to me by a very charming young lady!"

His gustatory achievements at the banquet have not come down in history; but Nellie was pleased to hear that on his return to the Gordon house, he fell enthusiastically upon the basket of choice fruits she had set in the library, and filled up on apples and ginger ale before going to bed.

The next morning, the President's valet had a hard time to get his master up and down for breakfast; but after one look at the table and sideboard, Mr. Taft announced firmly that he did not intend to be hurried. He started with grapefruit, heroically declined the variety of cereals offered him, but accepted shrimps and hominy with delight. Next he disposed of a potted partridge, then broiled venison, then a grilled partridge, then more venison. The cars arrived to take the President and his party to the parade. Worried messengers came in from time to time to remind the President that it was getting late, that if he didn't hurry he might not get to the reviewing stand on time. The President ate on, through waffles covered with butter and maple syrup, hot rolls and more venison. When at last he tore himself from the table Daisy assured her mother, after getting a view of him in profile, that she believed he had had a *good* breakfast. The compliments to his hostess and the appreciation of Southern hospitality which President Taft wrote down in the visitors' book have a ring of sincerity.

Pictures were taken in front of the Gordon house, which flew the President's own flag next to the Stars and Stripes. Mr. Taft fills most of the back seat of one of the long, open touring cars of the day. Daisy stands on the steps, a slender, graceful figure.

It was President Taft who afterwards related one incident of his visit to the Gordons in Savannah. There had been a heavy rain, and the red and blue of the flags and bunting with which business buildings and homes had been decorated in his honor had run very sadly. The President asked Willie why it was that the colors in the big flag on the Gordon house had not run at all.

Willie replied demurely, "Perhaps it is because these are Confederate colors. They never did run!"

CHAPTER XVII

———————— ☆ ————————

A LAST DUTY FOR WILLIE

BEIRNE GORDON, the son of Willie's brother George, was now in W. W. Gordon & Company along with Arthur. With these two young Gordons in the saddle, Willie was largely released from business cares. When the Southern heat began to be oppressive, he and Mama would go to Northern resorts. During the winter and spring, Papa spent much time at Belmont, his farm in the country north of Savannah, which he preferred to all places. When his English grandchildren, Peggy and Rowland Leigh, came to Savannah, he would insist that they go to Belmont too. He would see to it that they rode mule-back, that young Rowley drove the mule team in various farming operations. It was as though he felt that these descendants of a long and distinguished British line should have the feel and touch of their mother's native Georgia soil as well.

Nellie was as agile and energetic as ever. In 1910, when she was seventy-five, Daisy wrote her that "Canon Leigh has been chuckling over the word that you kicked an ornament off the mantelpiece to prove that you do not need Delsarte!" Released from housekeeping cares, which she had always hated, Nellie had applied herself zealously, in the 1900's, to rounding out the Kinzie family annals. She learned shorthand and typing after she was seventy in order to perform her tasks more expeditiously.

In 1901, Nellie had seen to the re-issuing of her mother's

book *Wau-Bun*, which had been out of print for many years, with Nellie's added notes about the Kinzies. In 1906, she had brought out a little book of poems, *Rosemary and Rue,* as a memorial to the long-dead, but never-forgotten, Alice. Then she had tackled a biography of her grandfather, John Kinzie, "The Father of Chicago." In this biography Nellie dealt fearlessly and honestly with aspects of the first John Kinzie's life which often are omitted from biographies written by descendants—a full account of the killing of the trader Lalime, of the family of illegitimate children John Kinzie had had prior to his marriage to Nellie's grandmother, Eleanor Lytle McKillip. Such things were part of the wilderness life of John Kinzie's day, and Nellie felt they should be recorded along with his bravery and many meritorious deeds.

It must have seemed to Willie and Nellie, as to the rest of the world, that all traces of Daisy's tragic experience had been wiped out. She had carefully kept from these "two dear little people," as she called them in her letters to Arthur, the unhappiness that would claim her from time to time. She had dreaded Christmas ever since the break with Willy Low. First there was the joint wedding anniversary of her parents and of Daisy and Willy Low, to be gotten past. "Our wedding date," Daisy had called it, with one of the few flashes of bitterness she ever showed, in writing Nellie on December 21, 1902, to have Agnes, Nellie's housekeeper, pack the linens from the Low house in Savannah and send them to Daisy. "They were given me before my marriage, so I think I am entitled to them." This was when Willy Low was refusing to consider a settlement, when Daisy was barred from Mealmore and Wellesbourne and could not consider anything in either place as belonging to her.

Then came Christmas itself, the day dedicated to families, to children. After Daisy began spending her winters in Savannah, we find her avoiding Christmas Day at the Gordon house. In 1907, she had started for India on the twenty-second. She wrote Arthur in 1908 that she would like to miss Christmas. Only the thought that "little Papa and Mama" might not be with them for many more Christmases enabled her to face the prospect at all. This had been one of the subtle signs that all was not as well with Daisy as she led her parents and friends to believe.

The winter of 1909, the pain she had thrust behind her so resolutely reasserted itself in a new and unaccustomed morbidness. Possibly the ending of her long, warm friendship with Sir Archibald Hunter had something to do with the despondency that suddenly assailed her, though she appears to have been the one who broke it off. She wrote Mabel, in the spring of 1910: "You will see Archie Hunter's engagement in Monday's papers. She is Lady Inverclyde, of the big place which Jim Ismay took one year. I am glad he is to settle at last, I wish them both the best of luck." Nevertheless there must have been a sense of forlornness for Daisy when Sir Archie passed out of her life. There is the testimony of a poem she wrote at this time, which she titled, "The Road":

> The road which led from you to me
> Is choked with thorns and overgrown.
> We walked together yesterday
> But now—I walk alone.
>
> The magic of the road is dead,
> The milestones marking memories
> Are moss grown, and our feet must
> Onward in separate ways tread.
>
> For life has paths that lead to power
> So high, two cannot walk abreast.
> You chose the high road, I the lower.
> God knows which road is best.

Not knowing of Sir Archie's attachment for Daisy and hers for him, some persons who have written about Daisy have assumed that this poem referred to her marriage, but by no stretch of the imagination can Willy Low have been considered to have chosen a high road which led to power, Daisy a lower one. The chronology, besides, fits the poem in with the decline of her relationship with Sir Archie. Menopause might have had a part in the picture, and Daisy's deafness would have increased her sensitiveness in this stormy period of a woman's life. Though she never referred to it except as it involved her in some funny misunderstanding, she evidently felt her handicap keenly, for she was always experimenting with some new treatment. It was easy to misinterpret remarks which she caught only in part.

What the record shows is that Daisy, as she drew near to fifty, looked back over her life, and saw that, alone of all the women of her line, she had failed as a wife, she had failed to bring children into the world. It did not occur to her that she had stood up under a spiritual testing such as no woman of her line had been called upon to undergo; that she had displayed courage and character and nobility unsurpassed by any ancestress, even by her Grandmother Juliette; that she had kept unimpaired her power to love, her kindness and generosity. Daisy spoke often about "callousness" through the bad years, as though what she dreaded above all was that her heart might lose its tenderness. It never did.

These things, however, she did not think of. To her, the triumphant wifehood and motherhood of her mother, her sisters, her sisters-in-law, began to seem a reproach.

She told Arthur, as her excuse for absenting herself at Christmas in 1909, that when all the Gordon women were together with their children, they assumed a superior air toward this one childless adult of the family. "I can see Mabel's attitude changing toward me even before she leaves England." Mabel, who would have suffered anything herself to keep Daisy from being hurt! Daisy felt that Arthur's love for her had diminished since he had acquired a lovely wife and child.

She turned, in a kind of desperation, to her father, throwing herself passionately into everything that interested him. The family dog now was a Mr. Dooley. Mr. Dooley got sick and Daisy stayed up all night to nurse him, because he was dear to Papa. She went with Papa to Belmont, rode horseback with him over the farm, inspecting the crops, visiting with Willie's overseer, Mr. Allen, and with Mrs. Allen. She was full of enthusiastic plans for improving the houses of the sharecroppers. She insisted on making a present of a dress to every Negro woman and girl on the place. She begged to be allowed to feed Willie's favorite cow.

Now it was an idiosyncrasy of Willie's, which Daisy shared, to have only the vaguest conception of time. He was likely to show up an hour or more late for a family meal, but his servants had strict orders that the horses, the cow, the dog and the cat should have their meals on the minute. When Daisy asked to feed the cow, Willie said, "You'll forget to." Daisy said, "Just watch me," then proceeded to forget all about the cow. Having been rebuked by Willie, "more in sorrow than in anger," she wrote some verses about the incident for the amusement of the family, claiming poetic license in order to have cow rhyme with Low:

> There was a General had a cow
>   But he had naught to give it,
> Except that sort of hedge, you know,
>   Which botanists call "privet."
>
> The hedge grew round a vacant lot,
>   Meant to be sold or rented.
> Like Naboth's vineyard was the spot,
>   The cow grew discontented.
>
> The General spoke to Mrs. Low,
>   Told her he thought it funny,
> That when she might have fed his cow,
>   She only thought of money.
>
> Then Mrs. Low was sad indeed,
>   She tried to compensate,
> The angry cow refused to feed
>   The General said, "Too late!
>
> "Insult my wife, my child, my horse,
>   My trusty dog, Bow-Wow,
> But insults I resent, of course,
>   When offered to my cow!"

This was the sort of "chaffing" the Gordons had always engaged in endlessly, with their father as freely as with other members of the family. Willie had never minded. But when the family laughed over her poem, Daisy was conscience-stricken. She wrote Papa a worried note of apology, hoping she hadn't hurt his feelings, saying the verses had been intended as a joke on herself, rather than on him.

Daisy was overly sensitive about Papa's feelings, because she had become supersensitive herself where Papa was concerned. We find in the files, in large, agitated handwriting, a cry wrung from Daisy's heart: "You did not say 'God bless you, my daughter' when I left you, and I missed your blessing—'Bless me too, Oh my Father!' Yours, Daisy. Tear up this sheet of paper, please."

Willie did not tear up the sheet of paper. Perhaps he held it long in his hand, read it over many times. When Daisy was a tiny girl and so many things were happening she could not understand; when she was hungry, frightened, ill, she must have cried often for her adored papa, but Papa had been far away. Now, out of her ravaged, desolate woman's heart, once more his little girl cried to him, and this time Papa would not fail her.

Beginning with Daisy's return to England after her visit to Savannah in the winter of 1909 and 1910, we have a series of remarkable letters from Willie to Daisy, very different in tone from those he had written hitherto. Willie was in his middle seventies when Daisy wrote this revealing note. Since he had grown to manhood, his life had been a record of duties accepted, obligations carried, of outstanding service to his fellow men and to his country. Yet perhaps Willie Gordon's finest act was his assumption of this last duty of his fatherhood.

It was never so stated—that was not Willie's way. But in his letters from now on, we see the little General exerting himself to take Daisy with him, in spirit, through everything he did, to throw about her the comfort and assurance of his love, to share with her his own peace.

Daisy thought herself a failure as a woman, that such gifts and qualities as she had were of no account. The first of these letters strives to make her feel her supreme importance to the person she loved best—himself.

"My darling daughter: When we sit down to a meal I keep expecting you to appear before the meal is ended.

"When I go out on the piazza I miss the mocking bird with his sociability and impertinent aggressiveness.

"When I see Mr. Dooley I wonder what you would think of his health and what orders you would give as to his food and medicine.

"But more than all I miss you when riding on horseback in the morning and both Mama and I miss you for bridge in the evening.

"You are correct in supposing 'a great calm *burst* upon us' when you departed, but while a calm is restful for a time, it grows monotonous and one longs for the return of a gale."

In a later letter he begs her to hurry back to Savannah. "I can't build the three-story hotel at Belmont nor put in the porcelain bathtubs and electric fans in the cabins of the sharecroppers until I have you to draw the plans for the workmen. Mostly though, I need you to massage my scalp and rub the fog out of my brains in the evenings."

A very long letter, bringing Daisy up to date in every happening of Belmont and the Gordon house, is "my last visit with you before Mama and I start for the North," the spring of 1910. The numerous temperature readings are due to the fact that Daisy had brought him an elegant new thermometer as a present. The frequent baths mentioned, we take it, had been Daisy's suggestion for her father's comfort.

"Baths

"Mrs. Allen frequently talks about you and your suggestions, especially about baths. The thermometer was 92 degrees at 3 P.M. yesterday over the water bucket on the shelf in the little entry between my room and the rooms in the rest of the house. This entry is the coolest place in the house.

"Being Sunday, I got up late (5:30 A.M.) today. The thermometer was 75 degrees.

"I took a sponge bath in the rubber tub and another bath when I got back at eleven from two hours' ride on horseback (with Mr. Allen) thru the river swamp—to see our cattle.

"When we got back thermometer was 89.

"At this hour (3:30 P.M.) a soaking summer shower is coming down and the thermometer is around 89.

"Mocking Birds

"There are two nests of them in the trees around the house and one nest near by. Just before dinner I went to the water faucet and found a mocking bird sitting on the side of my water pail taking a drink out of my pail.

"Quail

"In driving over the fields yesterday and in riding to and from the river swamp today we saw many pair, who evidently had nests near by. If Rowley [Leigh] comes over this winter he will have good sport, as no one has shot on the place for two years.

"Crops

"I wish you and Mabel could be here to see them.

"Oats

"We have just finished harvesting and nearly finished threshing. The yield will be a little over 3,000 bushels (30 bushels per acre) and we are selling them at 70 cents per bushel of 32 pounds, except what we reserve for feeding our mules and horses.

"Corn

"in the fields far from the house is 4 to 5 feet tall, near the house over 6 feet—all of it a rich green color.

"Cotton

"is from 6 to 10 inches tall (which is very small for this time of year) but is vigorous and healthy.

"Peggy Doots and Colt

"are at the Gordon Farm (near Savannah). The colt is as lively and as bad as he can be. He bites and kicks his Mama and anyone who goes into their paddock without bringing him something to eat—sugar preferred.

"Mr. Dooley

"has been clipped and seems entirely recovered from his fit."

And so through many pages. Willie's letters to Daisy from the North are full of his quiet humor, and his never-ending enjoyment of Nellie's performances, which he knew Daisy enjoyed equally. Nellie would write thirty letters in a morning, he said, "while at the same time brushing her teeth and putting up her back hair." He described the scene that took place every afternoon on the hotel veranda when Nellie would appear with her fancywork. The women would cluster about her as about a queen bee, admiring her beautiful stitches, listening enraptured to her stories, and no one would leave the circle until Nellie rose, indicating that the audience was over.

"Today Mama has gone motoring with some friends we have met in the hotel. Your Mama hates trips in motors, and going with the Willings prevented her from having her nap after lunch, but her motto is *Noblesse oblige*. I know she will entertain the Willings most amiably, but will be tired and cross tonight. In a general way, however, she has been behaving beautifully ever since we left Savannah—treating me with respect before strangers and rarely using 'cuss' words. She meets Chicago people here, and revels in telling all about Chicago as it was before her listeners had realized such a place existed."

In the very few years that now remained to Willie, these long letters of his to Daisy, crammed with homely incidents aimed often to divert her but primarily to make her feel that she was never out of Papa's thoughts, furnish a counterpoint to Daisy's restless and hectic life across the ocean. Daisy was deeply appreciative. Thanking Papa for some money he had sent her she said, "Now I feel rich. But the true riches of my life are your letters."

Daisy began to display her old spirit of making a frontal attack on her problems. By the end of September, she was thinking again of sculpturing—she called this "modelling"—about which she had spoken to Nellie in 1906. She wrote to Mabel on September twenty-ninth that she was planning to go to Savannah immediately, so that she could settle down to study this new objective when she got back to Paris. "For if I once start modelling I'll probably get interested and want to go on and not interrupt it to come to America."

Yet as though she could not bring herself to make the plunge into a more serious interest, Daisy did not return to Paris but crowded a host of other things in after her visit to Savannah. In early January we find her in Canada, the guest of Lord Grey, and witnessing brilliant spectacles such as ice carnivals and skating cotillions. Next she went to Egypt. She had already asked Gwendolyn Nash, whose family had rented the Low house in Savannah for several years, to go with her. Forty hours before they were to sail from New York, she invited Eleanor Nash to go too. Eleanor Arnett Nash has described the party's arrival at Alexandria. A sleek launch carrying port officials came through the jade water to the ship. The passengers crowded to the rail to see what important personage was being thus honored. J. Pierpont Morgan was on board, and assuming that this special gesture was for him, he stepped up to the gangway to embark on the launch. The sailor in charge said, "Sorry, sir, this launch is for Mrs. Low and party." Mr. Morgan stepped back and Daisy and the Nash girls swept grandly down the gangway into the launch.

George Hunter, Sir Archie's brother, was in charge of the Coast Guard and had arranged with the port officials for this courtesy. He, too, had remained a close friend, ever since his first meeting with Daisy in 1895, and after it became apparent that nothing would come of his brother's suit, had declared his love for the charming American. It disturbed him very much that his name had become involved with that of some lady or ladies. "He wrote me all about it," Daisy told Mabel, "but I had not heard the gossip, did not know the beautiful ladies involved, returned the letter to him, told him he had better burn it, and said I still consider it best that we should go our separate ways."

However, Daisy's friendship for George Hunter remained unimpaired. Daisy, when she got back to England, interested herself in furthering Hunter's military career, tackling her friend, Sir Francis Grenfell, a member of the army board of five which decided all army appointments. Daisy started obliquely by asking Sir Francis why the present sirdar, General Wingate, was "being kept on for life." By degrees she worked around to George Hunter, suggesting that General Wingate should step down as sirdar and Hunter be appointed in his place. Sir Francis knew that Hunter was to be given the command of Gibraltar, but the word could not be released yet, so he had to defend the army board as best he could against Daisy's attack. Later Jack Maxwell told her that Sir Francis Grenfell said he had lost three nights' sleep over the severity of Daisy's criticisms.

But it was some months before Daisy returned to England.

After the usual round of entertainment and festivities in Egypt, she teamed up with Minnie Davis, granddaughter of Daisy's Great-uncle General David Hunter, and the two set out to tour Spain and France by car. Minnie Davis was now a wealthy widow, spending much of her time in Europe. She and Daisy had resumed the friendship begun when Daisy had visited Great-uncle David in Washington at the age of sixteen. They ran into Rudyard Kipling, his wife and daughter Elsie, and explored the old fortified French town, Les Baux, together. In Monte Carlo they encountered the Earl of Warwick and his brother. "I find friends everywhere," Daisy wrote home. She darted about so much and met so many people en route that it is very hard to keep track of her. But finally she got back to Paris and at last settled down to the lessons in sculpturing which she had first started talking about in 1906.

Having done so, she threw herself into the enterprise with the ardor she brought to the mastery of every new skill, working at her modeling eight hours a day. She interrupted her routine only to show Aunt Eliza and her daughter Gulie the sights of Paris—Daisy could on no account fail Aunt Eliza—and said they enjoyed it so much that she was repaid. At first she was discouraged with her progress in the modeling and wrote Arthur: "I long, not for the words of the poet, but of my little mother, to express what I feel!"

But on April 12, 1911, she wrote Papa that "my teacher said, 'Excellent, I am astonished at your facility!' I am now in the heights of bliss, for though I will never do anything for public exhibition, yet if I only learn enough to work at home in leisure hours, my life will gain more serious interest." She made a gay account to Eleanor of her latest attempt to improve her hearing. "Mama continues to inquire whether my hearing is better. At first, I thought she was having me absently treated by a Christian Scientist at the rate of eighty dollars a treatment, but now I hear my osteopath Gorin has suggested the kind inquiries, so as you have a typewriter, will you please write out the following bulletin to be pasted on Mama's bedroom door next to the telephone, which is the spot she sees most frequently:

"PROGRESS, DAISY'S HEARING

"February 1st, heard a fog horn.

"March 1st, hearing improved, heard a camel when it rose.

"April 1st, hearing decidedly improved, heard the pantomime rehearsal, also the grass growing in the Bois.

"Have great hopes of hearing Gabriel blow his trumpet on the day of judgment.

"As a matter of fact I am better but it is not permanent. I vary horribly, some days deafer than ever. But my throat is two inches longer since Gorin rubbed the lump off my neck."

Whereupon Eleanor wrote some verses, of which Nellie sent a copy to all the relatives:

> Savannah braes are bonny
> When Gorin is in view,
> But it isn't very funny
> When your neck's put on askew.
> And it's almost past believing
> What an osteopath can do;
> For he tackled sister Daisy
> And made her over new.
>
> Her ear was like the adder,
> Her neck was like the goose,
> He limbered up her vertebrae,
> And made the muscles loose;
> Her frequent name was Crazy,
> Her face was fair to see,
> And our little sister Daisy
> Was as deaf as deaf could be.

By the end of a few weeks, the sculptor told Daisy he thought he had taught her all he could, that now she could proceed very well by herself.

Back in London she was caught up again in the old whirl of luncheons, dinners, balls, theater. Besides, the coronation of King George V was coming up and there was a frenzy of activity in connection with it. Daisy was planning to entertain Bill, Ellie, and their two children, and was begging Eleanor and her family to come. Daisy said that by converting the smoking room at 40 Grosvenor Street into a bedroom and having the servants sleep out, she could provide ten bedrooms. At the same time she was writing Mama that "I am so pressed and pushed from all sides that I hardly know how I can stand it."

There was little chance to work at modeling. But this new interest did form her first bond with the next of the series of famous British military men who were her special friends. She was full of her sculpturing, and when she found herself sitting, at a luncheon, beside General Sir Robert Baden-Powell, she started the conversation by pouring out her recent experiences in Paris, with the usual spate of funny anecdotes. To her great surprise, she learned that the hero of Mafeking and the idol of the British public was a sculptor too!

CHAPTER XVIII

————— ☆ —————

GENERAL SIR ROBERT
BADEN-POWELL

L ATER Daisy wrote Papa that she had hated General Baden-
Powell up to that time, "because I had not met him."
With her great loyalty to her friends, she had resented the fact
that Baden-Powell had emerged as the sole hero of Mafeking,
entirely putting in the shade Lord Mahon, who had liberated
Mafeking from the besieging army. "He was so lionized by
'the man in the street' that I considered he had stolen all of
General Mahon's thunder, and indeed my friend General
Mahon has been underrated, as Baden-Powell overrated. But
when one has met B.P., his vanity is excusable as he certainly
is a remarkable man. He is a genius as a soldier and he draws,
paints and models as well. He left the army against King Edward's wishes (but afterwards the King saw he was right) to
organize the Boy Scouts and now he has forty thousand boys
all over Great Britain, with branches in the U.S.A., France and
Germany. Little guttersnipes who in London became a danger
to the public under the name of 'Houligans', and in France the
same element from the slums under the name of 'Apaches' now
are growing up healthy, clean, orderly citizens."

General Sir Robert Baden-Powell—he did not become Lord
Baden-Powell until 1929—was as impressed by Daisy. He used
their common interest in sculpturing as his excuse to see more

of the charming American, and as quickly as possible. The day after their first meeting he wrote to remind her that he was always to be found at 32 Prince's Gate in London, and that if at any time she cared to come to take tea, his mother and sister would be delighted to welcome her. After tea he would take her to see his friend Signor Lanteri, who might be induced to give Daisy some further lessons in sculpturing.

The plan was soon carried out. Daisy joined a night class in sculpturing under Signor Lanteri and wrote Willie that "my teacher keeps encouraging me, which is lucky, as I am old and want *sugar*." She wrote Mabel that the girl who posed for the class looked starved and one night nearly fainted. "I was sure she was very hungry so last night I took thermos bottles of hot soup and milk and thick sandwiches of meat and bread. Mabel, that poor creature retired behind the screen in her rest periods and finished one quart bottle of mutton broth and a pint of milk and grew fat visibly under my eye!"

But their interest in sculpture, Daisy and Baden-Powell soon discovered, was only one of an almost unbelievable number of things they possessed in common. General Baden-Powell had a background of American wilderness and Indians quite as notable as that of Daisy's own early Kinzie ancestors, being descended from Captain John Smith on his mother's side. In fact he had made a bust of his famous ancestor which he took Daisy to see. John Smith's descendants in America however, had been Tories in the Revolution and had had to flee to England at its close. Somewhere along the way the spelling had been changed to Smyth. Daisy's good friend, Major Neville Smyth, was a cousin of Baden-Powell.

Brought up in England, Baden-Powell had taught himself the wilderness skills which Daisy's grandfather and great-grandfather had learned from the Indians; and this lore had formed the basis for his outstanding success as a soldier and for the founding of the Boy Scouts. His mother came from a family of naturalists, and used to take him for walks in the woods when he was a boy, telling him about the plants and animals, and teaching him to observe the wildlife about him. When the ancient Charterhouse school to which he went—Thackeray had been a Carthusian, as well as Addison and Steele and John Wesley—moved to Godalming, there was a near-by piece of woodland. Though it was out of bounds for the boys, young Robert used to steal away to the Copse as it was called, and here he perfected himself in such scouting skills as learning how to snare a rabbit and cook it over a tiny fire, or gliding through the woods without disturbing the wild creatures and without leaving any sign of his passing.

When he was sent out to India as a soldier, on the Afghan frontier which Daisy had once visited, he found these skills tremendously helpful, and established such a reputation that in Britain's war with the Ashantis in Africa in 1895, he was given command of a levy of natives to scout the country ahead of the troops. It was then that he started wearing the cowboy hat which he passed on to the Boy Scouts. The broad brim shaded his face and neck from the sun and protected his face from branches in the woods. The idea for the staff, also later accouterment for Boy Scouts, came from one carried by an engineer on the expedition with which he used to vault across the streams and through swamps. Since the staff was marked in inches and feet, it was always available as a measuring stick. On the scouting expeditions, the eating arrangements were almost identical with those Juliette Kinzie described when she and John Harris traveled over the prairie on horseback, except that the Kinzies used a biscuit for a plate, while Baden-Powell in Africa used one of his gaiters! And Baden-Powell had gloried in the wild life and in summoning resourcefulness to meet it, just as Juliette Kinzie had done.

Back in India in 1897, now a colonel in command of the Fifth Dragoon Guards, Baden-Powell found the British servicemen to be lacking in initiative. They were good at following orders and in carrying out routines, but helpless when it came to thinking out things on their own account. In order to increase their keenness and alertness, Baden-Powell broke up his command into small permanent units and began to train them in scouting; teaching them to track, to observe everything about them and then to figure out the meaning of the signs they saw.

It was these skills, and his original and unorthodox ideas, which enabled Baden-Powell to defend Mafeking so long with fifteen hundred men against a besieging army of nine thousand Boers. The defenders had only one decrepit old cannon, whereas the Boers were equipped with the latest Krupp weapons. At night the Mafeking garrison would push the old cannon from place to place and fire it, making the Boers think the town was ringed about by cannons. Encouraged by Baden-Powell, the whole populace of the town joined in the fun of outwitting the Boers. They erected dummy forts among the real ones, defended by realistic-looking dummy soldiers. Games and entertainments were held throughout the siege in sight of the Boers, to show how unworried the besieged were. Baden-Powell, who had always been greatly in demand as an entertainer at his various army stations, would masquerade as "Signor Paderewski" or a circus ringleader or a clown. He also cooked up many ingenious devices to disturb the slumbers of the Boers at night, by creeping among them undetected and providing constant little surprises.

Every hand was needed and a corps of boy messengers was formed to relieve the men for more important duties. The boys had a uniform, drilled regularly, and practiced carrying written messages and returning with oral ones. When the Boers made an attack, the boy messengers, or Cadets as they were called, carried messages back and forth under fire. A detachment of Boers being captured, the Cadets were allowed to disarm them and march them into town. Baden-Powell observed how these boys responded to the responsibility given them and how useful they made themselves. Thus one more piece was fitted into what was already shaping itself, unknown to Baden-Powell at that time, into a great new program for boys.

When the relieving force under Lord Mahon saw how lacking Mafeking was in any real defenses, and how the Boers could have taken the town at any time if they had not been scared off by Baden-Powell's inspired bluffing, their respect for Baden-Powell was tinged with awe.

By coincidence Baden-Powell's little book, *Aids to Scouting*, appeared on the bookstalls just as the news of the relief of Mafeking reached England, in a London gone mad from excitement and hero worship, with pictures of Baden-Powell exhibited everywhere, and flags hung up in his honor. A new word was coined in the English language, "mafficking," to describe the boisterous celebration in England. To his great surprise, Baden-Powell was besieged with letters from boys, asking how they might learn more about scouting, how they might become good scouts themselves. The rest is history.

One can imagine Daisy's delight in learning how the Indian skills in which her grandfather and great-grandfather had been supreme, had been turned to account in this latter day. General Baden-Powell, on his side, was equally intrigued by her stories of the Kinzies. Probably no one read *Wau-Bun* with keener interest—it was Nellie who sent him a copy, after Daisy had written the family of the amazing way in which his own background duplicated hers. He exclaimed to Daisy, "I say, what a fascinating book that is of your grandmother's. The soles of your boots must be worn thin if you inherit her adventurous and plucky spirit!"

And General Baden-Powell was skilled as well in the gentler arts which Daisy's Grandmother Juliette had introduced into the Kinzie strain. He had illustrated his book about the Matabele campaign with spirited sketches, as Juliette Kinzie had illustrated *Wau-Bun* with her sketches. Like Daisy, he reveled in amateur theatricals, and was a notable mimic. To cap it all, there is an amazing resemblance between a picture of Baden-Powell in his scouting clothes and Willie Gordon in his uniform and stiff campaign hat.

The many letters and notes from Baden-Powell to Daisy from their first meeting on show how eagerly he pursued this new friendship. It was not easy for the two to get together, for Baden-Powell was kept busy from morning until late at night between the demands of the booming Boy Scout movement and the public appearances in numerous causes required of a man of his prominence.

It appears that in the beginning of their acquaintance, Daisy was even more tightly scheduled than he because of her social engagements and visits to country houses. In order to show her his sketchbooks, Baden-Powell wangled an invitation to St. Donat's Castle in Wales, the property of Daisy's friends, Godfrey and Miriam Williams, where Daisy was spending Whitsuntide. He left his sketchbooks behind him and had to write Daisy to retrieve them for him from the drawing room at St. Donat's. This failing for leaving things, which Daisy had to so great a degree, must have been another bond between them.

In London, however, they would manage to snatch an hour or so together now and then, with Daisy attending a banquet where Sir Robert had to put in an appearance, and Baden-Powell slipping off to sit in Daisy's box at the opera, or to motor with her to some inn for tea, or to some picturesque castle. Baden-Powell loved castles, too, and would describe to Daisy the ones he visited on his many trips on Boy Scout affairs.

By dint of a great deal of advance planning, Baden-Powell managed to escort Daisy and Minnie Davis—Daisy still felt it desirable to have a woman companion when she appeared in public with members of the opposite sex—to the coronation of King George V, and Daisy was treated to a demonstration of Baden-Powell's great popularity. After they left Daisy's car at the City, they had to walk about a hundred yards. Baden-Powell was recognized and the thousands of people massed along the route the King and Queen were to take began cheering him wildly. *"I liked it!"* Daisy wrote Papa. Baden-Powell who was attired in the full uniform of the 13th Hussars, had to leave the ladies while he took the part assigned him in the services at the Cathedral, and went in the procession to the Guild Hall. But having delivered the King safely at the Guild Hall, he was free to give the ladies lunch at the Mercers' Hall, where he made his headquarters a good deal of the time, then show them the old Charterhouse School, where he had been a student, and the tomb of his ancestor, Captain John Smith. Baden-Powell also attended with Daisy and Minnie Davis a number of the brilliant social events which were held in connection with the Coronation and he enlivened these with his wit and talents as an entertainer.

But it was the character of this new friend that impressed Daisy most. "All of his portraits and all of his writings represent him in action, essentially a man of war, though never has any human being given me such a feeling of peace. He rushes from one engagement to another, though he doesn't strike me as restless or pushed or driven. It may be because in his own mind he is not personally seeking anything. His activities are for mankind and he has, perhaps, eliminated the effort to attain things for himself. When a man has conquered his enemies, they say death is the greatest conquest left, but isn't self even greater? The universe and the force that drives him to better it are the real objects of his existence. To him his own life, as a unit, is apparently unimportant."

Arthur has quoted from her diary of June 1, 1911: "Today, in the few moments I have had to myself, my mind has irresistibly dwelt on B.P. A sort of intuition comes over me that he believes I might make more out of life, and that he has *ideas* which, if I follow them, will open a more useful sphere of work before me in future."

On June seventeenth she wrote in her diary: "Again I met B.P. No doubt about his magnetism. I am not sure if he *knows* he can influence people, or if the charm of his presence is an unconscious one. I told him about my futile efforts to be of use, and the shame I feel when I think of how much I could do, yet how little I accomplish, and when thrown with a man who has made a success of everything, by contrast I feel that my life brings forth 'nothing but leaves.' A wasted life. He looked so kindly when he said, 'There are little stars that guide us on, although we do not realize it.' "

Now it was Daisy who was inviting Baden-Powell to all manner of entertainments which she thought he would enjoy, while he had to decline many of her invitations because of the press of his engagements. Sir Robert did, however, get to Lochs. They caught seventy-five trout in four days which pleased Sir Robert very much. And every night they played records on the Victrola Nellie had sent Daisy. "Sir Robert and Alix Beech did a pantomime while the Victrola made the music. Sir Robert and Alix looked as if they were singing and their pantomime was killing in the love scenes," Daisy wrote Mama.

It was during the interlude at Lochs that Daisy became interested in the Girl Guides. She wrote Papa, "The Girl Guides is a sort of outcome of the Boy Scouts. When Baden-Powell first formed the Boy Scouts, six thousand girls registered as Scouts. And as he could not have girls traipsing about over the country after his Boy Scouts, he got his sister, Miss Agnes Baden-Powell, to form a society of Girl Guides and the first law was that they must not even speak to a Boy Scout if they saw him in uniform. I like girls and I like the organization and the rules and pastimes, so if you find that I get very deeply interested you must not be surprised."

Sir Robert, knowing that Daisy was searching rather desperately for something to which to devote herself, urged her not to be in a hurry and to wait until she could see her line clearly

—"though it is difficult for me to give *you* advice as you have such a long head and sound ideas." This must have been balm to Daisy, who was not accustomed to hearing herself described in such terms. He also doubted that Daisy would be able to muster a troop in the sparsely settled glen. However, Daisy wrote Papa in August, 1911, "I am getting up a corp of Girl Guides here in this glen where the Highland Girls are so far from the world they remain ignorant in all details of nursing the sick and the way to feed and bring up delicate children."

Only seven girls could be found in the glen, but Daisy invited these to Lochs every Saturday afternoon, and although each had to come from a lonely and remote cottage—one walking seven miles!—still, come they did. In the beginning it might have been Daisy's delicious teas that brought them—hot buttered scones, thin bread and butter, strawberry jam and a variety of cakes. A good tea for her girls was Daisy's basic Scouting tenet then and subsequently. But there were also fascinating things to learn—the Guide Promise and Laws; the history of the British flag; how to tie knots. From this beginning the girls went on to knitting, cooking, first aid, and personal hygiene. A number of the young men who visited Ian Bullough at Meggernie and Daisy at Lochs were Guards officers. They taught the girls signaling, and the Highland lasses relayed messages from one lonely hilltop to another.

The families in this remote part of Scotland were so poor that the boys and girls were forced to leave home when they were very young in order to make a living. Usually, they went into factories in the big cities, which to these outdoor-bred children was equivalent to a death sentence. Many of them developed tuberculosis or some other fearful disease and died. Daisy studied ways by which the girls in her troop could make money at home. Raising chickens for the hunting lodges in the vicinity seemed a practical idea. Daisy saw that they were instructed in chicken lore, and they made a good thing out of chicken farming.

She personally taught the girls to card and spin wool. It was a great country for raising sheep but the raw wool was sold at a very low price. First Daisy learned how to spin, then taught the girls, who soon became so expert they could even spin in the dark. Then she found a market for their product in London. When it was time for her to leave Lochs she persuaded the village postmistress to take charge of the spinning project, which also became a remunerative one for the girls.

As the season at Lochs drew to a close, Daisy was toying with the idea of having a castle of her own. Her friends, the Godfrey Williams' of St. Donat's, had offered her one in Wales, free of all charge—its name, according to Daisy's spelling, being Aberpegwm. Daisy was strongly tempted, because she thought it was a place where she could settle down to serious work in sculpturing. Also, Aberpegwm was only an hour by car from the Fishguard Route, where steamers would let passengers from America disembark!

In the end, her new interest in the Girl Guides won out and she spent the entire fall and early winter in London, where she continued her night class in sculpturing; kept up her social activities; and started two troops of Girl Guides in London, one of them in Lambeth, a very poor section. She took her Victrola and records to the meetings in Lambeth, and the girls had never seen anything so wonderful. On December 14, she wrote Papa, she gave a tea for sixty people, including all the committees of Girl Guides in London, and entertained guests at a combined dinner and opera party. "However, I only gave them dinner and their opera tickets. I sneaked away to the modelling class after dinner."

Baden-Powell was going to America as part of a world tour to inspect and help the now-far-reaching Boy Scout movement. Daisy asked Mama to write a letter saying she would love to have him be the guest of the Gordons in Savannah. "Say you think he can get some sport. I will show him the letter. What he likes best is wild bird shooting, just what there is lots of at Bill's place at Myrtle Grove, and he *likes* roughing it. He is doing a lecture tour in America and may get near Savannah."

Daisy herself was planning a South American tour on her own way to America, after Christmas. There is no indication that she expected to be in Savannah when Baden-Powell was there, but was following her usual procedure with English friends whom she thought Willie and Nellie would enjoy, and who would enjoy the Gordon hospitality. Willie had considered her South American junket "the wildest flight you ever planned" until he learned that she wished to visit the Chalmers

Guthrie branches there, and knew the British Ambassador to Colombia very well. Then he approved. However, Castro stirred up a revolution, the road over the Andes was closed, so Daisy had to abandon that part of her trip.

Before leaving for America, she arranged to have her Girl Guide troops carried on in her absence. She selected Mrs. Mark Kerr, whom she barely knew at this time, as a suitable person to take charge of the Lambeth patrol and so informed Mrs. Kerr. This is the first recorded instance of Daisy's using her deafness to advantage in Girl Scouting, though there were to be many others. Mrs. Kerr replied that she could not possibly take over the troop as she had no time, did not live in London and was no good with girls.

"Then that is all settled," said Daisy cheerfully. "I have already told my girls you will take the meeting next Thursday. I shall be back myself in six months' time. I will pay for the girls' uniforms and any other expenses you may be put to, such as the tea every week after the meeting. Please give them a good one."

Baden-Powell wrote Daisy to ask when she would be going to America, and congratulated her on the splendid meeting she had held for the Girl Guide leaders. The letters from Baden-Powell to Daisy had been growing constantly more warm and personal. Apparently, Daisy had a way of hinting to him that some lady or other took a special interest in him, or he in her. He would make gallant disclaimers. On one such occasion, he replied that he had a better pebble on the beach than M—— R——, or hoped he did. Whereupon Daisy sent him a pebble she had picked up on the beach.

In the end, she and Baden-Powell sailed for America on the same ship, the *Arcadian*, which went by way of the West Indies. They must have made plans while on shipboard for Daisy to start the Girl Guides in America, for Baden-Powell wrote her the next month from New York that he had told Mrs. Van Dusen of Daisy's interest in the Girl Guides, had tried to interest Mrs. Andrew Carnegie in them and would give her name to women in Pittsburgh and Chicago who might help her get the organization started there.

There was also on board the *Arcadian* a charming young woman, Miss Olave Soames, traveling with her father. Daisy left the party at Jamaica. Before the cruise of the *Arcadian* was ended, Baden-Powell was engaged to Olave Soames. According to Baden-Powell's biographer, E. E. Reynolds, the engagement was kept secret for a year at the request of Mr. Soames, because of the considerable difference in age between Baden-Powell and Miss Soames. It would appear that Baden-Powell kept the engagement a secret from Daisy until just before his marriage.

It is here that the absence of Daisy's diaries is most regrettable, for the relationship between the founder of the Boy Scouts and the founder of the Girl Scouts is of general interest, and certainly was a matter of considerable importance in Daisy's life. She once confided to a dear friend that Baden-Powell had asked her to marry him, and that she had been strongly attracted to him, but had said no. She was fifty-one when she met him —Baden-Powell was fifty-four at this time—it would be impossible for her to give him children, and she thought it unfair to deprive him of the chance of children. This is entirely in keeping with Daisy's nature. The proposal, if one was made, must have been made before Sir Robert met Olave Soames on the *Arcadian*, for according to Mr. Reynolds, that romance blossomed quickly.

However, none of the documentary evidence available gives any indication that there had been a proposal of marriage. This is not conclusive in itself, since we know that letters were taken from the files, and we have no idea what letters were in the sealed package which presumably was destroyed unopened after Daisy's death. The impression created by the available letters from Baden-Powell to Daisy is that in the beginning Daisy must have had every reason to think that here was a potential suitor. The fact that after the first two letters he drops the opening, "My dear Mrs. Low" and begins with no salutation at all makes it seem that he did not like to use the formal "Mrs. Low" but did not feel at liberty to call her anything else. He persisted in finding opportunities to see her in the face of the many obstacles interposed by the full schedules of both; he was eager to introduce her to scenes he himself cherished. After the cruise of the *Arcadian*, he goes back again to, "My dear Mrs. Low," and thus continues throughout the correspondence between the two as long as Daisy lived.

This is a question that possibly can never be answered, though on the evidence at hand, we are sure of only one thing. Daisy left the *Arcadian* with a heightened enthusiasm for the Girl Guides. She had written to Mabel from Colon to get Peggy together with several of her young friends, whom Daisy named, and form a patrol. "For the Guide laws are good for rich or poor." She had also determined to bring the benefits of the new organization to the girls of America. And the place where she planned to start was her home city, Savannah.

CHAPTER XIX

———————— ☆ ————————

STARTING THE GIRL SCOUTS

THE VERY NIGHT Daisy arrived in Savannah, she phoned Miss Nina Anderson Pape, a distant cousin, who had visited Daisy at Wellesbourne and who was principal of a local girls' school. "Come right over," Daisy said. "I've got something for the girls of Savannah and all America and all the world and we're going to start it tonight!"

Miss Pape hurried over, eager as always to see Daisy, and curious to know what her latest wild idea might be. When Daisy told her about the Girl Guides, however, and how much the English girls enjoyed the opportunity for a taste of outdoor life, how many useful skills they learned, Miss Pape was impressed. Daisy had thought that some of the girls in Nina's school might be interested. Miss Pape had a better idea. A group of girls went every Saturday afternoon to the woods near Bonna Bella. Mr. Hoxie, a naturalist, had a camp there. He took the girls on walks through the woods, pointing out different shrubs, trees and birds to them. Often the girls would cook their supper over a campfire before going home. Here was a group already formed and made to order for the Guide program. Furthermore, Page Anderson was a member.

Daisy knew Page well. She was the young daughter of the very Cousin Randolph Anderson with whom Daisy had played as a child, and who had once braided taffy into Daisy's hair. Randolph's wife, too, was a good friend of Daisy's.

It was no trick at all for Daisy to get herself invited to mid-day dinner at the Andersons'. Knowing Daisy, they did not wait when she did not appear at mealtime, but started eating. When Daisy blew in, purposely late on this occasion, she was engaged in tying knots in a limp strip of leather. "I'm learning to tie knots for my Girl Guides," was her answer when they asked her about this strange occupation. Their further questions gradually elicited what the Girl Guides were, what exciting things they did, and how English girls were begging to be allowed to join. Soon Page Anderson was demanding to know why American girls were being denied these joys. Daisy replied that they needn't be if they were interested. Page flew off to inform the other members of the naturalist group that if they wanted her to, Cousin Daisy would see what she could do about helping them to become Girl Guides.

Daisy invited the girls to the Gordon house to talk things over. Margaret Gordon, calling on Nellie one afternoon, found her mother-in-law in the library having a tantrum because "Daisy has the back drawing-room full of little girls, and is making Morrison serve them a fussier tea than I would prepare for the President!"

The next Sunday, after church, Daisy buttonholed Page Anderson's mother, and informed her that she was to be the captain of the first Girl Guide patrol, as the troops were then called, which would be made up of Page and her friends. Daisy hurried off without giving Mrs. Anderson a chance to refuse. On March 12, 1912, sixteen girls were formally enrolled in two troops, Daisy having already enlisted her mother and ten friends to serve as the first board of counselors. The girls seemed to sense that this was a momentous occasion as they solemnly repeated the Promise after Daisy and then signed their names. But Daisy wrote down the first name herself, that of Bill's daughter, Daisy Gordon who later became Daisy Lawrence. Bill's family was living at Myrtle Grove plantation, twenty-three miles from Savannah, and young Daisy did not even know the patrols were being formed. Mrs. Randolph Anderson, willing or not, was made leader of the White Rose Patrol and Miss Van Diviere of the Carnations. Daisy had promised the girls that they might use the old carriage house and servant quarters at the rear of the garden of the Low house, a building of considerable size fronting on Drayton Street. She had it put in order for them and an imposing sign was placed over the door announcing that it was Girl Guide headquarters. She also promised them the use of a vacant lot she owned, across the street from the Low house, and started having a basketball court and tennis court installed.

It was the uniforms, however, which had the greatest appeal for the girls. The first ones were middy blouses and skirts of dark blue duck, with light blue sateen ties. Garbed in these dashing outfits, supplemented by long black cotton stockings and enormous black hair ribbons, the first Girl Guides attracted so much attention that all their friends immediately wanted to become Girl Guides too. Before long it was found that the dark blue showed marked contrast with the soil too plainly on picnics and camping trips and khaki color was substituted.

Daisy commandeered Eleanor Nash to take the Guides out driving. She informed Miss Sally McAlpin, another young friend, that she was to be executive secretary of the Girl Guides in Savannah. She apportioned other duties to other friends, and then took herself off to Myrtle Grove to visit Bill and his family and incidentally to break the news to her niece, Daisy Gordon, that she had become a Girl Guide.

The twelve-year-old Daisy was immediately on her guard. Named Margaret Eleanor when she was born, this niece was called Daisy ever afterwards because her older brother B. had insisted that his sister "looked just like Aunt Daisy." To distinguish the two Daisies from each other, the Gordons then proceeded to call the younger one Daisy Doots or just Doots, and thus we shall call her. Daisy Low had stood godmother to her namesake, and Doots had looked upon her, until recently, as a veritable fairy godmother. Every time Daisy came to Savannah she brought Doots some gorgeous present picked up on her travels: from India, a necklace of jade and seed pearls; from Egypt a necklace three thousand years old; a lace collar from Belgium. And always, whatever the present was, and wherever it came from, Aunt Daisy had a wonderful story to tell about it. The summer before, however, when Bill's whole family went to Germany to give young B. the benefit of treatments for his hearing, they had stopped over in London with Daisy, and Doots had been sadly disillusioned. It was at the time of the

Coronation of King George V, and Daisy said that Doots would get to sleep on a "coronation cot" which Doots had envisioned as a canopied four poster, royally emblazoned. When it turned out to be an army cot, Doots had dissolved in tears. To cheer her up, Daisy offered ginger beer as a great treat. The first taste convinced Doots that her Aunt Daisy was a woman of very queer ideas.

Now, when Aunt Daisy told Doots she had made her a Girl Guide, Doots was not going to be led up the garden path another time.

"You've made me a what?" Doots asked.

"A Girl Guide. All the girls in Savannah are going to be Guides."

"Why?"

"Because it's a wonderful thing to be," Daisy replied.

"How did you make me into a Guide?"

"I put your name down." Daisy was beginning to be impatient.

"You had no right to put my name down! You should have asked me first!" stormed Doots.

Ellie started to intervene, but Daisy had not been around nieces and nephews and children of friends all those years for nothing. She shrugged her shoulders. "It's not important. I just thought you'd like this chance of learning how to do things like cooking, and first aid and how to tie knots. And of course when you go back to Savannah and all the other girls are in uniforms with lots of badges, you're going to look rather silly. But if you're not interested—"

"Uniforms? Badges?" gasped Doots. "Do they have those things?"

"Why of course. You can't have Girl Guides without uniforms and badges."

"Aunt Daisy, do you think I could be a Guide?"

"I'll show you how to tie a square knot right now!" said Daisy, pulling out her strip of limp leather. And that was how Daisy Gordon Lawrence became America's first Girl Scout.

The next morning Daisy started modeling a head of Doots. (It is now in the Juliette Low Birthplace in Savannah.) A letter from Baden-Powell, written just before he started off for Australia and South Africa, congratulated Daisy on having started the Girl Guides so quickly and said she must have worked like a Trojan to do so. His praise sent Daisy hurrying back to her Guides in Savannah as soon as the head of Daisy Doots was finished. She left her niece a copy of the English handbook, which Doots studied diligently, although she found some of the English phraseology and practices difficult to puzzle out.

Soon Doots had an opportunity to use her first aid skills. Bill reported to Daisy, Senior, that "Our old horse Rollie playfully pushed one William Ferguson in the face with his left hind foot and jarred Ferguson badly. Daisy Doots rushed for the cotton and Listerine bottle and after binding up his wounds, prescribed whiskey for him. A big drink brought William to his senses. Ever since then every darky on the place has been flirting with Rollie's heels in the hope of getting the same treatment!" Doots was following in her grandmother's footsteps.

On Daisy Low's return to Savannah, she found that in her brief absence the two patrols had grown to six, with memberships varying from six to sixty. Inquiries were beginning to come from all over the United States. Daisy promptly began to think of setting up the Guides on a nationwide basis. She wrote Mabel that she did not plan to return to England until July, if her London houses were let, "as I am too keen about the movement to leave here until it is firmly established. You mustn't be bored with Girl Guides, as I can't think of anything else." When Mabel arrived in America on her next visit, and asked where Daisy was, Papa replied, "She is up in Washington, getting the Constitution of the United States altered to suit her Girl Guides." In actual fact, Daisy never found it necessary to alter the Constitution. If she had, undoubtedly we would have a Girl Scout amendment. She did, however, succeed later on in having the entry fee required of visitors waived for the delegates from abroad to the International Girl Scout Conference, after a valiant tussle with her ancient foes of the Department of Immigration.

That was a busy spring for Daisy. The Girl Guide movement was humming. In May, Willie and Nellie once more entertained President Taft, with Daisy's assistance. Then she had to dash off to England after all, to see to renting her houses. Miss Edith Johnston had been commandeered to serve as national secretary of the Girl Guides, Miss Sally McAlpin continuing as local secretary in Savannah. Daisy paid their modest salaries as she did all other expenses of the movement, out of her own pocket. In England, she learned everything there was to know about the Guides, and watched the English Guides with pride as they marched in the Empire Day parade.

Savannah girls were taking to the new movement with such enthusiasm that the newspapers became interested. Mama wrote Daisy that "a reporter"—the quotation marks are Nellie's —had come to see Nellie about them, and she had referred him to Sally McAlpin for one of the books of rules. "He was most anxious for a picture of you to accompany a quite elaborate article for the Sunday paper. I told him I would ask your father what he thought about that. Please remember the picture was given with your father's consent, uninfluenced by me. The story is all about you, it doesn't even mention your father! Papa sends you a copy and says to tell you 'you apparently do not have a father.' (Jealous!)"

For Papa to consent to having a photograph of his daughter appear in the public prints, to be a party to it, in fact, was an evidence of the delight the Gordons took in seeing Daisy so interested and happy. They all thought she would tire of her new enthusiasm before long, but that it was a fine thing for her while it lasted.

Papa wrote that he had ridden past the headquarters of the Girl Guides and "the rooms were packed with them like a swarm of bees. I don't know what they were doing, but apparently they were enjoying themselves. You are certainly giving a great deal of pleasure to a large number of individuals who would be unlikely to get it otherwise, and no doubt they will be improved in many ways." Daisy had great things to report to Sir Robert Baden-Powell when she had dinner with him, at his telegraphed request, on his return to London from his world tour.

Papa's next letters were from Belmont, where he had gone, following President Taft's visit, to get the usual refreshment for his soul that Belmont always gave him, before starting off with Mama to White Sulphur Springs, Virginia. They were the last letters Papa wrote Daisy from his beloved Belmont.

"The weather has been quite cool and you would have enjoyed driving over the fields with me or sitting on the piazza with me as I am doing now." He spoke with quiet satisfaction of the memorial at Yale, which was very near to his heart. "We have at last got the project in shape so that I think by June 13 we will be ready to submit our plans. It will be the first time any Northern institution has recognized any Confederates as entitled,to any recognition and honor."

The Civil War Memorial may be seen today in what was Woolsey Hall in 1912, but is now called Memorial Hall. Substantially as Willie described it to Daisy in the foregoing letter, it consists of two marble tablets with the names in gold letters of all Yale men, from North or South, who took part in what Willie always called the War between the States. The tablets are flanked on each side by two life-sized bas-relief figures by Henry Hering, representing "Courage," "Memory," "Peace," and "Devotion," each with a fitting inscription. The memorial was dedicated in 1915, three years after Willie's death, with Bill taking his father's place at the ceremony, upon the urgent plea of Yale University that Willie's son should make the presentation speech.

Daisy and Mabel both spent some time in White Sulphur Springs that summer with their parents, then Mabel returned to England. Daisy went up north to get her Girl Guides organized on a national basis. This she expected to do in about two months' time. She accepted an invitation from Papa to join him and Nellie at Briarcliff Manor, close to New York City, for September—"I want to be near the Girl Guide Headquarters in New York during September, but my real reason for chucking Scotland is to spend September with you and Mama." She would go on to Savannah with them in October, and there would be picked up by her friends of St. Donat's Castle, the Godfrey Williams', for a six months' cruise in "the biggest yacht in the world."

But all the plans went astray. Just as Mama was ready to start off on August 12 for Chicago to be the chief attraction at the centennial of the Fort Dearborn Massacre, Papa became ill. It was soon apparent that his condition was serious. Bill and Arthur hurried to White Sulphur Springs, Daisy got there as soon as she could. When the newspapers carried the word that Arthur and Bill had been called to their father's bedside, the

offices of W. W. Gordon & Company were besieged. Bierne
Gordon wrote Arthur: "You must have known how many
friends and admirers he had, but if the General could know
how often I am stopped on the street by people, of both colors,
that I never saw or heard of before, inquiring anxiously about
him, he would realize how much he is admired and loved in
this community." When Willie died, on September 11, 1912,
flags were flown at half-mast in Savannah. The papers carried
many columns of tribute to one of Georgia's most prominent
and best loved citizens. The Georgia Hussars escorted Willie
to his grave in Laurel Grove Cemetery.

For the first time in Nellie's life, she lost touch with reality,
her mind wandered. Daisy submerged her own terrible sense
of loss in concern and care for her mother. Arthur, who felt
the special solicitude for Nellie that Daisy displayed toward her
father, had never left her side throughout the long vigil and
was worn out. His wife, Margaret, had just given birth to their
son, Arthur. Daisy packed them all off to Atlantic City as soon
as the funeral was over. She wrote her brother there: "My darling boy: Dr. Jones says that Mamma's physical condition is
astonishing. Her heart, kidneys, liver, all are absolutely normal.
She is simply *stunned,* and physically exhausted. . . .

"When you think that emotional Mamma has never shed a
tear, or said a word but 'Oh, I thank God, he does not suffer
any more,' you may realize how crushed she is. She does not
even ask to see her letters! In fact, unless in pain, she talks
quite rationally on every subject, and as if Papa might come
into her room at any moment. I do not think that she is unhappy, and she has not even suggested going to Laurel Grove
so of course we also avoid it. Do not fret about her, darling.
This is God's merciful anodyne. The crisis will come when the
lover of her girlhood, the husband of her youth, the devoted
admirer and champion of her old age, has gone *and she knows
it.* She is so unselfish that she will agree that it is better for
her to suffer, so that he would be spared the pain of separation.
But the days and hours will be bitterly empty in spite of all our
love; for she never pretended for a moment that he was not
with her the first, and last, and that we were as nothing in comparison. I believe Papa thought that the triumph of his life!

For maternal love is the inheritance of the ages, but such love as Mamma gave him was a personal tribute."

Daisy decided it would be best to take Mama back to England with her, "and the sooner we can get on the way the better, as the nerves of all of us are extremely overwrought." The sea voyage did Mama a great deal of good. With her mind temporarily in abeyance, Nellie's sturdy little body, powered by the healthy instincts of her wilderness forebears, took charge. Nellie, who had claimed for years that she hated fresh air, lived on the deck in the daytime and even had her meals there. Eleanor's daughter, Lalla, and Mama's maid, Starr, had come too, so that Daisy was able to spend a good deal of time in her cabin "gathering strength for the sad meeting in England with poor little Mabel." Daisy wrote Arthur from shipboard: "At night Mama sometimes breaks down and her worst fears are that Papa may need her, or turn to someone else! Poor little soul, *she* needs him so desperately she believes he must be lost without her. I am so thankful she is no longer 'at odds' with me—on the contrary we are close to each other now."

When they arrived in England, and Mabel could take the responsibility for their mother, Daisy went to Harrogate to get relief, so she said, from rheumatism. Mabel wrote her there October 17: "Mama is better than she was. She demands food, sleeps eight hours a night and talks of Papa to me constantly. She cries over his letters, but quite quietly, and is evidently determined that if she must live, it shall be not only without pain, but bravely, for all of us. Of course she will have relapses, but there is something infinitely pathetic in her gratefulness, both for our love, and for what she has had. She says to me again and again how glad she is that Papa knew what friends you and she were this summer and how good you have been to her."

Mabel had been very worried about Daisy, having foreseen that "once you turned Mama over to me, and the tension relaxed, you were bound to collapse." This was the case. It was not rheumatism that had sent Daisy off to Harrogate but grief that she could keep in check no longer. True to her custom of hiding away when she was suffering, she had taken herself off so that Mama and Mabel should not be oppressed by her pain. Arthur, knowing how Daisy had depended on her father's love, tried to fill his father's place. Sending her a present for her fifty-second birthday, October 31, Arthur wrote: "It is my fervent wish that you may live for many long years to be the comfort to all of us that you have been in the past. You have often spoken to me about Papa being all you had, but that is not so, for you are part of our lives and we all call on you the more freely from the very fact that your home responsibilities are lighter. . . . I think Papa would like us all to grow closer together. . . . Write me often, dear, and tell me all you think and what your plans are."

When he did not hear from Daisy, he wrote her similar loving letters, trying to reach her in the black desolation that he sensed had claimed her. It was December 1, before she replied. "You are quite right, we must all put our shoulder to the wheel, bear up and help others. I haven't written because I don't think it helps to write when one is *ill*, it only weighs on others and accentuates my grief. That I should have lost, in Papa, the only human being who was indulgent to my faults, and took my part in all ways and always, is what I now feel. If I had a beautiful, devoted wife, children, an absorbing occupation in business, counterbalanced though it might be by worry for future success; if I were in the prime of manhood with a future stretching before me, I might grieve just as much for Papa but I would not despair." There is a long line after the word "despair," carried clear across the page.

Her letter continues: "There is no exact analogy between my case and the case of Papa's other children. In his justice, he tried to make up to me for all that I lacked. He loved me no more than the others, but he knew I needed him more, and in proportion I miss him more. . . . But as a matter of fact your letters have roused me out of a stupor of indifference, wakened me to the cowardice which has made me long, not only to die, but to be annihilated." Here is another long emphatic line "I forget the name of Job's best comforter, but he never succeeded in awakening in Job the right stiffness to stand up to his sorrows. Job continued to curse the day of his birth to the end, whereas you have made me feel glad that I was Papa's child, and I bless you for such love and sympathy as made you try to help me. . . . My love to Margaret. I daily thank God that He has given her to us all."

It may be that Daisy had had another blow to surmount just now, of which Arthur did not know. Baden-Powell had been in America again that fall, and Daisy had invited him to come to Savannah. She had been much concerned about this man who had put aside all considerations of self in promoting his program for the welfare of boys, she would send him analyses of his character and beg him to give more thought to his personal happiness. In a letter dated October 27, 1912, written from the train near Omaha, Baden-Powell regretted that he could not come to Savannah, and referred with grateful thanks to another complimentary analysis of his character, but assured Daisy she had been absolutely wrong in it. He denied, obliquely, Daisy's intimation that he might take a "lively young lady" to wife, saying that while he would like to slip out of harness some time and have a chance to play, he was tied to his work for the next two years at least, and that marriage did not "enter much" into his calculations.

Daisy must have written her letter before Papa's illness began in mid-August, when she was planning to be in Savannah in October, for she would not have been issuing invitations after Papa became gravely ill, and she and Nellie were aboard the *Olympic* on their way to England by the end of September. Perhaps the letter had been following Baden-Powell about the country, for there is no mention of Willie's death the month before. Sir Robert's answer presumably reached Daisy when she was at Harrogate, overcome by desperate grief, wishing not just for death, but for annihilation. In December, Baden-Powell wrote again to thank her for her very kind letter about his marriage to Olave Soames, and for the beautiful wedding present Daisy had sent them. By ironic coincidence, he and his bride were going to Gibraltar, to spend Christmas with George and Archibald Hunter!

Whatever Daisy's feelings were toward Baden-Powell, the letters show plainly that she had a great and sympathetic interest in him. At the very least, it must have given her some pain that he had kept her in the dark about his imminent marriage. Again, Daisy showed her generosity and nobility. The friendship with Baden-Powell became one between Daisy and husband and wife. She visited them at their home, they visited her. There are many affectionate personal letters to Daisy in the files from both Baden-Powells, in addition to the many devoted to Scout affairs. Whenever a child was born to them, Baden-Powell would write Daisy about it among the first, and she would send her heartfelt congratulations.

And if in the beginning, Daisy, as seems possible, had been attracted to the Girl Guides through the attraction she felt for Baden-Powell, the fact that he had married a "lively young lady" in no way diminished her interest in the work to which he had introduced her. From now on it was to claim everything she had to give, and was to bring its own reward. For not only had Daisy found at last something into which she could throw her vast array of unsuspected abilities. More than this—far, far more than this—in "her girls," Daisy was to find the children she had never had.

CHAPTER XX

———————— ☆ ————————

AS PAPA WOULD HAVE
WISHED IT

W ITH ARTHUR's loving help, Daisy got her emotions under
control and returned to London in December, taking
up her accustomed activities again. By this time Nellie had
emerged from her dazed condition. To her children's amazement, she, too, plunged into a full life. Eleanor, Daisy and Bill
could remember vividly the three years of depression Nellie had
gone through following Alice's death. No one had dreamed she
could rally so quickly from this still-heavier blow.

Daisy wrote Mabel on January 13, 1913, that "Mama has
never been in better health, and is leading the most active
schedule. It is partly because she thrives on excitement and is
in good condition, but it is also a way to forget sad thoughts.
She rushes at everything that can distract her mind. Thursday
we were invited to Crawley Court. It was at Queens Crawley
that Becky Sharp displayed her wit and charms. Our hosts
showed us where the old house used to stand and the door
through the wall, where Becky walked to the parsonage. We
got there at teatime and had four hours' steady talk, Mama and
I doing all the talking. . . .

' Mama was the center of all. She shone with brilliancy. It
was like what Papa used to say—'when I first met that inesti-
mable woman, she was standing on her head on the point of a

spear surrounded by fireworks.' To me, the effort of being entertaining *all* the time when I am visiting is fatiguing . . . but Mama loved it. In entertaining others, she entertained herself, and if you want to realize what a wonderful mother we possess, just read Second Samuel chapter XIX verses 32 to 41. Barzillia was only three years older than our mother, yet he pleaded his age as an excuse not to cross Jordan River, because he could not hear the singing of the men and women and could not enjoy what food he ate. Our mother doesn't hesitate to cross the Atlantic ocean. She not only hears singing voices, but like the lady who wore rings on her fingers and bells on her toes, she makes music wherever she goes."

That all this had been an act of sheer grit became plain when, a few days later, Nellie had a heart attack. Daisy wrote Mabel on the eighteenth: "Mama was perfectly well at the concert and looked so young and bright. She woke next morning with a violent pain and suffered all day, but is almost herself again. The doctors I called told her, 'Your heart is seventy-seven years old, all the rest of you is about thirty or forty years old, so you treat your heart badly and overwork it.' But they told me privately that the attack was not the result of exertion, but because she has been too brave since Papa's death. If she could sit and cry and talk to us it would be best, but she only weeps when she is alone at night, and a sleepless night will always be harmful. Dr. Porter says she is the most wonderful woman he ever saw. She will be as well as ever, but must adjust her life to the weak heart, rest one day a week and so on. Perhaps the heart attack will prove an actual advantage, if it makes Mama realize that there are limits to her endurance." Mama was homesick for Savannah, and the doctors said there was no reason why she should not sail on the twenty-third for America as she had planned. Daisy thought it had been a good thing for Nellie to come to England, but the time had come for her to return home. "Even if the associations are at first heartbreaking, yet she now longs for them."

And now, through one of those coincidences that seemed to abound in Daisy's life, another military hero moved into the place of close personal friend and adviser left vacant in Daisy's life by Baden-Powell's engagement and marriage. He was none other than Baden-Powell's cousin and Daisy's self-sacrificing host in India, Neville Smyth, now a colonel. Soon after Daisy got back to London from Harrogate, a note had arrived from him, saying that he was just in from Mesopotamia with his bags full of interesting curios he would like to show to Daisy. Might he call?

Daisy had heard from Neville Smyth at intervals since her Indian trip, from various corners of Asia and Africa. But he had given up soldiering for the time being, "to avoid dropping into a condition of comfortable self-complacency," he said, and had taken up flying, specializing in the Deperdussin monoplane which held the speed record of a phenomenal 105 miles an hour. Daisy saw him often, she consulted him about her personal problems; he took a great interest in her work with the Girl Guides, talked to them about flying, and helped Daisy in many other ways.

This modest holder of the Victoria Cross shows himself, by his letters, to have been, like his illustrious cousin, a man of cultivated mind and tastes, as well as sharing Baden-Powell's courage and spirit of adventure. Though the romantic overtones are lacking from his letters that one catches in Baden-Powell's earlier ones to Daisy, they bespeak a devoted thoughtfulness about her welfare. Daisy revealed to him, as she apparently never did to Baden-Powell, what a catastrophic loss Papa's death had been to her. She confessed her faults to him, and he wrote her: "I did not realize that you are erratic. But I will observe more closely from now on, and then decide whether it shocks my military instincts!" Like a true friend, Colonel Smyth never hesitated to point out weaknesses he saw in her plans. But like Papa, he was not disturbed by her quirks, and she took suggestions from him gracefully.

Daisy had thrown herself into the Girl Guide work more fervently than ever, and had a great new idea—which Baden-Powell approved heartily—to merge "her girls" in America with the already established Campfire Girls, and get Mrs. Woodrow Wilson, the wife of the new President, to head up the combined girls' organization. She wrote Colonel Smyth that Mrs. Wilson —the first wife of President Wilson—was from Savannah, which would make it all the cosier. He wrote back: "Your scheme is a grand one—to get Mrs. Wilson to combine all the Girl Guides. But *you* must be the 100-horsepower 'anzani,' or gnome engine that drives the aeroplane. The Girl Guides are the fuselage, and Mrs. Wilson the wings and empannage." (The empannage is the tail of an airplane.)

Daisy followed her mother to Savannah before long, visited all her troops and became acquainted with every member. She bought some lots near Bonna Bella to use for what is now called day-camping; and a launch so that "her girls" could have outings on the many rivers around Savannah. She took the first troop formed, the naturalist group of which Page Anderson was a member, on a five-day camping trip, where they followed as closely as they could the camping techniques of Daisy's Grandmother Juliette and of Baden-Powell.

The time had come, she felt, to set up a national headquarters, and also to get out a handbook for American girls. Daisy addressed herself to both tasks simultaneously. There is a difference of opinion as to who actually did the work on the first publication for the organization that was soon to be known as the Girl Scouts. Miss Agnes Baden-Powell had given Daisy permission to make use of the English handbook as she desired, and Daisy had retained W. J. Hoxie, the naturalist who had the camp near Bonna Bella, to write the chapters on camping and nature lore. Daisy's letters imply that he also revised the rest of the material, and his name alone is on the book, *How Girls Can Help Their Country,* which was issued by the Knickerbocker Press in 1913.

It has always been assumed, however, that Daisy herself did the adapting from the English handbook, and there are distinct Daisyish touches throughout. In the cooking section, girls are informed that "a most unwholesome food is stale fish," and that "boiling water is useful to dip your sardine into if you want to get his skin off, but do not dip him into the teakettle." The recipe for an omelette reads: "The true artist in omelettes is one who beats her eggs with a knife on a plate till they are so firm that, on turning the plate upside down, the whites keep sticking to it. A beginner told me she often used to let them drop on the floor; but such was her patience and persistence that she scraped up all the egg on to the plate again and continued beating. That is not really necessary for a good omelette, however." What the girl was supposed to do with her eggs after she had dropped them on the floor and then scraped them up again is not indicated.

Nevertheless, the handbook was received enthusiastically by the patrols, and the vision it gave of a new feminine future did a great deal to break down the restrictions then imposed on girls, especially in the South. Southern ladies were expected to do nothing more strenuous than "sit on a cushion and sew a fine seam," and their daughters were carefully shielded from a host of things considered unfeminine, including a more than rudimentary education. But the handbook pointed out that women had made a success in nursing, medicine, architecture—that they had even flown airplanes! Girls were inducted into the delights of outdoor life, vigorous sports, naturalizing. Careful Savannah parents allowed their daughters to do these things because, though Daisy might be odd in some ways, she was a Gordon, and undeniably a lady.

The Savannah troops practiced marching a great deal, and also played basketball on the vacant lot Daisy had put at their disposal; though they had to go to the headquarters to change into their basketball outfits—great wide bloomers and middy blouses—and put on long coats in order to cross the street. And they could not take off their coats until curtains, strung on wires around the lot, had been drawn, lest passersby should see their black-stockinged, early teen-age legs. But all this represented a considerable advance over what the girls would have been allowed to do if Daisy Low had not come along with her new program.

In the ensuing months, Daisy applied her hundred-horsepower engine to tending her Savannah Scouts, finishing up the handbook and getting it published, modeling a bust of Papa, setting up a national headquarters in the Munsey Building in Washington, D.C., with Edith Johnston in charge of it, and collecting illustrious names for her national board. In between times she interviewed Campfire Girls executives about her plan to amalgamate the organizations for young girls, suggesting the name "Girl Scouts" for the joint program. She began to refer to the Guides as Girl Scouts, the patrols as troops, and her fellow workers followed suit.

Mabel has said, "I think Daisy's never seeing difficulties, and being absolutely uninfluenced by arguments, were an advantage to her, as it worked out. The wonderful thing was that when she butted down a brick wall with her head, scattering brickbats on all around her, everyone realized it was never for herself but to accomplish what she thought was right."

In Washington, Genie Massey, her friend from Edge Hill Academy days, now Mrs. Oscar Underwood, took Daisy under her wing and saw that she met all the important people. Out of this kindness of Genie's came one of Daisy's most famous word confusions. To advance Daisy's work, the Underwoods took her with them to a reception at the White House. When the usher asked Genie for her name so he could announce her, for some reason she hesitated. Daisy filled the gap helpfully by saying, "Mr. and Mrs. Underbrush," and it was as Mr. and Mrs. Underbrush that the Senator from Alabama and his wife were announced. It is reported that Genie's husband was considerably annoyed, but Genie knew her old friend too well to be disturbed.

Eleanor was a great help, as well, interesting her close friend, Mrs. Corinne Roosevelt Robinson, Theodore Roosevelt's sister, in the Scouts, and Mrs. Thomas A. Edison. But what surprised Mabel, when she arrived from England, was to find her mother in Washington with Daisy, deeply implicated with Girl Scouting too! When Mabel spoke to Nellie about this, the reply was: "You ought to know that I don't give a damn about the Girl Scouts, and Eleanor doesn't either. We are so glad Daisy is sticking to her interest that we want to do everything we can." Her daughters, however, thought Nellie was reveling in this "stampede to Washington," as Daisy called it. The distinguished ladies Daisy drew into the Girl Scout movement paid flattering attentions to Nellie. Her letters from now on are filled with details of the work and of Daisy's plans.

But it was Daisy who got the spotlight. Wherever she went, these days, she was interviewed by reporters for the wire services as well as for the local newspapers. Juliette Low was becoming a national celebrity, and was in demand as a speaker. At a banquet in New York City, the chairman was August Belmont, who sat beside her. When he rose to introduce her, Daisy laid her large hearing aid on the table so that she could catch what he said. Mr. Belmont thought it was a camera with which she was planning to take a snap of him, and was so startled that he introduced her as Mrs. Loeb. But her name got in the papers properly. And every interview, every newspaper story about her, produced more inquiries about the Girl Scouts. Nellie was happy to be in the shadow of the erratic daughter whom people were beginning to refer to as a genius.

Daisy's first National Board of Councilors consisted of Mrs. W. J. Boardman, Mrs. Alfred Burleson, Mrs. James Marion Johnson, Mrs. Joseph R. Lamar, Mrs. Richard G. Lay, Mrs. John Van Rensselaer and Mrs. Oscar Underwood; very good names indeed in that day. At the first outing held by the Washington group, the prizes were distributed by Miss Martha Bowers, who was to become Mrs. Robert A. Taft. Mrs. Underwood and Mrs. Lamar went with Daisy to call on Mrs. Woodrow Wilson, and lay before her the plan to merge all American organizations for young girls into one, with Mrs. Wilson at the head. Mrs. Wilson was interested, and called some ladies together the next week at the White House, to discuss the idea.

But in the negotiations with the Campfire Girls, Daisy ran into a brick wall she could not batter down. Daisy's one stipulation was that the Girl Scout laws, or rules, should be part of the new organization. She thought them very clear and practical, and besides they followed the Boy Scout laws closely. The Campfire Girls refused to accept the laws and finally the merger plan fell through.

It was perhaps because of the emphasis Daisy placed on the Girl Scout rules that a parody of them was written in the visitors' book at Lochs by some irreverent hand. Though it is not signed, Daisy Lawrence has always suspected Rudyard Kipling, and it is the sort of chaffing Rud and Daisy used to exchange about each other's enterprises.

The Girl Scout laws read:

1. A Girl Scout's honor is to be trusted.
2. A Girl Scout is loyal.
3. A Girl Scout's duty is to be useful and to help others. (She should do at least one good turn to somebody every day.)
4. A Girl Scout is a friend to all, and a sister to every other Girl Scout no matter to what social class she may belong.
5. A Girl Scout is courteous.
6. A Girl Scout keeps herself pure.

7. A Girl Scout is a friend to animals.
8. A Girl Scout obeys orders.
9. A Girl Scout is cheerful.
10. A Girl Scout is thrifty.

The parody read:

MORAL

1. Seek Beauty and the boys will seek you.
2. Seize on to Health and the boys will seize on to you.
3. Follow truth—at a respectful distance.
4. Study Nature—she knows as much as most girls and has been at it longer.

PRACTICAL

5. Never trap in your own woods except for practice.
6. Cover your tracks. It may not seem necessary, but you cannot tell who may be following you.
7. Never come home by the same way you went.
8. If you keep an animal guessing, he will stop and look at you till he is sure of your intentions. Then you can be sure too.
9. Never stampede another girl's game and leave her traps alone.
10. A foul-hooked fish gives the most sport but a wounded bird is always picked up by a stranger. Kill clean.
11. If you want to have the brutes feed out of your hand learn to cook.
12. Noise and light never helped anyone yet except at a hotel.
13. Still-hunting is the best hunting but game gets up in the most unlikely places

SO

Wherever you may go and whomever you may meet and whatever you are doing
14. BE PREPARED.

Someone suggested it would be good publicity for the Girl Scouts if Daisy were presented to King George V and Queen Mary. Daisy's great friend, Eva Dugdale, was a lady-in-waiting to Queen Mary, Frank, her husband, an equerry, so it was only necessary for someone to pass the word along. At the end of May, Daisy, then in Savannah, was invited to appear at Court. Nellie wrote Mabel: "Daisy got her invitation to Court. I think she meant to accept it till I said I thought it would be a good plan—when she at once decided to decline! Perhaps it's just as well for it would have been a *rush!*"

But Daisy loved to rush, she accepted the invitation, and by June 10 she was in London arranging about her costume. There was no question this time of running over to Paris to buy a stunning new dress. Daisy was paying all the expenses of the American Girl Scouts, and also all the expenses for her Girl Guide patrols in England and Scotland. There were to be no more trailing negligees of real lace—Daisy from now on would have little time to wear them, anyway. She found she had a silver gown from last year that would do. She had a Court train made of silver tissue and Mabel loaned her a black scarf of real lace that Minnie Davis had given her, which was inserted in the middle of the train. As a widow, Daisy wore black plumes and a black veil. Mabel, now a member of a family that had attended English Courts for many generations, had arranged it all.

But when Daisy got a peep into the throne room from the stairs, she saw that not a single woman wore black feathers or a black veil except herself. "I cast about in my mind how I could retire, but having come three thousand miles to London to see the Queen I hated to miss seeing her." Daisy was carrying a white feather fan belonging to Mabel and was considering denuding it to decorate her head, when she saw Mrs. Asquith— Daisy always spelled this Askwith—in black with black feathers, and so Mabel's fan was spared. When Daisy got to the Lord Chamberlain, Frank Dugdale, who was among the courtiers, tried to make her giggle, but she "cut him dead and salaamed with dignity before the sovereigns."

Yet her desperate sense of loss remained unabated. She was avid for a ride in one of the record-breaking Deperdussin monoplanes, but Colonel Neville Smyth refused to take her up with him, considering the little plane too risky. Daisy managed her monoplane ride nevertheless, and Colonel Smyth upbraided her vigorously when he heard of it.

"Dear Mrs. Low: Nothing will ever make me acknowledge that I assisted you to fly in a Deperdussin monoplane with Norman Spratt, notorious as the pilot who takes the most risks. You did it yourself in spite of my efforts to put you off with a slow ride in a biplane." Daisy sent this on to a close friend with a note scribbled in the margin—"Return this and tell no one I've been flying. I wish I had been killed. It was a delicious experience."

She brought over to England the pony Willie had bought for his grandchildren to use, named Peggy Doots for the two granddaughters who were nearly the same age, and kept most of the time at Myrtle Grove, Bill's plantation. Cook and Sons, who attended to getting the horses of Colonel Smyth and Lord Mahon to and from India and other far places, took charge of transporting the pony, at considerable cost to Daisy. "I shall send it to the Huttons or to Muriel Worthington. All I want is to have the little pony happy, because Papa loved it."

In the end the pony went to Stoneleigh Abbey, the Leigh family estate, where Mabel's children, Peggy and Rowland, got the use of it. Daisy thought it only fair therefore, to pay Doots sixty dollars for her share in the pony. Doots, who by now had been working with the White Carnation Girl Scout Troop in Savannah and had become thoroughly imbued with the Girl Scout code, wrote an indignant letter in reply:

"I give Peggy Doots to Peggy and Rowley, as they gave her to me while I was at Myrtle Grove, and as I have had my share now I will not accept any money. If you look at rule 5 in the Scout Law, this is what you will find: 'A Scout is courteous. That is, is polite to all, but especially to women and children and old people and invalids, cripples, etc. *And she must not take any reward for being helpful or courteous!*' " Daisy felt that Papa would have approved of Doots' "independant" spirit, and the matter was allowed to rest there.

All the special tenderness Daisy had had for both her parents she now centered upon Nellie. Daisy had planned to pass up Lochs that summer because Eleanor had written that she was needed at the National Headquarters in Washington. "I have put my hand to the plough and I will not turn back." She would use the money instead to give an outing to seventy Girl

Guides. But she wrote Nellie a very loving letter saying that if her mother would like to come to Lochs, "I will let every Girl Guide or Scout wait until October." Nellie was the one thing that came ahead of the Girl Scouts in Daisy's life.

Arthur tried to take his father's place with Nellie, insofar as anyone could, just as he had tried to take his father's place with Daisy. The children knew their mother prayed every night to God to let her die soon, so that she might be reunited with her Willie. They respected this feeling while losing no opportunity to let her know how they treasured her. On her birthday the June following Willie's death, Arthur gave Nellie his father's traditional gift on this occasion. We have the little note that accompanied it, surely as beautiful and understanding an expression as any mother ever had from a son.

"MY PRECIOUS MOTHER:
"This is your birthday, and I know Papa wants me to bring the usual little purse, with the twenty-dollar goldpieces and his message of love and devotion. You always have been, and always will be, his comfort and pride and joy, and I am just as sure that he is with you today, as I am that I love you.

"I do not wish you many happy returns of the day, but I want you to know that I love and cherish you with all my heart and strength and that Margaret and Stuarty and little Son love you too."

Nellie was deeply affected by the love with which her children surrounded her. Her letters to them from now on are softer in tone and filled with loving expressions, some of them sounding like her own mother's letters in the early years of Nellie's wifehood. When the children suffered, she suffered with them. But she did not depart from her former character in any other way.

She knew it could not be many years until she would rejoin Willie. She did not want these years to be a burden to her children. And she knew how Willie had delighted in her wit and sparkle and unorthodox performances. Willie would have wanted her to get as much pleasure from the years remaining to her as she could, and she set herself to do that. Nellie had reached the age when the more original and uninhibited a bright, active woman is, the more she is appreciated by those around her. This was the kind of old age Nellie had been practicing for her whole life through, and she performed her rôle brilliantly. She liked to demonstrate that she was as agile as ever—Bill's wife, Ellie, used to say that at eighty, "Granny could still thread a No. 10 needle while standing on her head and whistling Yankee Doodle!"

It was in 1914, when Nellie was seventy-nine, that she wrote her reminiscences of her early childhood, quoted from earlier in this book, taking pains to stress what a very naughty little girl she had been. There was only one thing in her whole life she was prouder of, and that was that she had been born in Chicago.

Both the women to whom Willie Gordon had meant everything, tried to do what they knew he would have wanted them to. Nellie and Daisy drew very close after Willie's death, each trying to supply the need of the other for the deep, never-failing love he had given. Each entered ardently into the other's interests. Never again were they "at odds." But it was a sign of recovery for both that by July of the summer following Willie's death, Nellie was inquiring if Daisy had made off with her steamer rug—an area in which Daisy always remained sensitive. Daisy snapped back, though with more humor and less asperity than of old, "I did not steal your steamer rug as you so delicately suggest. Mine is a plaid, it's true, but 'It is not thy plaid, bonny though the colors be.' If your rug is gone, please inquire of the Star line, or even consult an astronomer, but don't accuse me of breaking the eighth commandment!"

Mother and daughter resumed their spirited and pleasurable fencing. Daisy was gleeful when she discovered a misspelled word in a letter from Nellie. She wrote Mabel: "There is only one 'l' in balance. Mama put two! I wrote and reproved her, explaining that I never use the word myself as I have not a balance anywhere, either in my actions or in my bank, but that I feel keenly how wrong it is to put two 'l's' in that word. I also wrote and asked her to get me a first edition of the Ten Commandments. I hear they are out of print, but I should like to have a set on hand for reference whenever she accuses me of fracturing one."

From now on until Nellie's death it is her comments—pride in her daughter's achievements, mingled with acerb criticisms—

that furnish the counterpoint to Daisy's still-hectic, but now-purposeful and triumphant course.

Daisy seems to have been particularly erratic and trying that summer. After having invited to Lochs Bill's son, B., her Gordon cousins John and Percy and others, she decided not to go to Lochs but to America. "But, Mama, you must not ask dates because should I change dates there may be more upheavals over my plans and I think I will just carry out what I consider best without consulting anybody. When we have such a short time to live it seems useless to get into a fever over plans, so in future I will not work myself up over arrangements or fuss at all. I shall do my best to give others pleasure and to do my duty and if I fail to meet the approval of everybody why I shall be able to bear it." That letter sent Nellie stamping and cussing around the house. When Daisy wrote Mabel that she was going to go to Lochs after all, having been persuaded by John and Percy Gordon to run up there in a car, but was sailing August twenty-eighth for America, Mabel advised Mama to "say nothing more to her about plans, for she cannot leave London the 19th, take two or three days to motor to Lochs, spend ten days there and sail the 28th! Expect her when she cables, not before!"

Daisy was evidently aware that she had irked her family. She sent them a very affectionate, complimentary letter she had received from Lady Warwick, writing on the margin: "I wish you would keep this and read it whenever you are all annoyed with me!"

Daisy, however, continued her untrammeled way. In September Edith Johnston, in the Washington Girl Scout Headquarters, received a cablegram telling her to be prepared to meet Daisy in "New York, Baltimore, Washington or Boston." The rendezvous was finally held in New York. It was then the decision was made to change the color of the Girl Scout uniforms to khaki, and plans were mapped out for extending the organization. Then Daisy was off to New Bedford, Massachusetts, to start setting up troops in New England. She wrote Bill: "I have crossed the Atlantic seven times in eleven months, have spent $1,500 on passage, and have nothing to show for it." But she rushed to Mama at Manchester, New Hampshire, when word came that Nellie had had another heart attack. "Mama said to the nurse at 4 A.M. on the 11th, 'At this hour, a year ago, my darling left me,' but did not talk of the anniversary to any of her children who were there with her. She is the most considerate and bravest woman I ever knew."

Not until Mama was definitely on the mend did Daisy return to her task of national organization, but then she accomplished wonders, bringing to bear all the abilities that had lain dormant through the "wasted" years. And those years proved not to have been wasted after all, because she had accumulated endless riches of friendships and old associations, and they paid priceless dividends to the Girl Scouts. Her cousin Percy Gordon, on whom she had had a girlish crush back in Etowah days, and with whom she had maintained an affectionate relationship ever since, had opened the New Bedford lead to her, which soon opened all New England. And every such opening brought new friends for herself and the Girl Scouts jointly. At New Bedford, it was Dorris Hough, who was to work in Girl Scouting for forty-three years, and was to become Daisy's close confidante. Out of New England came Mrs. J. J. Storrow, who was to mean much to Girl Scouting and to Daisy too. Of all Daisy's talents, it was her talent for friendship that had the most to do with making the Girl Scouts a thriving organization in so amazingly short a time.

After New England, Daisy went on to Chicago, where Nellie had advised her own old friends and her Skinner cousins of Daisy's coming, so that the way was all prepared. Daisy stayed at Hull House as the guest of Jane Addams, who set up meetings for her with important groups, even though Miss Addams was on the Council of the Campfire Girls.

Nellie wrote to Mabel proudly: "Daisy had a great success in Chicago. . . . There were notices in eight papers! She made an address at the Kinzie School where she had an enthusiastic reception and enrolled many new members." Then Daisy joined Nellie at White Springs, Florida, "arriving here a poor tired dirty little specimen," so Nellie wrote Mabel. But Nellie was impressed by the fact that even while recuperating in the mud baths at the Springs, Daisy recruited some new friends of her mother's, the Jacksons, for work in the Girl Scouts. By February, 1914, the patent for the trefoil, the Tenderfoot pin, came from the U. S. Patent Office and was framed and hung in the national office.

Daisy was looking forward to that summer of 1914 with a special eagerness. At last she was to have a castle of her own! She had rented Castle Menzies, which, like Meggernie, was in Perthshire, Scotland, and, also like Meggernie, came complete with ghost. Mama and Beth and Corty Parker were coming over to stay with her. Mabel would join them.

On June 22, Daisy wrote Nellie excitedly that the castle would be ready for occupancy that very night. "It is beautiful and glorious as Paradise. I am surprised at the way the furniture from 39 Grosvenor Street has filled the rooms—like the widow's cruse, it has daily increased so that with the Lochs furniture and the few things I brought from Savannah I have furnished *six* best bedrooms and servants' rooms. I have been lent nine old Fifteenth Century tapestries, fifteen to twenty feet long, which make the main rooms very grand. Everything is done up new, fresh blinds in the windows, new floors, new drains and with my nice furniture it all does look very nice." The George J. Goulds were her next neighbors. J. Gould was the tennis champion of the world. Corty would play on the Gould tennis court and she hoped J. Gould would play on hers. "I feel years younger and more peaceful than for years."

There was no hunting or fishing, however, since the fishing rights belonged to the Goulds. Also, after Daisy moved into the castle she found there was still some question about the drains. Upon receiving this word, Nellie wrote her: "Please understand that I could not visit any place where I was unable to shoot, fish and hunt. Besides, I am thinking of taking Buckingham Palace unless, as I now hope, I shall take a longer trip to a warmer climate, where the drains won't interest me."

By July, however, Mama and Eleanor and Mabel's son Rowland had joined Daisy at the castle, besides Beth and Corty Parker, and Daisy reported to Arthur that she herself was loving it more every day and every hour. "I dred the day when I, too, like Little Joe, must 'move on.' Mama says she *likes* my haunted castle."

But a bomb that had been thrown at Sarajevo changed everything. Germany invaded Belgium, and on August 4, Great Britain declared war on Germany. It was expected that Zeppelins would bomb the cities and German warships would shell the coastal towns. Daisy urged Mabel to come at once to the castle, prepared to stay for the duration. She got advice from her military friends, Lord Grenfell, Jack Maxwell, Lord Mahon and General Sir Archibald Hunter, whose name now reappears in the letters, as to the best course for the different members of her family then in England to pursue. Daisy was laying in stores, she had acquired an oil stove in case coal was unobtainable, and she assured Mabel that they would all be better off with her than anywhere else. "We can get lots of wood and game, and this glen does not lead to any important place." The agent for the castle had told Daisy unofficially that she might have it for another year. Mabel elected, however, to stay with her husband and family.

As Daisy realized that her food stores were going fast and would not last beyond November, she began to be anxious to get Mama, and Eleanor's two children off to America. (Eleanor had returned before war broke out.) Nellie had been seventy-nine her previous birthday, and Daisy dreaded war privations for her. But it was becoming very hard to get away from England, with English ships already warned that they might be taken over by the government on a minute's notice. President Wilson had promised safe transport to Americans, but Daisy feared a troopship would be uncomfortable for Mama, "unless she had the captain's cabin and messed with the officers!"

While her children fussed and stewed and tried to decide whether Mama would be worse off in Scotland or on the Atlantic Ocean, the Little Veteran, like the seasoned campaigner she was, thought the situation over, cabled Arthur, "Don't worry, returning American line shortly," and then explained her decision to her anxious daughters.

With Mama, Beth, Corty and Mama's maid, Starr, safely dispatched on an American ship, Daisy settled down to "sit tight" at Menzies until the war was over. She had no means of transportation except a bicycle—horses had been commandeered as soon as the war broke out, she was not allowed to take her car from the garage where she had placed it. Now at last she would be able to get some sculpturing done and live within her income. "I have groceries and stores to last the servants and me for six months, all the garden produce we can use, no one can fish for love or money, so the only bills I have are at the butcher's!"

Odd things about houses kept on happening to Daisy. In December, the Menzies creditors descended on the castle and Daisy was forced to flee back to London. She wrote Arthur, "I was thankful to get my furniture out, as all my things might have been seized to pay Lady Menzies' creditors!" It must have cost Daisy a good deal to renovate the rooms she used, move her furniture from London and Lochs and then back again, for so short a stay, but it was the last expensive whim in which she was to indulge herself.

CHAPTER XXI

———————— ☆ ————————

WORLD WAR I

Now at last Daisy could make return to her British friends for the loving kindness, the unswerving support, she had had from them in her own time of trouble. The lighthearted youths who had fished the streams and stalked the hills at Lochs with Daisy had gone immediately into combat and within a month of England's entrance into the war sad news was trickling back. Young Sir Francis Langston wrote Daisy in September of the deaths of a number of his friends and told her how often he and Hugh Grosvenor talked of the times at Lochs and longed to be back there again. "Do, Daisy dear, write me when you have a moment to spare. You can't think how one loves hearing about everything at home and you know how I love Meggernie and Lochs." And Daisy wrote and wrote to Sir Francis and the other young officers she knew among the Life Guards, the Coldstream Guards and the Black Watch.

To their parents, she gave the overflowing sympathy of her loving, understanding heart. They shared with her the letters they got from their boys at the front. They shared with her those letters it is the hard duty of a commanding officer to write, telling how well a son has fought, and as much as could be learned about the way he had come to his death; for Daisy shared their pride and their grief. And because the Gordons knew so many of these families and these youths, Daisy sent copies to Savannah, and in America, too, the young men of

England were mourned. Idris Williams, whose parents had entertained Daisy at St. Donat's Castle, coughed out his life with poison gas. David Bingham, the son of General Bingham, both the twin sons of Lady May Grey Egerton, both Grenfell twins and many other lads Daisy had watched grow up were among the casualties. When young John Kipling was killed in 1915, to Mama it was as though she had lost one of her own.

In January, 1915, Daisy returned to Savannah. She had intended to go with Rose Habersham to Belgium to help Herbert Hoover in the Belgian relief. Mr. Hoover had wanted two women to distribute clothing, as the young Rhodes scholars working under him knew nothing about children's garments. The execution of Nurse Edith Cavell by the Germans had put a stop to the plan. After her "murder," as Daisy called it, the English government would not allow any English women to go to Belgium. American women could go, however, if they would promise not to return to England until the end of the war, so that the Germans could not have the excuse that they were spies, or returning to England in order to carry information.

Daisy, anxious to be of greater service in the war and to get as close as she could to the fighting front, determined to regain her American citizenship, though warned by an English friend that "once you marry an Englishman, you stay English for the rest of your life." It was perhaps Daisy's investigation into the matter which led to the discovery that old Andrew had taken out American citizenship. The fact does not seem to have been known to his children, Willy Low had always considered himself an Englishman and so had everyone else. Born in Newport, Rhode Island, of a naturalized father, Willy Low had been an American all the time! It did not take Daisy long to establish her own citizenship under these circumstances, but by that time the jobs in Mr. Hoover's relief work had been filled. Daisy, however, in the meantime had become well acquainted with Mr. and Mrs. Hoover, and as a result Mrs. Hoover became deeply interested in the Girl Scouts. She was the third president of the national organization, assuming office in 1922. After that she became president of the board; and her husband's election to the presidency in 1928 literally "swept the Girl Scouts into the White House," giving the movement great impetus.

The war had cut heavily into Daisy's income from English securities, and she found that the Girl Scout organization had grown and grown. If it was to continue to exist, it must have funds. To support the movement for another year, Daisy sold her magnificent pearls. It was a noteworthy year for the Scouts. In 1915, the organization was incorporated as Girl Scouts under the code laws of the District of Columbia. The first constitution and by-laws were adopted. The first annual convention was held, a national council was formed and Juliette Low was named the first president. Sir Robert Baden-Powell thought the constitution very good and practical and suggested that Daisy might like to say in the bulletin the Girl Scouts of Washington, D.C., had just started that he was delighted to see that they had their own journal.

That June, Nellie celebrated her eightieth birthday. She had her photograph taken and sent one to each of her Goshen, Indiana, boys. Telegrams came from all parts of the United States, cablegrams from England. But a remembrance that surprised Nellie and touched her particularly, because of her long love affair with the City of Chicago, was a congratulatory letter from the pupils and principal of the Kinzie School, which had been named for her father, and which she herself had attended for a year. "They paid me such compliments that I am too modest to repeat them."

Daisy had stayed on in Savannah to help celebrate this event. Before leaving for England that summer, she dropped in on Anne Choate. The daughter of Mary Carter Clarke, Daisy's close chum at the Mesdemoiselles Charbonnier's and dear friend ever since, Anne had visited Daisy at Grosvenor Street, London, and had been courted there by Arthur Choate, who was Daisy's favorite among Anne's suitors. Now she lived on the Choate estate near Pleasantville, New York. One of the teachers in the Pleasantville high school had started a Girl Scout troop —that was the real reason for Daisy's visit, Anne Choate soon discovered. Would Anne take an interest in the troop? That is to say, pin on badges now and then? During luncheon, Mrs. Choate learned gradually that she would be expected to do a good many other things as well, including rounding up a local council. Among those Mrs. Choate asked to be on the council was her neighbor, Mrs. Josephine Daskam Bacon, a well-known writer. The upshot was that in spite of her protestations that she couldn't think of it, Anne Choate became vice-president of the national organization; succeeded Daisy as president when Daisy herself stepped down; and worked in the Girl Scouts from that time on. Josephine Daskam Bacon became the first editor of the Girl Scout magazine that was started in 1917 and has thrived ever since.

Daisy's voyage to Liverpool in June, 1915, on the liner *St. Paul,* was very different from her previous crossings. She thought the passengers the most interesting group she had ever traveled with, and the sinking of the *Lusitania* the month before added a spice of danger. Instead of the usual society and business folk, the ship's company was made up of brides going to join their husbands, hospital nurses, young Canadian wives with their babies, doctors, newspaper correspondents. The passengers were nervous and several ladies slept on board in "dress preservers"—presumably a Daisyism for life preservers. There was reason to be a bit nervous, for the *St. Paul* was torpedoed on its next trip.

Daisy found all her friends in England completely immersed in war work, Mabel holding an important position in the organization for Belgian Relief. Daisy wrote Arthur: "Yes, Mabel is indeed working too hard, but so is everybody in England. They're working partly because there is so much to do, and partly to deaden their anxieties and sorrow." Daisy herself, besides carrying on her Girl Guide and Girl Scout work, helped Mabel in the Belgian Relief, and took care of a number of Belgian families as her private responsibility.

Daisy did not allow the submarine menace to interrupt her schedule. By early 1916, she was back in America again and Nellie was boasting to Mabel that "Daisy's Scouts are booming! She has now *7,000 registered,* and she is doing many wonderful *stunts* for them. She has fitted up her camping house at Lowland in a most complete and artistic way and made it into a sort of tea house and has a ballroom where parties can come and dance. Quite wonderful!" A little later Nellie sent Mabel a résumé of Daisy's recent activities. "Left Princeton on hearing of Corty Parker's scarlet fever. Found she was not allowed to see Corty, so went to New York and did *stunts* for the Girl Scouts *(with great success).* Supposed to be staying at Anne

Choate's, but her letters dated 'Hotel Seville,' New York City. Wrote she would meet Bill in New York, Sunday, but went to Philadelphia, to make a speech for Girl Scouts. Went thence to Washington and had a big rally of Girl Scouts with all sorts of important people present, head of Boy Scouts in U.S., members of the Cabinet, etc., etc. Very fine. Arranged for *big ball* to be given by Scouts at 'Ranchers' (Washington) on March 4. Suddenly skipped off to Richmond to speak and whoop up Girl Scouts. Visiting people named *Walton* (*I* never heard of them nor has Margaret Gordon). Goes thence to Baltimore and thence?—God knows. . . . Apparently *never met Bill at all*. She seems to be imitating President Wilson about making speeches. That I should live to see the day one of my daughters would be speaking in public! It's time for my career to end!"

Daisy wrote Mabel that her reward for this strenuous program was "the marvelous strides the movement has made, and the response of the girls, who are so dear, and so grateful to me."

In April Mama was writing to Mabel, "Daisy has gone to New York again to interest people in her Scouts. She seems to be having a successful time with strong backing. Of course her letters are extremely amusing, in ways Daisy doesn't realize. The spelling particularly is unique. I do hope she will have no occasion to write any official notes unless she consults a dictionary. Her historical knowledge also is astounding, as when she quotes a remark of Madame de Maintenon to Louis IV, who lived centuries apart! Wireless? She seems to be associating, too, with Lieutenant Peary, who should be called the *Pole Cat* in my opinion!"

Daisy had been asked to lecture about the Girl Scouts, following an address by Lieutenant Peary of North Pole fame. "Lots of reporters swarmed around me and we will get the sort of publicity which will do more to spread the movement in New York than all the speeches."

When Daisy went back to England after this flurry of activity, her mother went with her. Nellie was making this trip at the age of eighty-one, across the submarine-infested Atlantic, in order to see Mabel. For a number of years, Mabel and Daisy had alternated their trips to America, so that one or the other would be at their parents' disposal a good share of the time. But now Mabel felt that her place was in her adopted country, doing the war work she had chosen and sharing the hardships and dangers with her husband, children and friends. So Mama was going to Mabel.

She kept a diary while she was in England, as was her custom when she went abroad, and the early part of it is filled with a good deal of grumbling at herself because her eyesight and hearing were not as good as they had been. "Went into Stoneleigh to church Sunday, never heard one word of the service. Deaf old fool! Won't try church any more." She castigated herself bitterly for not hearing, for "being stupid." At another time she wrote, "I do hope I won't have to go again to anyone's house to lunch or dine. I hate it and I am too deaf to enjoy it as well as too tired. I am not *up to* that sort of thing."

When she awoke one morning, her right arm was numb. She wrote in her diary: "It passed off in a measure, but I thought I would 'guard against any precaution until I was past all safety' as Cousin Dick used to say. If I am going to have a stroke of paralysis I hope I shall make a die of it." Daisy called a doctor, who told Nellie that "my blood pressure is that of a woman fifty years old, my strength is admirable, all my members are in first-class condition, I am likely to live twenty-five years longer. *(Too bad!)*. I am too fast, I must try to *go slow* and not rush things."

As soon as the doctor had left, Nellie got up and dressed and went shopping with Mabel. From then on, she carried out with zest a social schedule filled with luncheons, teas and dinners. There was a stream of visitors, friends of Daisy's who had become devoted to Nellie, and many of whom had visited the Gordons in Savannah. Nellie recorded in her diary proudly that in a single afternoon she had had eight callers. Occasionally the handwriting in her diary becomes shaky, as though her strength had failed, but in later sections goes back to its old vigor.

She watched the progress of the war with professional interest and the British drive on the Western Front that summer of 1916 reminded the Little Veteran of the "Confederate War," as she called it. "The British have broken through the third line of German line defences, now we must expect a few reverses, but not for long." She claimed that it was due to her failing eyesight that she mistook a young man she had never seen before for a relative of her granddaughter Lalla's husband and gave him a grandmotherly kiss. "As soon as I saw my mistake I ordered a whiskey and soda for him which obviated any fatal consequences. Really, at my age, I ought not to be so frivolous!"

Daisy was asked by the Y.M.C.A. and the military authorities to set up a hostel for the wives and relatives of wounded soldiers who passed through London on the way to see their men in the hospitals. Violet Stuart Wortly, a sister of Charles Guthrie, Mary Low's husband, joined with Daisy in this enterprise. Their task was to meet people at the train, feed and house them and forward them to their destinations, and Daisy loved it.

In late September Neville Smyth, now General Smyth, paid a flying visit to England. He told Daisy that in an assault on a strong point at Gallipoli, neither he nor his Australians slept for five days and five nights. "He looked very shaken and worn and I saw him only one morning, because he spent all his time at his own place at Cornwall, which he says is back a thousand miles in the time of King Arthur and where he can get quiet and rest. All the higher officers seem so worn out that they avoid plays and theaters or any crowd. George Hunter retired to his small farmhouse and sat still all his leave and would not even dine here. But the young officers like to go ahead and hunt, go to theaters and so on." Daisy made the leaves of her young friends as gay as she could manage.

But Nellie was getting homesick. "If I ever get back to Savannah I shall never leave it again," she declared. So as always when she could do something that would make Mama happy, Daisy left the hostel to Violet Wortly's care and in October took Nellie back to America, sailing on the *St. Louis*. They arrived a day sooner than they had expected because "our ship simply *flew* through the debatable ground, or rather sea, where German activity was rife."

Back in Savannah, Nellie wrote Mabel: "How delightful it is to be at home. The house looks lovely and my new cook is excellent. Daisy's house is perfectly charming."

Nellie's calm enjoyment of her home did not last very long. The day of the hotly contested election between Wilson and Hughes, Daisy wired Nellie that she would arrive in Savannah at two o'clock in the morning. "Of course she didn't remember that the time here is one hour later!" Mama wrote Mabel.

Nellie called the station to ask if any New York train was expected, and found one was due at two-fifteen and was on time. When Daisy didn't arrive on that Nellie went to bed. Daisy came in at three-thirty. Morrison, the butler, had gone to meet her and brought her home. When the exasperated Nellie asked Daisy how she came to choose that train, Daisy replied she thought that as it was election night Nellie would be up watching the returns. Nellie assured her she did not care a damn *who* was President of the United States, gave her daughter some supper, a hot bath and put her to bed. "She has been dashing around doing *stunts* ever since she got here. She seems to be very successful in all directions. She has meetings here, goes to Brunswick, goes to Atlanta, goes to Boston. I doubt whether she gets off for England on the twenty-fourth, but I make no comment," Nellie wrote Mabel.

Four days later Nellie was complaining to Mabel "I can hardly tell what I am writing. Daisy has gone off to Brunswick after the usual cyclone of departure and I feel like a rag doll with all the sawdust run out. I do not know how *she* lives through it all—losing things every hour—telephoning every minute—changing her plans every second! I suppose *she* enjoys it. I *don't*."

Daisy, as Mama had prophesied, did not get off on November twenty-fourth and was writing Mabel from New York on December second that "I want to arrive by the eighteenth but this octobus [evidently she means octopus] movement of Girl Scouts is growing by leaps and bounds, now claims all my attention, is getting too big to be manageable. Gratifying, but ties me down terribly."

But Daisy was on the *St. Louis* again on December 14, having managed during her short stay in America to move the National Girl Scout Headquarters from Washington to New York, and set up a national New York council. This council was made up entirely of old friends, Daisy wrote Mama happily: "Belle Marshall; Pink Price; Percy Gordon; Ted Coy; Anne Choate and Gammon and Spinach. Eleanor has christened me spinach because of my virdent green innocense." Mr. Gammon was the National Secretary, Edith Johnston having resigned.

Ted Coy had insisted that Daisy must no longer bear the financial burden for the organization. It is not known how much she spent in establishing the Girl Scouts, but it must have been a considerable sum, for in addition to her own traveling and hotel expenses, by her own wish she had paid all salaries, the rent for the National Headquarters, the cost of patents, uniforms and handbooks, for four years.

The outlay had necessitated many economies in her personal life, some of which were exceedingly annoying to her relatives and friends. Every scrap of food in her house had to be eaten before a fresh supply was ordered. The same tea cakes were presented again and again, left-overs kept appearing until guests learned to dispose of them in various novel ways. The electric lights must be turned off every time one left a room, and they could not be turned on at all on a dark afternoon. "I must save every penny for my Girl Scouts and no lights may go on until half-past five!" Her family figured that she perhaps saved a maximum of fifty dollars a year by these measures, while pouring out thousands.

What her relatives and guests did not realize was that there was method in these madnesses. Daisy had become publicity-conscious and an expert showman. Her economies were used to keep her Girl Scouts always in the minds of those about her. One of her stunts was to raid the kitchen for parsley and carrots and trim her hat with them before going to a fashionable luncheon party. As the party progressed, the parsley would begin to wilt, and the once perky carrots to droop.

"Oh, is my trimming sad?" she would ask, noting that her hat was being eyed with more than casual interest. "I can't afford to have this hat done over—I have to save all my money for my Girl Scouts. You know about the Scouts, don't you?" And she was off. Before the party was over she would be saying, "I *am* so glad you are interested. You're exactly the type of person we need on that committee." Turning her deaf ear to their refusals, her parting words would be, "That's marvelous! I shall expect you at the committee meeting on Wednesday."

But the war had made Daisy poor—she was complaining in 1917 that she was being asked to pay income tax on an income of five thousand pounds a year, of which she actually received only a few hundred pounds. She yielded to Mr. Coy's arguments, and the committee members had contributed $350 with which to start a fund-raising campaign. "Anne, Pink, Belle and I will write one hundred letters each asking people to become honorary members and subscribe $5.00 a year. Pink will attend to the Girl Scout shop. Anne said she would take over the job of getting a suitable new office and she and I secured *two* good rooms in the Harriman Bank Building, the best office building on Fifth Avenue! Anne is a personal friend of Mr. Harriman's widow, which made this possible. Ted Coy will collect funds from business men and Percy Gordon is tapping his St. Bartholomew Church parishioners, so you see how we are all working. Mama, you wouldn't believe how flourishing our Girl Scouts—yours and mine—are."

She wrote Arthur, from on board the *St. Louis,* that she had left the committee with a surplus in the bank of several hundred dollars, and that they were making enough from the sale of equipment to pay all the expenses. The Girl Scouts were on a sound financial basis. "I tell you these facts, not to boast, but because you were afraid, at one time, that I would spend all my own money on the Girl Scouts and then that would be the end of the movement."

Nellie seemed as vigorous as ever that Christmastime. She received more invitations than she could count, so she said, and though she declared she refused them all, she still went about a great deal. She wrote dozens of letters every day, Morrison having to take each one to the postoffice as soon as she had sealed it up, so that not a moment should be lost before it was on its way. In a letter to a distant cousin, Mary Wolcott Durham, she gave a picture of herself at the age of eighty-one and a half.

"I was greatly amused by the account you gave me in your last letter as to what you fancied me to be like, and I shall have to correct your impressions. In the first place, I am only five feet, one inch in height and weigh but 114 pounds, thus being far from the large dignified person of your imagination. In fact, if I ever attempted to stand on my dignity, I should surely fall off and break my neck.

"I have brown eyes, a fair complexion and my hair is the torment of my life, being very abundant, a yard long and only a little gray in front. I have only lost six of my thirty-two teeth and have never had a front tooth filled. I am growing a little deaf, which enrages me—but I never use spectacles to read, write or sew, though I cannot see across the street without far-sighted glasses. (But I can thread a No. 10 needle by candle light.) I regret to admit that I am very profane, but I consider swearing only vulgar and not wicked, since I keep within the limit given in the 3rd commandment, which only forbids 'taking the name of the Lord God in vain.' This recalls a good story on me. My little granddaughter said to her mother, 'Didn't you tell me it was very wicked to say "devil" and "damn"?' 'Of course I did,' replied her mother. 'Well,' said Daisy, 'my little Granny, she—' then Daisy stopped suddenly, swallowed hard and continued, 'she hates cold weather!'

"Our cousin Rudyard Kipling put me into one of his magazine stories, describing me as 'a little old lady with snapping black eyes, who used very bad language.' I wrote at once and thanked him, having recognized myself immediately.

"I love warmth and to sit by the fire in a comfortable chair with my book or work. I hate sermons and meetings. . . . I do not care for flowers. I do not take any interest in children—except those of my own family. I love everything witty and clever. My strict observance of the 5th commandment, which tells us to 'honor our father and mother,' has resulted in my 'living long in the land' according to the promise—unless it is because the Lord don't want me and the Devil don't want me either. At any rate, here I remain, very much against my will, for there is nothing I so sincerely desire in this world as to get out of it."

Daisy had expected that Mabel would take her place at Mama's side. But on her arrival in England on December twenty-second, she found Mabel still loathe to leave her war duties. Daisy wrote her on the thirty-first: "We will not always have our little mother and if I could take your place I would go back at once. But she gets tired of me, she is so brilliant. When I had, on two occasions, to suddenly leave my Girl Scouts and take Mama abroad, I honestly believed my movement was doomed. But I found others could keep the work going, although at the time I imagined I was really the only person in the U.S.A. who understood the training. We think ourselves indispensible but God provides a substitute. . . . If you knew how she counts the days of your coming you would not fail her."

A few weeks after Daisy wrote this letter, one of Nellie's granddaughters produced a girl child instead of the boy Nellie had set her heart on. Nellie indulged in a glorious tantrum, and it brought on a fearful attack of angina. Her life was despaired of, both Daisy and Mabel were sent for and were trying frantically to get passage from England.

Now Nellie's long, thick file among the Gordon papers is drawing to an end. There is only one letter more before the obituary columns from the newspapers, which close the record of her life. This last letter is to Daisy, and it is purely an expression of love. Nellie would have known how little that valiant heart of hers, that had loved so greatly and hated so fiercely, could now be counted on. She would have thought, "Perhaps Daisy will not get here in time." Nellie knew which of her children needed her most, which would miss her most. We can see the little old lady asking the nurse to prop her up against the pillows. She is so weak that her handwriting is like a child's scrawl. Painfully the few sentences are traced. "My darling: I meant to write you today but I am afraid I have missed the mails. I have been very ill but am on the mend but am still very weak. This is just to say I love you. Your own Mama." One can see the pen fall from the hand, the tired body slumped back against the pillows. "Bless me too, oh my Father." Nellie would have known of that cry from Daisy's heart to Willie, for Willie never had any secrets from Nellie. And now Nellie had given Daisy her blessing, too, and she would have been ready for death to come at any moment.

But this is not the last letter after all. There is one more to Daisy, slipped among the obituaries, and the first glance at it tells us that Nellie had rallied strongly. The handwriting is firm and the contents show that the old naughty Nellie is back in her best form. "I wrote a long funny letter to Eleanor by the last post. I am not so *funny* now. I don't seem to get well, perhaps because I don't try! . . . I am overwhelmed with messages and flowers. . . . Pink [Dr. Pinckney Waring] was making a great fuss because my tongue was so furred and giving me all sorts of nasty medicine. Before he got here next day, I got a cake of *sapolio* and my toothbrush and scrubbed my tongue until it was clean as a new pin. Pink was delighted and *surprised!* He hasn't found me out yet!"

Nellie, who had lived her life by a pattern all her own, was going to conduct her dying with the same individuality. She continued to be as naughty as a very old lady, close to death, could very well be, making all manner of trouble for her trained nurses, whom she chose to call "hussies" for some reason known only to herself. One day she said to Ellie, Bill's wife, "When I die, I don't want anybody to wear mourning, I don't want any tears. I want you to have a tremendous ball in this house. Invite all my old friends, and have a grand, gay time. I shall be so happy to be with my Willie again, everyone should celebrate." Ellie said, "But, Mama, while *you* might be happy to die, everyone else would be sorrowful, and in no mood for balls."

Nellie thought a minute, then said, "I suppose you are right."

However, there was a relapse. Nellie was still alive when Daisy and Mabel arrived from England, but had been in a coma for some days. Dr. Pinckney Waring warned them, "I doubt if she will recognize you or realize that you are here. But I will try and see if I can rouse her."

They tiptoed into the room, Dr. Waring leaned over the bed and said softly, "Mrs. Gordon, do you know who I am? Do you recognize me?"

Nellie's brown eyes flew open. "Why Pink Waring, of course I recognize you! I knew you before you were born!"

But it was getting very late for Nellie. Though she rallied again, there was another heart attack, and then another. Dr. Waring told the family the end might come at any time. They must decide about the arrangements that would have to be made. Nellie's five children were assembled in the library for this purpose, when suddenly the door was thrown open and in walked Mama in her nightgown, her eyes sparkling with mischief.

"I just want you to know you can stop talking about my funeral!" she told them. "I'm not dead yet! I got away from that hussy upstairs and came down to tell you so!"

Her startled children gaped at her. "But Mama, you shouldn't have walked down the stairs, you might have fallen!" one of them exclaimed.

"I didn't walk down the stairs. I slid down the banister!"

It was Nellie's last stunt. Arthur picked her up, carried the now feather-light little figure back upstairs and put Nellie gently on her bed. She never left it again. Nellie died on February 22, 1917. Her grandchildren say that as she died, her face took on the radiance of a bride, going to meet her bridegroom.

CHAPTER XXII

THE GIRL SCOUT MOVEMENT
GROWS UP

I N OCTOBER, 1918, Daisy was writing to Mabel from the Gordon house in Savannah. "For the first time since Mama's death I feel *at home*. My own house will never be as much my home as this house, and Bill and Ellie have made it look just as of old. Papa and Mama seem so very near to us all the time. Bill wrote me just what I now feel, that here of all places their spirit seems to abide.

"I occupy your room and Daisy has my room. I live my own life over again to see a young Daisy Gordon in my old room. She is such a dear and now she drives for the Red Cross motor corps and is making her work tell in Savannah. It seems so sad that all these young people have not had their fun first! If they had tasted of the lighthearted life you and I and all of us used to lead, I would be more resigned to the hard service they now give. But even if it does build up their character, I feel rebellious and just long to make up a house party and take all the nicest young people I know to Florida for tarpoon fishing or some sort of spree."

It was Bill who had kept the Gordon house in the family. After Nellie's death, it had appeared that none of the children wanted it. Eleanor and Mabel were firmly established in New Jersey and England, respectively. Daisy, Bill and Arthur all had their own homes in Savannah. Arthur had a horror of the place now that his mother was gone. The very thought of the house overwhelmed him with sadness, he said, and vowed he would never set foot in it again, much less live in it.

Daisy announced that she would sell the Low house and live henceforth in England. Bill said nothing. The children thought of converting the old home into an office building, or else moving it to the old Gordon farm on the outskirts of Savannah, and selling the valuable lot for a business site. They parceled out the furnishings each wanted—Daisy spoke for the gold drawing room curtains she had asked Mama to replace for President Taft's first visit, and that Nellie had declared so emphatically to be *sacred*.

Daisy stayed on in the house, while investigating the two possibilities for its disposal, and was still in Savannah in April, 1917, when the United States entered the war. Once more, circumstances changed over night. Civilian travel across the ocean was barred, Daisy could not get back to England. It also became impossible to carry out either project for the Gordon house because of the scarcity of materials and labor. When Bill learned this, he admitted to Daisy that it had broken his heart to think of the desecration of the old place, and he had kept silent only because it was the majority wish to get rid of it. Daisy wrote Mabel that "he has tried to be nice to me while I was getting figures about alterations and house moving, but he was perfectly impossible until he found out I had given up both ideas." It was arranged that Bill would buy the house from the others on the installment plan, Daisy offering to guarantee the payments.

The most important consequence of America's entrance into the war, however, from Daisy's standpoint, was that it set the Girl Scouts booming and mushrooming all over the country. The moment Congress approved President Wilson's decision that war should be declared on Germany, a special meeting of the National Girl Scout Board was called. They sent a telegram to the President offering any help the Girl Scouts could give in the emergency. Suddenly and simultaneously, it was realized in many parts of the United States that organized and trained groups of girls, even very young girls, could be of great assistance. Mr. Gammon, in the national office, was snowed under with requests for information about starting troops, finding leaders.

Anne Choate remembered that Dean J. E. Russell of Columbia University had once expressed interest in the Girl Scouts. She called on him and persuaded Dean Russell to come on the board. Dean Russell brought into the movement Mrs. V. Everett Macy, whose husband was a power in Westchester County, New York. Mrs. J. J. Storrow, a member of a prominent and wealthy Massachusetts family, who had worked in scouting in New England, came down to the New York office to see what was going on there. Daisy asked both these women to join the board. They had much to do with shaping the organization in its present form. Mrs. Storrow—"Aunt Helen" to the Girl Scouts—soon started the first national training camp for leaders. It continues today as Pine Tree Camp, Long Pond, near Plymouth, Massachusetts. Through Dean Russell, Columbia that summer offered training courses for Girl Scout captains. The name of Juliette Low appeared in the summer school prospectus as one of Columbia's instructors, though she never had learned, and never did learn to spell. Daisy wrote Mabel: "What would Mama say to that? Girl Scouts are now recognized as a definite force and the last Columbia class of one hundred and eighty has furnished the Scouts leaders throughout the entire country."

When the third National Convention was held in New York City on October 26, 1917, Daisy had a proud report to give. There was the tremendous growth of the organization. There was the newly established magazine, called *The Rally* at first, later *The American Girl.* She read a letter from Herbert Hoover commending the Girl Scouts for their help in the food conservation program. She had an inspiring and complimentary message from Sir Robert Baden-Powell. The second Mrs. Woodrow Wilson, formerly Mrs. Galt, had accepted the honorary presidency of the Girl Scouts. There was also a new handbook for Girl Scouts, this time indubitably written by Juliette Low and selling out as quickly as editions could be printed.

The Girl Scouts made a great name for themselves that winter and on through the war. They gathered in units at Red Cross sewing rooms; they helped in the canteens at the railroad stations; they acted as messengers; during the influenza epidemic that raged through the country they relieved overworked nurses. They planted back yard vegetable gardens by the thousands—in Boston, the Girl Scouts raised beans on the Common. And they sold Liberty Bonds by the millions. In the fourth Liberty Loan drive they stood sixth among the women's organizations in the sale of bonds.

It was too bad Nellie couldn't have seen her daughter now. Daisy was darting about the country, making speeches in nearly every large city in the United States and in many smaller ones, a stocky, indomitable figure in her Girl Scout uniform, in which she practically lived. Overly slender during her years of sorrow and trial and purposeless living, she had broadened and thickened since she had become happily occupied. The Girl Scout uniform of that day for women was about as unflattering as any costume could be, and particularly unflattering to those who, like Daisy, had a middle-aged spread; while the stiff, wide-brimmed hat would have extinguished the beauty of a Hebe. But Daisy wore the costume with pride, and what is more, got women like Mrs. Wilson, Mrs. Hoover and Mrs. Coolidge to wear it too, and have their pictures taken in it.

Daisy, as president of the Girl Scouts, had a special uniform. Like the girls' it was khaki-colored, but hers had a Norfolk type jacket and she wore a white shirt and black four-in-hand tie. Over her left shoulder was a fourragère of gold braid and attached to her leather belt were a Scout knife, a whistle and a tin drinking cup.

It dawned on Josephine Daskam Bacon one day that Juliette Low "*loved* that big hat; she *loved* that ridiculous whistle; she *loved* her whole uniform. She wasn't wearing them, as some of us were, because it was necessary or because it seemed best, *she loved to wear them!*"

The uniform gave Daisy a sense of identification with her adored father and the many fine men, close friends of hers, who were fighting across the sea. The knife and tin cup at her belt were the equipment in which her Grandmother Juliette, whom Baden-Powell found so admirable, had delighted when she started her perilous horseback trip to Chicago in 1830. Of course Daisy loved it all!

In her posed photographs of this time, made in her uniform, she even looks like an old campaigner. The soft, generous mouth of the bridal portrait has become a long, tight-lipped line above a determined chin; the heavy eyebrows could be those of a stern elderly general. She is only betrayed by the eyes that look out from beneath the stiff-brimmed hat. Full of love in her childhood, full of dreams as a bride, they are tortured now, and filled with anguished questionings. But in the snapshots made of her among "her girls," her ravaged face is so infused with sweetness and tenderness that it is beautiful.

By late October of 1918, Bill and his family were established in the Gordon house and Daisy was visiting them there. She had found her niece and namesake, Daisy Doots, together with the other Savannah Girl Scout alumnae, putting their training to use in the war effort in manifold ways. Jane Meldrim and Mildred Cunningham, the first captains of the two first Girl Scouts troops, had been responsible for forming the Savannah Red Cross, and for a year the Girl Scout headquarters was the Red Cross headquarters too. The work of these eighteen to twenty-year-olds was too important to permit Daisy's gathering them up and taking them tarpon fishing in Florida, as she would have liked to do. But she collected a group of the original Scouts and took them to Myrtle Grove for a picnic, where they toasted marshmallows over the fire, and Daisy read their palms and endowed them all with glowing futures.

She was in her own house on Armistice Day, November 11, writing Mabel, "It is glorious to live in the world today and share in the victory. Savannah has gone mad with delirious delight. . . . I can see from my front windows crowds and crowds of citizens, on foot, on bicycles, in motors, in street cars, with horns, pistols, drums, marching towards the Park! School girls enmasse, shipyard laborers, old men and children shouting for joy, women weeping with joy."

Now Daisy could get back to England, and she sailed in December, for her affairs there were sadly in need of attention. In London, a feverish gaiety was replacing the war shadows. Those who had lost loved ones were determined not to dampen the happiness of the more fortunate. There were dinners and parties galore. Daisy had previously told her American friends to have their army sons look her up when they were in London. Hardly a week passed that she did not have several American soldiers for guests. She introduced them to pretty English girls and made sure they had a good time.

There were still many scarcities in England. At a ball Lord and Lady Cork gave—for Sol had married at last—with all of Daisy's old friends there, Jack Maxwell, General Sir John Maxwell now, appeared in a skintight dress suit, a tucked shirt like the ones Willie Gordon had worn thirty years before, with three mother-of-pearl buttons down the front instead of pearl studs. When Daisy asked him how he dared appear in such a shirt he replied, "Any *manufactured* button is far more valuable than real pearls. They don't manufacture anything in England now." He looked critically at Daisy's diamond necklace. "Now if you had small lumps of coal around your neck, we might think you elegant!" At a costume ball, Daisy wore the costume she had had made for Lady Warwick's famous *bal poudre,* fourteen years before, representing the Honorable Mrs. Gilbert as Gainsborough had painted her. "I pinned my diamond swallows on the side of the black hat, and with powder and rouge I looked so nice that nobody recognized me!"

Strange new dances had come in, the bunny hug, the turkey trot. Mabel's daughter, Peggy Leigh, and her friends loved to go to Aunt Daisy's for tea, then push the rugs aside and dance to the phonograph. Daisy wrote to Bill in Savannah: "Everyone dances, it is a reaction from the awful four years. Staid old generals, old lords, and old ladies like myself included." She was inspired to write the following verses:

VETERANS' DANCE

Just step up and foot it with activity
Overcome your awkwardness and natural timidity
Cultivate a graceful gait in spite of your stupidity
Exercise your muscles—never mind your brain.

Try to bend your latter end with dexterous pomposity
Stretch a point and crack a joint with infinite velocity.
Come, advance and join the dance, quite a curiosity!
Thus shall every veteran eternal youth obtain.

But there was work to be done, too. Since the war's end, innumerable letters had been pouring into the Girl Guide office in London from many different countries. Where there had been Girl Guides before the war, they wanted fresh news about the program. Where there had not been Guides, they were anxious to organize. In some instances Boy Scouts wrote saying that their sisters wanted to get into the movement. Lady Baden-Powell, the Chief Guide at this time, felt there should be an international body which would link together the scattered groups of Guides in different countries. The International Council met for the first time in February of 1919 at Guide headquarters in London, with Juliette Low representing the Girl Scouts in America. She was able to report that her girls there now numbered forty thousand, and she also committed one of those *faux pas* which she enjoyed telling on herself.

One of the speakers was Miss Anstruther Thomson, for whom Daisy had great admiration, and to Daisy's dismay the audience was not applauding her. "I determined that I at least would show my appreciation, so, although I could not hear a word of what she was saying, I clapped and called, 'Hear, Hear!' every time she paused. It was only afterward that I found her speech had been all about me and must have sounded like this: 'Mrs. Low is a very remarkable woman.' (Hear, Hear! from D. L.) 'It is a marvelous piece of work to have founded the Girl Scouts of the United States.' Loud applause from me, while the audience remained in stony silence!"

There was another incident of the first International Council meeting of which Daisy did not speak, but which is highly significant. Evidently Katy Low, after she became mistress of Wellesbourne, gave Daisy the Wellesbourne visitors' book to which we have made reference. The last page but one records the little house party in 1904 when the Jack Maxwells and several members of the Low family had come to spend Willy Low's last Christmas with him. On the reverse side of this page are the signatures of the Girl Guide leaders who had come to the International Council meeting in 1919. It is as though Daisy had wished to close the book of her idle years with the names of these women who were engaged in helping the girls of many countries to grow up to more useful, more independent womanhood.

When Daisy returned to America in May, 1919, she brought Sir Robert and Lady Baden-Powell with her. As soon as the war ended she had started begging them to come and see for themselves what tremendous strides the American organization had made, and now they were here. She went with the Baden-Powells while Sir Robert spoke to enormous crowds in Washington, Baltimore, New York, Boston and Canada. In Washington, Lady Baden-Powell presented Daisy with the Silver Fish, the highest award of the British Girl Guides. A few days later Daisy received a jeweled Thanks Badge from her own girls, bought with pennies contributed by Girl Scouts all over the country.

Daisy found that great changes had taken place in the Girl Scout organization while she was in England. Mrs. V. E. Macy was now chairman of the board, and had brought Mrs. Jane Deeter Rippin as the new national secretary. These women saw that the organization had become too large and encompassed too many activities to be handled longer by volunteers. Camps had sprung up all over the country, many calling themselves "Girl Scout Camps" though they had little if anything to do with Girl Scouting. The time had come for trained professional workers, for standards and supervision. Daisy reviewed the plans and found them good. The Girl Scouts, she saw, could not be in better hands.

Daisy felt that her baby had grown up, it was time now for her to cut the apron strings. At the National Convention in January, 1920, she resigned as president, being known thereafter as "The Founder." Anne Choate became president—a choice most pleasing to Daisy. Freed of responsibility for the American organization, Daisy devoted herself to developing the movement on a world scale. She continued to represent the United States on the International Council of Girl Guides and Girl Scouts and attended all the international conventions. (These names were changed in 1924 to "World Order" and "World Conferences" to avoid confusion with the rapidly developing Russian Internationale.) After her income was restored, Daisy paid the expenses to the conferences of delegates from countries where the movement was newly established and was hampered for lack of funds.

Mrs. Mark Kerr has said that Daisy was not an easy person to have on a committee, because, unable to hear much that went on, she would follow a mental track of her own, then break into the discussion suddenly with a suggestion after the others had finished with the topic and gone on to something else. Sometimes, not having heard the original discussion correctly, her suggestion had little bearing on the matter, and it was hard to straighten her out.

"But with all this, it was worth while to stop and listen to what she had to say, for her remarks were always illuminating. She was that rarest of human beings, an original thinker; she had a fresh, unbiased approach to any problem—besides unbounded courage."

When Daisy sailed for the first International Conference, held at Oxford, England, in June, 1920, she took with her her namesake niece and goddaughter, Daisy Gordon, known in the family as Daisy Doots. A newspaper story about the departure of the Founder of the Girl Scouts and the first registered Girl Scout was Daisy Doots' first intimation that she herself rated this latter distinction. It came to her through her Aunt Daisy's thoughtfulness in writing her name down first on the list of girls who formed the pioneer troops in Savannah. It was to bring Daisy Doots many pleasurable and thrilling experiences.

However, the newspaper notice was also young Daisy's first intimation that they were going to England to attend a conference. She had thought she was being treated to a London season! Her spirits sank. And she got small comfort from her aunt when she confessed, the first night out, that just before leaving Savannah she had received a proposal of marriage from Samuel Lawrence, and already was wishing that she was back in Savannah where Sam was. Sam was a Bostonian, and worse yet, a Harvard graduate.

"Why, Doots, you can't think of marrying that man!" Aunt Daisy protested. "He's a Yankee!"

"Your own mother was a Yankee," Doots pointed out.

"She wasn't either! She married a Southerner and lived in the South all the rest of her life!"

"Well your grandmother was certainly a Yankee."

"Doots, how can you say such things! My Grandmother Kinzie was no Yankee. She came from Connecticut!"

But Aunt Daisy capitulated to Sam Lawrence as soon as she met him, whereupon he immediately ceased to be a Yankee.

Daisy's interest in the Girl Scouts in America remained as great as ever, and the Northern members saw a different side of their Founder when the National Convention was held in Savannah in 1922. She laid aside her military rôle and played the charming Southern hostess, entertaining in her own home and treating her guests to such food as they had never tasted before.

The principal difference made by her stepping out of office was that she spent more time among "her girls." The girls had always been the focal point of the work for Daisy. In the period of rapid expansion following America's entrance into World War I, when so much organizational planning had to be done, she was constantly reminding the board, "We mustn't lose sight of the girls. The girls must always come first!"

She had limitless faith in the capacities and judgment of the young. People often said to her, "How wonderful it must make you feel to have given something so fine to all those girls." Daisy would reply, "The Girl Scout movement caught on because it was what the girls wanted. The Angel Gabriel himself couldn't have made them take it if they hadn't!" She listened undisturbed when latecomers to the organization proposed projects that the veteran members considered unsound. "The girls will decide whether the plan is good or not, and reject it if it isn't. You can trust them to know."

From the beginning, she had kept in touch with the Savannah troops when she was away, writing them many letters, filled with quaint misspellings. Whenever she returned to Savannah, she made it a point to get acquainted with the new members. She followed the lives of the girls with a maternal interest. Now she made frequent visits to the Girl Scout camps in different parts of the country, going with the girls on their hikes, cooking with them over the outdoor fireplaces. At mealtime she would go from table to table, taking as lively a part in the girls' discussions as if she had been one of them, as in fact she was. Before and after meals and at all times during the day, she was kept busy reading palms. Dorris Hough says, "The girls took her prophecies very much to heart, and many a bit of shrewd wisdom was passed along under the guise of a 'fortune.'"

Daisy threw herself enthusiastically into the making of the first Girl Scout movie, *The Golden Eaglet*, thinking up enough plots and counterplots for any number of movies. Told that she was to be in the picture herself, reviewing a Girl Scout parade and pinning on the Golden Eagle Badge, the highest Girl Scout award, she immediately asked if instead she couldn't march in the parade, with the girls!

And the girls responded with that special worshipful adoration evoked in young hearts by adults who not only care about them, but understand and sympathize with them; and above all, believe in them. Though Daisy had become nationally famous as Juliette Low, she remained "Miss Daisy" to the Girl Scouts, and they had a special song for her, written to the tune of "Dixie." When she was expected at a camp, the girls would assemble by the road. As soon as her car came in view, they would start to sing,

> "Away down South in old Savannah
> First was raised the Girl Scout banner
> Daisy Low, Daisy Low, Daisy Low,
> Founder dear!

> "Now Scouting spreads to either ocean,
> Thousands bring you deep devotion,
> Daisy Low, Daisy Low, Daisy Low,
> Founder dear!

> "Away down South in Dixie,
> Daisy Low, Daisy Low,
> The Girl Scout band on every hand
> Are bringing praise together.
> Daisy Low, Daisy Low,
> Our love will leave you never;
> Daisy Low, Daisy Low
> Dwells in our hearts forever!"

When she was present, the only campfire program they would accept was stories by Miss Daisy. As they sat around the fire at night with the flames shooting high, she would tell them the legends and ghost stories of the many English and Scottish castles she had stayed in. Since Daisy more than half believed these herself, she made them very convincing. She would tell the Kinzie stories of early Wisconsin and Illinois that she had heard from her mother in her childhood; the Civil War stories Willie Gordon had told his children. Always saved to the last, for it was the story the girls loved best, was that of her Great-grandmother Eleanor Lytle Kinzie, Little Ship Under Full Sail, who had been captured by the Indians and lived among them for four years.

From her girls came love enough even for Daisy's hungry heart. She underwent no more periods of despair, such as Arthur had helped her through following Papa's death. At last she was able to read the wisdom of the whole design, to erase from her memory the bitter later years of her marriage to Willy Low, and restore there the image of the handsome young man whom she had loved and who had once loved her. She found her own inner peace, independent of family and friends.

From England, too, came appreciation of a kind very precious to Daisy. In 1922 an American woman, Mrs. Anne Archbold, gave the British Girl Guides a beautiful tract in New Forest, England, called Foxlease at that time, but now known as the Princess Mary Training Center, for Guide leaders. One cottage was set aside for the entertainment of Girl Guides and Girl Scouts of all nations, and it was turned over to Daisy to fix up as she pleased. She named the cottage The Link, to symbolize the bond between the British Guides and the Girl Scouts, and the bond between her two equally dear countries, which she hoped would draw always closer together. She gave much thought and time to furnishing and decorating the cottage, painting the interior herself with charming little medallions.

When Daisy went to Foxlease for the World Camp in 1924, she found that British Guides had had carved over the door of the cottage

JULIETTE LOW

UNITED STATES   GREAT BRITAIN

Dedicated to her, The Link is a memorial in England to the woman who "had no children of her own, and so devoted her great love of young people, first to her nieces and nephews and afterwards to her worldwide family of Scouts and Guides," as Daisy is described in the long tribute to her in the guest book of The Link.

CHAPTER XXIII

"SOMETHING FOR ALL
THE WORLD"

DAISY WAS so secretive about her last illness, in order to save those she loved anxiety and pain on her account, that such reports as exist are contradictory, in some respects, with regard to dates and sequences. There is good ground for believing, however, that she first detected signs of cancer in 1923, just as the Girl Scouts in America had reached a triumphant peak. They had received a Laura Spelman Rockefeller grant for the purpose of establishing leadership training classes in colleges and universities. Now this side of the organization and the formulating of standards were presided over by noted educators. Two new training camps had been added to the one founded by Mrs. J. J. Storrow in World War I—Camp Juliette Low at Cloudland, Georgia, on the top of Lookout Mountain, and Camp Chapparal at Redwood State Park, California. Because one little girl had so loved scouting, after her death her parents had given the Scouts more than one hundred acres of hilly, wooded land near Briarcliff, New York. Here Camp Andree had been erected as a model of what camping should be, in the end revolutionizing Girl Scout camping methods. The pleas of girls too young for the Scouts that they might have an organization had been heeded, and the Brownies had had their first conference.

It must have been at one of the happiest times of Daisy's life that she made her frightening discovery. She had promised to speak at a Girl Scout conference at Richmond, Virginia. Dr. Stuart McGuire, the brother of Daisy's beloved sister-in-law Margaret Gordon, Arthur's wife, and a dear friend of Daisy's as well, had a clinic there. According to Margaret Gordon, Daisy went to Richmond a week in advance of the conference and an operation was performed. Daisy was supposed to stay in bed for several weeks afterwards, but on the day of the Girl Scout conference she sent her nurse away on a trumped-up errand, dressed herself in her uniform, got out of the hospital undetected and into a taxi which fortunately was waiting by the door. She made her usual spirited, vivacious talk, giving the girls the inspiration they had counted on from her, returned to the hospital and collapsed. When Stuart McGuire heard of her escapade he said, "If the Girl Scout conference meant that much to her, I am glad she did it." The operation apparently was a complete success. After recovering from it Daisy went her usual vigorous way.

In January, 1924, when she was in England, symptoms reappeared. Daisy asked Peggy Leigh, Mabel's daughter, about doctors and hospitals. Peggy had nursed in hospitals during the war, and Peggy believes it was for this reason that she alone of the family was taken into Daisy's confidence. She had to promise that she would not breathe a word to her mother or anyone else. The doctor Peggy sent Daisy to advised an immediate and extensive operation, and one of England's leading surgeons was engaged to perform it.

The night before Daisy went to the nursing home for the operation, she gave a large dinner party and had never been gayer. But she had written a letter to each of her brothers and sisters and had given them to Sol Cork to send on in the event that "anything should happen to me." Afterwards she got them back from Sol, and the ones she wrote to Bill and Mabel remained among her papers. Years later Daisy Lawrence found them. Bill was dead, but in 1951, Mabel read the loving message her older sister had written to her on January 13, 1924:

"DARLING LITTLE SISTER:
Sol will give you this letter to explain why I *could* not go

into details with you about this operation. I want you to realize, Mabel, that I am *glad to die.* I look forward to seeing the
parents, Willy Low, Alice, Percy, Katy, Wayne and all the
people I have loved and lost. I've always dreaded growing old
and being a burden to my family. I am very glad to go when
I have set my house in order, when I have accomplished a
little good in the world, and when I have no ties that make
parting here on earth an agony. 'I know that my Redeemer
liveth.' I feel an inward and absolute conviction that I shall
behold little Papa and Mama glorified and glad to see me, so
you see, dear, you must realize that for me the passing into the
Promised Land is a joyful one. You and yours have always been
so good to me that I can't thank you enough.

"YOUR FAITHFUL DAISY"

Peggy Leigh went with Daisy to the nursing home, and the
day of the operation waited in the sitting room for "what
seemed like an eternity. I kept wondering how I would break
the news to Mother if Daisy did not get through the operation,
and my relief can be imagined when the burly surgeon came
in and told me Daisy was all right. She saw no one, not even
me, while she was in the nursing home and came back to
Grosvenor Street at the earliest possible moment. She had to
remain in bed a considerable time, but refused to have a nurse
and Bella [her maid] took care of her. A few months later Daisy
took a villa at Le Touquet and gave a large house party—needless to say, she was the life and soul of the party."

In April, Daisy embarked for America for the National Convention of Girl Scouts, held in Chicago in 1924. The Chicago
newspapers and hotels became practically delirious at having as
their city's guests an organization designed to perpetuate the
sturdy pioneer virtues, and its Founder, descended from Chicago's own Kinzie family. Daisy described many of the elaborate decorations to Mabel. At one banquet, the centerpiece
was a replica of Fort Dearborn and the Kinzie homestead, with
soldiers, settlers and Indians disposed about them, all done in
marzipan. "The papers are being very complimentary."

Daisy had had many extraordinary offers after she became
famous, but she thought that one resulting from the publicity
she received at the Chicago convention topped them all. A

Fort Dearborn exposition was being planned. The promoters, so they wrote Daisy, would "give all the history of those eventful years in pageants, parades and history plays. We want *you* to let us incorporate in our program a 'Juliette Kinzie Low' week—you to appear as the great-granddaughter of John Kinzie, and each day that week you will, in a loud voice, at certain hours of the day, tell the story of the Kinzie house, its being the first postoffice in Chicago and having been erected on the site where we mean to build a $7,000,000 office building. We can arrive at a satisfactory arrangement and you will accomplish much good." Daisy commented to Mabel, "Now I shan't have to sell my diamonds. And any time any of us run short of money, all we will have to do is come to Chicago and 'whoop it up' for the Kinzies, as Mama used to say." It is hardly necessary to add that Daisy declined this offer. After the Chicago convention, she whisked back to England for the World Camp, where she was as lively as the youngest delegate present.

None of her relatives or friends, with the exception of Peggy Leigh and Dr. Stuart McGuire, had had the faintest intimation that Daisy had been fighting cancer. Arthur's suspicions were aroused, however, when Daisy returned to Savannah the fall following the World Camp. Daisy told a man with whom she had some business dealings that she wanted the matter settled promptly, because she had only two more years to live. And she told Lige, a Negro butler, when he demurred at coming to work for her that "I haven't got long to live and I need you. If you don't come to me, I will haunt you after I am dead!" These statements reached Arthur, and he demanded to know what they meant. Daisy replied, "My saying this was based on the horoscope made for me in 1886, when I was told my life would end at the age of either fifty-five or sixty-five." Arthur laughed at his sister for being superstitious and thought no more of it. Daisy in fact died at the age of sixty-six.

It was obvious that winter that Daisy was not well, but she was so touchy about her health that no one dared mention it to her. Bill was suffering from high blood pressure and he and Daisy had violent disagreements. Her relations with Arthur were little better. In the early spring she went to Richmond to visit the Girl Scouts there, and also to see the fine home Stuart and Ruth McGuire had just built. On March 20, she felt she could at last explain to Arthur what the trouble had been.

"DEAREST ARTHUR:

"You will have devined that I have been very worried over my health, which will account for my silence and depression the night I took supper with you. Stuart has completely reassured me. . . . I expected to follow the advice of my English doctor, who removed a small lump from my neck and who told me to see a Washington or Johns Hopkins specialist if the lump reappeared. As I had to pass through Richmond, I decided to consult Stuart and await a telegram from the Johns Hopkins doctors there. I had no intention of letting Stuart into my case, but he at once convinced me it was too simple to bother a specialist with, and that he could take away the lump and make me as right as rain. I must say it has been a real pleasure to be here. The lump was the size of a pea. If, as I feared, I was in for a case of malignant growth, I would prefer not to be an object of worry to anyone. But now I can relieve my mind and I believe you will all be glad."

Daisy was most certainly fabricating about the small lump in her neck—the operation in England, in which both she and Peggy Leigh had feared she might die, had been much more serious than that. But the doctors must have told her that the growths were not malignant, otherwise Daisy would not have told Arthur about her previous fears. Herself reassured, Daisy lightheartedly begged Arthur to pay $300 at once into her account at the Savannah Bank and Trust Company, "or else they will sell up my pekinese puppy and my Rolls Royce Ford sedan car to pay the overdraft of twenty-five cents which they have written me three letters to remind me I owe them!"

From Richmond she went on to New York where she had "a hectic and beautiful time filled with luncheons and dinners and parties of all kinds." Mrs. Hoover gave a dinner at the Colony Club to twenty-nine Girl Scout regional directors and showed movies of the Girl Scout camps, which Mrs. Hoover had had made at her own expense. Daisy told her hostess that she had never enjoyed anything more than those movies "except the Moulin Rouge, where I once spent a glorious evening. She was not shocked."

Then Daisy went about showing a movie of the World Camp at Foxlease the preceding summer, running down to Macon, Georgia, to a regional meeting of Georgia, Alabama and Texas Girl Scouts, for which the Macon girls had made all the arrangements themselves. "They invited the delegates, they enlisted the Chamber of Commerce to back them, and arranged that one hundred citizens who had Girl Scouts in their families should entertain the visitors in their homes," she wrote Mabel. "Fancy, when you and I were twelve or fourteen years old, our swinging a big conference and collecting money to finance it and organizing motors for transport and committees for meeting arriving guests! This is the first conference ever run by girls alone. As their director, Miss Mitchell said, 'They did it as capably as grownups and talked less of what they did.' "

She was writing Mabel from Washington on June 6 that "every place I visit brings more luck to me in scouting. After the Boston convention . . . I went to Richmond and got a Girl Scout camp for leaders started. . . . Yesterday we had a big rally here in Washington, and then Mrs. Hoover and I and several others went to the White House and enrolled Mrs. Coolidge as a Girl Scout! She has promised to be honorary president. I pinned the Tenderfoot Badge on her and we all spent a happy afternoon together. Today I motor to Harrisburg for a Girl Scout rally."

Then to England for a meeting of the International Council of Girl Guides and Girl Scouts, where plans were made for the fourth World Camp, which was to be held in the summer of 1926. Daisy flared up indignantly when it was proposed that the camp be held in Switzerland. The first world conference outside England must come to the United States, she insisted. It was pointed out that many European delegates would not be able to afford so long a journey. Daisy countered with a promise that the Girl Scouts of America would pay the expenses for one delegate from every country where there were Girl Scouts or Girl Guides. Her offer was accepted. She sailed back to the United States on the *Olympic* to tell the American Girl Scouts what she had let them in for.

Daisy called Jane Deeter Rippin, the National Director, from the pier. "I have a wonderful new plan! I'll be up to Headquarters as soon as I get through Customs, and you shall hear all about it!" Soon Daisy appeared, with the air of one bringing great tidings. "Just think, Jane, we are going to have the World Camp here in America next year! Everything is arranged, I looked it all up on the boat coming over. The immigration restrictions won't matter a bit, for the delegates will only be visitors. Any other girls who want to can come too. I talked with the *Olympic*'s officers about sailing dates, and we can arrange it nicely for next May. We will have the meeting at Camp Macy. After that I want the delegates to visit Washington, Boston, Buffalo, Cincinnati, Chicago, St. Louis and Savannah. I especially want them to go to Savannah."

Mrs. Rippin felt as though someone had just pulled the rug out from under her. Camp Edith Macy, the gift of V. Everitt Macy to the Girl Scouts as a memorial to his wife, at this time was a large tract of virgin woodland, lying next to Camp Andree on the Hudson River. It was to be a camp some day, but as yet it had no buildings, no roads, no water supply. Weakly, Mrs. Rippin asked Daisy how many people they would have to entertain at Camp Macy. "Between three and four hundred I should say," replied Daisy calmly.

Mrs. Rippin pulled herself together. It would take several years to get Camp Edith Macy ready to hold four hundred people, she told Daisy. As yet there were not even blueprints for the many things that would have to be done. "Why don't we let them have the World Camp in Switzerland next summer? We can ask to have the World Camp here in 1928."

Daisy said, "Jane, if we don't have it next summer, I won't be here. But don't say a word to anyone."

Mrs. Rippin looked at Daisy, saw the marks of illness and pain in her face, knew that Daisy spoke truly. And she knew that Daisy wanted no sympathy. "Come and tell your plans to the executive committee at their meeting next week," she said softly. "I won't tell anyone if you don't want me to."

Daisy carried the executive committee with her by sheer force of will, and Jane Rippin set to work to bring Camp Macy into being. She has written: "It seemed that the very magnitude of the task rallied everyone to our assistance. . . . Girl Scout leaders in every part of the country wrote at once offering to help in any way. National committee members, staff and leaders gave everything they had. Girl Scouting was welded together as never before."

Daisy went to Washington, to get the visitor's entry fee waived in behalf of the foreign delegates. The hour hand fell off her watch, but she said it didn't matter. "I always know what *hour* it is—it's only *minutes* that I'm late as a rule." Late as she invariably was for appointments with senators, congressmen and Immigration officials, she nevertheless got the visitor's fee waived. She also persuaded the English and French authorities to waive visa fees for their nationals.

The army of devoted, capable Girl Scout workers she had brought into being could be counted upon to attend to all the other details. Daisy proceeded to Savannah, for there was something to be seen to there, and this was something she wanted to do herself. It was Bill, again, who had conceived the idea of breaking up the old Gordon farm, just outside Savannah, into building lots—an enterprise that was to prove very profitable to the heirs, and which resulted in the present suburb of Gordonston. Daisy had proposed setting aside a large wooded tract for a park, as a memorial to Willie and Nellie, wishing to bear the whole financial sacrifice herself—it represented a gift of something like $100,000 to the City of Savannah—because while her brothers and sisters had children to provide for, she had none. The others had insisted on sharing in the gift, but Daisy had assumed the responsibility for turning the land into a park. She planned to have the iron gates she had made for Wellesbourne brought over from England for the front entrance, and a handsome iron fence built around the entire park. Eleanor was to furnish an iron gate for the rear entrance. Daisy threw herself into getting these plans executed as quickly as possible.

When the pain struck, she hid herself away. What her relatives and all Savannah saw was the same enthusiastic, indomitable Daisy, still attempting the impossible and still carrying it off. In January, 1926, Arthur's eldest daughter, Mary Stuart, made her debut, and Daisy seized the opportunity for one of those occasions in which she took such delight—a gala party for young people. This one was to outdo all the many lovely parties the Low house had seen. She invited Sam and Daisy Lawrence to dinner and told them all about it.

"I'm going to give Stuarty a real cotillion, like the ones we used to have when I was a girl. I've ordered the nicest favors from New York—Japanese umbrellas, chiffon scarves and ivory fans for the girls, and packs of cards and enamel ash trays for the men. There will be comic favors besides. Bill and Arthur can explain how the cotillion is danced, for I doubt if the young people have ever seen one. I'll invite all the young crowd, of course, and all my own friends, I daresay we'll have at least three hundred people!"

Daisy Doots questioned that her aunt could get that many into her house and said so, but Daisy swept on, ignoring the interruption. "What a supper we'll have—terrapin stew, hot rolls, chicken salad, ices, lots of other things, just like the old days!"

"But Aunt Daisy," Doots objected more forcibly, "you can't possibly get more than ten people into your dining room at one time, with all that big furniture."

"Nothing could be easier," Daisy declared. "We'll put the big pieces in the basement and upstairs and use all the first floor for dancing. For the supper, we'll have tables set in the back garden. The grass there is green already and the camellias will be in bloom by the time of the party. I'll string Japanese lanterns around for lights."

"What if it rains?"

"Then we'll have a marquee. Why must you be such a pessimist, Doots? I want you two to help me. You will, won't you?" They said that of course they would.

It didn't rain, it turned unseasonably cold. Daisy's camellias, a late variety, remained tight little buds, and the day before the party the temperature dropped to the low twenties. Daisy Doots shivered at the very thought of the women, in their thin dresses and light dancing slippers, having to go out into the freezing garden for supper. That night she phoned her aunt. "You are going to call the party off, aren't you?"

"Certainly not!"

"Aunt Daisy, everyone will get pneumonia! How about your camellias—have they bloomed?" Doots added a bit maliciously.

"No, they haven't, but that doesn't matter—you'll see. You and Sam just be here early tomorrow morning. Wear old clothes and plenty of them and be prepared to stay a long time!"

The Low place was in a state of pandemonium when the Lawrences got there the next morning. Inside the house, furniture was being moved either up or down stairs, with floor polishers following in the wake of the furniture movers. Daisy, in a thin dressing gown, her long hair in a thick braid down her back, was flying from one group to another, exhorting each to more vigorous efforts. The back garden was swarming with men—plumbers, electricians, a corps engaged in putting up a marquee so huge it looked like a circus tent. Everyone was getting in everyone else's way, and occasionally the marquee would fall and envelop the plumbers and electricians.

Daisy thrust a paper at Doots. "Here is a list of people who have early camellias. They have said I may have all I need. You and Sam go and collect them in your car while the marquee is going up."

The mystified Lawrences obeyed, and soon had their car filled with camellias—a real sacrifice on the part of Daisy's friends, for it takes years for the growth to renew itself. When they got back to the house on Lafayette Square, there was some semblance of order. The tent was up and a canvas was spread over the icy ground. The plumbers had laid on gas pipes and at intervals throughout the large garden gas heaters were burning. Naked electric bulbs, hanging from wires spread through the trees, were being covered with Japanese lanterns. The back porch had become a miniature palm forest. The Lawrences marveled at what had been accomplished.

"Here are your camellia blossoms, hundreds of them. What do you want done with them?"

"Tie them on the camellia trees, of course!" Sam and Doots looked at each other, then shouted with delight. How could they have imagined that Aunt Daisy would let a little thing like a freeze keep her from having her outdoor party as planned? They spent the whole day tying blooms on the flowerless trees. And if occasionally white camellias appeared on a tree side by side with red or striped ones, no one noticed or cared. Underneath the great marquee the air was as warm as summer, and Savannah's young folk voted there had never been as splendid a party.

It was as though fate, which had dealt Daisy so many hard blows, had decided to crowd into the last year of her life the fruition of all her maturer dreams. Soon after the party, Savannah was moved to bestow signal honors on her. On February 12—Lincoln's birthday to the rest of America, but Georgia Day to Georgians—a large crowd assembled at the fountain in Forsythe Park to let Juliette Low know what her home folks thought of her. It was a beautiful day and the sun shone through the spray of the fountain, casting miniature rainbows everywhere. Colonel Reynolds Burt, commander of near-by Fort Screven, was there with his aide in behalf of the national government. There were representatives of the city and county, Boy Scouts and their leaders, the Savannah Girl Scout Council and many young women who had been in the earlier Girl Scout troops. The sidewalk leading to the speakers' platform was lined with the active Girl Scouts and their leaders. As Daisy walked to the platform, the girls strewed roses and hyacinths in her path.

If only Papa and Mama could have been there to see it! First Daisy was presented with a beautiful scroll from the City of Savannah, in appreciation of her services to her city, state and country. The scroll hangs today in the Juliette Low Birthplace. Then the Girl Scout Council presented her with a great basket of flowers, after which Nina Pape, the Savannah Girl Scout commissioner, read a telegram from Jane Rippin of the national organization, conveying to "our Founder, Juliette Low, our heartiest wishes and congratulations. She had the heart to resolve, the head to contrive, and the hand to execute." And finally Daisy Lawrence, the first registered Girl Scout, presented her aunt, in behalf of all the Girl Scouts in Savannah, with a beautiful silver coffee service and tray.

Here indeed was the "sugar" Daisy so craved. She wrote her niece Peggy Leigh how "in full uniform, dressed like a small kharki monkey," she had been given civic honors by the City of Savannah. She showed the coffee service to everyone who came to the house. She commissioned Peggy, then with the Jack Maxwells at Luxor, Egypt, to get her eighteen coffee cups in Egypt to go with the new silver service, and was very particular in her directions. "I want them in filagree silver stands or holders, larger if possible than the Turkish coffee cups this style. Jack will know of a merchant in the bazaars who can supply them. They must be *silver* not gilt."

Daisy, though she had a sure permonition that she had not much longer to live, behaved in other ways as though she looked forward to many more years. She promised Peggy Leigh that she would bring the favors left over from Mary Stuart's cotillion to England with her and give a cotillion for Peggy and her friends. She accepted an invitation to go riding in the Chevrolet Ellie, Bill's wife, had just bought and which she was learning to drive. To Ellie's surprise, the usually tardy Daisy was waiting in front of the house when Ellie drew up and watched critically while Ellie, a skilled handler of horses, pulled back on the wheel and said, "Whoa" when she wanted to stop, instead of stepping on the brake. Daisy, however, made no comment and got into the car when Ellie managed to bring it to a halt.

"I hope you're not afraid to ride with me," Ellie said as they started off. "For some reason, Bill and the children refuse to go in the car when I'm at the wheel."

Daisy leaned back wearily against the cushions. "No, I'm not afraid. The best part of my life is over. My work in the world is done. I'm ready to go at any time. Look out!" she screamed, as they missed a truck by inches. "You almost killed me, Ellie!"

"Why, you just said you didn't care, that you were ready to go!"

"Well I don't think it would be dignified for the Founder of the Girl Scouts to be killed by a garbage truck!" Daisy answered tartly.

Daisy had written Peggy Leigh that she was in "rude health." Because of Daisy's oddity about words, we cannot be sure whether she meant that her health was good or bad. But when she started for the World Camp that spring, she stopped over at Richmond and spent several weeks at the McGuire Clinic, writing Mabel that she had come down with influenza. "Stuart and Ruth are too good for words, but I am furious at missing the important Scout board meeting in St. Louis. I nearly lost my temper after Stuart said I could not travel, but Liza Hendry's saying, 'Manners and Behavior will carry you through' came to my aid. I am cultivating both!"

It is known that six months or more before her death, Stuart

McGuire told Daisy that her case was hopeless and her time was limited. It is Peggy Leigh's recollection that this interview took place in England, but it cannot be fitted in, at the time she gives it, with letters and with the time of Daisy's death. From the length of Daisy's stay at the McGuire Clinic in April, 1926, and subsequent events, it is logical to deduce that an exploratory operation may have been performed which revealed that nothing further could be done; and that it was Dr. Stuart McGuire's painful task to tell Daisy so. After Daisy's death he described the interview to his sister, Margaret Gordon. Daisy's face did not change. She made Stuart promise to say nothing to any of the Gordons, including Margaret, who would have told Arthur. She was thankful, she said, that she would be able to enjoy the World Conference the next month, and that the plans for the Memorial Park were far enough along so that she would be able to see it completed too.

Her first thought was that she would like to die in England. Then she said, "No, I want to die in Savannah, in the house where Willy Low and I were so happy, those months after our marriage. But I want to go to England and arrange my affairs there. Have I time?" And Stuart thought there would be time if she did not stay too long in England. He and his wife, Ruth, were going to England that summer. They would arrange to sail on the same steamer.

If Daisy had received her death sentence before the World Conference in 1926, she gave no hint of it. A radiant Juliette Low was at the pier in New York City when the *Olympic* docked, with Lady Baden-Powell and fifty-six foreign delegates, representing twenty-nine countries, on board. There was a triumphal tour up Fifth Avenue to a luncheon given by the Manhattan Girl Scout Council, then Daisy sailed with the visitors to Boston, where they were welcomed by the Governor of Massachusetts. Returning to New York, the fifty-six foreign and four hundred American delegates drove to Camp Macy in a motorcade, Daisy and Lady Baden-Powell in the leading car.

The camp stood completed and ready, though Mrs. Rippin said, "We bowed the plasterers out the back door while we welcomed our guests in at the front." The winding road up to the Great Hall was bright with the flags of many nations. As soon as Daisy had been greeted by the welcoming committee, she joined the receiving line and welcomed America's guests.

That evening Camp Macy was opened formally. Dean Russell of Columbia spoke of Mrs. Macy and told of the first hard beginnings of Scouting, of how he himself had first become interested in it because of the dauntless personality of Juliette Low. Then the international delegates lined up, each beside her country's flag, held by an American aide. One by one, the foreign delegates placed faggots on the fire in the huge fireplace of the Great Hall, telling briefly and poetically as they did so of the special gifts their countries brought to the world.

For a week the women and girls camped and worked and planned together. If Daisy was in pain, no one was allowed to suspect it. Her energy seemed boundless, her joy in the work and in the girls greater than ever before. Lady Baden-Powell said, "I shall never forget the hour when, awaiting the arrival of Sir Robert, Daisy Low, Anne Choate and I strolled along the sandy lane, the bushes swaying in the wind, and the country all ablaze with the glory of spring. How *happy* she was!"

Out of her excitement and enthusiasm, Daisy had told Nina Pape, when she phoned her in March, 1912, that she had "something for the girls of Savannah, the United States and the whole world!" She had lived to see her pronouncement realized.

Daisy collapsed at Eleanor's, where she went as soon as the conference ended, explaining it to the family as a recurrence of her influenza. She wrote Mabel that Eleanor had been down with it too. "I am very slow in getting well, the strain of this foreign nations camp has taken it out of me. While it lasted I never felt fatigued, it was too important to our organization and too gratifying to me to see every moment how successful it was, for me to know how tired *I* was! Now I am like B. Brand, I long to be a bed-ridden woman. . . . I am going to Savannah Monday, and until the gates at the Memorial Park are erected and the deeding of the land taken care of, I shall remain in Savannah."

On July 20, 1926, the cornerstone was laid for the gates of Gordonston Memorial Park, and the park was dedicated to Willie and Nellie. In the cornerstone Daisy placed the tools she had used in making the gates, and the stone pillars in which the gates are set have a daisy carved on each column.

But the pain was getting bad now. In her efforts to conceal her condition, Daisy's behavior became so incalculable and irritating that her brothers decided the honors that had been lavished on her must have gone to her head. By the time Daisy left for England, having witnessed the completion of the memorial into which she had poured her great love for her father and mother, Sam and Daisy Lawrence were the only members of the family who were speaking to her. They saw her off. When they got to the station, Daisy discovered she had left her jewel case behind. Sam and Doots dashed back to the Low house, jimmied open the locked wardrobe for which Daisy, Senior, had lost the key, and got back to the station just before the train pulled out. It was like all of Daisy's departures from Savannah. Only Dr. and Mrs. McGuire, who sailed with her from New York, knew that this was Daisy's last departure for her other beloved country.

On shipboard, Daisy carried on with her usual high spirits and took an active part in the social activities. For the fancy dress ball she inveigled the stewardess into giving her an old sheet and pillow slip, the bar steward into supplying her with empty whiskey, brandy and rum bottles. She draped herself in the sheet, cut eye-holes in the pillow slip and covered her head with it, tied the empty bottles on a rope around her waist. Calling herself "Departed Spirits," she won the prize for the most original costume.

It was a sad voyage for the McGuires, however, who were both devoted to Daisy. They tried to keep up a cheerful front, but it was difficult. One morning Daisy announced that she had a grievance. "Today is my birthday, and everyone seems to have forgotten it completely. I want a birthday party and a cake with lots of daisies on it." The McGuires, delighted to have something to do for their friend, alerted the whole ship's company and that night at dinner Daisy's place was piled high with packages. After she had opened them, the chef came striding among the tables bearing aloft a magnificent three-tiered cake that was literally covered with daisies.

The McGuires had been so busy getting up the party that it didn't occur to Stuart until the next day that there was something strange about this. "I didn't know your birthday was in the summer. I thought it was in October."

Daisy burst out laughing. "It is. Yesterday wasn't my birthday at all! But you and Ruth were so depressed and everything was so dull I thought what we all needed was a good birthday party to liven things up!"

In England, nothing in Daisy's manner indicated to her friends that she was making her last farewells to them. Mabel saw Daisy every day, and Daisy never once mentioned her illness. Even to Peggy Leigh, who was in the secret, she spoke of it only a few times. On one of these occasions, they were walking along a little trout stream near Batemans, where Daisy was visiting the Kiplings, when Daisy said suddenly, "Peggy, I want to ask you a question. I know that cancer research is going on all the time. I wonder if they see any hopes yet of finding a cure?"

Peggy, distressed, replied that it was only a question of time until a cure would be found, but at this moment they had nothing that was certain. Daisy said briskly, "I am quite sure you are right. I didn't really expect they had found anything," and began to talk about trout fishing. In between the visits with her friends, Daisy worked on a bust of her grandfather, W. W. Gordon I, which she planned to have cast in bronze as a present to the City of Savannah.

In October, her English doctor heard of a treatment being tried in Liverpool, which he thought might be helpful. Daisy asked Peggy Leigh to go to Liverpool and remain with her the ten days she was to be in the nursing home. To carry this out required elaborate scheming, for Daisy wanted no one to know that she was going to Liverpool, and it was difficult for Peggy to disappear for ten days, leaving no word of her whereabouts. Daisy solved the problem by saying she was taking Peggy off to Minehead for a little vacation. She spent her last birthday, October 31, 1926, in the nursing home in Liverpool, writing Mabel on November second: "When you see this address, you will think me a most deceitful woman. . . . Dr. Williamson thought my liver attack pointed to some internal trouble, undefined, and worked on Peggy to get me to consult Dr. Blair Bell, the great specialist in women! So instead of going to Minehead we came to Liverpool and Dr. Bell says as far as he can see there is no internal trouble, no growth or inflammation. . . . My appetite is *Kolosal*, my spirits high. I keep wondering what you were all saying at my birthday dinner. Don't tell anyone we are taking this wild goose chase off into the wilds of Liverpool. I believe two days would have been sufficient to test my lungs, lights and liver, but Dr. Bell, a dear old man, was so fascinated with Peggy that he said, 'I must keep your Aunt four days and *you* must stay with her!' He will no doubt propose to her before we leave."

What had actually become evident at the nursing home was that the treatments did not help. One day Daisy was resting on her bed, Peggy was standing looking out of the window, when to the young woman's horror she heard a low moaning sound. She turned quickly. "Are you suffering much, Aunt Daisy?"

Daisy smiled brightly. "That's only my baritone voice. Don't you recognize the tune? I was singing, 'Susie, oh my darling, I hope you never die-ie-ie; I hope you live forever, the apple of my eye-eye-eye.' " On her return from Minehead, Daisy reported to Mabel that she had had a thorough check-up and was "much encouraged."

Dreadfully ill now, Daisy knew there was little time to lose if she were to get back to Savannah. She told Mabel she was homesick for America and engaged early passage; she finished the bust of her grandfather and sent it to be cast. And ill as she was, she insisted upon going to see the *Charlot Revue* of 1926, for which her nephew, Rowland Leigh, had written some songs. She told Rowland that she wanted to take a party and since she was deaf, the seats must be in the front row of the stalls.

Young Rowland procured them, and on the evening of the performance, Daisy arrived with ten deaf people, all carrying ear machines and trumpets of different sizes and varieties. Daisy herself now had an electric one, which helped her hearing, but which had a bad habit of screaming when the electric connection was not made properly. She attached her machine to the bar of the orchestra and proceeded to enjoy herself, applauding Rowland's songs vociferously.

Young Rowland was behind the scenes that night. Halfway through the performance, André Charlot came rushing up to him. He said, "I am sure your aunt, the one you have told me so much about, is in the front row tonight. She and her friends have so many instruments, of so many kinds, that the company can't play to anyone else in the house!"

Mabel and Peggy accompanied Daisy on the boat train to Liverpool for her sailing. Mabel could see that her sister was very sick, but still had no suspicion that it was terminal cancer. Peggy has said, "How Aunt Daisy ever made the trip back to America I'll never know."

Arrived here, she went to Eleanor's at Hutton Park, New Jersey. She called Anne Choate on the phone. "I want you and Jane Rippin and Mrs. Lyman Delano to come to see me at once. I have a wonderful plan for the Girl Scouts!" The plan was Mrs. Hoover's really, Daisy wanted to set it in operation before she died. It was that regional conferences should be held by Girl Scouts of neighboring countries in the western hemisphere, just as regional conferences were held in the various parts of the United States, so that friendship bonds might be tightened throughout the Americas.

Daisy outlined the plan with all her old, bubbling enthusiasm and said, "We must get together right away with Central and South America. The meeting should be held in Hawaii, because it is so central."

"Hawaii? Central to the Americas?" Anne Choate queried. "Hawaii is in the middle of the Pacific Ocean!"

"Maybe I meant Haiti. But why should we bother about minor details?"

This last task for her Girl Scouts accomplished, Daisy went on to Richmond, where she had to stop and rest in the hospital to gather strength for her journey to Savannah. Here in Richmond she spent her last Christmas. She wrote cheery letters to her family, sent them all checks for Christmas presents, and said she was having a little spell of jaundice—her explanation for the yellow color which marked the last stages of her disease. But the truth could no longer be hidden. Arthur cabled Mabel: "Daisy has only six weeks to live." Mabel and Peggy started at once for America. Eleanor came from Hutton Park, Arthur and his wife, Margaret, from Savannah, to take Daisy back home.

When Daisy arrived at the Richmond station, where Eleanor,

Arthur and Margaret awaited her, she was sitting bolt upright in a wheelchair, talking and laughing with the porters and with the McGuires and other friends who had come to see her off. Clustered about her feet on the footrest of the chair were large pots of ferns.

"What are the ferns for?" Eleanor asked.

"They were sent to me in the hospital," Daisy explained, "And I am going to take them with me to Savannah."

"But there are lots of ferns in Savannah!"

"Not these ferns," replied Daisy firmly, and they went into the drawing room with Daisy, her maid Bella, her Pekingese and her numerous pieces of luggage.

Daisy had arrived back home with little time to spare. Only ten days remained, and they were days of grim suffering. But the suffering was lightened by the messages of love that poured in from all over the world. So many flowers came that Daisy remarked laughingly to Bella, "There won't be any left for the funeral if this keeps up!" The message that pleased her most, so much that she asked to have it buried with her, was a telegram from Anne Choate representing the Girl Scout National Council. "You are not only the first Girl Scout but the best Girl Scout of them all." One of the last letters Daisy wrote was to her dear old friend, Mary Carter Clarke of Mesdemoiselles Charbonnier days, whose daughter, Anne Choate, was also so dear to Daisy and had done so much to make the Girl Scouts grow and thrive. "We have loved each other many years, and our love will endure after death. . . . Give my love to Anne, and make her realize that when she took up Girl Scouts, she gave me one of the happiest hours of my life."

Daisy's one fear had been that she would not live to see the bronze casting of the bust of her Grandfather Gordon, which was on its way from England. She kept inquiring anxiously about the ship. It finally docked at noon on Saturday, which was a half holiday. Arthur drove at once to the pier, and got there just as the dock workers were leaving. He told them how very near death Daisy was, how much she wanted to see the bust. They went back to work, got the box out, the Customs officer helped Arthur to unpack it and cleared it. It was set up in Daisy's bedroom that afternoon, and she told Arthur the exact spot in the City Hall where she wished it to be placed.

And now there was just one thing more. Redheaded Bill, like Daisy, suffered from sensitiveness about his place in the family. After he had made a success of the Gordonston division, Arthur told Daisy that Bill had wept because neither Eleanor nor Mabel had answered his letters in which he had told them how well the sales were going and how much money it would make for each of them. "It shows how they feel about me," he had said to Arthur. Daisy had written at once to her sisters to "give him some sugar. I am writing him a most enthusiastic letter of appreciation. . . . His manner and temper are against him . . . he still holds *me* at arm's length. But he is just and fair and only wants to be appreciated."

Daisy could understand this very well. But during her previous stay in Savannah, between her own suffering and Bill's high blood pressure, they had quarreled bitterly. Bill, eating out his heart for his stricken sister, had stayed away because he thought she would not want to see him. Daisy had thought he did not wish to see her. The arrival of the bust furnished a happy way out of the difficulty. Daisy had Mabel phone Bill. Daisy wanted him to see the bust, she said, and give his opinion of it. She did not want it to go to the City Hall unless it had his approval.

Bill came, and weeping for their folly and their love for each other, they made their peace. That was on January 17, 1927, the day before she died. Then she sent for a lawyer and made some revisions in her will—bequests to all of her nieces and nephews and all of Willy Low's, to her servants and various friends. To Mabel she left her house at 40 Grosvenor Street, London, the Low house in Savannah to Bill, to be administered for the benefit of his deaf son, B. She canceled debts owed her by various persons. And she added a last paragraph: "I trust I have left no enmities; and I leave and bequeath to my family my frienoships, especially my beloved Girl Scouts."

All the Girl Scouts in Savannah lined the steps of Christ Church, where Bishop Reece conducted the funeral service. Daisy was buried in Laurel Grove Cemetery, beside the two "dear little people" she had loved best of all the world, in her Girl Scout uniform, adorned by the bright fourragère and her decoration of honor, the Silver Fish of the Girl Guides, the jeweled Thanks Badge of the Girl Scouts. In the breast pocket of the uniform there was a folded telegram. "You are not only the first Girl Scout, you are the best Girl Scout of them all."

It is her accolade.

EPILOGUE

Following Juliette Low's death, the Low house was bought by the National Society of Colonial Dames in the State of Georgia, and is the state headquarters of the organization. On stated days it is open to the public, or may be visited at any time if one is accompanied by a member of the Colonial Dames. Here may be seen Daisy's copy of the Healy portrait of Nellie as a young woman, the original Healy portraits of John Harris and Juliette Kinzie, and the desk where Thackeray worked on *The Virginians*. The Savannah Girl Scouts still have their headquarters in the roomy buildings at the rear of the property, these having been left to them by Daisy in her will.

The organization she founded has continued to grow as vigorously as Daisy could have wished. Approximately twelve million girls and adults have been Girl Scouts since the movement was started in 1912. At the time of Daisy's death in 1927, there were 167,925 members in the United States; at the time of writing this there are 2,860,050, with a million more in other countries. The world unity Daisy was so eager to advance is symbolized by Our Chalet in Switzerland, given by Mrs. J. J. Storrow as a meeting place for Girl Scouts and Girl Guides of all nations; and to further Daisy's last plan for her Scouts, a tightening of the bonds among the Americas, Mrs. Storrow has also given Mustera Cabaña in Cuernavaca, Mexico, for a permanent regional meeting place.

Few women have been as honored by the United States government as has Juliette Low since her death. In World War II, a Liberty ship was named for her, and christened at Savannah by Daisy Lawrence. Captain O'Toole of the S.S. *Juliette Low* wrote Daisy Lawrence that, on their third trip out, with a high priority cargo, in their haste to load and catch up with the convoy the deck cargo of thirty-five ton trucks had been only partially secured.

"When we got outside the harbor, the ship started to roll and those tanks started going places. Believe me, we had a time! Engineers, cooks, messboys, radio operators, even the purser were all out there with ropes, chains, cables and anything else that could be found, trying to secure those tanks.

"Several times I was tempted to turn back. But from all I have read of Juliette Low, nothing ever daunted *her*. When the going was toughest, that's when she went the hardest. . . . It was her spirit that kept us going, and General Eisenhower received a most valuable cargo on time."

In 1948, the United States government issued a Juliette Low postage stamp, carrying her picture in the uniform she doted on.

Her name goes on and on in Girl Scouting, and her stature increases with the years. Soon after her death, the Juliette Low World Friendship Fund was established to promote Girl Scouting and Girl Guiding throughout the world, "as a contribution to peace and goodwill." But the Girl Scouts wanted a tangible memorial to her as well, and in 1954 the Gordon house in Savannah was acquired for this purpose. Long before the formal opening and dedication in October, 1956, entire Scout troops were coming to visit the birthplace of Juliette Low.

There was some talk at first of calling it the Juliette Low Shrine, and Savannah folk who had known and loved Juliette Low and her family were relieved when it was christened The Birthplace instead. Daisy would not have recognized herself in the rôle of saint, and would have been the last to wish her life held up as an example for the young to follow. Nor was this a household of saints. It was a household of vivid, high-spirited people, with human failings. If there was a saint in this household, it was the quiet little Southern gentleman who expunged hatred and bitterness from his heart, and served loyally the government he once had fought.

But it is highly fitting that the Gordon house should be a place of pilgrimage and inspiration for youth. It has seen a great love between a man and woman, rare and tender love between brothers and sisters, between children and parents. Beneath its roof have been brought together the finest traditions of North and South and wild frontier; each of the generations it represents has met the challenges of its own time and place with the gay courage, nobility, and concern for others above concern for self which we count the best of the American heritage. It was through these qualities, and her family's unfailing love, that a troubled daughter of this house was enabled to turn mistakes and personal failure into a benefit for millions.

These traditions and this heritage the childless Juliette Low passed on to her own huge family of Girl Scouts, spread now into every nation, and made foster daughters of this house by her last will and testament as well as by her maternal love. And she added her unique contribution. The fun and gaiety of picnics and parties, which she enjoyed as long as she lived and which she felt should be the birthright of all the young; the ability to laugh at one's self; independence, gained through the full exercise of abilities; determination, to keep going and trying until the most crushing defeat is converted into victory.

Perhaps one day her dearest dream of all will be realized—a friendly world, brought about by a youth equipped with courage and love and laughter.